# International Production Networks in Asia

The economic crisis of 1997 called East Asia's economic miracle into question and generated widespread criticism of the region's developmental models. However, the cisis did little to alter the growing economic integration of the region, which is being forged through American, Japanese, and Chinese firms, which have created cross-border production networks – led by multinational corporations that span the entire value-chain in a number of industries. This book addresses the changing nature of high-tech industries in Asia, particularly in the electronics sector, where these networks are increasingly dsigned to foster and to exploit the region's highly heterogeneous technology, skills, and know-how.

Empirical studies of firms in the USA, Japan, Korea, Taiwan, and Singapore reveal that the organization of cross-border production networks has important competitive consequences. For technology-sensitive sectors such as electronic products, the definition of standards is a critical element of competition: product life cycles are short, and technological change is rapid and subject to disruptive innovations. In such markets, cost-competitiveness must be combined with product differentiation and speed to market. Cross-border networks allow firms to combine these very different market demands effectively. And despite fears that American firms were losing ground to their Asian competitors, the American electronics industry has perhaps been the most effective in mobilizing these networks to competitive advantage. These up-to-date findings will be invaluable to all those involved in high-tech production networks in the Asian Pacific market or corporate strategy, and to managers and policy-makers in Asia and the electronics industry.

**Michael Borrus** is the managing director of Petkevich & Partners, LLC. **Dieter Ernst** is a senior economist at the East–West Center, Honolulu, Hawaii, and a research professor at the Center for Technology, Innovation, and Culture (TIK), University of Oslo, Norway. **Stephan Haggard** is professor at the Graduate School of International Relations and Pacific Studies and research director at the UC Institute on Global Conflict and Cooperation.

# Routledge Advances in Asia-Pacific Business

# International Production Networks in Asia

Rivalry or riches?

**Edited by Michael Borrus, Dieter Ernst, and Stephan Haggard**

University of California
IGCC
Institute on Global Conflict and Cooperation

ROUTLEDGE
Taylor & Francis Group

London and New York

First published 2000
by Routledge
11 New Fetter Lane, London EC4P 4EE

Simultaneously published in the USA and Canada
by Routledge
29 West 35th Street, New York, NY 10001

*Routledge is an imprint of the Taylor & Francis Group*

Typeset in Baskerville by
Prepress Projects, Perth, Scotland
Printed and bound in Great Britain by
St Edmundsbury Press, Bury St Edmunds, Suffolk

*British Library Cataloguing in Publication Data*
A catalogue record for this book is available
from the British Library

*Library of Congress Cataloging in Publication Data*
International production networks in Asia: rivalry or riches?/edited
by Michael Borrus, Dieter Ernst, and Stephan Haggard.
    p. cm. – (Routledge advances in Asia-Pacific business)
    Includes bibliographical references and index.
    1. Electronics industries – Asia – Case studies.    2. Electronics
    industries – United States – Case studies. 3. Business networks –
    Asia – Case studies. Production management – Asia – Case
    studies. 5. Industrial organization – Asia – Case studies. 6.
    Technology transfer – Asia – Case studies. I. Borrus, Michael. II.
    Ernst, Dieter, 1942– . III. Haggard, Stephan. IV. Series
    HD9696.A3 A785    2000
    338.8'872138'095–dc21    99-087582
    CIP

ISBN 0–415–22170–6

# Contents

1   **Introduction: cross-border production networks and the
    industrial integration of the Asia–Pacific region**                   1
    MICHAEL BORRUS, DIETER ERNST, AND STEPHAN HAGGARD

2   **International competitiveness, regional integration, and
    corporate strategies in the East Asian electronics industry**         31
    PAOLO GUERRIERI

    US–Japan production networks, and the growth of
    Singapore's electronics industry**                                  176
    POH-KAM WONG

    *Introduction 176*
    *The rapid growth of the electronics industry in Singapore 177*
    *Competing and overlapping production networks of US and Japanese
        electronics firms 180*
    *The emergence of indigenous electronics firms 190*
    *Conclusion: how small economies can successfully ride the global
        technological waves 197*

8   **Japan and the United States in the Malaysian electronics
    sector**                                                            198
    GREG LINDEN

    *Foreign investment: policy and response 199*
    *MNC affiliate behavior in Malaysia 204*
    *Summary and conclusion 221*

9   **Convergence and diversity: how globalization reshapes
    Asian production networks**                                         226
    DIETER ERNST AND JOHN RAVENHILL

    *Introduction: does globalization lead to increasing convergence? 226*
    *International production networks and globalization: a conceptual
        framework 228*
    *Nationality and production networks 229*
    *Explaining national differences in production networks 234*
    *Forces of change: the opening up of Japanese production networks 237*
    *Partial convergence and persistent diversity: does nationality continue to
        matter? 246*

    *Index*                                                             257

# Illustrations

## Figure

## Tables

# Contributors

**Michael Borrus** is the managing director of Petkevich & Partners, LLC and was a founding co-director of the Berkeley Roundtable on the International Economy (BRIE) at the University of California, Berkeley, where he was also adjunct professor in the College of Engineering. Borrus is an honors graduate of Harvard Law School and a member of the California State Bar.

**Dieter Ernst** is a senior economist at the East-West Center, Honolulu, Hawaii, and research professor, Center for Technology, Innovation and Culture (TIK), University of Oslo, Norway.

**Paolo Guerrieri** is a professor in the Graduate School of Business at the National University of Singapore, a visiting professor of European economic integration at the University of Brussels, a senior advisor for the Istituto Affari Internazionali (Institute for Foreign Affairs), and has an association with the College of Europe, Natolin.

**Youngsoo Kim** is an assistant professor of finance, with research interests in asset pricing, investments and corporate finance, on the business faculty of the University of Alberta, Canada. He holds BBA (Korea University, 1978), MBA (Asian Institute of Management, Philippines, 1981), and PhD (Wharton School of Business, University of Pennsylvania, 1992) degrees.

**Stephan Haggard** is professor of international relations at the University of California, San Diego Graduate School of International Relations and Pacific Studies, and research director for international relations at the University of California Institute on Global Conflict and Cooperation. His interests are in international and comparative political economy. He is the author of *Pathways from the Periphery* (1990), *The Political Economy of Democratic Transitions* (1995), and the forthcoming *Politics of the Asian Financial Crisis*.

**Greg Linden** is a doctoral candidate in economics at the University of California, Berkeley. He is also a consultant on projects developing Asian industrial policy in high-technology industries.

**John Ravenhill** is chair of politics at the University of Edinburgh. He is also associate director of the Research School of Pacific and Asian Studies, Australian National University, as well as professor and head of its department of international relations.

**Poh-Kam Wong** is an associate professor in the business school of the National University of Singapore, where since 1992 he has been program director of the Master of Science Program in Management of Technology. He is concurrently the director of the Center for Management of Innovation and Technopreneurship (CMIT), a university-level research center. He obtained his BSc, MSc, EEng, and PhD degrees from MIT.

# Acknowledgements

For some time, the University of California Berkeley Roundtable on the International Economy (BRIE) has been examining regionalism in the Asia-Pacific and Western Europe (see <http://brie.berkeley.edu/~briewww/pubs/wp/index.html>). Much of the extant literature on this topic has focused on the causes and consequences of formal inter-governmental agreements. BRIE's research, led by Michael Borrus, Dieter Ernst, and John Zysman, paid greater attention to the underlying corporate decisions and new organizational forms that have driven integration at the level of the market. BRIE's work has shown how those market and corporate forces have strong political implications not only for economic outcomes and policy choices, but for security questions as well.

The University of California Institute on Global Conflict and Cooperation (IGCC) has also had a long-standing interest in regionalism, primarily in regional security processes and "track two" diplomacy. Under the directorship of Susan Shirk (1991–97), Stephan Haggard (1997–99), and now Peter Cowhey (1999 to present), IGCC has gradually broadened its *Innovations in International Cooperation* programs to include regional economic integration (see <http://www.ucsd.edu>). During the second half of the 1990s, BRIE and IGCC collaborated on several projects, including a companion volume to this, edited by Barry Naughton, entitled *The China Circle: Economics and Technology in the PRC, Taiwan, and Hong Kong* (Washington, D.C.: The Brookings Institution Press, 1998). The newest BRIE–IGCC venture, *Governing the Global E-conomy*, deepens this work (see <http://e-conomy.berkeley.edu>).

Michael Borrus and Dieter Ernst initiated the collaboration represented in this volume, and Ernst especially benefited from the intellectual support of George B. Richardson, Chris Freeman, Carlotta Perez, Keith Pavitt, Francois Chesnais, Bengt-Åke Lundvall, Peter Maskell, Lynn Mytelka, Esben Sloth Andersen, Gary Gereffi, and Rick Doner. Stephan Haggard was drawn into the project in his capacity as IGCC Research Director and Director, as well as through his own research on disk drive industry globalization (for the work of the Information Storage Industry Center at the University of California, San Diego, see <http://www-irps.ucsd.edu/~sloan/>).

This project would not have been possible without the generous support of a number of institutions. In addition to IGCC, these include the Pacific Rim Research Program, University of California Office of the President, Alfred P. Sloan Foundation, Copenhagen Business School, Council for Global Partnership, and Danish Social Science Research Council.

For their assistance in editing and production, we would like to thank MaryBeth Shubert and Ann Mine at BRIE for shepherding our disparate flock during early drafts. IGCC's senior (managing) editor, Jennifer Pournelle, nudged the project onward to the final book. Lynn Bush of The Page Group artfully compiled the manuscript for submission. University of California, San Diego undergraduate interns Amanda Harris and Erin Schultz, aided by the indomitable staff of the Graduate School of International Relations and Pacific Studies library, tirelessly pursued obscure reference queries.

Finally, our deep appreciation is due to Routledge acquisitions editor Victoria Smith for her vision and faith in the work.

Peter Cowhey, Director, IGCC
John Zysman, Co-Director, BRIE
May 2000

# Journal abbreviations

| | |
|---|---|
| AITR | Asia IT Report |
| BA | Business Asia |
| BT | Business Times |
| BW | Business Week |
| CENS | China Economic News Service |
| CJE | Cambridge Journal of Economics |
| CRN | Computer Reseller News |
| DJNS | Dow Jones News Service |
| ET | Electronics Times |
| FEER | Far Eastern Economic Review |
| FT | Financial Times |
| HBR | Harvard Business Review |
| IB | International Business |
| ICC | Industrial and Corporate Change |
| IEP | Information Economics and Policy |
| JEI | Journal of European Integration |
| JOC | Journal of Organizational Computing |
| KED | Korea Economic Daily |
| NNB | Nikkei News Bulletin |
| NST | New Straits Times |
| NW | Nikkei Weekly |
| PCC | PC/Computing |
| PDN | Penang Development News |
| RAPBR | Reuter Asia–Pacific Business Report Regional |
| RP | Research Policy |
| SCED | Structural Change and Economic Dynamics |
| SCMP | South China Morning Post |
| SEM | Samsung Jun-ki Sa-bo: Samsung Electro-Mechanics' Monthly Magazine |
| SEMM | Samsung Jun-ja Sa-bo: Samsung Electronics' Monthly Magazine |
| SMM | Samsung Sa-bo: Samsung Monthly Magazine |
| ST | The Straits Times |
| WSJ | Wall Street Journal |

# List of abbreviations

| | |
|---|---|
| ACS | Apple Computer Singapore |
| ADI | Automata Design Inc. |
| AFTA | ASEAN Free Trade Area |
| AMD | Advanced Micro Devices |
| AMS | Asia Matsushita Electric Singapore |
| APEC | Asia Pacific Economic Cooperation |
| APO | Asia Productivity Organization |
| ASDL | asymmetric digital subscriber loop |
| ASEAN | Association of South-East Asian Nations |
| ASIC | application-specific integrated circuits |
| AT&T | American Telephone and Telegraph Company |
| ATM | automated teller machine |
| ATT | advanced technology transfer |
| AV | audio-visual |
| BHQ | business headquarter |
| BIOS | basic input–output system |
| BRIE | Berkeley Roundtable on International Economy |
| CAS | Compaq Asia–Singapore |
| CD-R | compact disk-readable |
| CDROM | compact disk read-only memory |
| CE | consumer electronics |
| CEO | chief executive officer |
| CEPR | Center for Economic Policy Research (Stanford) |
| CMEA | Ministry of Economic Affairs, Taiwan |
| COCOM | Coordinating Committee for Multilateral Export Controls |
| CPN | cross-border production network |
| CPT | color picture tube |
| CPU | central processing unit |
| CRT | cathode ray tube |
| CS | center statellite |
| CTV | color television set |
| D&D | design and development |
| DEC | Digital Equipment Corporation |

| | |
|---|---|
| DRAM | dynamic random access memory |
| DRI | Danish Research Institute; direct response indicator |
| DRUID | Danish Research Unit for Industrial Dynamics |
| DVD | digital video disk |
| DY | deflection yokes |
| EC | European Community |
| EDB | Economic Development Board |
| EDP | electronic data processing |
| EIAJ | Electronics Industry Association of Japan |
| EIAK | Electronic Industry Association of Korea |
| EPABX | electronic private automatic branch exchanges |
| EPROM | erasable programmable read-only memories |
| ERSO | Electronic Research Service Organization |
| ESS | electronic switching exchanges |
| EU | European Union |
| FBT | flyback transformers |
| FDI | foreign direct investment |
| FSU | former Soviet Union |
| FTZ | free trade zone |
| FY | fiscal year |
| GATT | General Agreement on Tariffs and Trade |
| GE | General Electric |
| GNP | gross national product |
| GSM | Groupe Spécial Mobile; global system for mobile communications |
| GSP | generalized system of preferences |
| GTE | General Telephone and Electronics |
| HDD | hard disk drives |
| HEDS | Hitachi Electronic Devices Singapore |
| HMS | Harris Microwave Semiconductor |
| HP | Hewlett-Packard |
| HQ | headquarters |
| HRDF | Human Resources Development Fund |
| IBM | International Business Machines |
| IC | integrated circuit |
| ICC | International Chamber of Commerce |
| IECDF | International Economic Cooperation and Development Fund |
| IGCC | Institute on Global Conflict and Cooperation |
| IMF | International Monetary Fund |
| IPN | international production network |
| IPO | international procurement office |
| ISDN | integrated services digital network |
| ISEAS | Institute of SouthEast Asian Studies |
| ITRI | Industrial Technology Research Institute, Tapei, Taiwan |
| ITT | Integrated Telecom Technology |
| JACTIM | Japanese Chamber of Trade and Industry in Malaysia |

| | |
|---|---|
| JETRO | Japan External Trade Organization |
| JIT | just-in-time |
| KAIST | Korea Advanced Institute of Science and Technology |
| KIST | Korea Institute of Science and Technology |
| KSC | Korea Semiconductor Company |
| KTC | Korea Telecommunications Company |
| LAN | local area network |
| LC | liquid crystal |
| LCD | liquid crystal display |
| MAEI | Malaysian–American Electronics Industry |
| MEI | Matsushita Electric Industrial |
| MIC | Malaysian Industrial Classification |
| MIDA | Malaysian Industrial Development Authority |
| MIT | Massachusetts Institute of Technology |
| MITI | Ministry of International Trade and Industry |
| MNC | multinational corporation |
| MNE | multinational enterprise |
| MOEA | Ministry of Economic Affairs |
| MOS | metal oxide semiconductor |
| MWO | microwave oven |
| NAFTA | North American Free Trade Agreement |
| NBER | National Bureau of Economic Research |
| NCR | National Cash Register Corporation |
| NDKK | Nihon Desnhi Kikai Kogyokai |
| NEG | Nippon Electric Glass |
| NIC | newly industrializing country |
| NIE | newly industrializing economy |
| NSTB | National Science and Technology Board |
| OBM | original brand manufacturing |
| OC | overseas Chinese |
| ODM | original design manufacturing |
| OECD | Organization for Economic Cooperation and Development |
| OEM | original equipment manufacturing |
| OHQ | operational headquarters |
| OJT | on-the-job training |
| OPR | overseas production ratio |
| PABX | private automatic branch exchange |
| PAFTAD | Pacific Trade and Development Conference |
| PC | personal computer |
| PCB | printed circuit board |
| PCBA | printed circuit boards assembly |
| PDC | Penang Development Corporation |
| PLC | product life cycle |
| PSDC | Penang Skills Development Center |
| PSTN | public switched telephone network |
| R&D | research and development |

| | |
|---|---|
| RAM | random access memory |
| RCA | Radio Corporation of America |
| RF | radio frequency |
| RHQ | regional headquarters |
| RM | Malaysian Ringgit |
| ROAs | return on assets |
| ROM | read-only memory |
| ROS | return on sales |
| S&T | science and technology |
| SAIT | Samsung Advanced Institute of Technology |
| SC | Samsung Corning Company |
| SEC | Samsung Electronics Company; Securities and Exchange Commission |
| SED | Samsung Electron-Devices Company |
| SEM | Samsung Electro-Mechanics Company |
| SIE | systems and industrial engineering |
| SISA | Samsung Information Systems America Inc. |
| SITC | Standard International Trade Classifications |
| SME | small and medium-sized enterprises |
| SMT | surface-mount technology |
| SPEC | Sony Precision Engineering Center |
| SRAM | static random access memory |
| SRI | Stanford Research Institute |
| SSI | Samsung Semiconductor Inc. |
| SST | Samsung Semiconductor and Telecommunications Co. |
| STN | switched telephone network |
| SUM | Center for Development and the Environment (Oslo) |
| TDX | time division exchange |
| TFT | thin film transfer |
| TI | Texas Instruments |
| TNC | trans-national corporation |
| TQM | total quality management |
| TSE | Thai Samsung Electronics |
| TSEC | Tianjin Samsung Electronics |
| TSMC | Taiwan Semiconductor Manufacturing Corporation |
| UNCTAD | United Nations Conference on Trade and Development |
| UNCTC | United Nations Center on Transnational Corporations |
| VDP | vendor development program |
| VHS | video home system (videotape recording format) |
| WINTEL | WINdows + InTEL |
| WP | working paper |
| WPC | world product charter |
| XT | 1980s-era computer built around the INTEL 8086/8088 microprocessor |
| Y | yen |

# 1 Introduction

## Cross-border production networks and the industrial integration of the Asia–Pacific region

*Michael Borrus, Dieter Ernst, and Stephan Haggard*

The economic crisis of 1997 called East Asia's economic miracle into question and generated widespread criticism of the region's distinctive developmental models. The startling rapidity with which problems in one Asian economy were transmitted to others in part reflects similar weaknesses across countries: overvalued exchange rates, a run-up of unhedged, short-term, foreign debt, underdeveloped domestic financial intermediaries and weak regulatory oversight. In our view, contagion also reflected a deeper underlying fact about the region's economic development. Over the last two decades, driven neither by high politics as in the European Union (EU) nor by formal trade agreement as in North-American Free Trade Agreement (NAFTA), the economies in East Asia have become closely integrated at the level of production organization.

The massive literature on Asia's economic integration, most of it focusing on trade patterns and the investment and trade behavior of multinational corporations, has by and large missed this deeper level of industrial integration. Arm's-length trade, foreign direct investment, and even intra-firm trade do not fully capture the organizational structure of the region's major growth industries and markets. In electronics, textiles and apparel, autos, and other sectors, firms in the region are increasingly linked across borders in complex and ongoing relationships that extend beyond the boundary of the firm and span the entire value-chain in the given activity. The architecture of these "cross-border production networks," the way that technology, know-how, resources and control flow across them, and their implications for competition and cooperation in the region, are the subject of this book.[1]

By a lead firm's "cross-border production network" (CPN) we mean the inter- and intra-firm relationships through which the firm organizes the entire range of its business activities: from research and development (R&D), product definition and design, to supply of inputs, manufacturing (or production of a service), distribution, and support services. We thus include the entire network of cross-border relationships between a lead firm and its own affiliates and subsidiaries, but also its subcontractors, suppliers, service providers, or other firms participating in cooperative arrangements, such as standards-setting or R&D consortia. Choosing the CPN as the unit of analysis captures the cross-border operations of the lead firm itself, but also the proliferation of non-equity, non-arm's-length, inter-firm relationships in which significant value is added outside the lead-firm.

The value of studying CPNs is that they closely mirror the rapidly changing division of labor in the Asia–Pacific. In the electronics sector that is the subject of this book, CPNs are not simply constructed to access cheap factor inputs (resources or labor) or to gain access to expanding markets, two of the principle explanations for foreign direct investment. Although those factors may have motivated initial investment, CPNs are increasingly designed to both foster and exploit the region's highly heterogeneous *technological* capabilities. *Indeed, a central theme of our work is that CPNs are assembled to access locational advantages at each network node associated with the increasingly specialized technology, skills and know-how that are resident there.*

The origins of those specialized capabilities are multiple, and include both technology transfers from multinationals and increasing investment in process and product development on the part of firms in the region. However, the development of local technological capabilities has also been a primary objective of government industrial policies. The study of CPNs thus inevitably raises the question of the role of the state in fostering the region's rapid industrial transformation and its particular pattern of economic integration.

A second theme of our work is that CPNs come in many national flavors. Even when we control for industry or product, the relationships that make up a CPN can be arranged in a variety of ways, as can the accompanying flows of technology, know-how, resources and control. Some of these differences must be traced to characteristics of the lead firm in the CPN; individual firm strategies matter. However, the empirical chapters that follow argue that the CPNs emanating from the United States, Japan, Korea, Taiwan, and Singapore exhibit substantial differences that are ultimately rooted in national systems of production and innovation.

A third major theme of this book is that the organization of CPNs has important competitive consequences, particularly in technology-intensive sectors such as electronics. The electronics industry encompasses a range of different segments. But for an increasingly wide array of electronics products, the definition of standards is a critical element of competition; product life cycles are short and technological change is not only extraordinarily rapid but subject to periodic trajectory-disrupting innovations. In such "high-tech commodity" markets, cost competitiveness must be combined with product differentiation and speed to market. As Michael Borrus and Dieter Ernst show in Chapters 3 and 4, network forms of organization are an important explanation for the competitive resurgence of US electronics producers vis-à-vis their Japanese competitors. CPNs also explain Taiwan's success in the electronics sector (Ernst: Chapter 5) and help us understand why Singapore has prospered by positioning itself as the high value-added node for Southeast Asia's electronics (Poh Kam Wong: Chapter 6).

The fourth major theme of our work is that despite these competitive consequences of network organization, we have not seen convergence on a single organizational form; differences rooted in national origin have persisted. Indeed, the enduring differences in network character help to explain why some of the region's economies and industries have been able to adapt more rapidly than others to the stresses caused by the crises of 1998. It is conceivable that continued globalization and the sheer passage of time could decouple CPNs from their national origins. The crises of 1998 may well act as a catalyst for a new wave of foreign direct investment and for corporate restructuring and significant policy reforms throughout the region that would force greater convergence.[2] To date, however, the strong convergence predicted by many theorists of globalization has not occurred. Indeed, national differences endure over time despite operational convergence in some areas of CPN organization and behavior, as Ernst and Ravenhill suggest in the concluding chapter.

As several of the chapters make clear, over the long term, we expect that the Asia crisis and the structural changes associated with recovery from it will reinforce the production network patterns described in the book and the themes discussed above. In the short term, as Ernst and Ravenhill argue in Chapter 9, the real economic problems generated by the crisis appear to be deferring, and in some cases eroding, the technological and upgrading capabilities of some of the region's local suppliers. At the same time, however, post-crisis Asia has become even more of a base for networked production by American, Japanese and European multinational corporations (MNCs) given the decline in local currency-denominated costs. Indeed, foreign and the better capitalized indigenous MNCs are again investing heavily in now-cheap local assets. We hypothesize that the heterogeneous division of labor across the region will likely become even more elaborated as recovery proceeds in earnest. Variations in the severity and nature of the crisis across the region's countries will be one source of increasing differentiation. Long-term recovery will likely require even greater differentiation if it is to be sustained across the region as a whole.

Within the most affected economies of the region, including Japan, the crisis is resulting in a gradual process of corporate restructuring and rationalization. In principle, this will lead to increased opportunities for networked production structures as firms focus on core activities and supplement those cores with relationships rather than ownership patterns. This trend will likely be further reinforced as reliance on debt declines and reliance on securitized forms of finance (that enable less traditional production organization) increases. And because the Internet, electronic commerce and a more rapid regional adoption of information technologies are increasingly significant components of all of the region's recovery strategies, less integrated, more networked forms of production such as the kind we describe will be ever easier to embrace. We acknowledge, of course, that these are all empirical questions that await both the region's continuing recovery and further research.

We chose electronics as the focus of our analysis on both methodological and substantive grounds. Our focus on electronics raises questions of the applicability to other sectors. It should be emphasized, however, that the electronics industry itself represents a microcosm of sectoral differences: it covers a broad range of product markets that include truly high-tech products such as microprocessors as well as fairly conventional mass-produced commodities such as appliances and general-purpose computer memory. By focusing on the electronics industry, we are thus able to capture a great variety of sectoral characteristics that shape different approaches to the organization of CPNs.

Controlling for a broad industry sector also offers obvious advantages in conducting cross-national comparisons. Moreover, investment and trade in electronics dominates Asia's trade and investment flows in manufactures, and as Paolo Guerrieri shows in Chapter 2, electronics has been an important factor in regional integration.[3] Moreover, we expect that industrial practices characteristic of electronics are likely to diffuse to other sectors, just as cross-border network practices initially visible in the textile–apparel complex subsequently diffused and were later modified and deepened in the region's electronics industry.

## CPNs: a new form of competition and market organization?

To get at the new forms of market organization that are emerging in Asia and how they differ from traditional corporate forms, it is useful to consider an extreme case: the cross-border network controlled by US-owned Cisco Systems, the leading supplier of routers, switches and hubs for corporate communications networks.[4] Were Cisco to be organized like a traditional, vertically integrated, multidivisional producer of communications equipment – like the pre-Lucent Western Electric, Germany's Siemens or Japan's NEC – almost everything from the R&D at central corporate laboratories to product design, engineering, manufacturing, distribution, and service would be done by one affiliate or another, most located in the country of origin. The bulk of the underlying technologies, components, parts, software, and subsystems would be produced internally. The finished product would be sold directly to customers and control would be hierarchical and centralized.

In reality, Cisco looks nothing like this model. Cisco carries out no R&D in the conventional sense of a central corporate laboratory. It does carry out new product definition and software development at its headquarters in Silicon Valley. But the bulk of more conventional R&D and significant development work on some products is done through technology and product development alliances with key suppliers such as chip, design and software firms. Similarly, Cisco does none of its own volume manufacturing (although it does assemble prototypes and some low-volume, high-value models). Rather, the products are assembled entirely by independent "turnkey" contract manufacturers in California and Asia from components and manufacturing services [e.g. board-stuffing, printed circuit board (PCB) design] that flow from a variety of independent suppliers throughout Asia (including Taiwan, Korea, Japan, Singapore, Thailand, and Malaysia) and the United States . These suppliers are bound to Cisco through a variety of contractual arrangements; however, they do not typically involve an equity stake. Several independent companies in California produce to Cisco's technical specifications (i.e. its product standards), adding value in the form of products or services that interface in some fashion with Cisco's products. The final product is sold directly to customers but also through a variety of third-party channels, including value-added resellers and systems integrators. Third-party suppliers very frequently undertake after-sales service.

The product development and distribution relationships of Internet software producer Netscape Communications show a similar pattern. Product development is done in conjunction with a variety of independent development partners, such as Sun, Real Audio, Adobe, NEC Systems Laboratory, and others in Asia, which develop "plug-in" packages of software functionality (e.g. JavaScript applets, authoring tools, audio and video players) designed to work seamlessly with Netscape's browser–server products; without these products, the Netscape software would not be fully functional. The software is distributed directly to customers and through a variety of independent channels including original equipment manufacturers (OEMs), such as Netcom and Concentric, on-line service providers, such as Earthlink and Singapore's Pacific Internet, specialized retailers, such as EggHead Software, local systems integrators and value-added resellers, such as Hong Kong's Electronic Data Interchange Shop or Germany's Softlens, which provide Web set-up and services, and mass marketers such as Costco. The relationships that define the division of labor in Netscape's cross-border production network are mostly at odds with the traditional, vertically integrated form of business enterprise; Netscape controls none of its partners through ownership, fiat or resource allocation.

These limiting cases suggest that the new CPNs emerging in Asian electronics include not only increasingly far-flung intra-firm networks that have been extensively analyzed in the literature on foreign direct investment in the region, but a wide variety of new inter-firm relationships as well. These include supplier, buyer and customer networks,[5] but also producer networks, in which competing producers pool development and production capacities, standards coalitions among firms seeking to "lock-in" proprietary products, architectural or interface standards, technology cooperation networks and other strategic alliances. The external relationships that comprise a given firm's CPN include short-term supply contracts that approximate pure, arm's-length market relations. For example, procurement of some commodity subassemblies and components, where technical leadership can shift abruptly among suppliers between (and even within) product generations, is more likely to be short term and market based. However, we are particularly interested in CPNs that depart from this model, and in which traditionally core competencies, such as manufacturing or R&D, are conducted outside the lead firm on the basis of more stable, long-term alliances requiring more intimate involvement and greater trust.

Although there is no simple measure for the development of these new CPNs, one important indicator of the new organizational forms that are emerging is the increasing trend toward the outsourcing of production itself. Since the 1970s, it has been established practice for "brand name" companies in the garment, footwear, furniture, and toy industries to depend on CPNs for essentially all of their manufacturing requirements.[6] By contrast, the outsourcing of core manufacturing functions did not begin in earnest in the electronics industry until the mid-1980s. However, the trend has increased dramatically in the 1990s and shows no sign of abating. The scale and pace of these developments is suggested indirectly by the rapid growth of the contract manufacturing–production services segment of the industry, which has grown over the last decade from marginal revenues to $40 billion in 1995.[7] Outsourcing of supply and assembly to firms such as SCI Systems and Solectron now involves 10–20 percent of total product-level electronics manufacturing (up from less than 5 percent in 1982) and 40–50 percent of highly volatile electronics industry segments, such as PCs and modems.

Conversely, vertically integrated assemblers such as International Business Machines (IBM), Hewlett-Packard (HP), and Apple have disposed of captive production facilities and moved toward the new CPN model for a number of product lines. By 1994, 50 percent of HP's 20 million circuit boards and 11 percent of its 4.5 million final products were being assembled by contract manufacturers, as was fully 50 percent of Apple's production.[8] Some of the newest and most successful systems companies own *no* volume manufacturing at all, including Dell (PCs), Silicon Graphics (workstations), Cisco Systems (networking), Diebold (automatic teller machines), Digital Microwave (communications), Telebit (modems), LAM Research (equipment), and Octel (communications).

The emergence of contract production and CPNs in electronics and now, perhaps, automobiles turns the phenomenon from one confined to labor-intensive low- or middle-skill products in mature sectors to the most innovative and rapidly expanding sectors of the advanced industrial economies. Asia's well-developed local production and supply capabilities and their relatively open "merchant" character have put in place an infrastructure for global production strategies that drastically reduce the need for capital investment in production facilities by final electronic systems producers.[9] Such organizational developments call into question a number of existing approaches to foreign direct investment and modern theories of the firm.

## Theoretical considerations: explaining the network form

As John Stopford has observed, the emergence of CPNs shifts organizational focus "from the legal entity known as the firm to the contractual network of firms tied together by mutual long-term interest." (Stopford 1994: 21). Such network forms of industrial organization have generated an extensive literature.[10] How does that literature fare in explaining the new, loosely coupled organizational forms that we see in the electronics industry in the Asia–Pacific?

The literature on networks can be roughly grouped into two traditions of discourse (Alstyne 1996). One, anchored initially in business schools and subsequently in the microeconomics of organizations, centers on the attempt to explain the form and functioning of modern industrial enterprise, including tendencies to vertical integration (hierarchies) and disintegration (markets). Functional in explanatory form, these theories explain institutional design by reference to its implications for efficiency. The second, rooted in sociology and, secondarily in economic geography and comparative politics, elaborates the structure, characteristics and functioning of networks as a distinctive form of *social* organization.

The first tradition elaborates the rise of the large, vertically integrated, multidivisional, corporation, and the global spread of its modern MNC variants, and details their governance and operations.[11] In the nineteenth century the introduction of new production, transport and communications technologies vastly increased productivity, output, and ability to reach distant markets. The form of the modern corporation grew out of the need to manage the complex coordination problems posed by large-scale industrial production and marketing. Improving control over an increasingly complex and diverse production chain meant housing as many of those activities within the purview of the corporate administrative hierarchy as possible. In-house production meant lower transaction costs, much faster throughput, and greater economies of scale and scope.

Global market opportunities, declining transport and communications costs, and changing national policies eventually extended the reach of the modern corporation, first through trade and then direct investment. The seemingly organic development and inexorable cross-border reach of the modern corporation, in turn, spawned variations on the ideal typical form – e.g. affiliates with autonomous local ties, cross-border joint ventures, varied forms of outsourcing and contracting – and a lucrative cottage industry seeking to outline their determinants. John Dunning's (1993) "eclectic paradigm" (introduced originally in the mid-1970s) synthesized those determinants. Dunning argued that firms will locate wherever optimal for exploiting their defensible competitive advantages, choosing direct ownership whenever market transactions fail to realize the full value of those advantages, for example with intangible assets such as technological know-how.[12]

An important strand of this literature stylized economic history into formal theory by developing and elaborating Ronald Coase's hypothesis that transaction costs were key determinants of the optimal form of industrial organization.[13] Following Coase (1937), Oliver Williamson (1985) and others hypothesized that modern industrial organization arose because it minimized transaction costs. Because transactions involving significant irreversible investment are subject to the hold-up problem, they are best handled by a hierarchy. By contrast, we would expect a tendency to vertical disintegration and a return to market forms of organization when the costs of transacting and contracting fall. For example, Milgrom and Roberts (1990) have suggested that flexible machine tools and programmable, multitask production equipment have obviated the hold-up problem by permitting firms to produce a variety of outputs efficiently in small batches.[14]

The difficulties of operationalizing the transaction cost approach – and even identifying the meaning of "transaction costs" precisely – are notorious and well known. However, we wish to underscore two further difficulties with the transactions costs approach. As the literature on international supply-chain management suggests, it is by no means obvious that the costs of coordinating a large, geographically disperse network of independent suppliers is lower than vertical integration. In industries producing disk drives, several leading firms remain vertically integrated even as their operations have become geographically dispersed throughout Asia.

Rather, the *higher* transaction costs of managing a network of inter-firm relations must be offset by *other* advantages, such as economies of scale, flexibility, access to information, and the ability to focus resources on core competencies. For example, an investment by Cisco Systems in wholly owned assembly facilities that replaced its reliance on contract assemblers would reduce the transaction costs it currently incurs in coordinating with those assemblers. But it would also impose new costs (currently incurred by its contractors) associated with monitoring technical trends in assembly to keep facilities state-of-the-art. For Cisco Systems, investment in assembly capacity is likely to have much less payoff than expenditure of similar resources in broadening its product's technical capabilities and evolving its product standards in ways that lock in customers.

As this example suggests, the analysis of the determinants of institutional form must shift away from the narrow focus on transaction costs to the broader competitive environment in which firms operate. Although it is difficult if not impossible to generalize across all electronics segments, several fundamental changes in the industry help account for the adoption of network forms of organization.[15]

In the past, two stylized types of competitive strategies could be distinguished within the industry. For consumer electronics and components, competition centered primarily on cost reduction, with non-price competition reserved for a few, high value-added market niches, such as high-end audio equipment. In the computer industry, by contrast, the focus of competition was on product differentiation based on innovative product designs and market segmentation.

Today, however, a wide range of electronics products have become "high-tech commodities:" they combine the characteristics of mass production with extremely short product life cycles and highly volatile market demand. As a result, firms must combine product innovation and differentiation, and the learning and acquisition of specialized capabilities that implies, with high volumes, speed-to-market, competitive pricing, and the ability to penetrate new and uncharted markets. Mass production implies large investment thresholds to reap economies of scale, whereas short product life cycles imply the rapid depreciation of plant, equipment and R&D. The problems of squaring this strategic circle are compounded by periodic trajectory-disrupting innovations, so that leadership positions cannot be taken for granted.

These market conditions create pressures to move from partial globalization, characterized by a loose patchwork of stand-alone affiliates, joint ventures, and suppliers, to systemic globalization: the effort by a firm to network its own operations and inter-firm relationships worldwide, across both functions and locations. The demand both for scale and for closer, faster, and more cost-effective interactions between different stages of the value chain have been a driving force in shifting core functions, such as production, outside the boundaries of the firm into networks.

Our second criticism of the transaction cost approach to networks and vertical disintegration centers on the presumed efficiency gains from these organizational choices. This approach skips some of the more provocative chapters in the economic history of the modern corporation. Chandler's (1962) vibrant histories show that the quest for rents and market power via increased throughput and speed of coordination were more important in explaining hierarchy than the traditional emphasis on scale economies or efficiency. This book highlights these often overlooked dimensions of organizational choice. Like hierarchies, CPNs not only promise to improve efficiency but permit lead firms to sustain quasi-monopoly positions, generate market power through specialization, and raise entry barriers; these considerations are of particular concern for the integration of developing countries into CPNs.

Indeed, the cases suggest that competition in electronics in the era of CPNs is increasingly about developing and sustaining monopoly niches, whether through ownership and control of a *de facto* standard or by maintaining a differentiated product through the ability to add performance, functionality, and features or to improve costs faster than competitors. Profitability in electronics is almost purely a function of a firm's position in the resulting market structure; it is high when a quasi-monopoly position can be maintained, and weak and volatile everywhere else. Contrary to conventional wisdom, we find that electronics is not a simple story about firms finding profits by moving up a hypothetical value chain that starts in low value-added components and assembly and ends with services and content. As Intel demonstrates in components and Matsushita's recent desultory experience with MCA suggests in content creation, profits can be made or lost at any point in the value-chain. In electronics, then, CPNs are self-conscious efforts to structure markets in ways that increase profits by removing direct competitors, creating differentiation, erecting entry barriers, and, most significantly, assembling capabilities that other forms of business organization cannot match.

The second discursive tradition, with its emphasis on networks as unique forms of social organization, provides some tonic to the overdrawn dichotomy between markets and hierarchies. As Walter Powell (1990) has argued, the history of modern commerce is a story of enterprises with loose and permeable boundaries – e.g. guilds, trading companies, family associations – that do not fit neatly into a spectrum of organizational forms bounded by markets and hierarchies (Powell 1990: 298). Standard operating forms in a range of modern industries including construction, publishing, architecture, filmmaking, and the media have always fit uneasily into the market–hierarchy dichotomy. Nor is it entirely satisfying to say that these industries incorporate elements of both market and hierarchy; rather, Powell argues, they define a qualitatively different type of organization in which neither price signals nor command capture key relationships (Powell 1990: 330).

In particular, this second tradition views economic interactions as "embedded" in broader social relationships based on trust, reciprocity, and shared expectations that overcome opportunistic behavior and permit coordination.[16] The literature emphasizes how such forms of coordination are especially useful under conditions of high uncertainty, for mutual learning, and for adjusting rapidly to shifts in the environment, all features associated with the markets of concern here. The more complex the global market environment – the more subject to competitive ambiguity and rapid technical or market shifts – the more likely firms are to benefit from the trust and reciprocity of socially embedded networks.

The central problem with the sociological approach to networks has to do with the international rather than localized setting in which industries now operate.[17] Although it is possible to identify the discrete social institutions that support trust and reciprocity in northern Italian manufacturing, for example, what is the social foundation for such networks in the Asia–Pacific? Much of the literature on industrial districts and social networks has focused on an analysis of micro-interactions within a particular localized cluster. Yet, local clusters of knowledge creation can no longer exist in isolation: they are rapidly becoming internationalized through cross-border knowledge diffusion (Ernst 2000). They are also prone to erosion of existing knowledge clusters through information technology and globalization.

One answer, as we will spell out in somewhat more detail below, is the transnationalization of ethnic social networks, particularly within the Chinese diaspora.[18] However, it would be entirely impossible for Chinese firms – or firms of any nationality – to build CPNs in the electronics industry that are ethnically self-contained. Key technologies continue to be dominated by

Japanese and American firms, and end-markets for products are everywhere. Moreover, as Michael Borrus (Chapter 2) argues, American firms have been particularly adept at linking to Chinese networks, an outcome difficult to explain on the basis of sociological embeddedness. Thus, although we do not discount the role of transnational ethnic ties as the basis for the success of some Chinese enterprises, their importance in the overall structure of industries in the Asia–Pacific region has been exaggerated; because of the significant role played by American, Japanese, Korean, and, increasingly, European firms, they cannot capture the range of social ties that may be germane to understanding the development of the CPN form in the Asia–Pacific.

Rather, the case studies identify a different way in which embeddedness matters; foreign firms are increasingly tapping into *local* concentrations of technological and production capability that have in turn been fostered under conditions of social and political "embeddedness." Access to resources outside the firm is a key motive for building CPNs. It is also a principle reason why location decisions by firms tend to cluster where they can benefit from strong externalities generated by local networks, such as supportive infrastructures, specialized suppliers, skilled labor, supportive government institutions, and, above all, technological know-how.[19]

As illustrated by Chapters 5 and 7, CPNs incorporate and are linked with local capability clusters that have emerged out of both local social ties and policy-induced linkages among local firms, universities, government agencies, research institutions, and other public and quasi-public entities. The fact that CPNs both extend and incorporate these local networks underlines the conceptual ambiguity in the concept of "globalization": the most globalized firms depend heavily on capacities that benefit from *local* agglomeration economies.

Networks provide an especially effective means for tapping into locally developed technological capabilities.[20] Among the most significant of external resources for most firms is the specialized know-how embodied in other firms or locations. The extensive literature on the spread of inter-organizational partnerships thus emphasizes the central role of technological learning through such network connections.[21] But although technological know-how is increasingly exploited on a global basis through such partnerships, its *generation* remains to a substantial degree national and local.[22] The studies in this volume confirm patterns of increasing local and regional technical specialization as globalization proceeds. Indeed, a central theme of our work is that CPNs are assembled to access locational advantages at each network node associated with the increasingly specialized technology, skills, and know-how that are resident there.

In sum, new forms of CPNs are emerging that are only partly explained by reference to existing literatures on foreign investment or networks. CPNs are not motivated only by cheap factor costs or market access, although particular relations within a CPN may well be influenced by the need to surmount barriers to trade and investment. They are not confined to particular segments of an industry's value-chain such as supply of components or manufacturing. Nor are they confined to a limited number of routine relational forms such as outsourcing or joint ventures.

Nor is possible to explain CPNs solely with reference to changes in transactions costs or to social embeddedness. Rather, they represent efforts to develop new forms of organization that provide greater flexibility, responsiveness, risk-sharing, as well as efficiency under conditions of high market and technological uncertainty. CPNs embody efforts to develop relationships for exploiting complementary assets held by other firms, for example to develop something new that no partner could develop as effectively alone (within given constraints of time and cost) or because rationalization around areas of core competence requires contracting-out non-core functions. Most significantly, CPNs exploit locational advantages by organizing a division of labor across borders that re-assembles the industry value-chain through specialization at each node. To understand their distinctive form in Asia, therefore, requires an understanding of developments at each of those nodes.

## Enabling conditions: Asia's development and the emergence of CPNs[23]

CPNs emerged in a dense and highly elaborated form in Asia because the region's economic development occurred in phases that created unusually heterogeneous production capabilities and thus a high degree of intra-regional complementarity. Asia's long-term growth can be seen in terms of four developmental tiers. Japan occupies the first tier. Industrialization began in the nineteenth century, accelerated under military auspices during the late 1930s, and reached the advanced country frontier in the middle of the post-war era through self-conscious policies of technological catch-up, a large domestic market, and access to the American market for exports. The second tier consists of the newly industrializing countries (NICs): Taiwan, Singapore, Hong Kong and Korea. The so-called "Four Tigers" approached the advanced industrial frontier in some industry segments using strategies of extensive technological borrowing and export-led growth, and in the case of Singapore with a dominant role for foreign investment.

The third tier of later industrializers includes the major Southeast Asian countries of Malaysia, Thailand, the Philippines, and Indonesia. These countries began to emulate the first generation of NICs in the 1970s by pursuing more outward-oriented development strategies;[24] Malaysia and Thailand relied heavily on insertion into the networks created by Japanese, US, Korean, European, Taiwanese, and other overseas Chinese multinational corporations. To date, however, the extent of indigenous technological capacity in the "ASEAN four" remains substantially lower than in the four NICs.

The fourth tier is occupied by China, Southeast Asia's late-late developers, particularly Vietnam, and perhaps in the future India as well. China could in theory deepen the more inward-looking, dirigist strategies it has long pursued, and, despite extensive reforms, some elements of such a strategy remain visible. During the 1990s, however, the trend has clearly been toward a deeper incorporation into the region's trade and investment networks, with China already drawing foreign direct investment away from countries in the third tier.[25]

This tiered pattern of development created complementary capabilities across countries that were highly conducive to the emergence of regional production networks; indeed, the broad development history just sketched is mirrored in the evolution of CPNs in the region. To stylize a complex history, the beginnings of CPNs in electronics can be traced to the 1960s, when American and Japanese multinational firms established (or in some cases re-established) their presence in a number of Asian locations.[26] These investments took two basic forms. Outward-processing investments, which located first in Hong Kong and spread to Taiwan, Korea, and Singapore in the 1960s, established production units or contracted-out for narrowly defined activities that were intensive in the use of low-cost (and, initially, relatively low-skilled) labor. Simple electronic components and semiconductor packaging and testing are examples. Local value-added was largely limited to the wage bill, with little local sourcing; initial investments in these activities were often located in export-processing zones with few linkages to the local economy. By contrast, import-substituting investments, particularly in consumer electronics products in which the Japanese enjoyed advantages, established branch plants to circumvent tariff protection and to gain access to local markets; fans, air-conditioners, and refrigerators are examples.

Partly in response to the opportunities spawned by these investments, indigenous firms emerged and developed to produce components and subassemblies or to provide services. During the 1970s and 1980s, affiliates of US firms increasingly relied on local, and gradually regional, suppliers for specialized inputs. Backed in Korea, Taiwan, and Singapore by industry-specific industrial policies of various sorts, local firms strove to extend their range of production and to integrate forward and backward from their initial point in the production chain.

Product cycle and "flying geese" models predicted that the development of local capabilities would ultimately displace the multinationals in both home and foreign markets. Multinationals would cede low-end market segments to their lower cost competitors and move on to new products. In some cases, such as black and white televisions, such a process did occur. In a surprisingly large number of other segments, however, such a seamless transition did not take place; rather, a more complementary form of organization emerged. MNC affiliates continued to invest in production facilities, but relied on local and regional suppliers for a greater range of inputs, processes, and manufacturing steps. At the same time, the division of labor within Asia became more dense as suppliers from the second tier (e.g. Singapore, Hong Kong, Taiwan, and Korea) began to export to other Asian production sites, and finally extended their own operations into less developed parts of Asia (e.g. Malaysia, Indonesia, Thailand, southern China).

As the region's technological capabilities and labor skills deepened still further in the 1980s and 1990s, some MNCs focused increasingly on core competencies at home and the distinctive CPNs outlined above began to emerge. So developed had Asia's manufacturing capabilities become that the supply portion of the value-chain for some firms centered almost entirely in Asia. Moreover, production was no longer confined to wholly owned subsidiaries; rather, production itself was outsourced. The American firms that pursued this strategy concentrated almost entirely on product definition, development, and marketing. The very management of complex supply chains had itself become a core competence, and some firms, such as Compaq, even specialized in it. Production intermediaries such as Solectron built lucrative businesses by developing their own CPNs, packaging Asian supply capabilities with their own skills and providing full-service turnkey manufacturing capabilities to MNC customers. As Ernst shows in Chapter 5, a number of Asian firms entered this segment of the market as well.

It is important to underscore that the stylized history just sketched should not imply a linear, "stages" model nor a uniform pace to the developments across segments. The developments leading to more articulated CPNs overlap in particular countries and even in the experiences of individual MNCs; the emergence of new organizational forms did not necessarily replace existing ones. Rather, several forms coexist, representing in part different corporate production strategies (e.g. Stopford 1998; Ernst and Ravenhill, Chapter 9).

## Distinctions at the point of origin

More importantly, the structure and operation of CPNs in the region bore the imprint not only of their lead firm, but also of the lead firm's home country. Globalization has not eviscerated the analytic significance of national distinctions based on ownership and origin. American networks show modal characteristics that contrast with equally distinctive production networks under the control of Japanese, Taiwanese, Korean, and other Asian firms.

Moreover, the chapters that follow strongly suggest that these differences are competitively consequential. Differences in organizational form help explain why US electronics firms have prospered during the 1990s, while indigenous Asian firms have become significant players in a number of industry segments, and Japanese firms, whatever their previous successes and continuing strengths, have seen a reduction in their market share.

The following tables provide a typology of the major networks operating in the region – American, Japanese, Taiwanese, Singaporean, and Korean – based on the findings of the case studies. We have chosen to emphasize only those differential characteristics that seem to explain differences in competitive performance and market outcomes.

First, it is important to underscore that there are differences in the product mixes in which countries specialize. For example, US firms have a more pronounced presence in industrial electronics, Japanese firms still play a critical role in consumer products, as do Korean firms, whereas Taiwanese and Singaporean firms have established a strong specialization in PC electronics, including peripherals and components. However, there is no clear reason why these sectoral differences would necessarily produce diverse organizational forms; the case studies suggest strongly that even when we control for industry segment, the organization of production still differs in significant ways.

In the tables that follow, "accessibility" is an indicator of the openness of the network to outsiders and the willingness to develop relations beyond a limited set of partners. "Permanence" refers to the time-frame characterizing relationships among firms in the network, and whether the network involves relatively short-term relationships or longer-term ones built on trust and "repeat play." Together, as Table 1.1 implies, these factors help to explain the relative ability of the different networks to adjust to rapid market and technological shifts. In our view, the ability to adjust rapidly is perhaps *the* crucial performance variable in contemporary electronics markets.

"Governance" captures the extent of control exercised by headquarters or the lead network firm over affiliates and local network partners. The case studies have made a significant effort toward unraveling the question of control because of its implications for where value is captured, the existence of barriers to entry, and the developmental consequences networks have for the developing countries in the region.[27] Indicators of control include in the first instance the preference for vertical integration over more loosely coupled network forms, but also the role of headquarters in directing personnel, sourcing and other key managerial decisions of affiliates and network partners. Control over both product and process technology, and the willingness to transfer competencies constitute core elements of the governance structure. Thus, as a control indicator, the "supply base" variable is intended to capture the tendency for the lead firm to prefer domestic and affiliated partners over anyone who can meet price, quality, and delivery constraints. Taken together, as in Table 1.2, these variables help to explain the degree to which the different CPN forms exploit local technological and business capabilities throughout the region. In our view, the ability to exploit

*Table 1.1* Ability to adjust to market/technology shifts

| Permanence | Accessibility | |
| | *Open* | *Closed* |
| --- | --- | --- |
| *Fluid* | *Fast*<br>US, Taiwan | *Moderate*<br>Korea |
| *Long-term* | *Moderate*<br>Singapore | *Slow*<br>Japan |

*Table 1.2* Exploitation of Asian value-added

|  | Supply base | |
| --- | --- | --- |
| *Governance* | *Unaffiliated* | *Affiliated* |
| *Decentralized* | High<br>US | Moderate<br>Taiwan |
| *Centralized* | Moderate<br>Singapore | Low<br>Korea/Japan |

local specializations is a second crucial performance variable in electronics markets. Table 1.3 summarizes all of these features.

The US networks produce (and in some cases design and develop) increasingly sophisticated industrial electronics, such as hard disk drives (HDDs), PCs, InkJet Printers, and telecommunications products. Geographically, American investments are concentrated in the NICs, especially Singapore, but increasingly reach into the rest of Asia; for example, China is emerging as a separate regional focus for American CPN activity. However, the networks of American firms rely on an open, competitive supply architecture in which Japanese, Taiwanese, Singapore, and Korean firms, as well as other American firms based in the region, provide significant value-added. The US networks are more likely to exploit a complementary division of labor in which American firms specialize in "soft" competencies (definition, architecture, design, standards, and marketing) and Asian firms specialize in "hard" competencies (components, manufacturing stages, and design/development thereof). By increasing technical specialization throughout the production process, the Asian contribution to final output is *maximized*.

With respect to control, the US networks decentralize significant decisions to affiliates or partners. As Borrus argues in Chapter 3, the setting, maintenance, and evolution of *de facto* standards set in the domestic US launch market were the principle instruments used by US firms to preserve control over their inter-firm networks. As long as US firms maintained that role in the division of labor by defining the product and technology trajectory, customers were locked in to their standards, and it was extremely difficult for other firms in the network to challenge for the lead. US networks could be highly decentralized precisely because ownership of standards enabled devolution of responsibility to network partners without fear of losing control.

The Japanese networks, like the Korean, still mostly produce consumer audiovisual electronics, appliances, and components. In the late 1990s, however, unlike the Korean ones, the Japanese networks have rapidly expanded production of commodity industrial electronics products such as hard disk drives. Although Japanese networks span the region geographically, and Korean firms have begun to invest abroad aggressively in the late 1990s, both still rely on a largely domestic and affiliated supply base with surprisingly

Table 1.3 Typology of electronics production networks in Asia

| Characteristic | US owned | Japanese owned | Taiwanese owned | Korean owned | Singapore owned |
|---|---|---|---|---|---|
| Product mix | Sophisticated industrial electronics | Consumer and low-end components, commodity industrial | PC electronics | Consumer, some components | Disk drive and PC electronics |
| Accessibility | Open | Closed | Open | Closed | Open |
| Permanence | Fluid | Long term | Fluid | Long term | Long term |
| Ability to adjust to market/tech shifts | Fast | Slow | Moderate to fast | Slow | Moderate |
| Governance | Decentralized | Centralized | Centralized | Centralized | Centralized |
| Supply base preference | Anyone meeting price, quality, delivery constraints | Domestic and local affiliated | Domestic and local Chinese | Domestic | Local Chinese |
| Exploitation of intra-Asia value-added | Maximizes local Asian value-added | Maximizes Japanese value-added at home and locally; minimizes rest of Asia value-added | Maximizes Taiwanese value-added but exploits local Chinese value-added where necessary | Maximizes domestic Korean value-added | Maximizes high domestic and low local Asian value-added |

little value-added by other Asian producers. The division of labor across the network is more likely to be one in which domestic operations produce high-value, high-end products using sophisticated processes while offshore affiliations produce comparatively lower value, low-end products using simpler processes.[28] As a result, indigenous Asian (i.e. not Japanese/Korean) contribution is *minimized*, although, given relative levels of development, the Korean networks are much more dependent on partnerships, particularly with respect to core technologies.

In terms of internal organization, Japanese and Korean networks have tended to be relatively closed to outsiders, more centralized, and structured on stable, long-term business and traditional *keiretsu* or *chaebol* (i.e. group) relationships. Chapter 4, by Ernst, on Japan and Chapter 6, by Kim, on Korea show that, with control residing in their domestic-based manufacturing and core-component technologies, any significant devolution of responsibility to outsider partners risked creating a direct competitor; Japanese and Korean networks were thus centralized to avoid that outcome. More recently, as Japanese-affiliated local production has deepened (i.e. favored domestic suppliers have followed lead assemblers offshore), their networks (again, unlike the Koreans) have become more open and less centralized, although the contrast to the US degree of openness and decentralization is still quite stark.

In contrast to the American model, the Japanese and Korean CPNs are closed, cautious, centralized, long-term, and stable. Kim's work (Chapter 6)suggests that Korean networks are more likely than their Japanese counterparts to engage in short-term, opportunistic behavior. However, in general we find that the organizational structure of both Japanese and Korean networks results in cautious decision-making that has periodically proven costly in the region's rapidly changing electronics markets.

The emerging Taiwanese and Singaporean networks in Asian electronics take a different form, incorporating elements of both the American and the Japanese/Korean model and combining them in distinctive ways. With respect to products, the Taiwanese electronics industry has become heavily specialized in the PC business and related peripherals and components. Singapore's industry has established itself as a hub for the manufacture of a number of computer peripherals, such as disk drives, as well as components, but with an increasing move toward the high end of these product categories. The Taiwanese network relationships extend into Southeast Asia, but are increasingly China-centered. Ironically, they may end up with a China base as their global center, using demand and technical know-how in the Chinese market to achieve world-class scale, costs and innovation. Singapore firms have concentrated their reach in Southeast Asia, particularly in proximate regions such as the "growth triangle" containing Batam Island (Indonesia) and southern Malaysia. Less elaborately, Singaporean firms have, with government assistance, also forged ties with Chinese authorities and businesses.

Much like the Japanese and Koreans, Taiwanese and Singaporean networks retain in the home base high value-added products manufactured with more advanced processes, and offshore to cheaper production locations lower value-added products and simpler processes. However, like the Americans, these networks also seek to exploit a highly competitive supply base. Taiwanese networks, in particular, have self-consciously exploited indigenous specializations through local partners, typically other Chinese firms.

## Convergence, competitive outcomes, and the diffusion of CPNs

The distinctive features of the networks just outlined mirror in important ways the domestic competitive environments and political–economic systems of the home country of the lead firm in the network. The case studies seek to draw these links more closely, showing how patterns of regulation and industrial organization are extended transnationally through CPNs. For example, Korea's highly dirigist industrial policy, with a particular emphasis on channeling preferential credit to the heavy and chemical industries, contributed to the emergence of the distinctive *chaebol* form of business organization, a highly concentrated industrial structure, and a lesser role for small and medium-sized firms. In Taiwan, by contrast, the ruling Kuomintang initially feared concentrations of Taiwanese business power and relied to a greater extent on state-owned enterprises. The resulting industrial organization was less concentrated, and although large Taiwanese groups did emerge, they were complemented by a dense network of geographically dispersed small and medium-sized enterprises (Ernst, Chapter 5).

The important theoretical point is that these organizational forms do not always reflect optimal adaptations to the market environment at some subsequent point in time. Lead firms from all countries have invested abroad and formed CPNs in order to complement their domestic activities by exploiting location-specific advantages within the region, but they have varied in their capacity to do so.[29] The US network form helped US firms regain leadership in electronics markets during the 1990s, partly by reconstituting the architecture of supply to reduce dependence on Japanese rivals. Their own characteristic form helped both Taiwanese and Singaporean firms to keep abreast of the remarkable pace of technological advance in digital electronics markets while operating with extraordinarily thin margins and, by and large, without the economies of scale in investment and production widely believed necessary to stay competitive. For both, as for the American CPNs, the turn to skilled but cheaper indigenous Asian suppliers not only helped to lower overall production costs, but fierce competition within the supply base helped to reduce turnaround times and encouraged specialization and diversity along the supply chain that more effectively tracked market shifts. Growing Asian technical capabilities within their CPNs freed US firms to focus their efforts (and scarce resources) on new product definition, systems integration, software value-added, and distribution. Japanese and Korean firms have been slower to exploit these advantages, with consequences both for their positions within existing markets and for their ability to move into new segments.

Moreover, the studies suggest that these national distinctions between CPNs are slow to disappear with time: there is no ineluctable convergence of the different CPN types around some new global norm. To be sure, the evolution of each network – in terms of architecture, function, and role in international competition – has been strongly shaped by on-going interactions with other CPNs, by changes in the global strategies of the lead-firms, and by the force of competition leading to emulation of best practice. The studies provide clear instances of lead firms learning and adopting the network practices of other CPN types, as when Japanese electronics firms emulated US PC assemblers by establishing supply relations with Taiwanese firms (see Chapter 5). But the national distinctions that we highlight here are more enduring over time than the convergence theory would allow.

Partly as a consequence of its competitive success, the CPN form or organization nonetheless does appear to be spreading. It is most highly developed in industries that produce goods made up of a large number of components requiring complex final assembly stages, such as electronics, garments, and automobiles, and in regions such as Asia where heterogeneous production capabilities can be combined into unique packages of value creation. But intimations of the form are visible in other regions, and they are likely to be spread geographically, if only by the global investment of firms that adopt them or that provide turnkey CPN services. It is clear, for example, that by 1999, the form had spread rapidly into Europe, as firms such as Ericsson, Siemens, and Philips sell off production facilities to turnkey CPN service suppliers and then contract with them to form a new production network (e.g. Solectron 2000).

Technological changes are also facilitating the adoption of the loosely coupled CPN form in other sectors. Digital electronics is transforming products and processes in a wide range of other goods and services industries, and the more pervasive these technologies become, the more likely that CPN-like forms of corporate organization can become viable parts of corporate strategy. The spread of the Internet and electronic commerce, and the broader diffusion of information technology, have also had an effect on the adoption of the network form by enhancing the ability to transmit, process, and store information across organizational boundaries. As Antonelli argues, "the vertical integration structure of knowledge, characteristic since the Second World War, is being progressively replaced by the institutional creation of an information exchange market, based on real-time, on-line interaction between customers and producers," a structure conducive with, and supportive of, the network form of organization.[30] As already noted, there is ample precedent for the cross-sectoral diffusion of such "best practice" models. CPNs have already diffused from the textile–apparel complex into electronics.

Finally, Chapters 5, 7, and 8 all suggest that the CPN form will spread as much through the instigation of governments as of firms. The spatial location of investment, jobs, technology, and competencies is a major focus of policy initiative throughout the developing countries of Asia. Particularly in the wake of the currency crises of 1997–8, governments in the region are redefining policy to increase their attractiveness as sites for investment and to promote their insertion into the new production networks we have described. They are doing so with varying degrees of sophistication and intent. Both Taiwan and Singapore have facilitated the regional expansion of their CPNs by providing infrastructure and services in special economic zones in other countries, while simultaneously transforming both countries into higher value, complementary nodes.

The spread of CPNs across regions, sectors and to new players within the region suggests a range of questions for a successor research agenda. Is the electronics story in Asia a stand-alone tale, or the precursor to upheaval in other sectors and regions? As CPNs spread across sectors and to other regions, will they produce similar decisive impacts on market competition and economic development? How will the CPN adapt to new terrain? Will it vary across regions as consequentially as by the point of origin of the lead-firm? The work here suggests that so long as technological change continues at current rates, the CPN form is likely to spread outward and with significant variations as the network form is adapted both to the unique characteristics of different sectors and to the unique political economies of different regions.

## Implications for the Asia–Pacific region

Finally, our work has important implications for the burgeoning literature on regional integration in the Asia–Pacific region. With a few important exceptions, that literature has tended to focus either on the political–legal process centered on the Asia Pacific Economic Cooperation (APEC) or on underlying trade and investment flows.[31] However, our analysis suggests that the region is increasingly organized and integrated at the level of *corporate organization* as well, and that the dynamics traced here have important implications for both the political economy of the region and the trade and investment policies of particular countries.

First, our analysis has important implications for the debate over closed versus open regionalism.[32] The growth of Japanese investment in Asia between the mid-1980s and the early 1990s, and the recent growth of the so-called overseas Chinese networks have generated fears of a closed economic bloc in Asia, if only an informal one. As we have seen, however, American firms have knitted together their own CPNs in the region, networks that closely link the United States and Asia. Critics of free trade and "runaway shops" see such investment as evidence of declining American competitiveness. However, virtually the opposite is the case; American investment networks in Asia took advantage of the region's increasing technological capabilities and production capacity and allowed the United States to maintain a leadership position in the industry.

Of course, so far, there has been very little overlapping and rivalry between American and Japanese production networks in Asia: the Americans focused on PC-related products, whereas the Japanese focused on consumer electronics and appliances. This is now rapidly changing, as Japanese firms are shifting a variety of PC-related products to East Asia; they may now try to tap into the same set of regional supplier networks and capability clusters that, so far, have catered primarily to the needs of American firms (Encarnation 1992). This implies that for the first time, American and Japanese firms will have to compete for the same supply sources in East Asia. It remains to be seen whether the networks remain open and whether American computer companies will be able to retain control over them as Japanese vendors finally begin to target them.

Just as important, however, the long-standing US policy of maintaining an open market at home has played a key role in maintaining American advantage in exploiting the competitive potential of CPNs. As Chapter 3 by Borrus suggests, exposure to international competition has pushed numerous US industries, from finance to petrochemicals, to adopt new technologies quickly, making the United States the premier market for the launch of innovative new products; this was particularly true in electronics. A large, open market has allowed American firms to dominate product and standards definition in a range of products from business systems, to PCs, to a variety of communications equipment.

Because of the rapid growth of Asian markets, US trade policy has increasingly emphasized liberalizing trade and investment rules to allow American firms to operate more freely.[33] For an important range of sectors and countries, however, this strategy pushes on an open door. The middle-income countries that have played a successful role in the new CPNs have already liberalized rules governing trade and investment, either by adopting free trade and investment policies across the board (as in Hong Kong, Singapore, and increasingly Taiwan) or by adopting dualistic trade and investment policies in which the activities of key industries are freed, even as others remain sheltered; as Linden shows in Chapter 8, that was the model pursued in Malaysia. However, there is increasing evidence that those countries that have been slow to open up, such as Korea, or where there has been backsliding, as in Vietnam, have paid a high price by weakening their attractiveness as an investment site and reducing their participation in the networks we have outlined. The currency crises of 1997–8 have already given rise to a new wave of liberalization with respect both to trade and to the rules governing foreign direct investment, and we expect that this trend will continue even as controls on the capital account to deter over-reliance on short-term debt are embraced in some places.

Given the regional division of labor, APEC provides a natural forum for negotiating further liberalization and investment facilitation. However, the recent International Technology Agreement, which promises to eliminate trade barriers in a range of electronic products, shows that such regional developments can be used to wider effect and need not conflict with multilateral goals. The agreement was primarily a US–Europe creation, but European interest in the deal was heavily influenced by the rapid deepening of Asian electronics trade and investment.[34]

The new Asian networks also help explain the growing significance of a number of new issues on the multilateral and regional trade policy agenda. Although the new Asian CPNs flourish in an environment of free trade and investment, they also require strong protection for intellectual property. Given the increasingly close links between investment and trade, and the significance of national industrial policies in shaping the nature of network relations at each node, it is also not surprising that national policies with respect to product standards and competition are also gaining increased attention. In addition, the Asian financial crisis has highlighted the fact that these networks flourished in the context of relative macroeconomic and exchange rate stability. Only time will tell whether they can flourish under conditions of financial market volatility.

Finally, the new CPNs also influence the key trans-Pacific relationships between the United States, China, and Japan. Because of its size, Beijing believes it can exploit its large market to pursue an industrial strategy based on protection, restrictions on investment, forced technology transfer, and the creation of large industrial groups. China has also wielded its political influence to economic ends, playing US firms against their competitors and sanctioning government-to-government alliances that limit the participation of outsiders.

These strategies have reached their limits. As is shown in a parallel study to this project, China's attempt to foster national champions has generally been a failure; rather, it is the large number of relatively independent firms, including those integrated into the networks that we have described, that have spearheaded China's export drive.[35] The United States' bilateral trade deficit with China reflects in no small measure the offshore operations of overseas Chinese CPNs, and thus simply a shifting of exports from Taiwan and Hong Kong onto the mainland. The specter of a high technology, low-wage export powerhouse is thus exaggerated. Moreover, for China to continue to reap the benefits of foreign investment and the networks into which it is increasingly integrated, it will have to continue along its current reform path.

Japan's trade policies will also likely constitute a regional policy problem. Chapter 2, by Paolo Guerrieri, shows that the electronics trade in the region is still characterized by a marked triangular pattern, in which Japan's overseas investment produces for local consumption and for export to North American and European markets. The problem of Japan's structural surpluses are not unique to the United States; the China Circle and Southeast Asia remain heavily dependent on Japan, as does Korea. Japan provides much of the capital equipment on which industrial production is based and continues to dominate certain high-technology components.

The economic crisis of 1997 is likely to exacerbate these problems. Japan's continuing recession has meant a declining ability to serve as a locomotive for the region while reviving its temptation to refocus on exports. Indeed, despite historically large domestic stimulus packages introduced in 1998–9, Japan remains intransigent in maintaining much lower import levels than its wealth and size permit. It has told its neighbors not to expect Japan to substantially increase imports from them. Although there appears to be a narrow *fin de siècle* window for increased foreign direct investment (FDI) into Japan and increased acquisition by outsiders of domestic Japanese assets, we expect that window to become ever narrower when Japan's recovery finally proceeds. For the United States, the crisis has led to a marked increase in current account deficits. In the short run, these have been caused by a decline in exports to the region rather than a surge of imports. However, the competitive devaluations in the region coupled with the reality that exporting to the US market is the only recovery game in town, has, in short order, led to ballooning US imports from the region. The patterns outlined by Guerrieri are already thus being reinforced.[36]

The bilateral, sectoral strategy of dealing with Japan has yielded results by forcing dialogue on the range of anti-competitive practices that can hinder trade and investment. However, the closed and centralized nature of Japan's CPNs also raise the question of whether Japan's industrial organization is being exported to the region.[37] Given the disadvantages we see in this form of organization, this should not be seen as a major current threat. However, were technology markets to stabilize, Japanese CPNs could well become a major source of competitive advantage and of trade friction.

Indeed, despite the triumphalism in US pronouncements on Asia and on Japan post-crisis, we are quite hesitant to accord long-term competitive preference to the US CPN form. Competitive success among the different CPN types is highly context-dependent. In Chapters 3 and 4, both Borrus and Ernst outline scenarios under which the precise network characteristics that made Japanese firms vulnerable in the last round of market competition could be turned to competitive advantage under changed circumstances. We are prepared to hypothesize, however, that the loosely coupled CPN form we have outlined is likely to be a better adaptive fit to the competitive circumstances of those sectors of the electronics industry which, like the PC industry, are characterized by market volatility, rapid technological change, and the need for global reach.

## Notes

1  The concept of CPNs originated in work done at Berkeley Roundtable on International Economy (BRIE) by Borrus and Ernst. It has its conceptual roots in prior work on international production networks by Dieter Ernst, in studies prepared for the Organization for Economic Cooperation and Development (OECD) [such as *Networks, Market Structure and Technology Diffusion – A Conceptual Framework and Some Empirical Evidence*, report prepared for the OECD secretariat,

Paris: OECD, 1992; and "Network Transactions, Market Structure and Technological Diffusion – Implications for South-South Cooperation," in L. Mytelka (ed.), *South-South Cooperation in a Global Perspective*, Development Centre Documents, Paris: OECD, 1994]. The concept has been further developed in Ernst (1997a,b; 2000a–c).

2 This at least is the main conclusion of a survey of large MNCs, jointly undertaken by the United Nations Conference on Trade and Development (UNCTAD) secretariat and the International Chamber of Commerce (ICC) in February 1998 (UNCTAD 1998). More skeptical assessments can be found in F. Veneroso and R. Wade, "The Asian Financial Crisis: The Unrecognized Risk of the IMF's Asia Package," paper presented at the Nordic Research Seminar on the Economic Crisis in East and Southeast Asia, University of Oslo: Centre for Development and the Environment (SUM), January 23–24; K. S. Jomo, "Financial Liberalization, Crises, and Malaysian Policy Responses," paper presented at the Nordic Research Seminar on the Economic Crisis in East and Southeast Asia, University of Oslo: Centre for Development and the Environment (SUM), January 23–24 1998; and H. J. Chang (1998) "An Alternative View on Budgetary Reform in Korea. Dynamic Efficiency, Institutions and Political Economy," paper presented at a conference on "Korea's Transition to a High-Productivity Economy," Korea Studies Centre, University of Hawaii at Manoa, Honolulu, Hawaii, USA. A systemic analysis of how the Asian crisis is likely to affect the upgrading requirements of Asia's electronics industries can be found in Ernst (1998a,b; 2000).

3 For additional evidence that is based on a more disaggregated analysis, see Ernst and Guerrieri (1998).

4 For example, market analysts estimate that Cisco products account for approximately half of the router market in Asia. See, for example, Asia Pacific Research Group, http://www.aprg.com/routers.html.

5 On these relationships, see Gereffi and Korzeniewicz (1994).

6 Gereffi and Korzeniewicz, ibid. In this industry, fabric is produced, often in highly automated plants, in one place; cut and processed in another, and stitched and assembled and finished in still others. Many "assemblers" are simply product definition and marketing companies who provide design, distribution, and above all, brand names such as Nike.

7 See the work of Sturgeon (1998) and the relevant data sources cited there.

8 Apple has a long tradition in outsourcing production to companies such as SCI in order to reduce overhead and inventory costs while concentrating on marketing and design. For a detailed analysis, see Ernst (1997a: 39–42).

9 Sturgeon (1998) makes this point in great detail and argues that it is not confined to Asia. It remains to be seen, however, how well these arrangements survive the Asian crisis and the current transformation of these networks through the Internet. For instance, the crisis has substantially eroded the capacity of Asian suppliers, especially smaller ones, to finance the necessary upgrading of production facilities and R&D (Ernst 1999). As for the impact of the Internet, there are widespread concerns that this may place a premium on proximity to the big Western markets, eroding the competitiveness of Asian suppliers (Ernst 2000c).

10 For an excellent review of a large body of literature, see Powell and Smith-Doerr (1994: 368–402).

11 On the rise of the corporation, see, for example, Chandler (1962: note 14); on the MNC, see, for example, Vernon (1971); Dunning (1993), and Porter (1990).

12 Dunning (1993). Though admirably eclectic and multivariate, Dunning's focus on internalization to extract full value is clearly an application of the transactions cost framework.

13  The classic statements are Coase (1937), Williamson (1985, 1993: 107–156). The classic response is Powell (1990).
14  Milgrom and Roberts (1990).
15  The following paragraphs are based on Ernst (1997a).
16  See Granovetter (1985, 1990) and Biggart and Hamilton (1993).
17  We are sympathetic to the critique that such trust relations can be modeled as repeat-play games or as relationships with effective monitoring and sanctioning mechanisms, but this meta-theoretical debate is not relevant to our concerns.
18  For examples of this literature from different perspectives see Hamilton (1996), Kao (1993), and the historical essays of Gungwu (1991).
19  Porter (1990), provides an influential analysis of such clustering effects.
20  See, among others, Ghoshal and Barlett (1990), Levy and Dunning (1993), and Ernst (1997b).
21  See, among many others, Kogut (1988), Hagedoorn and Schakenraad (1990), Freeman (1991), Hamel (1991), Powell and Brantley (1992).
22  Archibugi and Michie (1995).
23  This subsection is drawn from Borrus and Zysman (1997).
24  See Bernard and Ravenhill (1995: 195–200).
25  On China's development and impacts on direct investment flows in the region, see Naughton (1997).
26  For an early analysis, see Tilton (1971), Lim (1978), and Ernst (1983).
27  Position in the network is thus just as important as the character of network ties, for networks can be as shaped by implicit hierarchies as more formally hierarchical structures. See Powell and Smith-Doerr (1994: 377), suggesting that power within a network lies in "structural position," i.e. in relative resources and access to exchange or other opportunities, citing work by, among others, Emerson, Cook, Pfeffer, and Salancik and Burt.
28  This is also a principal conclusion of Takayasu and Ishizaki (1995: 11), who call this "intrafirm product-to-product division of labor."
29  This is broadly consistent with work on the location decisions of multinationals. In addition to Dunning (1993), see Cantwell (1995).
30  Antonelli, "Localized Technological Change, New Information Technology and the Knowledge-Based Economy: the European Evidence," Manuscript, Universita di Torino, Laboratorio di Economia dell' Innovazione (1997: 3). For elaboration, see the discussion in Ernst and Lundvall (2000).
31  On the politics of the region, see Mack and Ravenhill (1994), Funabashi (1995) and Katzenstein (1997). On the economics, see Bergsten and Noland (1993), Chen and Drysdale (1995), and Dobson and Yue (1997).
32  For a summary, see Lawrence(1996).
33  See Haggard (1995).
34  See the analysis in Borrus and Cohen (1998)
35  Naughton (1997).
36  Note however that in the electronics industry substantial barriers exist to a rapid trade adjustment, delaying the expected export boom in electronics until mid-1999 (Ernst 2000e). Three barriers to an East Asian export boom in electronics are discussed: (1) supply-side constraints that result from limited access to trade finance, and from the cost-increasing impact of local currency depreciations in highly import-dependent countries; (2) demand-related constraints resulting from changing growth perspectives in East Asia's electronics export markets and a looming protectionist backlash; and (3) industry-specific constraints such as surplus capacity and price wars that periodically result in worsening terms of trade, magnifying supply-related constraints to an export expansion.
37  See Doner (1993) and Hatch and Yamamura (1997: 8, 1).

# References

Alstyne, M. van (1996) "The State of Network Organization: A Survey in Three Frameworks," *Journal of Organizational Computing*.

Archibugi, D. and Michie, J. (1995) "The Globalisation of Technology: a New Taxonomy," *Cambridge Journal of Economics*, 19, 121–40.

Asia Pacific Research Group. "Router Market," *Asia Market Trends*, [http://www.aprg.com/routers.html]

Bergsten, C. and Noland, M. (eds) (1993) *Pacific Dynamism and the International System*, Washington, DC: Institute for International Economics.

Bernard, M. and Ravenhill, J. (1995) "Beyond Product Cycles and Flying Geese: Regionalization, Hierarchy, and the Industrialization of East Asia," *World Politics*, 47(2): 171–209.

Biggart, N. and Hamilton, G. (1993) "On the Limits of Firm-based Theory to Explain Business Networks: The Western Bias of Neoclassical Economics," in N. Nohria and R. Eccles (eds) *Networks and Organization*, Boston: Harvard University Business School Press.

Borrus, M. and Cohen, S. (1998) "Why Now? A Transatlantic Initiative in Information Technology," in R. Steinberg and B. Stokes (eds) *Partners or Competitors? The Prospects for US–European Cooperation on Asian Trade*, Boulder, CO: Rowman and Littlefield.

Borrus, M. and Zysman, J. (1997) "Globalization with Borders: The Rise of Wintelism as the Future of Global Competition," *Industry and Innovation*, 4(2): 141–66.

Cantwell, J. (1995) "The Globalization of Technolgy: What Remains of the Product Cycle Model?" *Cambridge Journal of Economics*, 19(1): 155–74.

Chandler, A. (1962) *Strategy and Structure: Chapters in the History of the Industrial Enterprise*, Cambridge: Massachusetts Institute of Technology (MIT) Press.

Chen, E. K. Y. and Drysdale, P. (1995) *Corporate Links and Foreign Direct Investment in Asia and the Pacific*, Canberra: Harper Educational Publishers.

Coase, R. (1937) "The Nature of the Firm," *Economica*, 4: 386–405.

Dobson, W. and Yue, C. S. (1997) *Multinationals and East Asian Integration*, Ottawa and Singapore: International Development Research Center, Canada, and Institute of Southeast Asian Studies.

Doner, R. (1993) "Japanese Foreign Investment and the Creation of a Pacific Asian Region," in J. Frankel and M. Kahler (eds) *Regionalism and Rivalry*, Chicago: University of Chicago Press.

Dunning, J. (1993) *The Globalization of Business*, New York: Routledge.

Encarnation, D. (1992) *Rivals Beyond Trade*, Ithaca: Cornell University Press.

Ernst, D. (1983) *The Global Race in Microelectronics: Innovation and Corporate Strategies in a Period of Crisis*, Frankfurt: Campus.

—— (1997a) *Data Storage Industry Globalization Project Report 97-02*, San Diego: University of California Graduate School of International Relations and Pacific Studies.

—— (1997b) "Partners in the China Circle? The Asian Production Networks of Japanese Electronics Firms," in B. Naughton (ed.) *The China Circle*, Washington, DC: The Brookings Institution Press.

—— (1998a) "Catching-Up, Crisis and Industrial Upgrading. Evolutionary Aspects of Technological Learning in Korea's Electronics Industry," *Asia–Pacific Journal of Management*, 15(2): 247–284.

—— (1998b) "Destroying or Upgrading the Engine of Growth? The Reshaping of the Electronics Industry in East Asia After the Crisis," Background Study prepared for the World Bank report *East Asia – the Road to Recovery*, Washington, DC: The World Bank.

—— (1999) "Moving Beyond the Commodity Price Trap. Post-crisis Trade and Industrial Upgrading Options in East Asia's Electronics Industries."

—— (2000a) "Carriers of Cross-Border Knowledge Diffusion: Information Technology and Global Production Networks," paper presented at the Shumpeter 2000 Conference on Change Development and Transformation, Centre for Research on Innovation and Competition (CRIC), University of Manchester, 28 June–1 July 2000.

—— (2000b) "Globalization and the Changing Geography of Innovation Systems. A Policy Perspective on Global Production Networks," *Journal of the Economics of Innovation and New Technologies*, special issue: "Integrating Policy Perspectives in Research on Technology and Economic Growth," A. Bartzokas and M. Teabal (eds).

—— (2000c) "The Internationalization of Knowledge Support Functions: Global Production Networks in Information Industries," *Research Policy* (in press).

—— (2000d) "Placing the Net on the Web – Global Production Networks and Asia-Pacific Capability Formation," *Asia-Pacific Issues* 62, Honolulu: East-West Center.

—— (2000e) "Responses to the Crisis: Constraints to a Rapid Trade Adjustment in East Asia's Electronics Industry," in Ha-Joon Chang *et al.* (eds), *The Asian Crisis*, London: Macmillan.

Ernst, D. and Guerrieri, P. (1998) "International Production Networks and Changing Trade Patterns in East Asia: The Case of the Electronics Industry," *Oxford Development Studies*, 26(2).

Ernst, D. and Lundvall, B.-A. (2000) "Information Technology in the Learning Economy: Challenges for Developing Countries," in E. Reinert (ed.) *Evolutionary Economics and Spatial Income Inequality*, London: Edward Elgar.

Freeman, C. (1991) "Networks of Innovation: A Synthesis of Research Issues," *Research Policy* 20: 499–514.

Funabashi, Y. (1995) *Asia–Pacific Fusion: Japan's Role in APEC*, Washington, DC: Institute for International Economics.

Gereffi, G. and Korzeniewicz, M. (eds) (1994) *Commodity Chains and Global Competition*, Wesport CT: Praeger.

Ghoshal, S. and Barlett, C. (1990) "The Multinational Corporation as an Interorganizational Network," *Academy of Management Review* 15(4): 603–25.

Granovetter, M. (1985) "Economic Action and Social Structure: The Problem of Embeddedness," *American Journal of Sociology* 91(3): 481–510.

—— (1990) "The Old and the New Economic Sociology: A History and an Agenda," in R. Friedland and A. F. Robertson (eds) *Beyond the Marketplace: Rethinking Economy and Society*, New York: Aldine de Gruyter, 89–112.

Gungwu, W. (1991) *China and the Overseas Chinese*, Singapore: Times Academic Press.

Hagedoorn, J. and Schakenraad, J. (1990) "Inter-firm Partnerships and Cooperative Strategies in Core Technologies," in C. Freeman and L. Soete (eds) *New Exploration in the Economics of Technical Change*, London: Pinter, 3–37.

Haggard, S. (1995) *The Developing Nations and the Politics of Global Integration*, Washington, DC: The Brookings Institution.

Hamel, G. (1991) "Competition for Competence and Inter-partner Learning Within International Strategic Alliances," *Strategic Management Journal,* 12: 83–103.

Hamilton, G. (ed.) (1996) *Asian Business Networks*, Berlin: Walter de Gruyter.

Hatch, W. and Yamamura, K. (1997) *A Looming Entry Barrier: Japan's Production Networks in Asia*, Seattle, WA: National Bureau of Asian Research.

Kao, J. (1993) "The Worldwide Web of Chinese Business," *Harvard Business Review*, March–April: 24–36.

Katzenstein, P. (ed.) (1997) *Network Power*, Ithaca: Cornell University Press.

Kogut, B. (1988) "Joint Ventures: Theoretical and Empirical Perspective," *Strategic Management Journal*, 9: 319–32.

Lawrence, R. (1996) *Regionalism, Multilateralism and Deeper Integration*, Washington, DC: The Brookings Institution.

Levy, D. and Dunning, J. (1993) "International Production and Sourcing: Trends and Issues," STI Review, Paris: OECD.

Lim, L. (1978) "Women Workers in Multinational Corporations: The Case of the Electronics Industry in Malaysia and Singapore," Michigan Occasional Papers in Women's Studies, 9. Ann Arbor: Women's Studies Program, University of Michigan.

Mack, A. and Ravenhill, J. (eds) (1994) *Pacific Cooperation: Building Economic and Security Regimes in the Asia–Pacific Region*, Canberra: Allen and Unwin.

Milgrom, P. and Roberts, J. (1990) "The Economics of Modern Manufacturing: Technology, Strategy and Organization," *American Economic Review*, 80(3): 511–28.

Naughton, B. (1997) *The China Circle*, Washington, DC: Brookings.

Porter, M. (1990) *The Competitive Advantage of Nations*, New York: Free Press.

Powell, W. (1990) "Neither Market Nor Hierarchy: Network Forms of Organization," *Research in Organizational Behavior*, 12: 295–336.

Powell, W. and Brantley, P. (1992) "Competitive Cooperation in Biotechnology: Learning Through Networks?" in N. Nohria and R. G. Eccles (eds) *Networks and Organizations: Structure, Form and Action*, Boston: Harvard Business School Press, 366–94.

Powell, W. and Smith-Doerr, L. (1994) "Networks and Economic Life," in N. Smelser and R. Swedber (eds) *The Handbook of Economic Sociology*, Princeton: Princeton University Press.

Solectron (2000) "About Solectron. Site Profiles," http://www.solectron.com.

Stopford, J. (ed.) (1994) *Rejuvenating the Mature Business: The Competitive Challenge*, Boston, MA: Harvard Business School Press.

—— (1998) "Building Regional Networks: Japanese Investments in Asia," in S. Strange (ed.) *Globalisation and Capitalist Diversity: Experiences on the Asian Mainland*, Florence: European University Institute, pp. 104–130..

Sturgeon, T. (1998) "The Rise of the Global Locality," Ph.D. Dissertation, Berkeley, CA: University of California at Berkeley.

Takayasu, K.-I. and Ishizaki, Y. (1995) "The Changing International Division of Labor of Japanese Electronics Industry in Asia and Its Impact on the Japanese Economy," *RIM-Pacific Business and Industries*, 1(27): 2–21.

Tilton, J. (1971) *The International Diffusion of Technology; the Case of Semiconductors*, Washington, DC: Brookings Institution.

United Nations Conference on Trade and Development (1997) *World Investment Report*, Geneva: UNCTAD.

Vernon, R. (1971) *Sovereignty at Bay: the Multinational Spread of US Enterprises*, New York: Basic Books, 1971.

Wade, R. and Veneroso, F. (1998) "The Asian Crisis: The High Debt Model Versus the Wall Street Treasury IMF Complex," *New Left Review*, 228: 3–22.

Williamson, O. (1985) *The Economic Institutions of Capitalism: Firms, Markets and Relational Contracting*, London: Macmillan.

—— (1993) "Transaction Cost Economics and Organization Theory," *Industrial and Corporate Change*, 2(2): 107–56.

Zysman, J., Doherty, E. and Schwartz, A. (1997) "Tales from the Global Economy: Cross-National Production Networks and the Reorganization of the European Economy," *Structural Change and Economic Dynamics*, 8(1): 45–85.

# 2 International competitiveness, regional integration, and corporate strategies in the East Asian electronics industry[1]

*Paolo Guerrieri*

## Introduction

During the 1990s two basic trends emerged in East Asia's electronics industry. First, the competitiveness of East Asian countries[2] greatly improved, so that the region now accounts for a large proportion of the total world trade in many electronics sectors. Second, trade in electronic products *within* the East Asian region accelerated markedly during the 1990s. Since the first half of the 1980s there has been a sharp rise in intra-Asian trade and direct investment in the industry, mirroring a broader process of market- and firm-led regionalization.

Both trends have been interpreted in terms of the so called "flying geese" or "product cycle" model, in which Japan plays the role of the leading, innovative country, and the East Asian NICs and other Asian economies follow as second- and third-tier countries on the ladder of comparative advantage. This chapter provides another interpretation, based on the strengthening of the production networks in East Asia that have been described in the preceding chapter. It assesses trade patterns and the integration of the East Asian countries in electronic products since the 1980s by using an original trade database and taxonomy of trade flows in the electronics industry. The main purpose is to show that production networks based on strong intra-regional interdependence with respect to both inputs and sales have played a very significant role in the overall competitiveness and intra-regional trade in the electronics industry. These networks include those centered on Japanese firms, and also partly competing, partly complementary networks involving firms from the United States, the NICs, and even the ASEAN countries. The evolution of these networks has consequences not only for economic relations within East Asia, but also for the region's economic ties to the other two major areas, the United States and Europe.

This chapter is divided into three parts. The first section begins with an outline of the taxonomy and database for trade flows in the electronics industry and surveys the performance of the electronics industries since the 1980s in the major countries of East Asia: Japan, the NICs (Korea, Taiwan, Hong Kong, and Singapore), the ASEAN countries (Indonesia, the Philippines, Malaysia, and Thailand), and China. The second section evaluates intra-regional trade patterns in East Asia, providing a detailed historical and sectoral breakdown. The third section summarizes the chapter's main empirical findings and gives an explanation for them. The final section includes some concluding comments and prospects for the development of the East Asian region.

## The East Asian electronics industry: competitive position and regional integration

The competitive position of East Asian countries in the electronics industry as a whole has registered an extraordinary advance in terms of both Asia's share in world exports and Asia's standardized trade balances since the 1980s. By the mid-1990s East Asian countries controlled 50 percent of the world market, as opposed to only 23 percent at the beginning of the 1970s (see Table 2.1). East Asia as a whole also increased its trade surpluses with the rest of the world in both absolute and standardized terms throughout the period considered here, and especially from the mid-1980s to the mid-1990s (Tables 2.2 and 2.8).

If we look at the performance of individual East Asian economies, up until the mid-1980s Japan occupied a dominant position in terms of both growing market share and sectoral trade surpluses. By 1985, Japanese exports accounted for more than 28 percent of the world market. In the very short time since then, however, Japan's share in world electronics exports has diminished sharply to only 20 percent. The revaluation of the yen has led many Japanese firms to move the production of significant electronic products (particularly consumer electronics and electronics components) to other countries in the region, including Singapore, Malaysia, Thailand, and, more recently, China.

During the 1970s and 1980s, the market share of the East Asian NICs increased significantly. There were, however, marked differences across the East Asian NICs. Korean companies experienced a rapid growth in exports during most of the 1980s in both consumer electronics (color TVs and VCRs) and electronic components. In recent years, Hong Kong and Singapore have also significantly strengthened their competitive position in electronics, but in different product groups. In the case of Singapore this was due in part to the offshore transfer of production capacity by Japanese and American firms in sectors such as computer peripherals. However, in the more recent period (1990–4) the market share, and trade surpluses, of the East Asian NICs in electronics also decreased.

This development can largely be attributed to the progress of the ASEAN countries (Thailand, Malaysia, Indonesia, Philippines) and China on entering the world electronics markets, especially in consumer electronics. Among them, Malaysia has been able to strongly increase its market share and trade surplus from the late 1980s to the mid-1990s, mostly in consumer electronics. It benefited from a large influx of investment from Japanese firms and, more recently, also from East Asian NICs firms. Thailand has also attracted substantial FDI in the consumer electronics field, in particular from Japanese firms, and has strongly increased its export-oriented consumer electronics production, as in the case of TVs.

Finally, since the mid-1980s, China has advanced its position in consumer electronics in terms of both market share and trade surpluses. During the 1990s consumer electronics has become one of the country's strongest export sectors, partly as a result of the transfer of technology and production capabilities from Taiwan and Hong Kong (see Table 2.12).

The extraordinary advance of the East Asian countries in the electronics industry since the 1980s has naturally affected the position of both the United States and Europe. The US share in world electronics exports experienced a significant decline until the first half of the 1980s before stabilizing, whereas in Europe the decline in market share continued until the 1990s (Table 2.1). The United States, and more generally North America, has always been the largest contributor to Asia's trade surplus, whereas Europe has only recently registered increasing trade deficits with East Asia (Table 2.2).

Since the 1980s the trade pattern of East Asian economies in the electronics industry has exhibited a second important feature: a substantial increase in the share of intra-regional trade, especially of the intra-industry type (Japan External Trade Organization 1994). Table 2.3 shows the shares of various regions and countries in overall electronics exports to and imports from East Asia in selected years from 1970 to 1994; intra-regional trade has significantly increased over time for both exports and imports. The export share rose nearly 28 percentage points, from 11 percent in 1970 to 39 percent in 1994, and the intra-Asia share of imports increased even more (around 35 percentage points) from 31 percent in the early 1970s to 66 percent in the mid-1990s.

A closer examination of Table 2.3 reveals that behind the continuous increase in trade integration in Asia two phases can be distinguished. The first one covers the 1970s and the first half of the 1980s and is characterized by a strong increase in the intra-regional market share in East Asian imports and by a continuous dependence of the region on export markets in the United States and Europe.[3] Over that period Japan was an increasing source of exports for the East Asian countries (nearly 34 percent of East Asian imports originated there), whereas it represented a very marginal outlet for Asia's exports (only 1.5 percent by the mid-1980s). In the same period, North America (dominated by the United States) accounted for almost an equivalent share of electronics imports from Asian countries (nearly 30 percent) as Japan did, but it absorbed around 49 percent of their electronics exports.

The second phase, from the mid-1980s to the early 1990s, brought a substantial change in the regional integration of the East Asian electronics industry. Asia's export dependence on the US and European markets registered a significant overall decrease due to increased imports *within* Asia. Intra-regional imports rose from 57 to 66 percent from 1985 to 1994, and exports rose even more in the same period, from 21 to 39 percent.

Table 2.1 Share in world exports of selected countries and areas (percentage average for each subperiod)

| | Total electronics | | | Electronic data processing | | | Electronic components | | |
|---|---|---|---|---|---|---|---|---|---|
| | 1970–72 | 1984–86 | 1992–94 | 1979–82 | 1984–86 | 1992–94 | 1979–82 | 1984–86 | 1992–94 |
| Asia | 23.8 | 44.1 | 50.2 | 11.9 | 26.6 | 46.5 | 48.5 | 50.0 | 56.9 |
| Japan | 19.9 | 28.1 | 20.0 | 11.7 | 16.7 | 17.2 | 15.1 | 20.6 | 22.2 |
| *Asian NICs* | 3.1 | 13.3 | 21.9 | 0.2 | 9.6 | 23.9 | 22.2 | 18.5 | 24.0 |
| Singapore | 0.5 | 3.2 | 7.6 | 0.1 | 3.4 | 10.8 | 9.8 | 6.4 | 7.4 |
| Korea | 0.2 | 3.0 | 4.3 | 0.0 | 1.5 | 2.1 | 4.6 | 5.1 | 8.4 |
| Taiwan | 1.6 | 3.4 | 4.8 | 0.0 | 2.0 | 8.1 | 3.9 | 3.7 | 5.0 |
| Hong Kong | 1.5 | 4.0 | 5.5 | 0.1 | 2.9 | 3.3 | 4.7 | 3.8 | 3.8 |
| *ASEAN* | 0.0 | 2.0 | 6.1 | 0.0 | 0.1 | 4.1 | 10.3 | 10.2 | 9.8 |
| Thailand | 0.0 | 0.0 | 1.6 | 0.0 | 0.0 | 1.8 | 0.0 | 0.0 | 1.7 |
| Malaysia | 0.0 | 1.7 | 3.9 | 0.0 | 0.1 | 2.1 | 9.4 | 8.6 | 7.2 |
| Indonesia | 0.0 | 0.1 | 0.3 | 0.0 | 0.0 | 0.1 | 0.5 | 0.3 | 0.1 |
| Philippines | 0.0 | 0.2 | 0.3 | 0.0 | 0.0 | 0.1 | 0.4 | 1.3 | 0.8 |
| China | 0.0 | 0.3 | 1.8 | 0.0 | 0.1 | 0.9 | 0.0 | 0.0 | 0.3 |
| USA | 20.2 | 18.2 | 16.0 | 25.1 | 27.3 | 19.2 | 20.7 | 22.3 | 18.8 |
| EU (15) | 45.1 | 30.4 | 26.3 | 52.9 | 43.5 | 29.0 | 26.1 | 22.1 | 17.7 |

| | Consumer electronics | | | Office equipment | | | Telecommunications | | |
|---|---|---|---|---|---|---|---|---|---|
| | 1970–72 | 1984–86 | 1992–94 | 1979–82 | 1984–86 | 1992–94 | 1970–72 | 1984–86 | 1992–94 |
| Asia | 31.7 | 68.5 | 59.2 | 4.9 | 53.7 | 52.5 | 8.6 | 35.1 | 36.4 |
| Japan | 28.4 | 46.9 | 19.0 | 2.8 | 47.3 | 36.8 | 8.4 | 24.4 | 17.8 |
| *Asian NICs* | 3.0 | 19.3 | 26.0 | 2.0 | 5.6 | 10.8 | 0.2 | 9.9 | 11.9 |
| Singapore | 0.4 | 3.2 | 7.4 | 1.3 | 1.1 | 2.9 | 0.1 | 0.8 | 2.2 |
| Korea | 0.2 | 5.6 | 6.1 | 0.2 | 0.4 | 0.9 | 0.1 | 2.4 | 2.3 |
| Taiwan | 0.5 | 3.9 | 1.9 | 0.4 | 1.8 | 2.0 | 0.0 | 3.6 | 3.4 |
| Hong Kong | 2.1 | 7.0 | 11.0 | 0.1 | 2.5 | 5.1 | 0.1 | 3.4 | 4.3 |
| *ASEAN* | 0.0 | 0.9 | 8.8 | 0.0 | 0.4 | 3.0 | 0.0 | 0.2 | 4.1 |
| Thailand | 0.0 | 0.0 | 1.8 | 0.0 | 0.4 | 1.6 | 0.0 | 0.0 | 1.3 |
| Malaysia | 0.0 | 0.8 | 6.0 | 0.0 | 0.0 | 1.1 | 0.0 | 0.2 | 2.2 |
| Indonesia | 0.0 | 0.1 | 0.9 | 0.0 | 0.0 | 0.3 | 0.0 | 0.0 | 0.2 |
| Philippines | 0.0 | 0.0 | 0.1 | 0.0 | 0.0 | 0.0 | 0.0 | 0.0 | 0.3 |
| China | 0.0 | 1.0 | 4.9 | 0.0 | 0.3 | 1.8 | 0.0 | 0.4 | 2.3 |
| USA | 8.4 | 3.8 | 7.9 | 42.9 | 10.4 | 8.9 | 6.4 | 10.3 | 13.7 |
| EU (15) | 32.6 | 19.2 | 22.4 | 48.8 | 30.9 | 33.1 | 74.3 | 42.1 | 38.0 |

Source: Elaborations on OECD and UN data, from *SIE World Trade Database*.

Table 2.2 Asia: standardized bilateral trade balance with selected areas and countries*

| | Total electronics | | | Electronic data processing | | | Electronic components | | |
|---|---|---|---|---|---|---|---|---|---|
| | 1970–72 | 1984–86 | 1992–94 | 1970–72 | 1984–86 | 1992–94 | 1976–79 | 1984–86 | 1992–94 |
| World | 15.8 | 27.6 | 22.5 | 5.0 | 15.1 | 28.4 | 8.9 | 13.4 | 9.6 |
| North America | 10.8 | 16.4 | 11.1 | 1.3 | 8.6 | 15.6 | -0.8 | 5.7 | 3.7 |
| Japan | -2.1 | -4.5 | -4.9 | -0.5 | -1.7 | -1.5 | -5.4 | -6.8 | -10.6 |
| Asian NICs | 1.6 | 2.5 | 4.8 | 0.4 | 0.5 | 2.1 | 12.2 | 7.8 | 9.2 |
| Korea | 0.2 | 0.4 | -0.1 | 0.0 | 0.4 | 0.3 | 0.5 | 1.5 | -0.2 |
| Singapore | 0.3 | 0.8 | 1.8 | 0.1 | 0.2 | 1.3 | 3.2 | 1.7 | 3.5 |
| Taiwan | 0.5 | 0.5 | 0.7 | 0.1 | 0.2 | 0.0 | -0.4 | 2.2 | 3.0 |
| Hong Kong | 0.6 | 0.7 | 2.3 | 0.2 | -0.4 | 0.5 | 8.9 | 2.4 | 2.9 |
| China | 0.0 | 1.5 | 0.0 | 0.0 | 0.9 | 0.3 | 0.0 | 0.6 | 0.7 |
| ASEAN | 0.5 | 0.4 | -0.1 | 0.2 | 0.1 | -1.0 | -0.8 | -0.3 | 1.6 |
| Thailand | 0.1 | 0.1 | 0.1 | 0.0 | 0.0 | -0.5 | -1.0 | -0.2 | 0.4 |
| Malaysia | 0.1 | 0.3 | -0.3 | 0.0 | 0.1 | -0.4 | 0.2 | 0.5 | 1.0 |
| Indonesia | 0.1 | 0.1 | 0.1 | 0.0 | 0.0 | 0.0 | 0.0 | 0.0 | 0.0 |
| Philippines | 0.2 | -0.1 | 0.1 | 0.1 | 0.0 | -0.1 | 0.0 | -0.6 | 0.2 |
| EU (15) | 1.7 | 7.4 | 8.2 | 1.6 | 5.8 | 10.8 | 3.3 | 5.5 | 3.8 |

| | Consumer electronics | | | Office equipment | | | Telecommunications | | |
|---|---|---|---|---|---|---|---|---|---|
| | 1970–72 | 1984–86 | 1992–94 | 1970–72 | 1984–86 | 1992–94 | 1970–72 | 1984–86 | 1992–94 |
| World | 21.7 | 53.9 | 30.6 | -1.2 | 44.3 | 37.3 | 0.6 | 20.7 | 12.3 |
| North America | 13.8 | 31.9 | 14.0 | -0.1 | 25.1 | 19.4 | 2.1 | 17.0 | 8.0 |
| Japan | -3.5 | -6.8 | -4.3 | -0.1 | -4.1 | -5.8 | -1.6 | -3.5 | -4.4 |
| Asian NICs | 3.3 | 3.6 | 6.8 | 0.3 | 1.3 | 5.6 | 1.2 | 1.2 | 1.1 |
| Korea | 0.2 | -0.1 | -0.8 | 0.0 | 0.3 | 1.2 | 0.3 | 0.1 | -0.2 |
| Singapore | 0.9 | 1.4 | 2.0 | 0.0 | 0.3 | 1.6 | 0.1 | 0.5 | 0.7 |
| Taiwan | 0.5 | 0.3 | 0.6 | 0.2 | 0.3 | 0.7 | 0.7 | 0.3 | -0.6 |
| Hong Kong | 1.7 | 2.1 | 5.0 | 0.0 | 0.4 | 1.9 | 0.2 | 0.3 | 1.3 |
| China | 0.0 | 2.2 | -3.1 | 0.0 | 1.5 | -0.3 | 0.0 | 0.8 | 1.7 |
| ASEAN | 0.6 | 0.6 | -1.3 | 0.1 | 0.6 | 0.0 | 0.5 | 1.5 | 0.4 |
| Thailand | 0.2 | 0.2 | 0.2 | 0.0 | 0.2 | 0.0 | 0.2 | 0.6 | 0.4 |
| Malaysia | 0.1 | 0.3 | -1.8 | 0.0 | 0.2 | -0.2 | 0.2 | 0.7 | -0.4 |
| Indonesia | 0.0 | 0.1 | 0.2 | 0.0 | 0.3 | 0.2 | 0.1 | 0.1 | 0.3 |
| Philippines | 0.3 | 0.1 | 0.1 | 0.0 | -0.1 | 0.2 | 0.0 | 0.1 | 0.2 |
| EU (15) | 4.0 | 13.6 | 11.3 | -1.7 | 15.2 | 13.3 | -4.2 | -1.5 | 1.9 |

*Trade balance expressed as percentage of total world trade in each single product group (STB).

STB = $X_i - M_i/W_i \times 100$ where $X_i$ = total export product group i; $M_i$ = total import product group i; $W_i$ = total trade product group i.
Source: Elaborations on OECD and UN data, from *SIE World Trade Database*.

*Table 2.3* Asia: geographic trade composition (total electronics)*

|  | 1970 | 1980 | 1985 | 1990 | 1992 | 1994 |
|---|---|---|---|---|---|---|
| **Export** | | | | | | |
| World | 100 | 100 | 100 | 100 | 100 | 100 |
| Asia | 11.0 | 19.9 | 21.5 | 28.1 | 32.5 | 39.0 |
| Asia (without Japan) | 10.6 | 18.1 | 19.9 | 24.6 | 29.1 | 33.9 |
| Japan | 0.5 | 1.8 | 1.6 | 3.5 | 3.4 | 5.1 |
| Asian NICs | 8.0 | 12.7 | 11.0 | 18.0 | 20.7 | 22.1 |
| China | 0.0 | 1.6 | 6.1 | 2.6 | 3.4 | 4.2 |
| ASEAN | 2.5 | 3.8 | 2.7 | 4.0 | 5.0 | 7.6 |
| NAFTA | 58.9 | 35.3 | 49.7 | 37.7 | 36.2 | 35.0 |
| North America | 58.5 | 34.8 | 49.3 | 37.1 | 35.5 | 34.0 |
| APEC | 71.5 | 57.2 | 73.6 | 67.7 | 70.4 | 75.6 |
| Total Europe | 15.5 | 27.1 | 20.3 | 27.7 | 22.6 | 19.9 |
| EU (15) | 12.6 | 25.2 | 19.0 | 25.8 | 21.3 | 19.0 |
| **Import** | | | | | | |
| World | 100 | 100 | 100 | 100 | 100 | 100 |
| Asia | 31.1 | 47.5 | 57.1 | 59.5 | 64.8 | 66.6 |
| Asia (without Japan) | 3.5 | 19.4 | 23.9 | 33.1 | 37.6 | 42.1 |
| Japan | 27.6 | 28.2 | 33.2 | 26.4 | 27.2 | 24.5 |
| Asian NICs | 3.3 | 13.5 | 17.4 | 18.5 | 20.4 | 22.1 |
| China | 0.0 | 0.4 | 1.4 | 6.2 | 7.2 | 7.4 |
| ASEAN | 0.2 | 5.5 | 5.1 | 8.5 | 10.0 | 12.7 |
| NAFTA | 35.0 | 35.3 | 31.0 | 28.9 | 24.6 | 22.7 |
| North America | 35.0 | 35.1 | 30.8 | 28.8 | 24.5 | 22.6 |
| APEC | 66.6 | 83.0 | 88.3 | 88.8 | 89.8 | 89.7 |
| Total Europe | 33.2 | 15.6 | 10.2 | 10.6 | 8.3 | 9.5 |
| EU (15) | 23.8 | 12.4 | 8.4 | 7.6 | 6.1 | 7.8 |

*Asian export (import) toward a given area or country divided by world Asian export (import), as a percentage.

Source: Elaboration on OECD and UN data, from *SIE World Trade Database*.

Both trends outlined above, that is the strengthening of East Asia's competitive position and the rapid increase in regional trade integration, have been explained using the so-called "flying geese" or "product cycle" model of Asian development (Cohen and Guerrieri 1994; Hobday 1995). This approach explains the shift in the location of production from one country to another in terms of changing competitiveness as industries mature (Akamatsu 1961; Vernon 1966; 1979). In the application of the product cycle model to East Asia, the lead role is typically assigned to Japan, both as a source of technology and as an outlet market. As an industry segment matures, however, production shifts to the NICs, then to the other East Asian countries at lower stages of development.

If we look at the electronics industry as a complex mix of products with different technology and skilled labor contents, the flying geese model can be applied to the East Asian trade pattern in electronics as a whole. As Japanese labor costs increased and the yen appreciated, production capabilities and technology were transferred from Japan to the East Asian NICs, then to the ASEAN countries and China, which in turn exported electronics back to Japan as well as to other countries. As the NICs registered wage increases and upgraded their production to more technology-intensive electronics products, they also moved part of their electronics production and technology to ASEAN and Chinese producers.

The evidence reported above on the performance of individual East Asian economies and their sequential "gains" in different electronics sectors would seem to confirm this interpretation. But as a number of other scholars have noted, this first impression can be misleading (Park and Won-am 1991; Ernst 1994b; Hobday 1995; Ravenhill 1995; Ernst and Guerrieri 1998). The model of a seamless transfer of capabilities overlooks a number of distinctive features of East Asia's development in the electronics sector, including the networks analyzed in this book. When the electronics trade data were disaggregated further, somewhat different patterns of regional integration emerged.

## Regional integration: differentiating the industry

Electronics is a complex and highly differentiated industry that comprises both technology-intensive and labor-intensive products. With the purpose of assessing different patterns in East Asian trade integration across industry segments, we adopt a taxonomy first introduced by Ernst and O'Connor (1992). They distinguished five product categories: (1) electronic data processing equipment, (2) electronic office equipment, (3) telecommunications equipment, (4) electronic components, and (5) consumer electronics. For the purpose of this analysis, we combine the first three product categories into a single one, industrial electronic products. By calculating the geographical composition of trade flows in East Asia in each of these categories since the 1980s, a more nuanced portrait of the changing division of labor in the region will be gained.

*Industrial electronic products* (encompassing electronic data processing equipment, office electronic equipment, and telecommunications equipment) covers a heterogeneous group of products, ranging from personal computers, terminal and transmission equipment to peripheral equipment, such as disk drives, printers, keyboards, switching systems, and office equipment, such as photocopying machines. In this group, East Asia as a whole has recently increased intra-regional imports yet has maintained a very high external export dependence on the US and European markets. In the electronic data processing segment, for example (Table 2.4), the share of imports emanating from Asia rose substantially from 32 to 63 percent in the period 1985–94, reflecting the lengthening of the supply chain in the computer industry and the dramatic growth of intra-regional trade in peripherals. This development lowered Asia's previous dependence on imports from the United States. But the role of the United States and Europe as outlet markets for East Asian exports has remained highly significant through the first half of the 1990s, with an increase in the relative share of the European market in the most recent period. By the mid-1990s the United States and Europe as a whole still accounted for almost 70 percent of East Asia's exports of personal computers and peripheral equipment (Table 2.4). This pattern was reflected in recent years in the substantial increase of Asia's trade surplus (standardized) in electronic data processing compared with the United States and Europe (see Table 2.8). Singapore and Taiwan greatly contributed to this result by sharply improving their share of world trade in electronic data processing equipment, particularly in computer peripherals (see Tables 2.1, 2.11, and 2.12). By contrast, Korea lagged behind, as shown by the decrease in Korean world export market share and the stagnation of electronic data processing in the total exports (see Tables 2.1 and 2.11).

In the *industrial electronic products* group, Asia as a whole registered the most impressive performance in terms of export growth. Furthermore, by 1994

*Table 2.4*  Asia: geographic trade composition (electronic data processing)*

|                      | 1970 | 1980 | 1985 | 1990 | 1992 | 1994 |
|----------------------|------|------|------|------|------|------|
| *Export*             |      |      |      |      |      |      |
| World                | 100  | 100  | 100  | 100  | 100  | 100  |
| Asia                 | 4.0  | 18.6 | 14.5 | 17.5 | 20.0 | 25.7 |
| Asia (without Japan) | 4.0  | 17.1 | 13.6 | 15.4 | 17.7 | 21.7 |
| Japan                | 0.0  | 1.5  | 0.9  | 2.1  | 2.2  | 3.9  |
| Asian NICs           | 2.3  | 11.1 | 6.9  | 11.5 | 12.6 | 14.7 |
| China                | 0.0  | 2.7  | 4.8  | 1.3  | 2.1  | 2.6  |
| ASEAN                | 1.7  | 3.2  | 1.8  | 2.7  | 3.1  | 4.4  |
| NAFTA                | 46.3 | 48.2 | 55.3 | 48.8 | 45.8 | 45.4 |
| North America        | 45.7 | 47.5 | 55.1 | 48.6 | 45.6 | 44.9 |
| APEC                 | 54.2 | 73.1 | 73.7 | 68.7 | 68.0 | 73.5 |
| Total Europe         | 36.0 | 20.2 | 24.3 | 29.9 | 28.2 | 24.9 |
| EU (15)              | 32.9 | 19.1 | 23.7 | 28.8 | 27.2 | 24.3 |
| *Import*             |      |      |      |      |      |      |
| World                | 100  | 100  | 100  | 100  | 100  | 100  |
| Asia                 | 4.8  | 13.4 | 32.7 | 47.0 | 55.7 | 62.7 |
| Asia (without Japan) | 0.6  | 3.6  | 17.0 | 30.3 | 38.8 | 47.5 |
| Japan                | 4.2  | 9.8  | 15.7 | 16.7 | 16.9 | 15.2 |
| Asian NICs           | 0.2  | 3.1  | 13.7 | 19.9 | 21.9 | 25.5 |
| China                | 0.0  | 0.0  | 0.6  | 1.5  | 4.0  | 5.0  |
| ASEAN                | 0.4  | 0.5  | 2.7  | 8.9  | 12.9 | 16.9 |
| NAFTA                | 64.4 | 67.3 | 55.2 | 45.2 | 35.4 | 28.6 |
| North America        | 64.4 | 67.0 | 54.7 | 44.8 | 35.2 | 28.6 |
| APEC                 | 69.5 | 81.0 | 88.3 | 92.9 | 92.2 | 92.6 |
| Total Europe         | 30.0 | 12.6 | 7.7  | 5.9  | 5.8  | 6.6  |
| EU (15)              | 28.4 | 12.4 | 7.3  | 5.7  | 5.6  | 6.5  |

*Asian export (import) toward a given area or country divided by world Asian export (import), in percentage.

Source: Elaboration on OECD and UN data, from *SIE World Trade Database*.

industrial electronics had replaced consumer electronics as the leading export item for Japan and a few East Asian NICs, in particular Singapore and Taiwan (see Tables 2.11 and 2.12).

It is also interesting to look at the shifts in intra-regional sources of trade flows for electronic data processing equipment. Table 2.4 reveals that Japan's share of intra-regional East Asian imports remained almost stable from the mid-1980s up to the mid-1990s. This occurred despite the fact that the periodic appreciation of the yen not only weakened Japan's competitiveness but led to a great expansion of Japanese direct investment in East Asia in products related to personal computers and peripheral items, investment characterized by a strong export orientation toward third countries, particularly the United States and Europe (Ernst 1994a). The share of the other East Asian countries has increased substantially during the same period (from 17 percent of all East Asian imports by the mid-1980s to more than 47 percent in 1994). Two ASEAN economies, Malaysia and Thailand, which increased their exports mainly to Singapore and other East Asian NICs, offered the largest contributions to this increase. In both countries this trend was due to the huge influx of foreign investment from Japan, the other East Asian NICs, and the United States (Takeuchi 1993). In the mid-1990s, China also increased her intra-regional exports, up to 5 percentage points, mainly by exporting to Hong Kong, and from there to the United States and Europe.

The case of *consumer electronics* provides a very different picture of regional trade integration in East Asia (Table 2.5). For many East Asian countries, including Japan, consumer electronics provided the initial entry point into the electronics industry. This product group comprises both labor-intensive and volume-intensive standard products, such as audio products, TVs, VCRs, microwave ovens (MWOs), electronic toys, and games. The share of East Asian imports originating from within the region has remained extra-ordinarily high, more than 75 percent, over the past fifteen years. By contrast, Asia's export dependence on markets in the United States and Europe has decreased during the past ten years because of the expansion of demand within the region. Whereas domestic markets in the region accounted for under 20 percent of East Asia's exports of consumer electronics in 1985, their share of exports rose to more than 39 percent in 1994. Hence, Asia's (standardized) trade surplus has also significantly decreased towards the United States and Europe in the same period (see Table 2.9).

Major shifts have also occurred in the distribution of trade flows within the Asian region in the consumer electronics field. Japan's share of East Asia's imports from the region shrank from 57 percent in 1985 to only 29 percent by the mid-1990s owing to the massive expansion of its own export-oriented FDI in this sector. With the revaluation of the yen, Japanese firms shifted the production of many consumer electronic products (particularly TVs and VCRs) towards countries in Southeast Asia, including Singapore, Malaysia, Thailand, and, more recently, China (Urata 1993). The East Asian NICs, which have also intensively invested in other East Asian countries in consumer

*Table 2.5* Asia: geographic trade composition (consumer electronics)*

|  | 1970 | 1980 | 1985 | 1990 | 1992 | 1994 |
|---|---|---|---|---|---|---|
| *Export* | | | | | | |
| World | 100 | 100 | 100 | 100 | 100 | 100 |
| Asia | 14.6 | 14.9 | 19.2 | 26.7 | 33.4 | 39.1 |
| Asia (without Japan) | 13.9 | 13.8 | 18.2 | 23.8 | 29.3 | 31.9 |
| Japan | 0.7 | 1.0 | 1.0 | 2.9 | 4.1 | 7.2 |
| China | 0.1 | 2.0 | 7.6 | 2.9 | 4.2 | 5.5 |
| ASEAN | 2.0 | 1.8 | 1.3 | 2.5 | 4.0 | 6.2 |
| NAFTA | 51.3 | 29.6 | 48.4 | 29.0 | 29.3 | 28.1 |
| North America | 50.7 | 29.2 | 48.3 | 28.2 | 28.2 | 26.6 |
| APEC | 67.9 | 46.5 | 69.9 | 57.6 | 64.5 | 69.0 |
| Total Europe | 16.3 | 31.0 | 20.5 | 32.4 | 21.6 | 20.3 |
| EU (15) | 11.8 | 28.5 | 18.7 | 29.0 | 19.9 | 19.1 |
| *Import* | | | | | | |
| World | 100 | 100 | 100 | 100 | 100 | 100 |
| Asia | 39.0 | 77.4 | 84.9 | 76.6 | 79.2 | 81.0 |
| Asia (without Japan) | 3.4 | 24.6 | 27.5 | 49.1 | 48.9 | 56.1 |
| Japan | 35.6 | 52.8 | 57.4 | 27.6 | 30.4 | 24.9 |
| Asian NICs | 3.1 | 22.7 | 21.6 | 21.0 | 17.4 | 17.3 |
| China | 0.0 | 1.2 | 4.1 | 19.0 | 20.1 | 21.5 |
| ASEAN | 0.3 | 0.7 | 1.7 | 9.1 | 11.3 | 17.3 |
| NAFTA | 14.4 | 6.2 | 5.4 | 8.0 | 8.2 | 7.9 |
| North America | 14.4 | 6.2 | 5.4 | 8.0 | 8.2 | 7.9 |
| APEC | 53.6 | 83.8 | 90.4 | 85.0 | 87.8 | 89.2 |
| Total Europe | 46.2 | 15.5 | 9.3 | 14.5 | 11.1 | 10.2 |
| EU (15) | 11.3 | 5.6 | 3.1 | 3.0 | 2.3 | 2.8 |

*Asian export (import) toward a given area or country divided by world Asian export (import), as a percentage.

Source: Elaboration on OECD and UN data, from *SIE World Trade Database*.

electronics, have also seen a decrease in their share of intra-regional imports in the same period (from 21 percent to 17 percent), after continuous increases over the previous fifteen years.

These developments can largely be attributed to the entry of the ASEAN countries and China into the world market for consumer electronics. The intra-regional share of the ASEAN countries increased substantially between 1985 and 1994, accounting for more than 17 percent of total intra-regional imports. China experienced the largest gains, increasing its share of Asia's consumer electronics imports to more than 21 percent (up from 4.1 percent in 1985), mainly through its growing trade integration with Hong Kong. Consumer electronics accounted for nearly 54 percent of China's overall electronics exports in 1994, and although by a decreasing value they were by far the dominant item in China's electronics exports by the mid-1990s (see Table 2.2).

A third picture of East Asian regional trade integration is evident in *electronic components*. This is a heterogeneous product group ranging from low

*Table 2.6* Asia: geographic trade composition (electronic components)*

|  | 1980 | 1985 | 1990 | 1992 | 1994 |
|---|---|---|---|---|---|
| *Export* | | | | | |
| World | 100 | 100 | 100 | 100 | 100 |
| Asia | 39.8 | 38.9 | 49.6 | 54.0 | 56.3 |
| Asia (without Japan) | 34.7 | 33.8 | 41.6 | 48.6 | 50.5 |
| Japan | 5.2 | 5.1 | 8.0 | 5.4 | 5.8 |
| Asian NICs | 24.8 | 24.6 | 33.2 | 37.8 | 35.9 |
| China | 0.3 | 2.1 | 1.1 | 1.3 | 1.9 |
| ASEAN | 9.6 | 7.1 | 7.3 | 9.5 | 12.7 |
| NAFTA | 41.9 | 41.8 | 33.1 | 30.8 | 29.6 |
| North America | 41.6 | 41.6 | 32.7 | 30.4 | 29.0 |
| APEC | 82.1 | 81.3 | 83.2 | 85.2 | 86.4 |
| Total Europe | 16.7 | 17.6 | 15.7 | 12.5 | 12.7 |
| EU (15) | 16.1 | 17.0 | 15.0 | 11.6 | 12.1 |
| *Import* | | | | | |
| World | 100 | 100 | 100 | 100 | 100 |
| Asia | 44.8 | 51.2 | 56.4 | 63.4 | 65.7 |
| Asia (without Japan) | 27.4 | 27.0 | 26.3 | 33.4 | 36.9 |
| Japan | 17.4 | 24.2 | 30.1 | 30.0 | 28.8 |
| Asian NICs | 13.6 | 14.9 | 16.4 | 23.6 | 25.9 |
| China | 0.0 | 0.1 | 0.3 | 0.5 | 0.6 |
| ASEAN | 13.8 | 12.0 | 9.6 | 9.3 | 10.4 |
| NAFTA | 46.8 | 40.3 | 34.8 | 29.5 | 26.9 |
| North America | 46.8 | 40.3 | 34.8 | 29.4 | 26.8 |
| APEC | 91.6 | 91.6 | 91.4 | 92.9 | 92.6 |
| Total Europe | 8.2 | 6.8 | 8.3 | 5.9 | 6.7 |
| EU (15) | 7.9 | 6.7 | 8.2 | 5.7 | 6.5 |

*Asian export (import) toward a given area or country divided by world Asian export (import), as a percentage.

Source: Elaboration on OECD and UN data, from *SIE World Trade Database*.

value-added products to the most sophisticated ones that perform critical functions for virtually all other electronics products, such as semiconductors, integrated circuits, microprocessors, and electronic microassemblies. This composite mix is reflected to a large extent in the localization and distribution of the electronics component industries within East Asia. In this product group, trade regionalization increased in terms of both exports and imports, and intra-regional shares of both East Asian exports and imports increased by almost the same amount (Table 2.6). By the mid-1990s more than 56 percent of East Asian exports of electronic components went to other East Asian markets (compared with 39 percent at the beginning of the 1980s), and 65 percent of East Asian imports originated within the region (up from 44 percent in 1980), again reflecting the development of dense production networks within the region. As a result, Asia's external dependence on both export to and imports from North America and Europe decreased throughout the more recent period, with a corresponding decrease in Asia's trade surplus (in standardized terms) toward the other two major regions (see Table 2.9).

With regard to the distribution of trade flows within the East Asian region, during the 1990s Japan has replaced the United States and become the largest supplier of electronic components in the region. Japan's specialization in electronics components has also rapidly increased since the mid-1980s (see Table 2.11). However, unlike the other two segments outlined above, Japan's share of East Asian imports of electronic components has also maintained high values in recent years (Table 2.6). The East Asian NICs as a group have emerged as a major market for Japan. But Japan is also a very important customer for electronic components produced in the NICs, such as computer memory. ASEAN countries have recently achieved significant progress in components exports as well, to a large extent by assembling semiconductor devices. Malaysia is by far the most important producer and exporter of the ASEAN economies, although more recently Thailand has come on the scene.

Nonetheless, Japan's trade surplus (standardized) compared with the other East Asian countries has strongly increased throughout the 1990s in this segment (see Table 2.9) owing to the increasing import dependence of all major NICs (Singapore, Korea, and Taiwan) on Japanese electronics components (see Tables 2.11 and 2.12). Moreover, the trade surplus of ASEAN countries as a whole drastically diminished from the mid-1980s to the mid-1990s because of a similar increase in the import dependence on high value-added Japanese components (see Table 2.9).

## Regional integration and trade balances in Asia

Further insights into Asia's regional trade integration can be gained by looking at the trade balance of the East Asian countries across the sectors just outlined. East Asia as a whole substantially increased its trade surplus in electronics in absolute terms in the period from the mid-1980s to the mid-1990s (Table 2.7), registering only a marginal decrease in standardized terms (Table 2.2). The sectoral composition of Asia's trade surplus, however, changed significantly in the recent period. The (standardized) trade surplus with the United States and Europe in industrial electronics has increased strongly in more recent years (Table 2.8), thus largely compensating for the slow growth in East Asia's trade surplus in consumer electronics (Table 2.9).

As noted above, Japan accounted for most of the Asian trade surplus. Although North America registered the highest deficit during the first half of the 1980s, by the mid-1990s North America and Europe contributed almost equally to Japan's positive trade balance. But Japan also saw a huge increase in its surplus *vis-à-vis* the rest of Asia (Table 2.7). The three regional areas (North America, Europe, and Asia) differ significantly, however, in terms of the sectoral composition of their trade deficits with Japan. The United States and Europe have witnessed increasing trade deficits in industrial electronics, particularly data processing equipment, since the second half of the 1980s,

Table 2.7 Overall and bilateral cumulative trade balances of Asia, Japan, and the Asian NICs (total electronics) (current US dollar)

| Export from | Export to | | | | | | |
|---|---|---|---|---|---|---|---|
| | World | Asia | Japan | Asian NICs | ASEAN | North America | Europe |
| *Cumulative trade balances from 1980 to 1994 in US dollars (millions)* | | | | | | | |
| Asia | 877.317 | | −153.637 | 136.128 | 4.137 | 435.487 | 323.740 |
| Japan | 683.259 | 153.637 | | 116.916 | 22.355 | 260.095 | 197.818 |
| Asian NICs | 184.297 | −136.128 | −116.916 | | −16.449 | 156.182 | 116.750 |
| *Cumulative trade balances from 1980 to 1986 in US dollars (millions)* | | | | | | | |
| Asia | 211.323 | | −32.410 | 21.254 | 3.937 | 110.386 | 64.329 |
| Japan | 194.576 | 32.410 | | 23.177 | 4.607 | 79.842 | 52.387 |
| Asian NICs | 31.698 | −21.254 | −23.177 | | 37.622 | 31.589 | 13.059 |
| *Cumulative trade balances from 1980 to 1994 in US dollars (millions)* | | | | | | | |
| Asia | 665.993 | | −121.227 | 122.026 | 0.201 | 325.101 | 259.411 |
| Japan | 488.683 | 121.227 | | 93.739 | 17.748 | 180.253 | 145.431 |
| Asian NICs | 152.600 | −122.026 | −93.739 | | −16.487 | 124.593 | 103.692 |

Source: Elaborations on UN and OECD trade data, from *SIE World Trade Database*.

*Table 2.8* Overall and bilateral cumulative trade balances of Asia, Japan, and the Asian NICs (electronic data processing) (current US dollar)

| Export from | Export to | | | | | | |
|---|---|---|---|---|---|---|---|
| | World | Asia | Japan | Asian NICs | ASEAN | North America | Europe |
| *Cumulative trade balances from 1980 to 1994 in US dollars (millions)* | | | | | | | |
| Asia | 264.979 | | −14.252 | 17.059 | −5.115 | 142.915 | 110.950 |
| Japan | 144.945 | 14.252 | | 12.882 | 0.413 | 71.508 | 53.130 |
| Asian NICs | 117.019 | −17.059 | −12.882 | | −4.776 | 69.873 | 55.195 |
| *Cumulative trade balances from 1980 to 1986 in US dollars (millions)* | | | | | | | |
| Asia | 144.945 | | −2.836 | 1.135 | 0.328 | 11.961 | 9.102 |
| Japan | 20.587 | 2.836 | | 2.178 | 0.259 | 9.195 | 6.957 |
| Asian NICs | 4.854 | −1.135 | −2.178 | | 0.075 | 3.864 | 2.516 |
| *Cumulative trade balances from 1987 to 1994 in US dollars (millions)* | | | | | | | |
| Asia | 242.789 | | −11.416 | 15.924 | −5.443 | 130.954 | 101.849 |
| Japan | 124.358 | 11.416 | | 10.704 | 0.154 | 62.313 | 46.173 |
| Asian NICs | 112.165 | −15.924 | −10.704 | | −4.851 | 66.009 | 52.678 |

Source: Elaborations on UN and OECD trade data, from *SIE World Trade Database.*

Table 2.9 Overall and bilateral cumulative trade balances of Asia, Japan, and the Asian NICs (consumer electronics) (current US dollar)

| Export from | Export to | | | | | | |
|---|---|---|---|---|---|---|---|
| | World | Asia | Japan | Asian NICs | ASEAN | North America | Europe |
| *Cumulative trade balances from 1980 to 1994 in US dollars (millions)* | | | | | | | |
| Asia | 337.408 | | –3.961 | 55.866 | –3.599 | 158.626 | 118.426 |
| Japan | 221.950 | 3.961 | | 29.205 | 3.005 | 85.053 | 63.018 |
| Asian NICs | 76.324 | –55.866 | –29.205 | | –6.713 | 57.013 | 43.442 |
| *Cumulative trade balances from 1980 to 1986 in US dollars (millions)* | | | | | | | |
| Asia | 221.950 | | –12.760 | 8.449 | 1.977 | 60.737 | 37.069 |
| Japan | 100.584 | 12.760 | | 8.839 | 1.255 | 41.367 | 28.009 |
| Asian NICs | 25.338 | –8.603 | –8.839 | | 0.708 | 18.993 | 8.749 |
| *Cumulative trade balances from 1987 to 1994 in US dollars (millions)* | | | | | | | |
| Asia | 215.590 | | –26.849 | 47.264 | –5.576 | 97.889 | 81.357 |
| Japan | 121.366 | 26.849 | | 20.366 | 1.749 | 43.686 | 35.009 |
| Asian NICs | 50.986 | –47.264 | –20.366 | | –7.421 | 38.020 | 34.693 |

Source: Elaborations on UN and OECD trade data, from *SIE World Trade Database*.

*Table 2.10* Overall and bilateral cumulative trade balances of Asia, Japan, and the Asian NICs (electronic components) (current US dollar)

| Export from | Export to | | | | | North America | Europe |
|---|---|---|---|---|---|---|---|
| | World | Asia | Japan | Asian NICs | ASEAN | | |
| *Cumulative trade balances from 1980 to 1994 in US dollars (millions)* | | | | | | | |
| Asia | 73.012 | | −67.426 | 47.858 | 5.101 | 25.504 | 31.271 |
| Japan | 111.426 | 67.426 | | 52.986 | 13.134 | 2.259 | 17.432 |
| Asian NICs | −34.492 | −47.858 | −52.986 | | −0.696 | 2.816 | 8.778 |
| *Cumulative trade balances from 1980 to 1986 in US dollars (millions)* | | | | | | | |
| Asia | 111.426 | | −8.600 | 6.549 | −0.786 | 5.208 | 6.486 |
| Japan | 16.907 | 8.600 | | 7.277 | 1.135 | 4.294 | 3.196 |
| Asian NICs | −3.989 | −6.549 | −7.277 | | −1.266 | 0.457 | 1.999 |
| *Cumulative trade balances from 1987 to 1994 in US dollars (millions)* | | | | | | | |
| Asia | 59.026 | | −58.826 | 41.309 | 5.887 | 20.297 | 24.784 |
| Japan | 94.519 | 58.826 | | 45.709 | 11.998 | 18.300 | 14.236 |
| Asian NICs | −30.503 | −41.309 | −45.709 | | −0.569 | 2.359 | 6.780 |

Source: Elaborations on UN and OECD trade data, from *SIE World Trade Database.*

whereas their trade deficits in consumer electronics, although increasing in absolute terms, have slowed down. In the same period East Asian countries, especially the East Asian NICs, have experienced increasing deficits towards Japan, especially in electronic components (Table 2.10). As a consequence, the "bilateral" trade deficit of the East Asian region towards Japan has risen substantially for the electronics industry as a whole.

On the other hand, the East Asian NICs were able to generate a substantial trade surplus with the rest of the world, especially with respect to the United States and Europe. This surplus was mostly concentrated in consumer electronics and, more recently, in industrial electronic products (particularly computers). In 1994 the ASEAN economies, particularly Thailand and Malaysia, were also able to accumulate a trade surplus in electronics, mostly in consumer electronics, toward the United States, and, to a lesser extent, Europe. Again, this is due mainly to the influx of FDI from Japan, but also from the other East Asian NICs and the United States (Ernst and Guerrieri 1998).

Thus, most Asian countries have been running large and increasing trade deficits with Japan in the recent period and symmetrical (though not entirely compensating) trade surpluses with the United States and Europe. This confirms that the Japanese market has remained a poor outlet for Asian electronics exports up to the end of the period considered here. The share of Asian electronics exports destined outside the region, to the United States and Europe, was fully ten times higher than that shipped to Japan by the mid-1990s.

To summarize the data presented here, both the competitiveness and the regional trade integration of the electronics industry in East Asia has undeniably increased during the 1990s. However, overall trends mask very different patterns across segments – industrial electronics, consumer electronics and electronics components – some of which do not fit the flying geese model. First, the data confirm that East Asian countries are still heavily dependent on the United States and, more recently, on Europe for their electronics exports, especially for industrial electronics products. Japan is still a marginal market outlet for exports from the Asian NICs and ASEAN, in no way playing the role of "lead goose" with respect to absorption of the region's exports. The result is increasingly large trade deficits in electronics for the United States and Europe, and symmetrical trade surpluses for Japan and other Asian countries. Asia has also experienced large trade imbalances with Japan, however. In sum, we find a triangular trade configuration with Asia as a whole running surpluses with the United States and Europe, but with Asia outside Japan also running deficits with Japan.

Second, the evidence on intra-regional imports in industrial electronics and electronic components shows that East Asian countries and firms located there increasingly rely on the region for supplies of components, equipment, and technology for many electronics products. There is no doubt that the growth in regional investment flows in East Asia is closely linked with this regional pattern of manufacturing production, technology, and trade, since a large proportion of trade integration derives from intra-company transactions (Park and Won-am 1991; Urata 1993) as well as the looser network forms outlined in the chapters which follow.

Japanese CPNs are an important force in creating this pattern. Japanese FDI has been growing dramatically since the mid-1980s, more than in all previous years, and the electronics industry has accounted for a large share of the total Japanese FDI in East Asia (Yoshitomi 1994). In recent years, an increasing number of Japanese firms (not only multinationals but also medium-sized firms) have moved production off shore. As Ernst shows in Chapter 4, these firms have built up regional networks and intra-industry and intra-firm trade linkages (Yoshitomi 1994; Graham and Anzai 1994).

The expansion of Japan's peculiar production networks in East Asia helps explain the increasing dependence of the East Asian economies on Japanese electronics components and technology during the late 1990s. Throughout the 1980s Japan experienced a substantial shift in the product composition of its electronics exports from consumer electronics to components and industrial electronics, especially electronic data processing equipment (Table 2.11). Meanwhile, the NICs became more dependent on Japan for imports of precisely those products: industrial electronics and especially electronic components (Tables 2.12 and 2.13) (Takeuchi 1994).

The increasing technological dependence of the NICs explains why their trade deficit with respect to Japan increased during the 1990s despite the rapid growth of the their exports to Japan.[4] However, these patterns also indirectly confirm the "closed nature" of Japanese regional production networks in East Asia. The data are consonant with very high component imports on the part of East Asian affiliates of Japanese firms from their parent companies and the limited links between affiliates and local firms in the region.[5]

However, a third and most significant finding is to show that East Asia's performance in electronics is not due only – or even mostly – to Japanese CPNs. US firms have always been an important competing source of technology, foreign investment, and capital goods for both the Asian NICs and the ASEAN economies. This is confirmed by the evidence on trade in electronic components and electronic data processing equipment in the period considered here, but also by the very large deficits that the United States runs in the electronics sector more generally. As Borrus outlines in Chapter 3, these deficits reflect not only exports from the subsidiaries of Japanese firms, nor arm's-length purchases from firms located in other countries in the region, but the development of an alternative supply base in the NICs and ASEAN fostered by the "open" network organization of American companies. This architecture has been particularly favorable to the transfer of technology and the fostering of local capabilities in the region.

The changing composition of electronics exports and trade specialization in the NICs confirms this structural transformation (Tables 2.11, 2.12, and

*Table 2.11* Trade composition of the electronics industry in Japan, Singapore, and Korea*

| Declaring country | Exports | | | Imports | | |
|---|---|---|---|---|---|---|
| | *1980* | *1987* | *1994* | *1980* | *1987* | *1994* |
| *Japan* | | | | | | |
| Electronic data processing | 4.8 | 23.9 | 28.5 | 37.8 | 35.4 | 34.3 |
| Office equipment | 14.2 | 10.4 | 8.5 | 5.2 | 2.9 | 2.4 |
| Telecommunication | 3.0 | 6.3 | 5.6 | 1.4 | 4.1 | 4.6 |
| Electronic components | 9.4 | 13.6 | 28.9 | 27.3 | 25.3 | 27.4 |
| Consumer electronics | 57.6 | 32.1 | 17.3 | 13.8 | 18.4 | 20.2 |
| Medical equipment | 1.1 | 1.7 | 1.7 | 8.3 | 8.4 | 4.6 |
| Other | 9.9 | 12.0 | 9.5 | 6.2 | 5.5 | 6.5 |
| Total electronics | 100.0 | 100.0 | 100.0 | 100.0 | 100.0 | 100.0 |
| *Singapore* | | | | | | |
| Electronic data processing | 2.0 | 37.4 | 46.7 | 37.8 | 35.4 | 34.3 |
| Office equipment | 3.7 | 1.8 | 1.5 | 5.2 | 2.9 | 2.4 |
| Telecommunication | 1.4 | 1.6 | 2.0 | 1.4 | 4.1 | 4.6 |
| Electronic components | 42.2 | 25.8 | 24.2 | 27.3 | 25.3 | 27.4 |
| Consumer electronics | 40.8 | 24.8 | 19.2 | 13.8 | 18.4 | 20.2 |
| Medical equipment | 0.3 | 0.2 | 0.2 | 8.3 | 8.4 | 4.6 |
| Other | 9.6 | 8.4 | 6.3 | 6.2 | 5.5 | 6.5 |
| Total electronics | 100.0 | 100.0 | 100.0 | 100.0 | 100.0 | 100.0 |
| *Korea* | | | | | | |
| Electronic data processing | 3.3 | 16.5 | 14.5 | 11.8 | 16.7 | 17.5 |
| Office equipment | 1.9 | 1.1 | 0.9 | 2.8 | 2.8 | 5.1 |
| Telecommunication | 1.3 | 5.0 | 3.3 | 9.2 | 1.6 | 3.0 |
| Electronic components | 28.9 | 23.0 | 46.6 | 43.7 | 53.7 | 52.1 |
| Consumer electronics | 59.6 | 48.1 | 26.1 | 17.2 | 14.2 | 9.3 |
| Medical equipment | 0.1 | 0.1 | 0.2 | 2.7 | 1.8 | 3.1 |
| Other | 4.9 | 6.2 | 8.4 | 12.5 | 9.3 | 10.1 |
| Total electronics | 100.0 | 100.0 | 100.0 | 100.0 | 100.0 | 100.0 |

*Percentage shares of the sectoral groups in total electronics exports (or imports) of each country and area.

Source: Elaborations on OECD and UN data, from *SIE World Trade Database*.

2.13), which is analyzed in detail in Chapters 4, 6, and 7, by Ernst, Wong, and Kim respectively. Taiwan and Singapore show a deep restructuring in the product composition of their electronics exports during the 1990s, from consumer electronics to industrial electronics (especially electronic data processing equipment), whereas Korea has strengthened its specialization in terms of electronic components and consumer electronics. Only Hong Kong has maintained a relatively backward trade pattern mainly concentrated in the consumer electronics exports. Moreover, the successful export growth of the East Asian NICs is due largely to their own indigenous efforts and the growth of local firms; Singapore constitutes the exception, where MNCs have dominated production and exports. The data are thus consonant with an

*Table 2.12* Trade composition of the electronics industry in Taiwan, Hong Kong, and China*

| Declaring country | Exports | | | Imports | | |
|---|---|---|---|---|---|---|
| | *1980* | *1987* | *1994* | *1980* | *1987* | *1994* |
| *Taiwan* | | | | | | |
| Electronic data processing | 2.1 | 25.9 | 56.1 | 11.3 | 19.1 | 18.1 |
| Office equipment | 4.0 | 4.6 | 1.8 | 3.0 | 2.1 | 2.7 |
| Telecommunication | 1.7 | 5.1 | 4.4 | 11.6 | 5.0 | 2.3 |
| Electronic components | 16.5 | 12.1 | 26.3 | 30.4 | 43.9 | 62.9 |
| Consumer electronics | 56.9 | 26.2 | 6.2 | 20.6 | 17.2 | 8.7 |
| Medical equipment | 0.1 | 0.1 | 0.2 | 2.4 | 1.7 | 1.2 |
| Other | 18.6 | 25.9 | 5.1 | 20.7 | 11.0 | 4.3 |
| Total electronics | 100.0 | 100.0 | 100.0 | 100.0 | 100.0 | 100.0 |
| *Hong Kong* | | | | | | |
| Electronic data processing | 10.2 | 17.0 | 18.9 | 15.6 | 13.5 | 15.5 |
| Office equipment | 3.7 | 4.4 | 4.6 | 4.6 | 4.4 | 3.3 |
| Telecommunication | 0.4 | 4.7 | 4.8 | 4.4 | 4.9 | 4.3 |
| Electronic components | 14.3 | 16.2 | 16.0 | 26.7 | 29.2 | 25.8 |
| Consumer electronics | 67.4 | 45.5 | 41.9 | 43.1 | 39.9 | 38.9 |
| Medical equipment | 0.2 | 0.6 | 0.6 | 0.4 | 0.8 | 0.7 |
| Other | 4.0 | 11.6 | 13.2 | 5.2 | 7.2 | 11.5 |
| Total electronics | 100.0 | 100.0 | 100.0 | 100.0 | 100.0 | 100.0 |
| *China* | | | | | | |
| Electronic data processing | 1.8 | 3.8 | 18.6 | 16.4 | 20.3 | 15.9 |
| Office equipment | 5.8 | 5.3 | 5.0 | 4.5 | 3.3 | 2.0 |
| Telecommunication | 0.9 | 7.9 | 9.3 | 1.7 | 10.7 | 25.0 |
| Electronic components | 2.5 | 1.0 | 4.5 | 3.5 | 6.3 | 20.1 |
| Consumer electronics | 63.3 | 75.0 | 54.4 | 59.8 | 22.3 | 17.5 |
| Medical equipment | 1.2 | 0.3 | 0.3 | 4.0 | 4.5 | 2.0 |
| Other | 24.6 | 6.6 | 7.9 | 10.0 | 32.7 | 17.4 |
| Total electronics | 100.0 | 100.0 | 100.0 | 100.0 | 100.0 | 100.0 |

*Percentage shares of the sectoral groups in total electronics exports (or imports) of each country and area.

Source: Elaborations on OECD and UN data, from *SIE World Trade Database*.

explanation that sees the upgrading of the electronics production structure of the NICs as a result of their insertion into networks of both American and Japanese firms. Over time, national firms in all of the NICs have developed their own, independent networks, which have contributed to the extension of CPNs in ASEAN and China.

## Conclusion

This chapter has dealt with East Asia's trade pattern in the electronics industry during the past fifteen years, providing evidence of the great

*Table 2.13* Trade composition in the electronics industry in ASEAN, Thailand, and Malaysia*

| Declaring country | Exports | | | Imports | | |
|---|---|---|---|---|---|---|
| | 1980 | 1987 | 1994 | 1980 | 1987 | 1994 |
| *ASEAN* | | | | | | |
| Electronic data processing | 0.1 | 5.7 | 23.8 | 4.3 | 13.1 | 16.2 |
| Office equipment | 0.4 | 0.1 | 2.3 | 5.7 | 2.0 | 1.5 |
| Telecommunication | 0.2 | 0.4 | 4.1 | 11.7 | 4.6 | 6.0 |
| Electronic components | 89.3 | 76.4 | 33.4 | 52.2 | 59.8 | 53.6 |
| Consumer electronics | 6.0 | 13.6 | 30.9 | 15.8 | 7.1 | 11.4 |
| Medical equipment | 0.1 | 0.0 | 0.0 | 1.1 | 0.9 | 0.7 |
| Other | 3.9 | 3.8 | 5.5 | 9.2 | 12.5 | 10.6 |
| Total electronics | 100.0 | 100.0 | 100.0 | 100.0 | 100.0 | 100.0 |
| *Thailand* | | | | | | |
| Electronic data processing | 0.6 | 20.1 | 40.6 | 3.7 | 44.4 | 26.7 |
| Office equipment | 24.1 | 0.2 | 4.9 | 14.9 | 2.2 | 2.3 |
| Telecommunication | 2.4 | 0.3 | 4.4 | 24.0 | 6.3 | 6.4 |
| Electronic components | 0.1 | 77.3 | 23.2 | 13.9 | 11.1 | 38.5 |
| Consumer electronics | 64.0 | 1.2 | 22.9 | 15.3 | 7.2 | 13.9 |
| Medical equipment | 1.1 | 0.1 | 0.0 | 4.1 | 2.1 | 1.2 |
| Other | 7.7 | 0.8 | 4.0 | 24.2 | 26.7 | 10.9 |
| Total electronics | 100.0 | 100.0 | 100.0 | 100.0 | 100.0 | 100.0 |
| *Malaysia* | | | | | | |
| Electronic data processing | 0.0 | 0.8 | 19.6 | 2.5 | 4.3 | 11.5 |
| Office equipment | 0.1 | 0.1 | 1.2 | 2.4 | 0.9 | 0.7 |
| Telecommunication | 0.2 | 0.5 | 3.8 | 6.4 | 2.7 | 2.1 |
| Electronic components | 91.6 | 75.3 | 37.5 | 71.3 | 75.8 | 65.9 |
| Consumer electronics | 4.6 | 17.7 | 33.0 | 12.0 | 7.7 | 10.8 |
| Medical Equipment | 0.1 | 0.0 | 0.0 | 0.3 | 0.3 | 0.3 |
| Other | 3.3 | 5.5 | 4.8 | 5.1 | 8.1 | 8.8 |
| Total electronics | 100.0 | 100.0 | 100.0 | 100.0 | 100.0 | 100.0 |

*Percentage shares of the sectoral groups in total electronics exports (or imports) of each country and area.

Source: Elaborations on OECD and UN data, from *SIE World Trade Database*.

improvement in the competitiveness of East Asian countries, on one hand, and the strong acceleration of intra-regional trade on the other. At first, the patterns described appear to conform to a broad product cycle model in which capabilities are transferred as both foreign and local firms exploit changing comparative advantage. But they are not in line with an interpretation of the region's growth in which Japan plays the role of lead innovator or "goose"; indeed, the closed nature of Japan's networks has arguably inhibited the development of other locations in the region. Rather, they are compatible with regional production networks based on strong intra-regional interdependence with respect to inputs and sales and stemming from the divergent global production strategies of firms that have their headquarters in different countries.

Japanese firms operating in Japan have moved out of consumer electronics production but have maintained substantial production capabilities on-shore in industrial electronics and components. At the same time, they have invested heavily in the region, partly to service growing local demand (which is visible in evidence of growing absorption of exports within the region) and partly to export to third markets. However, the pattern of trade in these networks is consonant with Ernst's analysis in Chapter 5; apart from certain components, Japan is not a major absorber of the region's exports. Moreover, it remains a significant exporter not only to the United States and Europe but to other Asian countries. As Ernst shows in Chapter 5, these exports encompass both arm's-length transactions, and the heavy reliance of Japanese affiliates on inputs from Japan.

American firms and their Asian affiliates and network partners also play a major role in the trans-Pacific trade in electronics, but in a way quite different from Japan's, as Borrus shows in Chapter 3. It is the American CPNs, as well as Japanese firms, that have contributed to the "bilateral" trade imbalances between East Asia and the United States.

Moreover, as the studies about Korea, Taiwan, and Singapore demonstrate in different ways, these networks have contributed to the development of indigenous Asian firms that have subsequently developed their own distinctive networks. As Ernst shows in Chapter 5, there is significant debate over how far these firms can go in penetrating Japanese, American, and European markets on their own. However, the disaggregated data on particular industry segments, as well as the case studies of Korea, Taiwan, and Singapore, show that these firms and networks have established central positions as providers of what might be called "electronic intermediates" that are fueling the deepening industrial integration of the region. The following chapters parse the character of Asia's emerging industrial integration in detail.

## Appendix

Data on the trade flows of the Asian countries selected above were aggregated by using an original systems and industrial engineering trade database (*SIE World Trade Database*) derived from the OECD as well as the United Nations trade statistics (see Guerrieri 1993, 1994). The *SIE World Trade Database* provides detailed information about the export and import of 400 product groups in eighty-three countries. The database includes trade statistics for the twenty-four OECD countries, the newly industrializing countries (NICs), the other developing countries, and the former CMEA countries, and makes it possible to examine and analyze the entire world trade matrix. The sources for the basic trade statistics of the SIE world trade are the official publications of the OECD and the United Nations and are provided on magnetic tapes.

The SIE database is organized in different product group classifications at various levels of disaggregation (400 product groups, ninety-eight sectors, twenty-five categories, five branches) according to the three Standard International Trade Classifications (SITCs), Revised, Revision 2, Revision 3, defined by the Statistical Office of the UN for the periods 1961–75, 1978–87, and 1988 onwards. Thus, the main advantage of the *SIE World Trade Database* is that it allows us to use extremely disaggregated time series for products groups, given its system of correspondence between the SITC Revised, the SITC Revision 2, and the SITC Revision 3.

## Notes

1 In addition to the sponsors listed in the introduction, this chapter has benefited from the support of the Italian National Research Council under its project "Technological Change and Industrial Growth."
2 In terms of geographic disaggregation, the East Asian countries will be here classified into the following groups: (a) Japan; (b) Asian NICs (Hong Kong, Singapore, South Korea, and Taiwan) (c) the four ASEAN economies (Indonesia, Malaysia, Philippines, and Thailand); (d) China.
3 For an extensive analysis, see Ernst and Guerrieri (1998).
4 For a similar perspective see Ishizaki (1993).
5 For a detailed analysis see Ernst (1994a), Borrus (1994), and Baba and Hatashima (1994).

## References

Akamatsu, K. (1961) "A Theory of Unbalanced Growth in the World Economy," *Weltwirtschaftliches Archiv*, 86(2).
Baba, Y. and Hatashima, H. (1994) "Capability Transfer of Japanese Electronics Firms to the Pacific Rim Nations: Towards Open Global Manufacturing?" BRIE and Asia Foundation Conference on Japanese Production Network in Asia, San Francisco, September.
Borrus, M. (1994) "Building an Alternative Supply Base in East Asia: Regional Production Networks of US Electronics Firms," University of California at Berkeley, CA: Berkeley Roundtable on the International Economy, University of California at Berkeley (BRIE).
Cohen, S. and Guerrieri, P. (1994) "The Variable Geometry of Asian Trade," in E. Doherty (ed.) *Japanese Investment in Asia. International Production Strategies in a Rapidly Changing World*, San Francisco: The Asia Foundation and BRIE.
Ernst, D. (1994a) "Carriers of Regionalization: The East Asian Production Networks of Japanese Electronics Firms," *Working Paper 73*, University of California at Berkeley: BRIE.
—— (1994b) *What are the Limits to the Korean Model? The Korean Electronics Industry under Pressure*, Berkeley, CA: BRIE.
Ernst, D. and O'Connor, D. (1992) *Competing in the Electronics Industry. The Experiences of Newly Industrializing Economies*, Paris: OECD.
Ernst, D. and Guerrieri, P. (1998) "International Production Networks and Changing Trade Patterns in East Asia: the Case of Electronics Industry," *Oxford Development Studies* 26(2).

Graham, E. and Anzai, N. T. (1994) "Is Japan's Direct Investment Creating an Asian Economic Bloc?", Washington DC: Institute for International Economics.

Guerrieri, P. (1993) "Patterns of Technological Capability and International Trade Performance: an Empirical Analysis," in M. Kreinin (ed.) *The Political Economy of International Commercial Policy: Issues for the 1990s*, London and New York: Taylor & Francis.

—— (1994) "International Competitiveness, Trade Integration and Technological Interdependence," in C. Bradford (ed.) *The New Paradigm of Systemic Competitiveness: Toward More Integrated Policies in Latin America*, Paris: OECD.

Hobday, M. (1995), *Innovation in East Asia*, Cheltenham, UK: Edward Elgar.

Ishizaki, 1 Y. (1993) "Recent Trends in Asia-Pacific Trade: Expansion and Structural Changes," *RIM: Pacific Business and Industries* 3(21).

JETRO (1994) *JETRO White Paper on Foreign Direct Investment*, Tokyo.

Kodama, F. and Kiba, T. (1994) "The Emerging Trajectory of International Technology Transfer," Asia/Pacific Research Center.

Noland, M. (1990) *Pacific Basin Developing Countries: Prospects for the Future*, Washington DC: Institute for International Economics.

Park, Y. C. and Won-Am, P. (1991) "Changing Japanese Trade Patterns and the East Asian NICs," in Paul Krugman (ed.) *Trade with Japan: Has the Door Opened Wider?* Chicago and London: The University of Chicago Press, pp. 85–120.

Ravenhill, J. (1995) "Competing Logic of Regionalism in the Asia Pacific," *Journal of European Integration*, 28: 2–3.

Takeuchi, J. (1993) "Foreign Direct Investment in ASEAN by Small- and Medium-Sized Japanese Companies and Its Effects on Local Supporting Industries," *RIM: Pacific Business and Industries*, 4(22): 36–57.

Takeuchi J. (1994) "Some Observations on Japanese Foreign Direct Investments and International Production Strategies," BRIE and Asia Foundation Conference on Japanese Production Network in Asia, San Francisco, September.

Urata S. (1993) "Changing Patterns of Direct Investment and the Implications for Trade and Development," in C. Bergsten and M. Noland (eds) *Pacific Dynamism and the International Economic System*, Washington, DC: Institute for International Economics.

Vernon, R. (1966) "International Investment and International Trade in the Product Cycle," *Quarterly Journal of Economics*, 80: 190–207.

—— (1979) "The Product Cycle Hypothesis in a New International Environment," *Oxford Bulletin of Economics and Statistics*, 41: 255–268.

Yamazawa, I. (1990) *Economic Development and International Trade. The Japanese Model*, Honolulu, Hawaii: Resource Systems Institute.

Yoshitomi, M. (1994) "Building New United States – Pacific Asia Economic Relationship for the Post-Uruguay Round Era," in *Economic Cooperation and Challenges in the Pacific*, Berkeley: Korea Economic Institute of America.

# 3 The resurgence of US electronics

## Asian production networks and the rise of Wintelism

*Michael Borrus*

The electronics industry of the late 1990s bears only a passing resemblance to that of a decade earlier. Some of the names are the same – IBM, NEC, Toshiba, Digital Equipment Corporation (DEC), Matsushita, Siemens – but those big, vertically integrated assemblers of electronic systems no longer control the industry.[1] In their stead a new generation of firms has arisen, mostly but not exclusively American owned, who exercise the kind of market power (and have attained the market capitalization) that is but a passing memory for more traditional firms: Microsoft, Intel, Cisco, Oracle, Netscape, Cadence, Dell, Applied Materials, 3COM, SAP, Sun, Qualcomm, Octel. The new firms look nothing like the old leaders. Most are specialists operating within one (occasionally more) horizontal slice of the electronics industry value-chain rather than full-line systems firms who vertically integrate the value-chain. Most control key technical specifications that have been accepted in the market as *de facto* standards. Most operate with network forms of production organization. Almost all produce software, albeit often embedded in a hardware product. All deliver value-added services. Despite the similarities, they also differ in important respects. For example, Intel invests heavily in fabrication and assembly, whereas Cisco and Dell rely exclusively on contract manufacturers. Netscape and Sun widely license their technical standards; SAP and Cadence do not.

As the names have changed, so has the global competitive game. The early 1980s saw a widely heralded battle for dominance of world electronics markets between Japanese and American industries.[2] Through innovations in processes and manufacturing, Japanese producers had taken over consumer electronics and a range of component technologies including displays, precision mechanical parts, and semiconductor memory. US firms have been increasingly forced to rely on Japanese rivals for the supply of the underlying technologies, processes, and manufacturing know-how necessary to produce electronics systems.[3] In consumer electronics, such thoroughgoing technology dependence had been a first step toward market exit even for such powerhouses as General Electric (GE) and RCA. Dependence has meant that US firms were far enough removed from the technological state of the art to impede new product development, and that their principal competitors could dictate time-to-market, product cost, and feature quality. US leadership in computers, communications, and professional electronics was threatened with a similar, debilitating, dependence.

A decade later things looked decidedly different. The new generation of US firms was almost everywhere ascendant and the Japanese were on the defensive and seeking alliances with the new market leaders. This breathtaking reversal of industrial fortunes was not the result of careful planning. Built in equal parts of serendipity, entrepreneurial innovation, desperate experimentation, inter-firm cooperation, and policy intervention, the competitive strategies pioneered largely by American firms were rather surprising. US firms constructed an alternative supplier base in Asia to the Japanese for components, processes and manufacturing know-how, in effect commodifying their areas of greatest dependence. Simultaneously, they reasserted control over new product development by de-coupling the key technical standards that defined new products from commodity technology inputs, and then aggressively guarded those standards through strengthened intellectual property protection. This strategy relied on the development of cross-border production networks (CPNs) concentrated in Asia coupled with the re-emergence of the United States as the principal launch market for new information technology products. In combination, these efforts defined a new form of competition: "Wintelism."[4]

Wintelism is characterized by several major elements.[5] The vertical disintegration of the industry's value-chain is the first element, one partly induced by government policy. Vertical disintegration had the effect of shifting market power from traditional, vertically integrated system assemblers to suppliers of hardware and software technologies, product definition, and producer services. The second element was increased specialization by independent producers in each segment of the value-chain, with American firms exercising market power through development and evolution of key technical specifications that are accepted as *de facto* market standards. These firms utilize strategies of continuous innovation (incremental increases in functionality, performance, features, or quality within generations, and radical increases between generations) to lock in an installed base of customers. In turn, they leverage that installed base by broadening outward from their core area of value-chain specialization to seize increasing value-added opportunities in neighboring parts of the value-chain or in related industries. Thus, for example, Cadence moved from being a seller of integrated circuits (IC) design tools to integrated electronics design systems and services; Microsoft moved from PC operating systems to applications, server operating systems, network services, information services, transactions, and even content.

CPNs are the organizational counterpart to Wintelism, a new organization of production in which lead firms exploit the increasing technical specialization throughout the value-chain by producers in disparate geographic locations around the world. Wintelism could not have succeeded without the extensive inter-firm relationships with Asian-based producers that comprised the CPNs of American-owned firms. Those cross-border ties permitted US-owned firms to exploit the growing technical sophistication and competitive strength of indigenous producers initially in Taiwan, Singapore, and Korea, and later throughout Southeast Asia, in selected cities of India, and along the coastal provinces of mainland China. The unique heterogeneity of Asia's regional economy, with different tiers of nations (Japan, Four Tigers, ASEAN, and coastal China, interior China, and India) at different stages of development provided the fertile ground for technical and production specialization that enabled the creation of CPNs; e.g. software in Bangelore, process engineering in Singapore, component assembly in Malaysia, printed circuit board (PCB) assembly in coastal China, semiconductor memory in Korea, digital design and final assembly in Taiwan. This chapter explores the development of American-led CPNs in greater detail, outlining the rise of Wintelist business strategies and the development of the CPN organizational form.

## The origins of Wintelism and the new dynamics of competition

During the 1990s, the terms of competition in the electronics industry have shifted away from the big final assemblers such as IBM and Siemens, whose past dominance was built through vertically integrated control of technologies and manufacturing. The character of the shift in market power is suggested in the advertisements of PC producers such as IBM, Toshiba, Compaq, or Siemens–Nixdorf, whose systems are nearly identical and which emphasize components or software that have become *de facto* market standards – "Intel Inside," or "Microsoft Windows installed" – rather than unique features of their own brands.

The pre-Wintel electronics industry was dominated by assemblers, i.e. systems producers who designed, marketed, and assembled the final product, with almost all value-chain functions carried out in-house, and principally within the producer's home country. Such producers, e.g. GE, RCA and IBM, prospered with quite traditional advantages of scale and vertical integration. IBM dominated the computer segment of the electronics industry and extended its franchise into Europe and Asia in pursuit of new markets. Similar strategies produced dominant players such as Western Electric and Siemens in the telecommunications segment of the market.

Also starting in the 1960s, in the course of attempting to emulate IBM in structure and strategy, Japanese producers such as Matsushita and Hitachi began to overturn established American positions in the consumer electronics market. Similar to Toyota and other Japanese car manufacturers, they did so by applying lean production principles in order to innovate in traditional consumer electronics products with all solid-state televisions. As in car manufacturing, adoption of lean production techniques enabled Japanese electronics firms to create new and distinctive market segments by the late 1970s, such as the Walkman, VCR, and Camcorder. By the early 1980s, Japanese firms were poised to challenge US leadership in other electronic markets. Here too, however, the dominant market position still lay with the final product assemblers who controlled consumer product definition, the most important underlying component technologies, and usually both the supply and the distribution chains. Their competitive strength was the ability to manufacture high quality at consumer price points with some degree of product variety.

By the early 1980s, essentially all electronics product markets were dominated by large-scale producers such as IBM, Siemens, Matsushita, NEC, and Toshiba. They produced fully proprietary systems whose key product standards – i.e. the technical specifications that describe the system architecture and enable the pieces of the system to inter-operate as a whole and with each other – were either fully "closed" or fully "open." A fully open standard is one in which the technical information necessary to implement the standard is in the public domain, fully available on a non-discriminatory and timely basis to anyone. This was the case with most consumer and many communications interface standards such as TV or fax broadcast standards. With the relevant technical information in the public domain, products such as TVs and radios built to such open standards became commodities in which scale, quality, and cost were the defining features of competition in highly contested markets.

By contrast, telecommunications and computer firms built to "closed" standards in which the relevant technical information was owned as intellectual property and *not* made available to anyone other than through legally permissible reverse engineering. IBM's mainframe computers epitomized such proprietary, closed systems. Here, too, vertical control over technologies and manufacturing was essential, especially in the early stages of competition when new systems were introduced. But once established in the market, competition centered on developing an installed base of customers who could be locked in to a firm's product line. In the open standards case, lock in was impossible; with all products built to implement the same standard, users could seamlessly switch between them. With closed standards, the costs of switching could be very high indeed, requiring, for example, rewriting an existing base of software and retraining all users. Large installed bases were decisive over time in these competitions, as all of IBM's competitors discovered. Firms who had them had lower per unit costs for succeeding generations than the competition, since such costs (e.g. of development or marketing) could be amortized over more locked-in users. In sum, *with both closed and open systems, vertical control over technologies and manufacturing was the key to market success*. For closed systems, it was necessary to lock customers into proprietary standards; for open systems, it permitted firms to compete on implementation, quality, and price.

This era of proprietary systems built to open or closed standards lasted until the early 1980s. Throughout there were shifts in market structure, attacks on established incumbents, a myriad of new entrants, and, not least, significant policy interventions, including trade protection, antitrust actions and government procurement, that shaped market outcomes. Some of those changes, such as the emergence of independent (so-called "merchant") component suppliers, began to undermine the logic of competition rooted in ownership and vertical control of technology. These firms created the evolutionary ground for the emergence of Wintelism.

## The origins of Wintelism

Wintelism's roots can be traced to the merchant character of the domestic US semiconductor industry, the first crucial step in the disintegration of the electronics industry's value-chain and one strongly influenced by policy. After an incubation period during the 1950s in which several critical technical developments were diffused by antitrust constraints on Bell Laboratories and by military spending, government defense and space procurement at premium prices provided the initial launch market for the new technology in the 1960s. As costs fell with large-scale federal procurement, initial commercial applications spun off into the computer industry where antitrust constraints further prevented IBM from monopolizing the application of the technology. Through antitrust-induced licensing, labor mobility (in typically flexible US labor markets), tax-advantaged venture capital, and federal procurement contracts, the policy helped to foster the emergence of "merchant" chip firms who specialized in developing and selling semiconductor components to assemblers of final products.

Because their basic role was to diffuse chip technology as widely as possible, merchant semiconductor firms fostered other specialized producers throughout the electronics value-chain. In effect, they pioneered and instigated a gradual process of vertical disintegration throughout the American electronics industry. Final assemblers no longer needed to be vertically integrated into component production on the IBM=ATT model. Instead, they could focus on system definition and assembly. Specialization in one part of the value-chain bred specialization in other parts: throughout the 1960s and 1970s, specialized producers of semiconductor equipment and materials emerged, as did producers of software and systems integrators higher up the value-chain. The whole process was accelerated by the competitive entry of Japanese producers who helped to eliminate traditional vertically integrated players from the US market.

In the struggle to break loose from IBM's dominant model and to react to Japan's ascent, new product strategies emerged. The pioneering product was, of course, the PC. But the extraordinary pace of technical progress and ever-improving price/performance soon made the underlying microelectronics technologies increasingly pervasive, transforming just about everything from telecommunications switches to automobiles and medical instruments. By the mid-1980s, new electronics product markets began to converge on a cost-effective, common technological foundation of networkable, microprocessor-based systems, of which the PC was only emblematic.

Such systems enabled a dramatic shift in the character of electronics products: from the prior era's proprietary systems built to fully open or closed standards, to the Wintelist era's "open-but-owned" systems built to "restricted" standards. In the new systems, key product standards, especially the interface specifications that permit interoperability with the operating system or system hardware, are owned as intellectual property but made available to others in the value-chain who produce complementary or competing components, systems, or software products. Hence the systems are "open-but-owned."[6] The relevant technical standards are licensed rather than published, with either the universe of licensees, the degree of documentation of the technical specifications, or the permissible uses, restricted in some fashion. Very often, changes can be made unilaterally by the standard holder in ways that affect availability and timing of access to the interface specification, as Microsoft is routinely accused of doing by its licensee competitors. Open-but-owned systems combined competitive elements from both product types of the prior era. The standards are licensed in order to create commodity-like competition around system elements chosen by the licensor (e.g. around assembled PCs built to Intel processor architecture standards), whereas their evolution is controlled by the owner to build an installed base and to lock in customers and the value-added licensees.

The shift to open-but-owned systems was accelerated by two factors that helped to spread and consolidate Wintelist business strategies. From the supply side, the increasing cost and complexity of continuing innovation made it increasingly difficult for any one company, even IBM, to maintain ownership and control over all of the relevant technologies. The increasing expense of technological advance demanded specialization to maintain the pace of innovation. But the specialized technical elements had to fit together at the end of the day into workable systems. The former demanded ownership to recoup costs; the latter demanded openness for system integrity.

Second, and more critical, major industrial users in the United States, such as banks, brokerages and insurance companies, aerospace, automobile and petrochemical producers, began aggressively to move their business operations onto integrated corporate data communications networks, a process that was well under way by the early 1980s.[7] In pioneering such complex hybrid networks (i.e. using an integrated mix of owned and purchased facilities and services), major corporations were inevitably operating in a multivendor environment as they attempted to tie together computer systems from some vendors with communications systems from others, with databases and software from still others. Consequently, they began to demand that all of their vendors deliver increasing levels of interoperability in the complex systems being delivered.

Again, American public policy set the context: over three decades from the 1950s through the 1980s, US policy gradually deregulated American Telephone and Telegraph Company (AT&T) and introduced competition into the domestic US market for communications services and equipment. That, in turn, provided the communications facilities and services from which industrial users would piece together their information networks. Industrial demand stimulated a burst of innovation in both development and usage of network equipment and services, creating broad market opportunities for new firms such as Cisco Systems and Novell. Users could pick and choose among the most innovative equipment and services from multiple vendors to knit together their information networks. But the pieces from multiple vendors had to fit together; they had to be open enough to enable end-to-end interoperability of the corporate communications infrastructure. Suppliers responded with open-but-owned systems: "open" at the interface to permit interconnection of systems from other vendors, but "owned" to reap a return from innovation. In short, users demanded highly functional and interoperable systems, US policy stimulated provision of them, and both further encouraged the value-chain specialization with open-but-owned standards that are the hallmarks of Wintelism.

But the move to open-but-owned systems and value-chain specialization was legitimized, as perhaps it only could have been, by IBM with the IBM PC.[8] In order to get to market fast and to exploit a market window opened by Apple (who had adopted a quite traditional proprietary systems strategy), IBM pieced together the first open-but-owned PC using its own proprietary BIOS (basic input–output system) and a variety of components and software from numerous third-party vendors. It invited cloning to establish the market. Once firmly entrenched, IBM intended to bring the product back in-house and make it increasingly proprietary. It presumed that its brand conjoined with a traditional strategy of unsurpassed scale, and vertical control of technology and manufacturing would fend off the clones. It was wrong. Unfortunately for the computer giant, it permitted key standards in its PC to be owned by others (especially Intel for the microprocessor architecture, and Microsoft for the operating system) who innovated at the furious pace that focus and specialization permitted. Gradually, they took control of the evolution of the PC's key standards. In concert with the clone-makers, Intel and Microsoft wrested control from IBM of the PC itself. Strategies to set and control the evolution of *de facto* standards were developed. Business speed (e.g. rapid product cycles, fast time to market) was rewarded. Wintelism was born.

## The new terms of competition

In this new epoch, firms located anywhere in the temporarily disintegrated value-chain can control the evolution of key standards and in that way define the terms of competition not just in their particular segment but in other segments and often, critically, in final product markets as well. Market power has shifted from the assemblers such as Compaq, Gateway, IBM, or Toshiba, to key producers of components (Intel); operating systems (Microsoft); applications (SAP, Adobe, Octel); interfaces (Netscape); languages (Sun's Java); and to product definition companies such as Cisco Systems. What all of these firms have in common is that from quite different vantage points in the informatics value-chain they all own key technical specifications that have been accepted as *de facto* product standards in the market. Each beat rival standards. In winning, each created a universe of licensees who produce to its standard and add value to its use, just as applications software firms such as WordPerfect, PC assemblers such as Compaq, peripherals producers such as Canon, or content providers such as Grolier's all produce to Microsoft's Windows operating system standards. Each standard owner maintains a growing installed base of customers who use the products that conform to the standards. Each has been careful to evolve the standards by adding incremental improvements in performance, functionality, features, quality, or costs within product generations and dramatic improvements between generations (while remaining backwardly compatible with past versions). In that way, each has effectively "locked in" their customer base and their licensees in the sense explored earlier. Given the customer's investment in all of the conforming products and in how to use them effectively, the customer will normally be unwilling to switch to competing standards unless they offer truly radical and compensatory improvements in price, performance, and functionality. Switching will not occur unless it is even more costly to stay put.[9]

Each Wintelist standard-holder has also effectively shaped the terms of competition in its core market segment. Once the competition to create an open-but-owned *de facto* standard is initially settled, the losers' strategies must shift to one (or a combination) of a relatively limited menu of alternatives. These include strategies: to sell into the market created by the standard-holder and to differentiate products on traditional bases of cost, performance, functionality, reputation, control of marketing and distribution, after-sales services and the like; to wrest control of the standard over time by evolving it ahead of the creator (as Intel and Microsoft did to IBM); to devise a competing alternative standard that can wrest part of the overall market away from the incumbent (as Microsoft is successfully doing to Netscape in the browser market); to force greater openness and less opportunity to exercise the prerogatives of ownership, by causing industry standards bodies or public policies to embrace a *de facto* standard and set non-discriminatory conditions on its use (as happened with Local Area Network standards and in the UNIX operating system market), and always to confine the standard-holder to the markets he currently dominates, if necessary via antitrust attack (of the kind currently focused on Microsoft).

Competitions to set and control the evolution of *de facto* standards do not always lead to dominant, Wintelist winners, but they do tend in that direction. A brief exploration of the economic characteristics of standards competitions will suggest why.[10] All standards are carriers of technical information in a codified form, around which related industrial and consumption activities can coalesce with heightened predictability and lowered risk: those who produce or use products that implement the standard form of a complementary and reinforcing community or network. The universe of conforming products constitutes the standard network's installed base. In general, the bigger the network the greater the benefits for users and producers (i.e. network externalities or simply, "network effects"). Thus, for example, Microsoft's standard PC operating system, Windows 95, drew together a variety of producers of complementary products from PCs and peripherals to applications software and information services into a network with all of the users whose computers run the operating system. The universe of such machines is Microsoft's installed base for Windows 95. Network effects made adopting Windows 95 increasingly attractive as others jumped aboard (the so-called bandwagon effect),[11] and, consequently, Windows 95 became the dominant PC operating system within only one or two years of its introduction.

As the Microsoft example implies, Wintelist standards are more than mere information vectors. In facilitating the organization of related industrial activities and in creating opportunities for consumption, standards also shape market structure and the terms of exchange.[12] Standards shape market structure, among other ways, by altering relative costs among producers, inducing demand pattern changes, raising or lowering entry barriers, creating opportunities for economies of scale and scope, facilitating a division of labor, and generating opportunities for network externalities in both production and use. For example, World Wide Web standards and the Netscape Navigator family of browsers for interfacing with the Web have had all of these effects. Their adoption altered costs among existing players, facilitating market entry by some, making market entry more expensive for those with other approaches (e.g. CompuServe or Prodigy, who had built expensive proprietary approaches), and ultimately forcing even Microsoft to reorient its entire PC strategy around integrating its operating system with Internet Explorer, its competing browser. By focusing demand from content creators, information services providers and potential consumers on a single set of standards, they permitted a wide range of new software and equipment producers (including those, such as Cisco, who produce the underlying infrastructure equipment) to reach additional scale and prosper. They facilitated an increasingly intricate division of labor, for example permitting specialization in production, before and after production of content, in pointcasting, and tailored delivery of information services and content, in the production of a growing variety of complementary software (browser plug-ins) and equipment (network computers). Perhaps most important, they are facilitating the emergence of communities of users that cross national boundaries and of a truly global network.

The coexistence of large potential gains that rise with size, manipulable costs, and influence over market structure and the terms of exchange give to standards battles many of the characteristics of competitions to develop and commercialize new technologies.[13]

Because market conditions are anything but the perfectly competitive equilibrium of neoclassical models, choices of standards are highly dependent on initial starting points, available resources, market context, and event sequence. Advantages can accrue to early movers (whether innovators or imitators, producers or users) who in turn can influence the choices of later players as the market structure shifts. The timing and pattern of developments – choices made by both producers and especially lead-users – can significantly influence the choice of standards in ways that are difficult to reverse (so-called "path dependence").[14] Seemingly small choices can have big consequences, as occurred with Sony's choice of focusing the initial recording capability of its Betamax VCR around hour-long TV shows rather than the multiple-hour sporting events that initially drove surging sales of the rival VHS standard. This small choice proved decisive in negating Sony's early lead in installed bases.[15] As installed bases and the size of the associated standards network grows, players can acquire monopoly-like market power with lock-in. This is true even for products conforming to more open standards, wherever producers can maintain the differentiable features thus creating market niches over which they can act like a quasi-monopolist. Indeed, equipment from almost all producers of open computer platforms that run some version of UNIX will inter-operate better within the brand than across brands, even though all brands conform to the common standards.

The economic characteristics outlined permit multiple competitive equilibria to emerge, but Wintelist open-but-owned standards tend toward quasi-monopoly or oligopoly outcomes. Such standards permit the standard owner to manipulate its competitive environment in unprecedented ways. The aim is to establish a quasi-monopoly position, maintain high and rising barriers to entry and with them high and rising switching costs for one's locked-in customers, thus reaping standards-based rents in the market. By favoring one set of producers or users at the expense of another – which can only be done when evolution of the standard and access to it is controlled through ownership – standard holders can directly influence the allocation of available benefits.

The actions of one standard owner thus directly influence the returns to a rival.[16] Market competition consists of strategic thrusts over pricing, licensing, and other assets that anticipate and forestall rival moves while attempting to structure the market to the standard owner's advantage. As market power begins to accrue with installed bases, the possibilities for manipulation grow commensurately. Over time, there are large opportunities for entry deterrence and competitive pre-emption of rivals: enormous up-front sunk costs associated with creating an alternative to the existing standard (as the Power PC alliance of IBM–Apple–Motorola showed in its futile attempt to dislodge Microsoft–Intel dominance), existing scale and scope economies that must be overcome, the likelihood that the established standard holder will engage in pre-emptive investment (as Intel has done), and predatory pricing (Microsoft's offering of Internet Explorer for free).

In essence, Wintelist standards competitions are market processes in which the players vie for the available consumer and producer surpluses stemming from the achievement of standardization. The winners – like Microsoft and Intel in PCs – establish *de facto* standards monopolies and become wildly profitable as more and more of the available surplus accrues to them through consumer lock-in and exit of competitors. And those circumstances can tolerate a high degree of user dissatisfaction, as essentially all users of Microsoft operating systems are by now aware: barely adequate performance or functionality is in most cases more than sufficient to continue the locked-in relationship, especially where a large investment in complementary products such as applications programs and associated learning has occurred. In those circumstances, upgrades and follow-on need not be better or even as good as a rival's products; they need only be adequate to deter the switch.

Such Wintelist strategies effectively attenuate the link between market power and the *ownership* of the assets of production that characterized the prior era of competition, and at the extremes, as with a firm like Cisco Systems, can completely decouple control of final markets from the ownership of manufacturing assets. For Wintelist firms, the ownership and manipulation of their *de facto* standards are considerably more effective barriers to entry than the barriers of scale and vertical control over technology and production in the prior era because they are far harder to duplicate. It still remains true that you cannot control what you cannot produce.[17] But the ways of implementing and controlling production have changed. Wintelism has an organizational counterpart: a distinctive system of production, the cross-border production network.

## US FDI and the creation of a regional supply base[18]

By the end of the 1970s, US electronics firms were almost completely dependent on Japanese competitors for the supply of the underlying component technologies (for example tuners, picture tubes, recording heads, miniature motors) necessary to produce consumer electronics products.[19] In most cases, thoroughgoing technology dependence was a first step toward market exit. US firms were far enough removed from the technological state of the art to impede new product development, and, as a result, their principal competitors could dictate the time-to-market, product cost, and feature quality. Under those circumstances, profits were minimal if any were to be had at all. By 1980 most major US firms had exited the consumer segment of the market, and the remaining players like GE and RCA survived largely by putting their brands on Japanese OEM production. A few years later, even RCA and GE, who had created most of the consumer electronic technologies that Japanese firms perfected, left the business.

The loss of the high-volume demand of consumer electronics eroded the US *supply base* for the other segments of the electronics industry, and threatened them with an equally, competitively constraining *architecture of supply*.[20] The supply base is the local capability to supply the component, machinery, materials, and control technologies (e.g. software) and the associated know-how that producers use to develop and manufacture products. The architecture of supply is the structure of the markets and other organized interactions (such as joint development) through which underlying technologies reach producers. In effect, US producers of industrial electronics such as computers and communications were in danger of becoming dependent on their Japanese competitors for memory chips, displays, precision components, and a wealth of the other essential technologies and associated manufacturing skills that went into electronic systems.[21] The only alternative to increasing dependence on a closed oligopoly of rivals was to make the supply architecture more open and competitive. In conjunction with government policies and local private investors in Asia, US firms gradually turned their Asian production networks into a flexible alternative to Japanese suppliers.

The transformation from affiliates based on low-cost labor to an alternative supply base occurred in three stages: an initial stage from the late 1960s to late 1970s during which US firms established their presence through foreign direct investments; a second stage in which their Asian affiliates developed extensive local relationships in the shadow of the dollar appreciation from 1980–5; and a third stage from the late 1980s through the early 1990s, when the technical capabilities in their regional production networks were significantly upgraded and local affiliates gained global product responsibilities. The US progression from simple assembly affiliate to technologically able Asian production network contrasts sharply with the development pattern of Japanese investments in the region over the same time period. A brief review of key developments in each of the three stages will highlight the differences.[22]

After an earlier round of market access investments by a few large US MNCs (notably IBM, GE, and RCA), most US electronics firms in the 1960s sought not market access but cheap production locations in Asia. US investment was led by US chipmakers, then consumer electronics and calculator producers, and finally, toward the end of the 1970s, producers of industrial electronic systems like computers and peripherals. Most of the US investments in this first stage established local assembly affiliates. Cheap but disciplined Asian labor permitted US firms to compete on price at home and in Europe. Right from the start, then, the Asian affiliates of US electronics firms were established as part of a multinational production network to serve advanced country markets. By contrast, as Ernst suggests in Chapter 4, most Japanese investment into Asia in this period, led by consumer electronics and appliance makers, was aimed at serving nascent local markets behind tariff walls. Japanese investment was often turnkey, with knock-down kits exported from Japan for local final assembly and sale in the local affiliate's domestic market. While the Japanese and US investments in this first stage were both oriented to simple assembly and superficially appear similar, the vastly different markets being served pulled their respective investments in divergent directions.

Consider the resulting logic of sunk investment for the two sets of firms. Because their Asian affiliates were integrated into a production operation serving advanced country markets, US firms upgraded their Asian investments in line with the pace of development of the lead market being served, the US market. In essence, they upgraded in line with US rather than local product cycles. By contrast, Japanese firms were led to upgrade the technological capacities of their Asian investments only at the slower pace necessary to serve lagging local markets. As local US affiliates became more sophisticated through several rounds of reinvestment, a division of labor premised on increasing local technical specialization developed throughout the US firms' global production operations. Local needs began to diverge from those elsewhere in the United States and the overall operations and affiliates of firms were sought out, and, where necessary, local partners were trained to meet them.

To be sure, the growth of local autonomy and relationships was constrained by overall corporate strategies (e.g. where economies of scale dictated a global rather than local sourcing arrangement), but over time US investments still led to greater technology transfer and increasing technological capabilities for locals. By contrast, stuck in developing market product cycles, offshore Japanese affiliates benefited from no such incentives to upgrade and no need to develop local supply relationships. Japanese firms served the domestic and US markets wholly from home. Whatever their lagging Asian affiliates needed could be easily supplied from Japan. As local Asian markets demanded the marginally more sophisticated goods whose product cycles had already peaked in the advanced countries, the entire production capability for those could also be transferred from Japan. Overall, less technology was transferred, and even that remained locked up within the Japanese firms' more limited circle of relations.

Thus, during the second stage (1980–5) US-owned assembly platforms were upgraded and enhanced technically to include more value-added, e.g. from assembly to test in chips, from hand to automation assembly techniques, from simple assembly of PCBs to more complex subsystems and final assembly in industrial electronics. As they gained more autonomy, US affiliates began to source more parts and components locally (a range of mechanical parts, monitors, discrete chips, and power supplies). As US affiliates developed and as the US industry exited the consumer segment, local electronics producers in places like Taiwan began to concentrate more and more of their own investment (and their government's attentions) on industrial electronics.[23] As these developments occurred, the contour began to appear of an ever more elaborate and deepening technical division of labor between US and

Asian-based operations, bound together in production networks serving US firms' advanced country markets. In essence, a new supply base was being created in Asia under the control of US and local, but not Japanese capital.

Indeed, while Asia's indigenous electronics capabilities (excluding Japan) developed in close symbiosis with the strategies and activities of American MNCs, they were driven by local private investment and supported by government policies. Outside of Korea (where the *chaebol* dominated domestic electronics development), resident ethnic Chinese investors played the principal, private entrepreneurial role in the China circle, Singapore, and later in Malaysia, Indonesia, and Thailand. During this period, in the NICs (and later in Southeast Asia) governments provided a panoply of fiscal and tax incentives, invested heavily in modern infrastructure, generic technology development, and the technical upgrading of the work force, engaged in selective strategic trade interventions, and in some cases, even provided market intelligence and product development roadmaps.[24] The aims were both to plug into the developing multinational production networks in the region and to use them as a lever toward autonomous capabilities. The result, by the end of the 1980s, was burgeoning indigenous electronics production throughout the region, with most of it outside of Korea, under the control of overseas Chinese (OC) capital.[25]

Not surprisingly, given its strong ties in this period to US producers, as OC electronics activity began to emerge it was concentrated in the PC and PC-related product markets. In turn, the nerve centers of OC activity in PC electronics in this era were Taiwan and Singapore, the home bases for emerging Asia–Pacific MNCs like the former's Acer and the latter's Creative Technologies.[26] Taiwanese producers were at the heart of the nascent alternative supply base. Ultimately, their position would crystallize in the third period, culminating in the mid-1990s, as Chapter 5, by Ernst, suggests, with significant to dominant world market shares in fourteen PC-related supply categories. As Chapter 7 by Poh-kam Wong suggests, Singapore based OC producers similarly began to emerge in this second period as significant suppliers of hard disk drive-related components and services, and of multimedia sound cards, PC subassemblies and PC assembly services (Callon 1995).

By contrast to the US and OC developments in this second phase, the pattern of Japanese investment led to a dual production structure under the control of Japanese firms and premised on traditional product cycles. Sophisticated products were produced at home with sophisticated processes to serve advanced country markets, whereas lower end products were produced with simple processes in regional affiliates to serve local Asian markets. Both sets of operations sourced from a common supply base, located largely in Japan and controlled, directly or indirectly, by Japan's major electronics companies. Where Japanese companies responded to government or commercial pressures to localize, they did so, as Ernst suggests in Chapter 4, from within their established supply base by transplanting the operation of an affiliated domestic Japanese supplier, not by sourcing significant value-added locally from the emerging Asian supply base. In short, the Japanese production networks boasted redundant investment and remained relatively closed, even as the US networks became more open and entwined with indigenous producers, with each link in the US network chains becoming more specialized.

These trends were fully elaborated during the third stage, from 1985 to the early 1990s. At home, US firms focused scarce corporate resources more intensely on new product definition and the associated skills (design, architectures, software) necessary to create, maintain, and evolve *de facto* market standards. In turn, they upgraded their Asian affiliates, giving them greater responsibility for hardware value-added and manufacturing and significantly increased local sourcing of components, parts, and subassemblies. They often contracted-out design and manufacture of some boards, components, and, toward the end of the period, even entire systems. During this period, the Asian affiliates of US firms continued to migrate from PCB to final assembly with increased automation; to increase both component production and final system value-added; and to assume global responsibility for higher value-added systems (for example from monochrome desktops to color notebook PCs). Their production networks extended to more and more capable local Asian producers who became increasingly skilled suppliers of components, subassemblies and, in some cases, entire systems. Even in the areas of memory chips and displays, where Japanese firms remained important suppliers to US firms, there was sufficient competition from other Asian sources (such as Korea in memory chips) or sufficient political pressure to keep the supply architecture open.

Major US producers of PCs such as Apple illustrate these developments well.[27] Apple Computer Singapore (ACS) opened a PCB assembly plant for the Apple II PC in 1981. By 1983, nine local companies were contract-manufacturing PCBs for the Apple IIe and Lisa PCs. By 1985, ACS was upgraded to include final assembly of Apple IIes for the world market. From 1989, ACS was expanded and upgraded to begin some component design work. In 1990 ACS assumed final assembly responsibility for two of three new Macintosh PCs (and PCBs for the third) and designed (locally) and manufactured associated monitors. By then, essentially all components were sourced in Asia, except the US-fabricated microprocessor. ACS's 130 major suppliers included local firms like Gul Technologies and Tri-M. ACS had also demonstrated that its growing technical prowess could pay competitive dividends in speeding up the time to market: it was able to move from design to production roll-out in up to half the time of Apple's other facilities. By 1992, ACS assumed responsibility for final assembly for all Asia–Pacific markets, including Japan, and was designing and supplying boards globally, manufacturing monitors and some peripherals, and designing chips. Over $1 billion was being procured annually in Asia through ACS. In 1993, ACS set up a design center for Macs for high-volume desktop products, Apple's only hardware design center outside the United States. By 1994, ACS had become the center for distribution, logistics, sales, and marketing for the Asia–Pacific region, and was assembling the MacClassic II, LC III and IV, mid-range Centris, and Quadra 800 for global distribution. Regional sourcing reached $2 billion, half from Japan [liquid crystal displays (LCDs), peripherals, memory, HDDs], another quarter from Singapore, $250–500 million in Taiwan for OEM desktops, monitors, PCBs, PowerBooks, Digital Assistants, and chips. Korea's Goldstar also supplied monitors. By late 1994, ACS had begun to design the motherboard and tooling, and to assemble the multimedia system, for the Mac LC 630 PC for worldwide export. Two new Mac products completely designed and manufactured at ACS were launched in 1995.

The progression of other major US electronics players in Asia with respect to local sourcing and value-added is broadly similar.[28] For example, Compaq Asia (hereafter CAS for Compaq Asia-Singapore) established its Singapore factory in 1986 for PCB assembly of components sourced from Asia (including Japan) and for desktop PCs to be final assembled in the United States. By 1994, after terminating an OEM relationship with Japan's Citizen Watch, CAS was designing and manufacturing all notebook and portable PCs for worldwide consumption, and all desktop PCs for the Asia–Pacific region. Similarly, Hewlett-Packard's Singapore operations evolved from the assembly of calculators in 1977 to the global responsibility for portable printers and Pentium desktop PCs and servers, using local manufacturing for process design, tooling development, and chip design. Motorola's Singapore operations evolved from simple PCB assembly of pagers and private radio systems destined for the United States in 1983 to worldwide mandates for design, development, and automated manufacture of double-sided six-layer PCBs, for design and development of integrated circuits for disk drives and other peripherals, for some R&D, and for sourcing of at least $500 million of parts and components within the region. Similar kinds of stories can be told about AT&T for telecommunications products, about IBM and DEC for PCs and peripherals, about Maxtor, Connor, Seagate, and Western Digital for HDDs, and about TI, Intel, and National Semiconductor for chips.

As US Asia-based affiliates upgraded and specialized in this way during the third period, their indigenous suppliers followed suit, as Chapters 5, 6, and 7 suggest. So successful were the NIC suppliers that they enabled American Wintelist producers like Dell and Cisco to dispense with essentially all investment in underlying component technologies and manufacturing capacity. In turn, by leveraging their link into the US production networks and the global distribution capabilities thereby provided, the strongest indigenous Asian producers began to control their own production networks. For example, in the early 1990s, intense competition and growing needs for scale-intensive investment forced a shakeout and consolidation among Taiwanese and Hong Kong-based electronics firms.[29] Firms like ACER, the Formosa Plastics Group, and Tatung began to accumulate an extensive indigenous supply base of thousands of small and medium-sized design, component parts, subassembly and assembly houses throughout the China Circle and extending into Southeast Asia. These firms formed an intricate subcontracting structure of affiliated and family enterprises which comprised the local production network and supply base. The numerous small firms aligned vertically with the few larger scale enterprises that acted as intermediaries for foreign MNC customers.[30] Designs and key components would flow down from the large-scale enterprises; more labor-intensive production activities would flow up along the subcontract network leading to final assembly.

Toward the end of the third period, in response to steep rises in factor input costs in the NICs, and exacerbated by currency appreciation, the indigenous production networks became more and more regionalized. For example, Table 3.1 suggests the extent to which considerable PC-related production is now being carried on by Taiwanese MNCs within the region but outside of Taiwan. As Table 3.1 suggests, production outside of Taiwan but in the Asian regional networks accounted for increasing shares of total production under Taiwanese control, approaching one-quarter of the total in 1995. Effective regionalization of the production networks of indigenous producers helped to articulate further the emerging division of labor in electronics within Asia as a whole. Assembly and component activities were transplanted to mainland China and Southeast Asia, and higher value-added specializations within the disaggregated value-chain were developed at home in the NICs (e.g. digital design in Taiwan, leading-edge memory in Korea, advanced processes in Singapore).

In sum, by the early 1990s, the division of labor between the United States and Asia, and within Asia between affiliates and local producers, deepened significantly, and US firms effectively exploited increased technical specialization in Asia. In stark contrast, up until the end of 1993, Japanese firms still controlled their Asian affiliates' major decision-making and sourcing activities from Japan. More low-end process/product technology had been offshored, including production of audio systems (cassette recorders, headphones, low-end tuners, etc.), under 20-inch televisions and some VCR models, cameras, calculators, and appliances like microwave ovens. Local

*Table 3.1* Domestic versus offshore production value of Taiwan's electronics industry, 1992–5 (~ millions)

|  | *1992* | *1993* | *1994* | *1995 (est.)* |
|---|---|---|---|---|
| Domestic production | 8391 | 9693 | 11579 | 13139 |
| Offshore production | 973 | 1691 | 3003 | 4279 |
| Offshore/domestic (%) | 11.60 | 17.45 | 25.93 | 32.57 |

Source: MIC/III.

Asian content had risen toward 60 percent, but core technological inputs like magnetrons, chips, and recording heads were exclusively sourced from Japan, and the 60 percent "local" content was mostly supplied by the offshore branch plants of traditional domestic Japanese suppliers. Local design activities were invariably to tailor Japanese product concepts for local Asian markets, and global mandates for advanced products, let alone their design, development, and manufacture, were nowhere to be found outside of Japan. In contrast to US producers, for example, Japanese PC producers sourced displays, memory, some microprocessors, drives, power and mechanical components, plastics, and PCBs from Japan (or in the case of some low-end components, from offshore affiliates), and carried out PCB and final assembly, and essentially all advanced design and development in Japan. In short, Japanese firms intensified rather than rationalized their dual production structure, and, by exclusion from their production networks, failed to benefit from increasing, cheaper, and faster technical capabilities in the rest of Asia.

## Conclusion: Wintelism, CPNs and the future of competition

Wintelism and CPNs have been very important to the outcome of competition in the electronics industry. They were the principal means by which the US electronics industry recovered from its mid-1980s nadir in competition with Japanese firms to re-emerge as the global technical and market leader by the mid-1990s; they were also the enablers that permitted indigenous electronics producers to emerge and prosper in the rest of Asia. Wintelism shifted the industry's product market strategies away from final assembly and toward the distinctive value-added products backed by standards strategies in which American innovations and entrepreneurial companies were strong. Simultaneously, the American CPNs created an alternative supply base in Asia, an alternative to reliance on Japanese competitors for underlying component technologies and manufacturing capabilities. By exploiting an ever more intricate and flexible division of labor *based not on cheap factor endowments but on increasing local technical specialization in Asia* – a division enabled by Wintelist product strategies – CPNs helped to lower production costs and turnaround times while keeping pace with rapid technological progress and responding rapidly to unpredictable market shifts. Also, the networks spawned Asian-based direct competitors to Japanese firms in several of their stronghold markets (e.g. memory chips, consumer electronics, and displays).

Taken together, Wintelism and CPNs enabled a new generation of US firms to pioneer a new form of competition in electronics: one that grew out of the distinctively American market environment and was adapted to overseas opportunities. It is a form of competition in which "core assets" are the intellectual property and know-how associated with setting, maintaining, and continuously evolving a *de facto* market standard, a process that requires perpetual improvements in product features, functionality, performance, costs, and quality. And the core managerial skill has become orchestrating the CPN itself: managing the continuously changing sets of external relationships and melding them with the relatively more stable core of internal activities in order to access relevant technologies, design, develop, and manufacture the products, and get them from product concept to order fulfillment in minimal time.

For Wintelist American firms the innovations in product concept and corporate organization appear to have fulfilled the single most important strategic imperative of competition in high-technology markets: developing and sustaining monopoly niches, whether through ownership and control of a *de facto* standard or by maintaining a differentiated product through the ability to add performance, functionality, features or to improve costs faster than their competitors. Profitability and market capitalization in electronics are almost purely a function of achieving such market structures, high where a quasi-monopoly position can be maintained in fast-growing markets, low or non-existent everywhere else. As Intel and Dell demonstrate in components and PC distribution, and Sony and Symantec demonstrate in their recent struggles with content creation (Columbia Pictures) and software, respectively, profits can be won or lost at any point in the value-chain if the market is structured accordingly. Future competitive battles in electronics will continue to center around the creation of and defense against a quasi-monopoly position, as the concerted attack by Silicon Valley on Microsoft's position and practices demonstrates.

It is also instructive that traditionally vertically integrated assemblers like HP, Motorola and, more recently, IBM have been the first among the traditional players to embrace the new form of competition. That fact suggests the hypothesis that in a globalizing world economy, new, epochal forms of competition like those described here will increasingly originate in a firm's ability to exploit location-specific advantages at its point of origin and to fill in complementary elements as necessary with relationships that exploit location-specific advantages elsewhere.[31] Thus, for example, the shape and character of US firm CPNs clearly reflect the advantages they derive from their point of origin in the US launch market: the setting, maintenance, and evolution of *de facto* standards set in the domestic US launch market was the principal instrument used by US firms to structure and preserve control over their inter-firm networks. So long as US firms maintained that role in the division of labor – by defining and executing an evolutionary path for improved performance, functionality, and cost that kept customers and licensees locked in to their standards – it was extremely difficult for other firms in the network to challenge for the lead. US networks could be relatively decentralized because control over standards enabled devolution of responsibility for significant value-added to partners without fear of losing the ability to orchestrate the network. By contrast, with control residing in their domestic-based manufacturing and core-component technologies, any significant devolution of responsibility by Japanese firms over those competencies to outside partners risked creating a direct competitor. Japanese networks had to be centralized to avoid that outcome.

For most firms, new forms of competition are initially linked to the domestic point of origin because that is where development of new product or process concepts and associated launch market opportunities are most developed, where local capacities and technical specialization are still exploited most fully, where the initial patterns of constraint and opportunity to which firms respond are first set.[32] But, increasingly, the future of competition will lie in the ability to exploit complementary capabilities originating elsewhere in the world, to combine them effectively and thereby generate innovations in strategy and organization. Already, as other chapters in the book suggest, there are signs that the Japanese and indigenous Asian producers are adapting to the US-inspired innovations suggested here. As they adjust, we can expect the newly dominant position of the resurgent US industry to be assailed with even newer forms of competition emanating from Asia. And there is little doubt that the deep industrial integration and increased technical specialization that Wintelist American strategies and CPNs helped to foster in Asia will be principal elements of the coming counterattack.

## Notes

1  As discussed later, a few of the traditional firms, notably Hewlett-Packard and up until recently Motorola, have adjusted quite well to the new competitive game.

2  As an important piece of the overall debate of US competitiveness, there is a voluminous literature covering that era of competition. In addition to numerous government studies in the United States and abroad, representative academic work includes Tyson and Zysman (1982) and Dertouzos *et al.* (1989).

3  See, for example, the discussion of sequential increasing supply dependence in consumer electronics in Consumer Electronics Sector Working Group (1988).

4  For an earlier version of the argument that argues for its general applicability as a model of industrial behavior, see Borrus and Zysman (1997). The name is derived from widespread usage of "WINTEL" (WINdows + InTEL) within the PC industry to connote the market power held jointly by Microsoft Windows operating systems and Intel microprocessor architectures.

5  To the elements discussed here, I would add another: the rapid embrace of Internet standards to transform legacy corporate data and communications networks, to enable Wintelist strategies, and to speed up CPN formation and management. This element is being explored in on-going BRIE work.

6  The "open-but-owned" rubric was first suggested in conversations with Robert Spinrad, Vice President of Technology Analysis and Development at Xerox.

7  This point and the following account are drawn from Bar and Borrus (1989).

8  There are numerous accounts of this period. Representative are Chposky and Leonsis (1988) and Cringely (1992).

9  The argument which follows draws in part from Bar *et al.* (1995).

10  For a brief but dense and suggestive economic analysis of standards, see Antonelli (1994). That issue of *IEP*, edited by Antonelli, was devoted to the economics of standards and contains many fine contributions. See, also David and Greenstein (1990), Katz and Shapiro (1994), and Besen and Farrell (1994).

11  See, for example, Farrell and Saloner (1986) and Katz and Shapiro (1986).
12  See the discussion by Antonelli (1994: 201–2)
13  Antonelli remarks that in modeling the emergence of *de facto* standards, the economics of technical change and of standards are so intertwined that they really cannot be separated. Ibid. p. 205.
14  On the concept of path-dependence, see Arthur (1985).
15  See the account in Gabel (1991: 67–70).
16  For more detail on the economics of this point, see David and Greenstein (1990: 1–23) and the sources cited there.
17  Cohen and Zysman (1987).
18  This section reproduces material first published in Borrus (1997).
19  See the discussion of sequential increasing supply dependence in consumer electronics in Consumer Electronics Sector Working Group (1988).
20  For an extended discussion of the supply base and architecture of supply concepts, see Borrus (1993).
21  For the broad range of major component technologies involved, see the discussion in Borrus, ibid.
22  The characterization of US FDI is based on the BRIE US Electronics FDI database, compiled from public sources and maintained by Greg Linden, supplemented by industry conversations, and reviewed by senior managers with Asia responsibility from most of the firms mentioned in the text. The characterization of Japanese electronics FDI in Asia which follows is consistent with, and in part draws on Chapter 4 by Ernst, as well as from Takayasu and Ishizaki (1995).
23  On the progression from consumer to industrial electronics in Taiwan, see also Callon (1994). More generally, on the development of Taiwan's information technology industry, see Kraemer and Dedrick (1995).
24  There were, of course, tremendous variations in the role played by state policy and in the policies themselves, in the different countries of the region. In highlighting a few commonalties, I do not mean to slight those differences. The active role played in general by governments in the region has been explored in detail in a variety of scholarly works. See, for example, Wade (1990), Haggard (1988). More recently, see the excellent contributions in MacIntyre (1994).
25  In focusing on OC electronics producers, I am ignoring the significant regional investment by the Korean *chaebol* who emerged during this period as major, regionwide producers of consumer electronics and components. See, for example, Bloom (1993).
26  Hong Kong was at best a distant third most important NIC site for MNC or indigenous electronics production. Moreover, its relative importance declined as PC investment spread into Southeast Asia and mainland China – though Hong Kong undoubtedly played an important role in helping to channel Taiwanese investment onto the mainland during the third period, described below.
27  Based on press accounts, company annual reports and SEC filings as compiled by Greg Linden in the BRIE Asia FDI Database. See Linden (1994a).
28  For Compaq, see Linden (1994b); for Hewlett-Packard, see Linden (1994c); for Motorola, see Linden (1994d).
29  The resulting industry concentration was most visible in Taiwan's largest domestic product sectors, notably monitors, PCs, and PCBs, where the top ten indigenous producers now account for over 70 percent of the market. See the discussion in Chung (1997).
30  For elaboration on the following, see, for example, Shieh (1991) and Levy and Kuo (1990). I have also drawn on an excellent paper by one of my graduate students (Chen 1994).

31  This is broadly consistent with work on the location decisions of multinationals. In addition to Porter (1990) and Dunning (1998) see Cantwell (1995).
32  I argue this at greater length in *Left for Dead* (Borrus 1997).

# References

Antonelli, C. (ed.) (1994) "Localized Technological Change and the Evolution of Standards as Economic Institutions," *Information Economics and Policy,* 6(3–4): 195–216.

Arthur, W. B. (1985) "Competing Technologies and Lock-in by Historical Events: The Dynamics of Allocation Under Increasing Returns," *CEPR Publication* 43, Stanford: Center for Economic Policy Research (CEPR).

Bar, F. and Borrus, M. (1989) "Information Networks and Competitive Advantage: Issues for Government Policy and Corporate Strategy Development," *Final Report for the OECD,* Paris: OECD.

Bar, F., Borrus, M. and Steinberg, R. (1995) "Islands in the Bit Stream: Charting the NII Interoperability Debate," BRE WP 79, Berkeley, CA: BRE.

Besen, S. and Farrell, J. (1994) "Choosing How to Compete: Strategies and Tactics in Standardization," *Journal of Economic Perspectives,* 8(2): 117–131.

Bloom, M. (1993) "Globalization and the Korean Electronics Industry," *Pacific Review.* 6(2): 119–126.

Borrus, M. (1993) "The Regional Architecture of Global Electronics: Trajectories, Linkages, and Access to Technology," in P. Gourevitch and P. Guerrieri (eds) *New Challenges to International Cooperation: Adjustment of Firms. Policies, and Organizations to Global Competition*, San Diego: University of California at San Diego.

—— (1997) "Left for Dead: Asian Production Networks and the Revival of US Electronics," in B. Naughton (ed.) *The China Circle*, Washington, DC: Brookings.

Borrus, M. and Zysman, J. (1997) "Globalization with Borders: The Rise of Wintelism as the Future of Global Competition," *Industry and Innovation,* 4(2): 141–66.

Callon, S. (1995) "Different Paths: The Rise of Taiwan and Singapore in the Global Personal Computer Industry," Asia/Pacific Research Center WP 105, Stanford: Asia/Pacific Research Center, Institute for International Studies.

Cantwell, J. (1995) "The Globalization of Technolgy: What Remains of the Product Cycle Model?" *Cambridge Journal of Economics* 19(1): 155–74.

Chposky, J. and Leonsis, T. (1988) *Blue Magic: The People. Power and Politics Behind the IBM Personal Computer*, New York: Facts on File.

Chen, F. (1994) *From Comparative Advantage to Competitive Advantage: A Case Study of Taiwan's Electronics Industry,* Unpublished manuscript.

Chung, C. (1997) "Division of Labor Across the Taiwan Strait: Macro Overview and Analysis of the Electronics Industry," in B. Naughton (ed.) *The China Circle,* Washington, DC: The Brookings Institution Press.

Cohen, S. and Zysman, J. (1987) *Manufacturing Matters: The Myth of the Post Industrial Economy,* New York: Basic Books.

Consumer Electronics Sector Working Group (1988) "The Decline of US Consumer Electronics Manufacturing: History, Hypotheses, Remedies," in Working Papers of the *MIT Commission on Industrial Productivity*, Cambridge, MA: MIT Press.

Cringely, R. (1992) *Accidental Empires: How the Boys of Silicon Valley Make Their Millions, Battle Foreign Competition, and Still Can't Get a Date*, Reading MA: Addison-Wesley.

David, P. and Greenstein, S. (1990) "The Economics of Compatibility Standards: An Introduction to Recent Research," *CEPR Technical Paper* 207, Stanford: Center for Economic Policy Research.

Dertouzos, M. and MIT Commission on Industrial Productivity (1989) *Made in America: Regaining the Productive Edge,* Cambridge, MA: MIT Press.

Dunning, J. (1988) *Multinationals. Technology and Competitiveness,* London: Unwin Hyman.

Farrell, J. and Saloner, G. (1986) "Installed Base and Compatibility: Innovation, Product Preannouncements and Predation," *American Economic Review* 76: 940–955.

Gabel, L. (1991) *Competitive Strategies for Product Standards: The Strategic Use of Compatibility Standards for Competitive Advantage,* London: McGraw Hill.

Haggard, S. (1988) *Pathways from the Periphery: The Politics of Growth in the Newly Industrializing Countries,* Ithaca: Cornell University Press.

Katz, M. and Shapiro, C. (1994) "Systems Competition and Network Effects," *Journal of Economic Perspectives* 8(2): 93–115.

—— (1986) "Technology Adoption in the Presence of Network Externalities," *Journal of Political Economy* 94(4): 822–41.

Kraemer, K. and Dedrick, J. (1995) "Entrepreneurship, Flexibility, and Policy Coordination: Taiwan's Information Technology Industry," Irvine: Center for Research on Information Technology and Organizations.

Levy, B. and Kuo, W.-J. (1990) "The Strategic Orientation of Firms and the Performance of Korea and Taiwan in Frontier Industries: Lessons from Comparative Case Studies of Keyboard and Personal Computer Assembly," *World Development* 19, 4: 363–74.

Linden, G. (1994a) "Apple Computer East Asian Manufacturing Affiliates," Unpublished summary, November 7.

—— (1994b) "Compaq East Asian Manufacturing Affiliates," Unpublished summary, November 7.

—— (1994c) "Hewlett-Packard East Asian Manufacturing Affiliates," Unpublished summary, November 7.

—— (1994d) "Motorola East Asian Manufacturing Affiliates," Unpublished summary, November 7.

MacIntyre, A. (ed.) (1994) *Business and Government in Industrializing Asia,* Ithaca: Cornell University Press.

Porter, M. (1990) *The Competitive Advantage of Nations,* London: Macmillan.

Shieh, G. S. (1991) "Network Labor Process: The Subcontracting Networks in Manufacturing Industries of Taiwan," *Academia Sinica Bulletin of the Institute of Ethnology,* 71.

Takayasu, K. and Yukiko Ishizaki, Y. (1995) "The Changing International Division of Labor of Japanese Electronics Industry in Asia and Its Impact on the Japanese Economy," *RIM: Pacific Business and Industries* 1(27): 2–21.

Tyson, L. and Zysman, J. (eds) (1982) *American Industry in International Competition,* Ithaca NY: Cornell University Press.

Wade, R. (1990) *Governing the Market: Economic Theory and the Role of Government in East Asian Industrialization,* Princeton: Princeton University Press.

# 4 Evolutionary aspects

## The Asian production networks of Japanese electronics firms

*Dieter Ernst*

## Introduction

Like their American counterparts, Japanese electronics firms have developed substantial international production networks (IPNs) in Asia.[1] This chapter examines how far Japanese firms have cloned key features of American IPNs or developed substantially different international production activities. As we shall see, there have been substantial differences that mirror important characteristics of the respective national political economies. Those differences have had significant competitive effects.

I proceed in four steps. First, I provide an overview of the internationalization of the Japanese electronics industry up to 1991, i.e. before the bursting of the bubble economy. I briefly describe two peculiar features of Japanese IPNs that distinguish them from the networks established by American firms – their closed and Japan-centered governance structures and their asymmetric trade relations. Second, I discuss some of the causes for these differences. Although nationality is only one factor determining the nature of Japan's IPNs, aspects of domestic industrial organization do spill over into foreign operations.

In the third section, I describe the factors that are gradually forcing Japanese firms to open up their Asian production networks. While the "bursting of the bubble economy" and the yen appreciation have acted as powerful catalysts, more fundamental forces are also at work. The closed and Japan-centered nature of the country's production networks originally was a great strength. It enabled Japanese electronics firms to rapidly ramp up export platform production in Asia and to sustain international market share expansion. Yet it also came at a heavy cost. Far-reaching changes in the domestic production system associated with yen appreciation and recession forced rapid changes in IPNs. Of equal importance, however, were changes within East Asia. As the region improved its production and innovation capabilities and became a leading growth market for electronics products and services, Japanese firms needed to exploit these opportunities.

I conclude with a brief review of some recent changes in the organization of Japanese production networks in Asia. Overall, the Japanese case suggests that changes in the organization of international production are path-dependent. Industry- and product-specific factors, firm-level characteristics and locational advantages of the host economies matter, but the significance of national characteristics persists.

## The Asian production networks of Japanese electronics firms during the early 1990s

Three distinctive features characterize the Asian production networks of Japanese electronics firms prior to the early 1990s: (1) heavy geographic concentration; (2) closed, headquarters-centered governance structures; and (3) asymmetric trade links with East Asia (Ernst 1994a). While the first feature constitutes an important similarity with American IPNs in the electronics industry, the other two features do not.

### *Locational patterns*

As Encarnation (1995) has shown, Japanese investments in general are more geographically dispersed across Asia than American ones. This was also true for the electronics industry, because until the mid-1980s Japanese affiliates produced primarily for protected local markets. Once the focus shifted to export-platform production, Japanese electronics firms invested heavily in "mega-plants" concentrated in a handful of industrial sites in Malaysia, Taiwan, Singapore, and Thailand. In 1993, these four countries together accounted for two-thirds of all Japanese affiliates in Asia: Malaysia had the highest share (24 percent), followed by Taiwan (17 percent), Singapore (13 percent), and Thailand (12 percent).[2]

With regard to location, similarities thus have been stronger than differences; US electronics firms have also concentrated their Asian production networks in Singapore, Malaysia, Taiwan, and Thailand. For both Japan and the United States, Singapore often is the apex, performing critical support and coordination functions; Taiwan and South Korea are suppliers of precision components and sources of OEM (original equipment manufacturing) supply; and Malaysia and Thailand are the preferred locations for volume manufacturing.

### *Governance: control and coordination*

The governance structures that determine whether control over international production networks is centralized or decentralized are highly sensitive to peculiar features of national institutions and markets (Chandler 1990). There is a broad consensus that Japanese companies, once they moved abroad, were less obsessed with equity control than American companies (Dobson 1995, 38; Graham and Anzai 1994; Petri 1993). Most production took place as part of joint ventures with local partners. This is a reflection of important differences in the domestic capital markets of both countries and the fact that Japanese firms have had, until quite recently, ample access to patient capital. Some observers also claim that Japanese firms, especially in East Asia, are more willing to engage in joint ventures and other forms of inter-firm cooperation than American companies because of *domestic* relations with suppliers. "[A]ccustomed to operating in their home market through an extensive network of cooperation agreements, [Japanese firms] show a higher propensity to enter partnerships in Asia than American firms" (Lasserre and Schuette 1995: 176; Abegglen 1994).

As long as their objective was the penetration of protected domestic markets, Japanese subsidiaries in Asia had relatively strong local roots; local content was substantial, and this gave rise to a first generation of domestic support industries. At the same time, these subsidiaries often had considerable leeway with respect to the main objective: how to reap the windfall profits available in highly protected domestic markets.

The Matsushita group provides an example. Its core company Matsushita Electric Industrial (MEI) arguably is "...the company most deeply involved in East Asian electronics, and most representative of the Japanese approach."(Abegglen 1994: 221). Matsushita's involvement in East Asia started in the early 1960s with minority joint ventures strictly targeted at heavily protected domestic markets. The so-called "mini-Matsus" originally produced simple products like batteries, radios, electric fans, rice cookers and other low-end home appliances, small TV sets and some related components. As minority joint ventures, most of these local affiliates had considerable decision autonomy not only for employment, work practices, and salary, but also on how to organize production, support services (quality control and maintenance) and procurement. Decision autonomy was probably most pronounced in the choice of marketing approaches and distribution channels. Considerable local linkages developed from these investments, and local value-added increased sharply, often, however, at the expense of cost efficiency and quality.

Once their objective shifted from the penetration of domestic markets to exports, Matsushita increasingly relied on 100 percent affiliates or at least majority joint ventures. Local linkages declined as components were procured either directly from Japan or from Matsushita's affiliates within the region. This general pattern has been followed by all Japanese electronics firms: as they shift to export platform production, they close their Asian production networks to outsiders by centralizing almost all strategic decision-making and high value-added activities in Japan. Until a few years ago, sourcing components from independent local suppliers played a very marginal role, and was restricted to technically simple low-end components and support activities; almost all high value-added components were imported from Japan.[3] This heavy dependence on Japan appears to have reached its peak by 1992.[4] Between fiscal year (FY) 1991 and FY 1992, East Asian affiliates of Japanese electronics firms increased their procurement from Japan from less than 40 percent to nearly 47 percent, much higher than the average share of 38 percent reported for all industries. While the share of intra-regional procurement has stagnated at around 15 percent, there has been a substantial decline in local purchases from nearly 44 percent to less than 37 percent.[5]

The closed and Japan-centered nature of the Asian production networks of Japanese electronics firms extends well beyond the sphere of procurement. Japanese electronics firms rely much less on local managers and engineers in their Asian affiliates than their American and European counterparts do, leaving Asian affiliates little scope for autonomous decisions. Japanese electronics firms routinely engage in sound and systematic "on-the-job" training. Most of the training however remains restricted to simple operational capabilities required for production and maintenance.[6]

We also find only a limited transfer of the Japanese production model to Asian affiliates of Japanese electronics firms. In most affiliates, seniority-based wage systems, job rotation, "life-long" employment, quality control circles, and just-in-time (JIT) management approaches play an insignificant role. Often a crude Fordism prevails, at least during the initial phase of production.[7] This contrasts with the situation in the United States and Europe, where Japanese firms have made serious attempts to transfer key elements of their domestic production system and to adapt them to the peculiarities of local institutions and labor markets. In contrast to the situation in Asia, Japanese IPNs in the United States and Europe have undergone a certain limited convergence with the investment patterns of American and European firms (Abo 1993; Encarnation and Mason 1994; and Gittelman and Graham 1994).

The issue of governance structure thus leaves us with a few puzzles. In contrast to a general perception that Japanese firms are more willing to engage in partnerships in East Asia, we find that this has not been the case in the electronics industry. Early partnerships serving local markets gave way to highly centralized and closed governance structures as production moved toward exports for third markets.

## Trade patterns[8]

Two aspects of the Asian production networks of Japanese electronics firms are important to Japan's trade links with East Asia: (1) a heavy reliance on intra-firm trade; and (2) a consistently high and growing trade surplus. Both features are in stark contrast to the US pattern. American electronics firms in Asia rely much more on arm's-length trade, and US trade links with East Asia in the electronics industry are characterized by a large and rapidly growing trade deficit.

Ministry of International Trade and Industry (MITI) data for 1992 show the trade of Asian affiliates of Japanese electronics firms with Japan to be overwhelmingly dominated by intra-firm trade: 85 percent of the affiliates' purchases and almost 90 percent of sales were intra-firm.[9] Such heavy reliance on intra-firm trade is a reflection of the closed and Japan-centered nature of

Japanese production networks in Asia; the organization of international production shapes international trade patterns.[10] Comparable data (though not specifically for the electronics industry) indicate that intra-firm trade plays a much less prominent role in Japan's trade links with North America and Europe (Encarnation 1995: 28–29). A heavy reliance on intra-firm trade also sets Japanese IPNs apart from the trade patterns that characterize the Asian production networks of American firms. In 1992, arm's-length transactions accounted for well over 80 percent of all US exports to Asia and all US imports from Asia (Encarnation 1995: 28–29).

The implications of these patterns for control and competitiveness are not clear. Encarnation (1995: 28) correctly states that intra-firm trade enables multinational enterprises (MNEs) to exercise tight control over their subsidiaries, supply sources, and markets, but US MNEs have developed more sophisticated (indirect) forms of control. Inter-firm production networks enable them better to balance the advantages of size with the advantages of decentralization.[11] In the PC industry, for example, a substantial share of procurement relies on subcontractors and contract manufacturers. These suppliers are formally independent, even though they remain dependent on leading partners.

Moreover, it is not clear that a heavy reliance on intra-firm trade proves a long-term advantage. Compared with arm's-length transactions, intra-firm trade reduces transaction costs and provides opportunities for transfer-pricing. Yet there is also a body of literature that argues that organizational integration, of which a high level of intra-firm trade is an important manifestation, has substantial disadvantages. It may constrain a firm's capacity to utilize capabilities and access markets that exist outside the boundary of the firm, and can reduce speed-to-market and the capacity to react flexibly to changes in demand and technology. A high share of intra-firm trade also generates severe trade imbalances and trade frictions, and can limit the transfer of capabilities to host economies.

This brings us to the second peculiar feature of Japan's trade links with East Asia in the electronics industry – its controversial trade surpluses. Japan has a consistently high and growing trade surplus with East Asia in the electronics industry, whereas for the United States, a huge and rapidly growing trade deficit prevails. Such radical differences in trade behavior can be attributed in part to traditional macroeconomic factors such as exchange rates, factor endowments, and growth differentials. However, one complementary explanation lies in some peculiar features of American and Japanese IPNs in East Asia.

Table 4.1 indicates that a high dependence on component imports is the main cause for Japan's trade surplus with East Asia. Of even greater importance, this share has risen drastically over time. In 1993, Japan's trade surplus in components with Malaysia ($1.4 billion) was responsible for almost 82 percent of its total bilateral trade surplus in electronics ($1.7 billion). In Taiwan, Japan's trade surplus in components ($2.5 billion) was responsible

*Table 4.1* Japan's trade balances in electronics: Taiwan, Singapore, Malaysia, 1980–93

|  | 1980 | 1985 | 1990 | 1993 |
|---|---|---|---|---|
| *Billion US dollars versus Taiwan* |  |  |  |  |
| Total electronics | 0.3 | 0.6 | 2.2 | 3.5 |
| Electronic data processing | 0 | 0.07 | 0.4 | 0.4 |
| Electrical components | 0.1 | 0.2 | 1.2 | 2.5 |
| Consumer electronics | 0.1 | 0.1 | 0.4 | 0.2 |
| *versus Singapore* |  |  |  |  |
| Total electronics | 0.6 | 0.9 | 2.9 | 4.8 |
| Electronic data processing | 0 | 0 | 0.1 | 0.3 |
| Electrical components | 0.1 | 0.3 | 1.1 | 2.5 |
| Consumer electronics | 0.3 | 0.3 | 1.1 | 1.1 |
| *versus Malaysia* |  |  |  |  |
| Total electronics | 0.1 | 0.3 | 0.8 | 1.7 |
| Electronic data processing | 0 | 0 | 0 | 0 |
| Electrical components | 0.1 | 0.1 | 0.5 | 1.4 |
| Consumer electronics | 0 | 0.1 | 0.1 | 0.1 |

Source: Ernst *et al.* (1998) "International Production Networks and Changing Trade Patterns in East Asia. The Case of the Electronics Industry," *Oxford Development Studies*, 26(2).

*Table 4.2* US trade balances in electronics: Taiwan, Singapore, Malaysia, 1980–93

|  | 1980 | 1985 | 1990 | 1993 |
|---|---|---|---|---|
| *Billion US dollars versus Taiwan* |  |  |  |  |
| Total electronics | −0.9 | 2.2 | 3.4 | −5.1 |
| Electronic data Processing |  | −0.1 | −2.5 | −4.7 |
| Electrical components |  | −0.1 | 0 | 0.1 |
| Consumer electronics |  | −0.6 | −0.9 | −0.2 |
| *versus Singapore* |  |  |  |  |
| Total electronics | −0.8 | −1.3 | −4.3 | −5.2 |
| Electronic data Processing | 0 | −0.4 | −3.4 | −5.6 |
| Electrical components | −0.5 | −0.2 | 0 | 0.8 |
| Consumer Electronics | −0.1 | −0.3 | −0.2 | −0.2 |
| *versus Malaysia* |  |  |  |  |
| Total electronics | −0.7 | −0.5 | −1.4 | −4.8 |
| Electric data processing | 0 | 0 | 0.002 | −1.3 |
| Electrical components | −0.7 | −0.3 | −0.1 | −0.6 |
| Consumer electronics | 0 | −0.1 | −0.8 | −2.2 |

Source: Ernst *et al.* (1998) "International Production Networks and Changing Trade Patterns in East Asia. The Case of the Electronics Industry," *Oxford Development Studies*, 26(2).

for almost 72 percent of its total bilateral trade surplus in electronics. And even in Singapore this share was quite substantial, $2.5 billion out of $4.8 billion or 52 percent (Table 4.2).

By contrast, the United States ran large bilateral trade deficits with the same three Asian countries, also its most important production sites. The US trade deficit in electronics with both Taiwan and Singapore is attributable in part to the IPNs of US computer companies. In the case of Singapore, these networks comprise both US subsidiaries and a variety of subcontracting and contract manufacturing activities; in the case of Taiwan, a large share is due to a variety of OEM/ODM (original equipment manufacturing)/turnkey production arrangements. For both countries, electronic data processing (EDP) accounts for the lion's share of the deficit.

Malaysia continues to play an important role as an offshore assembly base for integrated circuits (ICs), producing a small US deficit in components of roughly $600 million. Over the last decade, American hard disk drive manufacturers have also established a variety of export platform activities in Malaysia, which is the main reason for the $1.3 billion US trade deficit for EDP. Consumer electronics (CE), however, is responsible for the largest deficit with Malaysia. Increasing exports to the United States from Japanese subsidiaries present in the country since 1985 are the main cause. While in 1985 the US trade deficit with Malaysia in CE was insignificant, it is now responsible for almost half of the total US trade deficit in electronics with this country.

## Explaining Japanese production networks in Asia

Why have Japanese electronics firms adopted a different approach to the organization of their Asian production networks than American and European firms? And why have they organized their Asian production networks differently from their production networks in North America and Europe? I suggest that nationality of ownership does matter, and can be traced to definable institutional features of the Japanese production system, particularly the absence of tight financial control and a domestic bias of the procurement system. Yet these national characteristics must be placed in the context of other industry and even firm-specific factors. First, until the early 1990s, Japanese firms focused on very different product groups and markets from American firms, i.e. consumer electronics and household appliances. Second, as latecomers to international production, it took Japanese firms time to develop the capacity to manage IPNs. As a result, networks were organized in a highly centralized manner to minimize risk. Third, East Asia's close proximity to Japan enabled Japanese firms to implement centralized and Japan-centered IPNs in a relatively efficient fashion. And, finally, firm size and strategic focus have shaped the organization of Japanese IPNs.

## Peculiar features of the domestic Japanese production system

There is no doubt that certain basic features of the domestic Japanese production system have shaped the organization of Japanese IPNs in East Asia.[12] First, until the "bursting of the bubble economy" in 1991, one of the key features of corporate governance in Japan has been a lack of tight financial control (Dobson 1995; Stopford 1998; Kester 1996) that has forced Japanese firms to establish other forms of control.

Kester (1996: 118) distinguishes two types of corporate governance: those associated with the separation of ownership and control (the control of "agency costs"), and those associated with the establishment and maintenance of contractual exchange among separate enterprises. Kester (1996) shows that

> the chief shortcoming of Japanese governance is its low ability to control...agency costs.... In modern Japanese business history, controlling agency costs has been of second-order importance.... So long as attractive real growth opportunities were abundant and product and factor market rivalry was fierce, corporate managers were unlikely to deploy resources in a highly disciplined way. High rates of real growth, moreover, can do much to attenuate disputes among corporate stakeholders by relieving pressures to compare one group's gains to those of another from a zero-sum perspective. So long as growth could be sustained, virtually all stakeholders benefited and conflict among them could be held to a minimum.
>
> (Kester 1996: 126–7)

Japanese corporate governance thus differs fundamentally from the American approach where elaborate capital-budgeting and financial-planning systems since the Second World War have become a key feature (Baldwin and Clark 1994). It is this fundamental difference in corporate governance rather than differences in the relative cost of capital (alleged or real) that explain why Japanese firms had better access than their US rivals to patient capital.[13] This gave rise to high rates of capital investment and encouraged firms to develop overextended product portfolios. There was little pressure to control the use of capital: financial control mechanisms remained quite loose and embryonic compared with the sophisticated US techniques of global cash flow management.

The absence of tight financial control has had important consequences for the organization of Japanese IPNs. Japanese firms have been reluctant to let locals participate in decision-making and have relied heavily on expatriates to establish indirect centralized control. As a result, most decisions taken at the level of the affiliate require continuous interaction with the management of the parent company. Japanese firms claim that one major reason for not increasing more rapidly the share of local managers in East Asia is that very few local candidates know enough Japanese. The main issue, however, is that local managers and engineers remain confined to marginal roles in the decision-making process. A survey conducted for the Asia Productivity Organization in 1992 shows that local managers in no case were entitled to make their own decisions, and typically were supporting the implementation of given decisions (Shiraki 1993). This obviously has a number of negative consequences. Not only does it lead to a "…high propensity of [local] white-collar employees for frustration" (Shiraki 1993: 96), it stifles local initiative and on-the-spot learning possibilities, leads to costly duplication and overlapping of activities, limits the flexibility of subsidiaries to adapt to local market conditions, and constrains their ability to mobilize and exploit local capabilities. Moreover, Japanese subsidiaries have a low reputation among local managers and engineers, advantaging American and European rivals.

A second characteristic of Japan's domestic production system is a strong local bias in procurement. Barriers to entry and exit into a firm's supplier networks are very high, which in turn has given rise to structural rigidities in the procurement system; these biases are replicated when Japanese firms go multinational.

Japanese procurement decisions are made by individual product divisions and profit centers in the parent through procurement offices that have strong ties with domestic suppliers. Procurement engineers have been trained to handle the multi-layered networks of Japanese suppliers, but have neither the incentive nor the expertise to search for, qualify, and upgrade foreign suppliers, including East Asia. Under this system, it is difficult for managers of affiliates to override decisions made by the procurement offices in Japan. For example, once an affiliate locates and qualifies a local supplier, it can take up to nine months for the part to be approved by the parent company. This has constrained the speed with which Japanese electronics firms can increase their component sourcing within the region. The result has been a highly Japan-centered procurement system in which most suppliers are Japanese firms that are either captives (i.e. *de facto* part of a business group or "keiretsu") or highly dependent on one or a small number of key customer firms.

### Industry-specific factors: a different product mix

Nationality is not, of course, the only variable of significance in explaining the nature of Japanese IPNs. Some of the observed differences in organization are explained by the very different product mix that Japanese and American electronics firms have shifted to Asia. American firms in Asia have concentrated on ICs (especially microprocessors and logic devices) and PC-related products since the late 1960s, whereas Japanese firms, almost without exception, have focused on lower end consumer electronics and related components. Microprocessors and PC-related products are highly differentiated products that require close and fast interaction with sophisticated customers. TV sets and household appliances, on the other hand, are homogeneous products. As we argue in the introduction, American semiconductor firms and computer companies have sought new markets based on the capacity to define and control international product and architectural standards (Christensen 1993; Ernst 1997a). This is in stark contrast to the Japanese strategy, which seeks to expand international market share for relatively mature products through price competition, control of some key components, and rapid product differentiation (Ernst and O'Connor 1992, Chapter 2).

This divergence in the product mix had a number of important implications. First, there is very limited overlap between American and Japanese IPNs in Asia. In Malaysia, for example, there is limited interaction between the production networks established by American IC vendors such as Intel and Motorola and Japanese consumer electronics firms such as Matsushita, Sony, and Sanyo. Second, the strategic rationale for developing Asian production networks differs across product groups. For instance, American semiconductor merchant firms established offshore chip assembly plants in Asia in the late 1960s to avoid the heavy capital outlays that would have been necessary for factory automation at home. Only much later did they become concerned with pre-empting possible attacks by Japanese firms through rapid cost reduction (Ernst 1983; 1987).

Japanese consumer electronics producers were faced with a very different challenge; they had hesitated too long in moving production of these products to East Asia (Ernst and O'Connor 1992). Under the impact of the yen appreciation, they risked losing market share in the United States and Europe, especially to the aggressive new competitors from Korea. A quick response on a massive scale was required to roll back these new challengers. Production ramp-up had to occur quickly, and cost and quality had to be tightly controlled. Under such conditions, centralized management control was a perfectly rational choice. Developing local capabilities and linkages through "trial-and-error" would have been a time-consuming process, and thus had to be discarded.

Third, we find that specific features of consumer electronics are important for the organization of Japanese production networks. Lower end consumer devices have a variety of characteristics that are conducive for the establishment of global export platform mega-plants. They are homogeneous products with large economies of scale in which close interaction with customers is not required. They are characterized by a high divisibility. Different stages in the value-chain can be easily separated, and fundamental changes in design methodology and the shift from metallic to plastic parts have facilitated offshore production, even for relatively complex components such as drums, video heads, and small motors.[14] With but few exceptions (such as picture tubes), most components and subassemblies are also characterized by low transportation costs, and can be easily moved between different locations.[15]

### The vintage factor: latecomers in international production

Latecomers to international production are likely to differ in their organizational approaches from firms that have had a much longer learning experience. We know from innovation theory that firms need time to develop their capabilities;[16] this is even more true for international production. Stopford (1998: 2), for instance, argues that "...firms progress over time from the simplest to more complex forms [of international production networks] as they learn how to manage [them]." Such learning also takes place in the foreign affiliates: "As skills and resources accumulate within the various foreign units, new options and more complex projects can be undertaken without relying heavily on the parent organization for help and guidance (ibid. 16).

There is ample empirical evidence that Japanese firms in general are laggards in international production compared with their American and European counterparts. A survey conducted by JETRO (the Japanese External Trade Organization) in December 1995 found that the ratio of overseas production as a percentage of total output, the so-called overseas production ratio (OPR), was 26 percent for American firms, 16 percent for European firms, yet only 8 percent for Japanese firms.

Compared with all manufacturing, Japanese electronics firms have been substantially more exposed to international production. Yet they still lag behind their American and European rivals.[17] This is true even for early pioneers in international production, such as Sanyo and Sony. American PC companies, by contrast, generate roughly 40–50 percent of their total production value in East Asia. Seagate, the current market leader for hard disk drives, is estimated to generate around 75 percent of its overall production value in East Asia, primarily in the triangle that comprises Singapore, Malaysia, and Thailand. European electronics multinationals have fairly high OPRs, but only in the last decade have major European electronics firms discovered East Asia (Lasserre and Schuette 1995). We estimate that during the early 1990s major European electronics firms generated roughly 15–20 percent of their total production value in Asia.[18]

### Economic geography: the role of proximity

A third factor that explains the closed and Japan-centered nature of Japanese production networks in Asia is proximity, which has facilitated centralized control. The scope for centralized control diminishes with increasing distance; once a firm extends its value-chain across national boundaries, it is faced with complex coordination problems and the risk of abrupt disruptions.[19] Firms have had only limited success reducing the likelihood of such disruptions (Levy 1994; 1995). While production-related disruptions decline with increasing product maturity, demand-related disruptions and abrupt changes in management decisions brought on by financial markets do not.

Japanese firms are in a much better position to manage these risks than

American and European firms. Japanese firms can control their East Asian affiliates from Tokyo, because the region is part of the same time zone; American firms never had this option. Owing to their proximity to East Asia, Japanese firms are able to establish closer contacts than US firms with their subsidiaries, suppliers, and critical customers in East Asia.

### Firm-specific features

Finally, firm-specific features also play an important role in shaping the organization of international production; I focus here on two: size and strategic focus.[20]

One of the peculiar features of Japan's international production networks in electronics is the substantial role played by small and medium-sized enterprises (SMEs).[21] SMEs have higher OPRs than their large, vertically integrated counterparts. This is true for smaller firms that produce final products but have a quite narrow product focus, such as Aiwa (whose OPR exceeds 85 percent) or Uniden (with an OPR close to 100 percent), but it is also true for the hundreds of relatively small subcontractors and component suppliers that have moved production offshore to Southeast Asia and China.

This finding is somewhat surprising. Small firms have limited resources and capabilities, many of them lack strong proprietary assets, and international production involves transaction costs that most SMEs may simply be too small to shoulder. Small firms can bypass such size-related barriers to internationalization if they are part of a network centered around a core firm that reduces the transaction costs involved in international production, such as the hierarchical supplier networks that traditionally have characterized the Japanese electronics industry. Small firms can also compensate for their size-related disadvantages by limiting the geographic scope of their foreign investments. While large firms have dispersed their production activities around the world, medium-sized firms cluster their overseas operations in Taiwan, Korea, and Singapore; small firms are concentrated mainly in Taiwan, but recently have expanded into China. Despite a rapid growth of international production, smaller Japanese electronics firms rely on a very limited international division of labor.

Even if product and size are held constant, however, it is important to underline that substantial differences may remain across firms. This can be seen by looking at consumer electronics and comparing Sanyo, the pioneer in establishing Asian production networks, with the Matsushita group and Sony.

Sanyo's founder was the brother-in-law of Konosuke Matsushita, who took over most of the operations of the Matsushita group when it was broken up under the US Occupation Authority. In Japan, Sanyo always remained a second-tier competitor, and compensated with an aggressive early shift into international production. In the early 1970s, Sanyo developed the so-called "one-third" strategy for manufacturing capacity – one-third domestic manufacture for the domestic market; one-third domestic manufacture for foreign markets (especially higher-end segments); and one-third foreign manufacture for foreign markets. Sanyo aggressively focused its international production and sourcing on East Asia in the second half of the 1970s, much earlier than any of its Japanese rivals.

Matsushita Electric Industrial Co. Ltd (MEI) is the world's largest manufacturer of consumer electronics and household appliances. Since the mid-1980s, it has diversified aggressively into communications and factory automation equipment, semiconductors, and video software, with the result that today the share of industrial electronics and electronics components in its overall sales is roughly equal to the share of consumer and household goods. For quite some time, this giant conglomerate has been run like a loose network of (almost) independent business units, with headquarters playing the neutral role of an arbiter. As long as markets kept growing, this loose network organization was widely considered to be a great strength, as it enabled the company to remain reasonably flexible despite its huge size (Imai 1988). However, as demand growth slowed the hidden costs of excessive decentralization and decision autonomy, such as duplication, foregone economies of scale and self-generated price pressures became apparent.

Matsushita's core competencies traditionally have been size-related advantages in distribution and high-end manufacturing (in specialized affiliates like Matsushita Kotobuki). It had tight control over the domestic distribution channels for consumer electronics, and thus its expansion activities in East Asia were geared more to the heavily protected domestic markets than to the establishment of low-cost export platform production. Once Matsushita decided to move to export platform production, however, it was able to do so on a massive scale, rapidly neutralizing whatever first-mover advantages Sanyo may have developed.

Sony, together with Sanyo, has one of the highest OPRs among large diversified Japanese electronics firms; yet, its overseas production has remained focused almost exclusively on the United States and Europe. Only since the late 1980s has the company begun to invest seriously in the development of an Asian production network. Sony's approach to international production reflects some peculiar features of this company that have shaped its strategy. In 1952, when Sony purchased a license for Western Electric's transistor patent and began to produce transistor radios under the model name Sony, the company decided to focus on the high-income and high-growth markets in the United States and Europe. Right from the beginning, the firm sought to develop its own brand name image. Akio Morita, the company's charismatic co-founder, spent considerable time and energy on developing direct links with large US retailers to ensure that Sony's products would receive sufficient floor space.

Owing to the tremendous success of this strategy, Sony was under much less pressure to internationalize than its rivals, who lacked similar image recognition and concentrated on Asian markets. Sony was also reluctant to shift to export platform production in East Asia and invested heavily in the automation of its European and North American plants, including those in Mexico. Today Sony's Asian production networks are still relatively underdeveloped, but they are also much less burdened than Sanyo and Matsushita with "deadwood," surplus capacities and duplication.

## Causes for change

### *The yen appreciation and the bursting of the bubble economy*

The year 1991 constitutes an important watershed. The combined effect of accelerating yen appreciation and the bursting of the bubble economy forced firms to cut costs at every stage of the value-chain and to rationalize existing IPNs by opening up their Asian production networks. From around 240 in 1985, the yen's exchange rate to the US dollar experienced a breathtaking dive to below eighty in the summer of 1995 before increasing again to around 110 in the first half of 1996. As a result, Japanese affiliates in East Asia paid steeply rising prices for components and production equipment imported from Japan, wiping out any advantages from lower labor costs. Particularly hard hit were companies such as Sony, which continued to rely heavily on components shipped from Japan.[22] Localization of component sourcing in Asia thus became a necessary prerequisite for sustaining international market share.

The appreciation of the yen also led to a rapid increase in cheap "reverse imports" from East Asia into Japan; this occurred not only in TV sets and audio-visual (AV) equipment but also in an increasing variety of components and computer-related products. For example, in 1994 almost all of Fujitsu's PC-related parts and components were sourced in Japan; in the first quarter of 1995, Fujitsu estimates that 95 percent of the parts for the PCs sold in Japan were imported (most of them from East Asia).[23]

The yen appreciation and the bursting of the bubble economy exposed the hidden costs of closed and Japan-centered Asian production networks. But much more fundamental forces are at work, including the deepening of regional capabilities, the rapid growth of markets, and changes in Japan's domestic production system.

### *Changes in the domestic production system: a move towards systemic rationalization*

Confronted with drastic changes in technology as well as in its major markets, the Japanese electronics industry is undergoing a period of turmoil. Two fundamental changes in technology are upsetting prevailing market structures. First, digitalization implies that performance features of consumer devices are defined by integrated circuits, with the result that market leadership positions based on analog technology can no longer be taken for granted. Second, the spread of "multimedia" applications implies a convergence of computing, communications, and consumer-related technologies. Computer companies have entered competition for consumer mass markets, and software and entertainment programming capabilities have grown in significance.[24]

Japan's big integrated electronics makers have been able to strengthen their position in the consumer sector. For example, Toshiba recently succeeded in establishing its DVD (digital video disk) format as the *de facto* industry standard for the next generation of recording disks, and traditional leaders in the consumer electronics industry, especially the Matsushita group, Sony, and Sanyo, have transformed themselves into integrated electronics makers by strengthening their position in components, computers and telecommunications. Particularly noteworthy in this context are the aggressive strategies pursued by both Matsushita and Sony to become leaders in display technology.

Pressures have been particularly intense for smaller companies with a much more limited product focus. The typical example is Aiwa, which has radically reduced its product mix and which now produces 87 percent of its overall production value abroad, mostly in East Asia. This extreme reliance on overseas production has not guaranteed success. Aiwa failed to complement overseas production with product upgrading and differentiation; as a result, the benefits of overseas production have been wiped out by increased competition from low-cost competitors, especially in Korea and China (*FT*, 15 May 1996).

Although experimentation and "strategic drift" continue to prevail to some extent, most firms appear to be committed to moving toward what I will call "systemic rationalization" – the attempt to move beyond partial rationalization of individual business functions (such as factory automation or JIT procurement systems) to generate closer, faster, and more cost-effective interactions between all stages of the value-chain across all production locations (Ernst 1997a, Chapters II and IV). This effort involves at least three organizational changes of significance to IPNs.

First, Japanese electronics firms are implementing for the first time formal financial control systems; performance is now measured for every plant and every business unit. Tighter financial control is expected to slim down "fat" product portfolios and reduce excessive investment outlays. With stringent financial control systems in place, parent companies are now granting greater local decision autonomy, which, sooner or later, will erode the centralized governance structure that has characterized Japanese IPNs.

Second, Japanese firms are introducing a strategy of procurement rationalization and internationalization to reduce dependence on high-cost domestic supply sources and to generate larger economies of scale. Rationalization means paring down a company's supply base. Internationalization means that a firm can choose the best suppliers in the world, in terms of cost, quality and delivery performance, no matter where their operations are located. Rationalization and internationalization together mean that the size of each contract on average is likely to increase. As a result, the client firm can request that each supplier offers more favorable unit prices and delivery schedules. If the contract is big enough, the client firm may even be able to ask the supplier to set up shop at a particular location.

Firms must make important changes if they wish to reap the potentially huge scale economies of international procurement. For example, procurement decisions for low-volume, low-cost commodities (especially those with high transportation costs) can be left to regional headquarters or even to individual affiliates. Within the firm, procurement decisions need to be based on close and continuous interaction among purchasing, engineering, finance, and quality assurance. Improved inter-firm networking and administration are thus increasingly crucial to the effective implementation of inter-firm networks.

Third, Japanese electronics firms are experimenting with new approaches to innovation management, which, again, may have far-reaching implications for the organization of their Asian production networks. Japanese firms are well known for their capacity to reduce the development cycle for new products and thus to accelerate speed-to-market for products that remain within a given technology paradigm.[25] Continuous refinement of product design and process engineering have been hallmarks of the Japanese approach to innovation management. However, recent research has highlighted that international innovation management strategies of Japanese electronics firms lack a clear focus and have been plagued by costly trial and error methods.[26] Compared with their American and European counterparts, Japanese firms are still at a relatively early stage of R&D internationalization, and so far have very limited experience in organizing international R&D networks. Moreover, in their attempts to internationalize R&D, Japanese firms face even greater cross-cultural communication problems than for manufacturing, and have failed to integrate ideas and concepts developed abroad into the firm's domestic R&D agenda.[27] Japanese firms are finding it more difficult than their American and European counterparts to recruit first-class non-Japanese researchers, remain reluctant to localize the management of their overseas R&D activities, and thus have failed to fully tap into local and regional science and technology communities.

Our interest here is to understand why Japanese firms have decided to expand their overseas R&D activities in Asia and to what degree these activities differ from those they pursue in the United States and Europe.[28] Both in the United States and in Europe, Japanese electronics firms seek to improve their access to international technology networks by expanding overseas basic research centers and establishing "satellite R&D centers" that conduct cooperative research with foreign companies, universities, and research institutes. Japanese electronics firms, for example, are under increasing pressure to speed up the growth of their accumulated patent portfolios. They know that the fastest way to do this is to complement their domestic R&D activities by establishing a center in one of those "regional clusters" (Porter 1990) where innovation capabilities and R&D infrastructure are concentrated.

In Asia, the innovation management strategies of Japanese electronics firms are shaped by a very different set of objectives – to provide adequate support activities for their expanding IPNs. Overwhelmingly, these networks consist of mass production-type assembly and related component manufacturing. The main driving force for relocating R&D activities to East Asia is this current shift from proprietary components to standard components that can be sourced at lower cost from local or regional suppliers. In order to achieve this goal, Japanese electronics firms have been forced to upgrade their regional and local support services and establish on the spot a capacity for continuous re-design or so-called "adaptive engineering."

Since the early 1990s, Japanese firms have attached greater importance to market intelligence and product customization. Asia is increasingly characterized by heterogeneous demand patterns and highly segmented product markets; as a result, Japanese firms have had to adapt their Asian production networks to the idiosyncrasies of each of these markets. These developments "...require high degrees of local adaptation of products, integration of products with local services, and close relationships with component suppliers" (Branscomb and Kodama 1993: 86).[29] Local affiliates require a capacity for continuous product customization, adaptive engineering and some development activities. According to Kuniji Osabe, the head of Canon's R&D Planning Center, "...the best way to create products which meet local market needs is to perform local research with local talent."[30]

A third important objective for Japanese electronics firms is to tap into existing pools of lower- cost human resources. Most countries in Asia pursue aggressive policies to increase the supply of engineers and scientists, especially for software engineering and certain basic assembly technologies, circuit designs and system engineering and integration (Ernst 1997b).

As a location for Japanese overseas R&D activities, Asia still lags well behind the United States and Europe, where most of these activities remain concentrated. In Asia, R&D has centered on training, some basic manufacturing support services, product customization, and software engineering. Most of these activities are integrated into manufacturing affiliates, and thus do not show up on a count of "R&D centers." On the other hand, there is reason to believe that many of the reported "R&D centers" may not undertake any research at all. Japanese firms are now under increasing pressure from host country governments and firms to broaden the scope of transferred capabilities and thus have a tendency to use the term "R&D" rather loosely to include mundane and routine production-related engineering tasks.

## Recent changes

Do the causal forces just outlined imply that Japanese electronics firms will replicate the US model of international production? Recent changes in the organization of Japan's Asian production networks show rapid expansion, important shifts in their location, and moves towards broadening and deepening, although these efforts have been plagued by substantial constraints in implementation. These changes are reflected in Japan's trade links with East Asia. Yet despite the opening of Japan's IPNs in Asia, a number of important organizational differences persist when compared with the regional operations of American firms.

## Towards an emerging regional division of labor

In 1988 Asia accounted for roughly two-thirds of the total number of overseas investments of Japanese manufacturing companies; five years later this share had shot up to more than 90 percent (JETRO 1995: 20). SMEs, most of them suppliers of components and other intermediate goods to large MNEs, are driving this shift to Asia. For most of these firms, investing in East Asia is a defensive move: firms no longer able to supply at competitive prices from their Japanese home base are desperately searching for new low-cost locations in Asia. Much of this investment has moved into China, helping fuel the "China fever" that raged through Japanese industry between 1992 and 1995.

Between 1985 and 1993, nearly half of the total increase in Japanese manufacturing FDI in East Asia went into electronics (Yoshitomi 1994: 16). As a result, by 1993 almost 60 percent of all foreign affiliates of Japanese electronics firms were located in East Asia, and 70 percent of overseas employment was in East Asia.[31] At the same time, there has been a vast increase in the share of China in the investment of Japanese electronics firms abroad. From the measly 0.6 percent of 1990 (the year after the Tiananmen Square massacre), it has reached almost 7 percent, and is quickly approaching the 7.7 percent of ASEAN.[32] In addition to manufacturing affiliates, Japanese electronics firms are beginning to enter sourcing arrangements with Chinese counterparts. Although in sheer numbers the shift to China clearly dominates, Japanese electronics firms have also expanded their production networks into Indonesia, India, Vietnam, Myamar, and the Asian republics of the former Soviet Union (FSU).[33]

Two important complementary changes have remained largely unnoticed.[34] First, Japanese subsidiaries in ASEAN, especially in Malaysia and Thailand, have substantially upgraded and rationalized their production lines. The share of ASEAN-based Japanese subsidiaries in the investment of all Japanese overseas subsidiaries increased from less than 17 percent in 1989 to more than 32 percent in 1992 (MITI 1994a). Most of these investments were funded locally. Between 1989 and 1992, the ratio of reinvestments of Japanese affiliates to Japan's total FDI increased from 35 to 60 percent for ASEAN affiliates and from 54 to 80 percent for newly industrializing economy (NIE) affiliates, far exceeding the ratios that were reported for the United States and Europe, which increased from 15 (1989) to 24 percent (1992) and from 10 to 17 percent respectively (MITI 1994a).

Investments of this size were possible because of the high profitability of Japanese affiliates in Asia. In FY 1992, the ratio of ordinary profit to sales of Japanese overseas manufacturing affiliates was 5.1 percent in ASEAN and 5.6 percent in the Asian NIEs; this is in sharp contrast with the situation in the United States and Europe, where these ratios were minus 0.2 percent and minus 2.5 percent respectively. Profitability has important implications for the governance structure. Japanese overseas affiliates are now much less dependent on their parent companies for investment funds, although Japanese parent companies increasingly depend on the transfer of profits back from foreign affiliates, and are actively devising new transfer-pricing techniques.[35]

The second change is the revitalization of Asian affiliates of Japanese component suppliers, especially in South Korea and Taiwan. Most of these affiliates were set up during the 1960s to supply components for domestic market-oriented consumer production lines, first for Japanese set-makers but later also for local firms. Massive investments have automated existing facilities and broadened the range of components to include those required for industrial electronics. These upgraded affiliates now serve as platforms for exports back to Japan and the Asian affiliates.

These changes have important consequences for the pattern of regional specialization in Japan's East Asian networks in the electronics industry. Singapore and Hong Kong compete for the position of regional headquarters (and major support functions like procurement, testing, engineering services and training). South Korea and Taiwan compete for OEM contracts and as suppliers of precision components. Malaysia and Thailand, and now also the Philippines, are preferred locations for volume production, especially of mid-level and some higher end products. China, Indonesia, and (possibly) Vietnam compete for low-end assembly and simple components manufacturing.[36]

We are already seeing the effects of such regional specialization. The shift of Japanese FDI from the four first-tier NIEs to ASEAN during the late 1980s led to a considerable increase in the share of intra-regional trade. JETRO estimates that a one-unit increase in Japanese investment in ASEAN results in a 1.85-unit increase in exports to the region, most of them components and capital equipment. This compares with an estimated 0.46-unit increase per each 1-unit increase in Japanese investment in the four first-tier NIEs (JETRO 1995, 23).

However, for the time being, the spread of Japanese production networks into new locations has given rise to serious problems, such as the serious duplication of production capacity and product lines witnessed since the massive wave of investment into China. The case of the Matsushita group, which since 1992 has aggressively expanded its China presence and now has nineteen affiliates in the country, nicely illustrates these problems.[37] Matsushita's joint venture in Beijing for TV picture tubes is widely considered to be a major test case for Japanese FDI in China and has received quite privileged treatment. Nevertheless, serious problems have emerged. Owing to very weak local supplier industries, 15 percent of the components used (all of them key components) have to be imported from Japan. The yen appreciation has pushed up the price for these components, leading to a severe profit squeeze. In addition, labor costs have drastically increased – wages now approach Thai levels – while productivity continues to lag. Probably the most serious problem results from unexpected limits to the growth of the domestic market. Roughly one-fifth of the thirteen million TV sets sold per year in China are smuggled across the borders, many of them, ironically, produced by Japanese affiliates in Southeast Asia. Furthermore, demand for lower end TV sets is already reaching saturation. Almost 90 percent of China's urban households are now estimated to have such TV sets. As a result, Matsushita has had to radically change its strategic focus. Instead of aiming primarily at the domestic market, which was the original motivation, an increasing share of production will have to go into exports. Given the massive production capacities that Matsushita has in place in ASEAN (especially in Malaysia), this is likely to generate serious overcapacity.

These new developments compound structural adjustment problems that were never adequately addressed after the earlier wave of investments in ASEAN during the 1980s. Take, again, the example of Matsushita. One key feature of Matsushita's Asian production network is the coexistence of "mini-Matsus," oriented towards the domestic market, and more recent export-oriented affiliates in the same countries. The same type of product is often produced at both facilities but at very different productivity and quality levels. In principle, as Salter (1960) has shown, plants of very different vintages can coexist competitively as long as they are producing different qualities for different market segments at different prices. Low productivity production for the domestic market can be highly profitable as long as the domestic market remains protected; however, it may not prove so as domestic consumer electronics markets are opened up to international competition.[38] As we have seen, substantial surplus capacities exist in the region, especially for consumer electronics products. Under such conditions, a "dual production structure," although very costly, will be difficult to overcome, given the considerable sunk investments.[39]

### Broadening and deepening the networks

The quantitative expansion of Japanese electronics firms has given rise to new and serious adjustment problems with which Japanese firms are still struggling. One possible solution would be to broaden and deepen the Asian production networks. Broadening implies the addition of new products and transfer to East Asia earlier in the product life cycle. Deepening implies the spread of forward and backward linkages across the region and the consequent diffusion of required capabilities and support industries. To the degree that either change materializes, it is likely to lead to more decentralized governance structures.

Let us look first at some evidence of broadening. Japanese electronics firms now produce and source a much greater variety of products and services in East Asia. Japanese firms are involved in a variety of final assembly projects for PCs, and they have drastically increased their OEM purchases from the region. They may now try to tap into the same set of regional supplier networks that have so far catered primarily to the needs of American firms, and which were an important factor in the capacity of American computer companies to consolidate their market leadership (Ernst and O'Connor 1992; Borrus Chapter 3). Whether American computer companies will retain control over these precious supplier networks now that Japanese PC vendors are beginning to target them remains to be seen.

Broadening also implies that production of new products is shifted overseas at a much earlier stage of the product life cycle. As conceptualized in the product life cycle (PLC) theory, international production traditionally moved overseas only once a product had reached a certain degree of maturity; newer, leading-edge products normally remained confined to domestic production.[40] This is no longer the case today, as we can see from the computer industry, in which product cycles have been cut ruthlessly and time-to-market has become the single most important determinant of competitive success. An incremental and sequential process has been accelerated by product cycles as short as nine months. It simply does not make sense for PC vendors to transfer production to East Asia one year after the launch of a new product. In order to amortize such investment, computer firms must now shift the production of new products to Asia at the beginning of the product cycle.

Technological change has acted as another crucial enabling factor for an early transfer of the production of sophisticated products. Since the mid-1980s, fundamental changes in design methodology and the shift from metallic to plastic parts have facilitated the transfer of production of complex products to overseas locations. This finding runs counter to much of the established wisdom that argues that the spread of microelectronics and new materials will make it more difficult to transfer industrial production to developing countries (Ernst 1997a).

The deepening of an international production network implies that an increasing number of stages of the value-chain are shifted overseas. Two activities are of particular importance – changes in the procurement system, and the partial redeployment of some R&D functions. Japanese electronics companies are being challenged to reduce the dependence of their various Asian production subsidiaries on high-cost imports from Japan without losing too much in terms of quality, speed, and reliability of delivery.

Hitachi, a behemoth whose consolidated sales today equal roughly 2 percent of gross national product (GNP) in Japan, provides an example.[41] Although Hitachi started as a producer of heavy electrical equipment, today close to half of its sales are generated by its two largest divisions, information systems and electronics. Earlier than many of its Japanese rivals, Hitachi developed a fairly sophisticated approach to international procurement. In the early 1970s, Hitachi was among the first Japanese electronics firm to set up overseas procurement bases in the United States and Hong Kong; in 1979, a European procurement base was added in Germany. Since 1989, Hitachi has shifted focus from arm's-length imports to reverse imports from foreign affiliates and to OEM imports from technical tie-ups with foreign companies, and has begun to provide assistance to cut prime costs and to train foreign suppliers.

Hitachi made only limited attempts to deepen its international procurement function until a major corporate reorganization in August 1993. In Singapore Hitachi established a Center for the Promotion of Procurement in Asia. Although Hitachi's international procurement offices (IPOs) previously had been staffed primarily by buying agents, in the new center engineers (both from Hitachi and from its suppliers) will be involved throughout all stages of the procurement decision, including component design and materials specification. The center thus would act as a mechanism for bringing foreign suppliers into Hitachi's internal design processes, for shifting to longer term supply arrangements, and for coordinating Hitachi's procurement plans with the sales efforts of different host governments.

Policy incentives provided by both the Japanese government and by various host countries in the region also have induced Hitachi to open up its international procurement activities in Asia. For instance, tax incentives for import promotion developed by the Japanese government have helped Hitachi reduce the cost of importing components from East Asia.[42] At the same time, Hitachi, Matsushita, and others have closely cooperated, for example, with Malaysian government programs for promoting domestic industries

Important changes have also occurred in the role of Japanese component suppliers. Those firms that produce relatively complex and higher value-added components have substantially increased their investment in East Asia, primarily in Malaysia and Thailand, but also in China. In order to amortize their investment outlays and to gain economies of scale, these affiliates are actively searching for new clients, and frequently supply a number of Japanese firms as well as American, Korean, and some European firms (Ernst 1997b).

It is necessary to stress the irreversible nature of most of these changes brought about by the yen appreciation. By generating a substantial amount of new sunk investment in East Asia, the yen appreciation has imposed major changes both in the domestic production system and in the Asian supplier networks. It would be very difficult for Japanese electronics firms to return to the status quo ante now that the yen has depreciated again.

A second critical element in regional restructuring is the transfer of R&D facilities to the region. I distinguish five categories: (1) adaptive engineering, i.e. engineering activities that go beyond basic manufacturing support services and include the incremental adaptation and improvement of products and processes;[43] (2) circuit design; (3) software engineering; (4) product development, for the local or regional markets; and (5) generic technology development, i.e. research aimed at major innovations with the potential for productivity enhancement and the creation of new product markets.

Out of a total of forty-five projects, only one falls into category 5. Matsushita's audiovisual information research center, established in Singapore 1990, develops compression technology videophones and multimedia. Eleven projects are reported in category 4, product development, but the category is problematic because we cannot distinguish to what degree it might actually consist of simple adaptive engineering. The result is that our classification probably underestimates the degree to which Japanese electronics firms' R&D operations concentrate on relatively simple engineering activities.

The largest share of Japanese electronics R&D activities in East Asia falls into two categories, software engineering (with fifteen cases) and circuit design (with eleven cases). Both are essentially support services required to enter or expand the region's domestic markets. Japanese computer manufacturers, for example, can improve the market position in China with the development of Chinese-language programs. Circuit design activities are mostly dedicated to ASICs (application-specific integrated circuits) for consumer devices or telecommunications equipment sold in the domestic or regional markets. Both Singapore and Hong Kong have recently emerged as regional IC design centers for consumer devices. Japanese firms are concentrating limited resources at home on higher value-added products related to computing, multimedia and networking applications, and thus are eager to redeploy design and engineering functions linked to AV equipment and home appliances. For example, Sharp's IC design center in Singapore concentrates primarily on the programming of microcontrollers embedded in home appliances; however, Sharp intends to begin outsourcing design work from Japan on a much larger scale.[44]

### Future prospects

We have seen that globalization in East Asia has led to important changes in the scope and depth of Japanese production networks. Yet fundamental implementation constraints are likely to slow down the pace of change. First, it will not be easy to establish a consistent regional strategy for East Asia to guide the reorganization of Japanese Asian production networks. Second, even if a firm succeeds in sorting out the trade-offs involved in developing a regional strategy, it will have to tackle a more fundamental constraint that results from basic rigidities in the domestic Japanese production system.

In the reorganization of their Asian production networks, Japanese electronics firms have been struggling to cope with a number of conflicting requirements. One of the most immediate concerns is market penetration, especially for companies with a substantial stake in consumer electronics. Japanese firms are eager to exploit the rapid expansion of East Asian markets, which requires a greater focus on the idiosyncrasies of individual countries. Within each country, reorganization strives to improve specialization and to gradually develop "local integrated production systems." At the same time,

Japanese companies are equally attracted by supply-side factors such as East Asia's lower labor costs, as well as other capabilities that are increasingly difficult to mobilize at home. Tapping into these resources requires a regional strategy based on specialization among individual Asian affiliates and between them and their local suppliers, which implies concentrating the production of a single product family in one factory that supplies the whole region.

In turn, these regional strategies may conflict with a firm's global strategy. Some of the firms that we interviewed have established global information networks that link overseas affiliates with the parent company for crucial stages of the value chain, such as product design, production, procurement, and inventory control, in order to ensure that East Asian affiliates have access to the same information not only as sister affiliates in the United States but also as the parent company. There is still a huge gap between this objective and its implementation.

Japanese electronics firms thus face a basic dilemma. If they continue to rely on closed and highly centralized regional production networks, they may create increasingly non-competitive domestic and overseas production systems. If, on the other hand, Japanese networks open up too quickly, the resultant transfer of technology and capabilities may create new competitors, not only for low-end, labor-intensive products but increasingly for mid-level and some higher end products as well.[45] The nature of these changes and evaluation of initial responses to them in light of the Asia crisis are further explored in Chapter 9.

## Notes

1  In a related study (Ernst 1998), I show how the evolution of Japanese production networks in Asia has affected the formation of local capabilities in the region. Ernst, in this volume, discusses the impact of IPNs on capability formation in Taiwan's computer industry, while Ernst and Ravenhill (Chapter 9) address convergence and diversity. Other related studies are Ernst (1997) (a comparative analysis of the evolution of American and Japanese IPNs in the electronics industry; Ernst and Ravenhill (1999) (a comparative analysis of the impact of American and Japanese IPNs on local capability formation in Asia); and Ernst and Guerrieri (1998) (which analyzes implications for Asia's trade links with the United States and Japan in the electronics industry).
2  Computed from data in Nihon Desnhi Kikai Kogyokai (NDKK) 1994.
3  Japanese electronics affiliates in Asia rely much more heavily on component imports from Japan than similar affiliates in North America and Europe. Although the share of components in Japan's electronics exports to Asia has exceeded 30 percent, it has been less than 15 percent for Japan's electronics exports to North America and Europe. MITI (1994b: 6).
4  MITI data on the purchasing patterns of East Asian subsidiaries of Japanese electronics firms, as reported in Yoshitomi (1994) and Graham and Anzai (1994, Tables 5 and 6).
5  It is important to add that much of the "intra-regional" and "local" sourcing essentially takes place in three forms: (1) the affiliate produces the components in-house – an approach pioneered early on by Sanyo; (2) the affiliate procures

the component from one of its sister affiliates in the region; (3) the affiliate requests its Japanese subcontractors to establish a plant within the region.

6  Probably the best sources for the limited capability transfer are the annual surveys of the Japanese Chamber of Commerce in Malaysia (JACTIM). The 1994 survey for instance documents that Japanese firms are actively pursuing the transfer of production, labor management, and financial management capabilities. For marketing, management control and product development, capability transfer has remained very limited. (Tonan Nagamatsu, chairman of the trade and investment committee of JACTIM, and vice president of the Sumitomo group in Malaysia, as quoted in *BT*, Malaysia, August 12 1994, p. 1.

7  Similar findings are reported in Tachiki (1994), Sedgewick (1995), and UNCTAD (1995).

8  The following draws on Ernst and Guerrieri (1998).

9  As reported in Yoshitomo (1994: Table 10).

10  The chain of causation appears to work both ways. Changes in the organization of international production have led to changes in the composition of international trade. Such change in trade patterns, in turn, invites and shapes further changes in the organization of international production.

11  Inter-firm networks are defined to include five different arrangements: (1) supplier networks (consignment assembly, subcontracting, and a variety of so-called "original equipment manufacturing," "original design manufacturing," "contract manufacturing" and "turnkey production" arrangements); (2) customer networks (links with local distributors, value-added resellers, and end users); (3) producer networks (a variety of co-production arrangements like "second-sourcing," etc.); (4) standard coalitions; and (5) technology cooperation networks. See Ernst (1994b).

12  For a more detailed discussion, see Abo (1993) and Stopford (1998).

13  Throughout the 1980s, comparative costs of capital were cited as an important reason for the decline in US competitiveness relative to Japan. See, for example, Hatsopoulos and Brooks (1986). More recent research, summarized in Baldwin and Clark (1994), has raised doubts about the validity of this explanation.

14  For instance, the shift from metallic to plastic parts has reduced the importance of precision mechanical engineering. And the spread of standard ICs and PCBs has led to a substantial reduction in the number of components required for each system. At the same time, this has increased the scope for factory automation, especially so-called surface mount assembly techniques. For a detailed analysis, see Ernst (1997).

15  For a systematic analysis of minimum economies of scale for consumer electronics devices, see Ernst and O'Connor (1992, Chapters 3 and 4).

16  For a review of this literature, see Ernst *et al.* (1998).

17  For an excellent analysis of why Japanese electronics firms postponed overseas production, see Tachiki and Aoki (1991) and Tejima (1994, 1996).

18  Among these companies, Philips stands out as a pioneer in international production. With 90 percent of total sales being generated abroad, and 40 percent outside Europe, it had to develop early on an extended and sophisticated international production network. Already, by 1988, roughly one-quarter of all Philips products were made in East Asia. This compares with 15 percent during the early 1980s (Ernst 1997).

19  Four sources of disruption can be discerned: those caused by suppliers, either through late delivery or through the delivery of defective materials; unforeseen fluctuations in demand and abrupt changes in demand patterns; a variety of production problems that result from the transfer of immature products and production processes; and abrupt changes in management decisions such as last-minute corrections of product launch dates and performance features.

20  For a detailed analysis, see Ernst (1997).
21  Good sources are Takeuchi (1993) and various studies of the Small and Medium Enterprise Agency (Tokyo), especially its Medium and Small Enterprise White Papers.
22  Sanyo and Aiwa (which is affiliated to the Sony group) currently are the leaders in procurement localization among Japanese set-makers in East Asia. [Based on phone interview with the Electronics Industry Association of Japan (EIAJ) February 1996.]
23  Based on telephone interview with Fujitsu, May 22 1996.
24  Success cases are Packard Bell and Taiwan's Acer group, but increasingly also market leaders like Compaq and IBM.
25  Relevant sources are Imai (1988); Mowery and Rosenberg (1990); Clark and Fujimoto (1991); Kenney and Florida (1993); Branscomb and Kodama (1993).
26  The following account is based on Abe (1992), and interviews in the *Japanese Electronics Industry*, November 1993 and June 1995.
27  An interesting account of such cross-cultural communication problems and an agenda for required changes can be found in the *Hitachi Research Institute* 1994.
28  There is now a rich literature on why a firm would want to engage in overseas R&D activities. Good overviews are Granstrand *et al.* (1993); and Archibugi and Pianta (1996).
29  This is the main reason for the recent expansion of so-called "Design & Development (D&D)" activities of Japanese firms into East Asia.
30  Interview at Canon, November 1993. Branscomb and Kodama (1993, 87) quote an NEC R&D manager, "NEC sees new products becoming increasingly dependent on the ability to adapt to local culture and customs."
31  Computed from data in NDKK 1994.
32  MOF figures, as quoted in JETRO (1995, 17).
33  For case studies on Indonesia and Vietnam, see the relevant chapters in Ernst, *et al.* (eds) (1998).
34  MOF figures of Japanese FDI do not report reinvestments by overseas affiliates, nor do they provide a sufficiently fine-grained sectoral disaggregation. This is now changing: both the Export–Import Bank of Japan's Research Institute for International Investment and Development and the most recent Overseas Investment Statistics Overview by MITI include such information. For an early pioneering contribution, see Tejima (1994).
35  Interviews in *Japanese Electronics Industry*, June 1995.
36  Fujitsu established in early 1996 a PCB assembly plant in Vietnam, which could pave the way for further Japanese investments.
37  So far, Matsushita's Chinese affiliates play a marginal role, accounting for less than 5 percent of total international production; the lion's share of Matsushita's total international production value, 60 percent worth $6 billion, is still generated in ASEAN. The goal is to raise China's share to roughly 20–25 percent by the year 2000. Author's interviews, June 1995.
38  In response to the challenge of investment and trade diversion away from ASEAN to China, ASEAN are now pursuing with much greater resolve the establishment of a regional free-trade zone, called ASEAN Free Trade Area (AFTA), and the consumer electronics sector is one of the first to be targeted for tariff reduction.
39  Interviews at Matsushita were conducted in November 1993 and June 1995.
40  For critical assessments of the product cycle model, see Cantwell (1995) and Bernard and Ravenhill (1995).
41  The following is based on interviews with Hitachi in November 1993.
42  The irony is that these incentives were originally developed in response to pressures from various US administrations to increase the domestic market share

for US companies, while in reality they have facilitated overdue organizational adaptations of Japanese firms.
43 Basic manufacturing support services are defined to include activities like calibration and testing, die and tool services (preventive) maintenance and repair, and quality control.
44 Based on interviews at Sharp headquarters, in June 1995.
45 For a fascinating analysis of the chances of "hollowing-out," which concludes that this is not a serious threat, see Ishiyama (1995). The author is Director of economic research at IBM Japan.

## References

Abe, T. (1992) "Overseas R&D Activities of Japanese Companies" (in Japanese), *The Journal of Science Policy and Research Management*, Tokyo, 7(2).

Abegglen, J. C. (1994) *Sea Change. Pacific Asia as the New World Industrial Center*, New York: The Free Press.

Abo, T. (ed.) (1993) *Hybrid Factory. The Japanese Production System in the United States*, New York: Oxford University Press.

Archibugi, D. and Pianta, M. (1996) " Innovation Surveys and Patents as Technology Indicators: the State of the Art," in *Innovation, Patents and Technological Strategies*, Paris: OECD.

Baldwin, C. Y. and Clark, K. B. (1994) "Capital-Budgeting Systems and Capabilities Investments in US Companies after the Second World War," *Business History Review*, 1 (Spring).

Bernard, M. and Ravenhill, J. (1995) "Beyond Product Cycles and Flying Geese. Regionalization, Hierarchy, and the Industrialization of East Asia," *World Politics*, 47(January): 171–209.

Branscomb, L. M. and Kodama, F. (1993) *Japanese Innovation Strategy. Technical Support for Business Visions*, CSIA Occasional Paper 10, Center for Science and International Affairs, Harvard University

Cantwell, J. (1995) "The Globalisation of Technology: What Remains of the Product Cycle Model?" *Cambridge Journal of Economics*, 19: 155–174.

Chandler, A. (1990) *Scale and Scope: The Dynamics of Industrial Capitalism*, Cambridge, MA: Belknap Press.

Christensen, C. M. (1993) "The Rigid Disk Drive Industry: A History of Commercial and Technological Turbulence," *Business History Review*, 67(Winter): 531–583.

Clark, K. and Fujimoto, T. (1991) *Product Development Performance: Strategy, Organization, and Management in the World Auto Industry*, Boston, MA: Harvard Business School Press.

Dobson, W. (1995) "East Asian Integration: Synergies between Firm Strategies and Government Policy," manuscript, University of Toronto, Centre for International Business.

Encarnation, D. (1995) "Does Ownership Matter? American and Japanese Multinationals in East Asia," manuscript, Cambridge, MA: MIT Press.

Encarnation, D. and Mason, M. (eds) (1994) *Does Ownership Matter?*, Oxford: Clarendon Press.

Ernst, D. (1983) *The Global Race in Microelectronics*, Frankfurt and New York: Campus Publishers.

—— (1987) "U.S.–Japanese Competition and the Worldwide Restructuring of the Electronics Industry," in J. Henderson and M. Castells (eds) *Global Restructuring and Territorial Development*, London: Sage Publications.

—— (1994a) "Carriers of Regionalization? The East Asian Production Networks of Japanese Electronics Firms," Working Paper 73, University of California at Berkeley: BRIE.

—— (1994b) "Network Transactions, Market Structure and Technological Diffusion – Implications for South-South Cooperation," in L. Mytelka (ed.) *South-South Cooperation in a Global Perspective*, Paris: OECD.

—— (1997) " Partners for the China Circle? The Asian Production Networks of Japanese Electronics Firms," in B. Naughton (ed.) *The China Circle*, The Brookings Institution Press.

—— (1998) "Catching-up, Crisis and Industrial Upgrading. Evolutionary Aspects of Technological Learning in Koreas's Electronics Industry," *Asia-Pacific Journal of Management*, 15(2).

Ernst, D. and Guerrieri, P. (1998) "International Production Networks and Changing Trade Patterns in East Asia. The Case of the Electronics Industry," *Oxford Development Studies*, 26(2).

Ernst, D. and O'Connor, D. (1992) *Competing in the Electronics Industry. The Experience of Newly Industrialising Economies*, Paris: OECD.

Ernst, D. and Ravenhill, J. (1999) "Globalization, Convergence, and the Transformation of International Production Networks in Electronics in East Aisa," *Business and Politics*, 1(1).

Ernst, D., Mytelka, L. and Ganiatsos, T. (1997) "Technological Capabilities in the Context of Export-Led Growth – A Conceptual Framework," in D. Ernst, T. Ganiatsos and L. Mytelka (eds) *Technological Capabilities and Export Success – Lessons from East Asia*, London: Routledge.

Ernst, D., Ganiatsos, T. and Mytelka, L. (eds) (1997) *Technological Capabilities and Export Success – Lessons from East Asia*, London: Routledge.

Gittelman, M. and Graham, E. (1994) "The Performance and Structure of Japanese Affiliates in the European Community," in D. Encarnation and M. Mason (eds) *Does Ownership Matter?*, Oxford: Clarendon Press.

Graham, E. and Anzai, N. T. (1994) "Is Japanese Direct Investment Creating an Asian Economic Bloc?" Washington, DC: Institute for International Economics.

Granstrand, O. Håkanson, L. and Sjoelander, S. (1993) "Internationalization of R&D – a Survey of Some Recent Research," *Research Policy*, 22.

Hatsopoulos, G. N. and Brooks, S. H. (1986) "The Gap in the Cost of Capital: Causes, Effects and Remedies," in R. Landau and D. W. Jorgenson (eds) *Technology and Economic Policy*, Cambridge, MA: Balinger Publ. Co.

Imai, K. (1988) "Patterns of Innovation and Entrepreneurship in Japan," paper presented to the Second Congress of the International Schumpeter Society, Siena.

Ishiyama, Y. (1995) "Is Japan Hollowing Out?" manuscript, Ecole Nationale des Ponts et Chausées, Paris: Graduate School of International Business.

JETRO (1995) *JETRO White Paper on Foreign Direct Investment*, Tokyo: Japan External Trade Organization.

Kenney, M. and Florida, R. (1993) *Beyond Mass Production. The Japanese System and its Transfer to the US*. New York: Oxford University Press.

Kester, W. C. (1996) "American and Japanese Corporate Governance: Convergence to Best Practice?" in Berger and Dore (eds) *National Diversity and Global Capitalism*, Ithaca and London: Cornell University Press.

Lasserre, P. and Schuette, H. (1995) *Strategies for Asia Pacific*, New York University Press.

Levy, D. (1994) "CCT's International Supply Chain," Harvard Business School Case Study, Harvard Business School.

—— (1995) "International Sourcing and Supply Chain Stability," *Journal of International Business Studies*, second quarter.

MITI (1994a) *White Paper on International Trade and Industry*, Tokyo.

MITI (1994b) *Overseas Investment Statistics Overview*, Tokyo.

Mowery, D. and Rosenberg, N. (1990) *Technology and the Pursuit of Economic Growth*, Cambridge, UK; New York: Cambridge University Press.

Nakayama, W., Boulton, W., and Pecht, M. (1999) *The Japanese Electronics Industry*, Boca Raton, FL: Chapman & Hall, CRC Press.

Nelson, R. (ed.) (1993) *National Innovation Systems*, London: Oxford University Press.

OECD (1992) *Technology and the Economy. The Key Relationships*, Paris.

Petri, P. A. (1993) "The East Asian Trading Bloc: An Analytical History," in J. Fraenkel and M. Kahler (eds) *Regionalism and Rivalry. Japan and the United States in Pacific Asia*, Chicago: National Bureau of Economic Research.

—— (1995) "The Interdependence of Trade and Investment in the Pacific," in E. K. Y. Chen and P. Drysdale (eds) *Corporate Links and Foreign Direct Investment in Asia and the Pacific*, Pymble: Harper Educational.

Porter, M. E. (1990) *The Competitive Advantage of Nations*, London: The Macmillan Press.

Salter, W. E. G. (1960) *Productivity and Technical Change*, Cambridge, Cambridge University Press.

Sedgewick, M. W. (1995) "Does Japanese Management Travel in Asia? Managerial Technology Transfer and Japanese Multinationals," paper prepared for conference "Does Ownership Matter? Japanese Multinationals in Asia," MIT-Japan Program, MIT, September.

Shiraki, M (1993) "A Comparative Study of Human Resources Development in Asian Settings: Problems and Strategies of Japanese Companies," in *Report on APO Top Management Forum: Human-Centered Management*, Tokyo: Asia Productivity Organization.

Stopford, J. (1998) "Building Regional Networks: Japanese Investments in Asia," in S. Strange (ed.) *Globalisation and Capitalist Diversity; Experiences on the Asian Mainland*, Florence: European University Institute, pp. 104–130.

Tachiki, D. (1994) "Extending the Human Capital Formation Process: Transnational Corporations and Post-Employment Training," *RIM: Pacific Business and Industries*, 23(1): 33–44.

Tachiki, D. and Aoki, A. (1991) "The Globalization of Japanese Business Activities," *RIM: Pacific Business and Industries*, 20(1).

Takeuchi, J. (1993) "Foreign Direct Investment in ASEAN by Small- and Medium-sized Japanese Companies and its Effects on Local Supporting Industries, *RIM: Pacific Business and Industries*, 4(22): 36–57.

Tejima, S. (1994) "The Recent Trends of Japanese Foreign Direct Investment and Prospects in the 1990s based on the Japan EXIM Bank's Survey Implemented in FY 1993," *EXIM Review*, 14(1): 82. Tokyo: Research Institute for International Investment and Development.

—— (1996) "Toward More Open Corporate Strategies: Will Japanese Firms Take Those Strategies to East Asia?" manuscript, Tokyo: Research Institute for International Development and Development, The Export–Import Bank of Japan.
UNCTAD (1995) *1995 World Investment Report*, Geneva: UNCTAD
Yoshitomi, M. (1994) "Building New United States – Pacific Asia Economic Relationship for the Post-Uruguay Round Era," paper presented at the fifth United States – Korea Symposium, University of California at Berkeley: Korea Economic Institute of America.

# 5 What permits David to grow in the shadow of Goliath?

## The Taiwanese model in the computer industry

*Dieter Ernst*

It would seem self-evident that small companies would not be competitive in a knowledge-intensive industry that is highly globalized.[1] Small firms, by definition, have limited resources and capabilities and thus are unlikely to possess substantial ownership advantages. They also have a limited capacity to influence and shape the development of markets, market structure, and technological change. One would thus expect SMEs to be ill-equipped to compete in an industry that requires a broad range of fairly demanding technological and organizational capabilities.

The disadvantages of small size for firms are compounded if they come from small countries. Small nations are confronted with four types of size-related disadvantages:[2] (1) the small domestic market places tight restrictions on the ability to function as a buffer against heavy fluctuations in international demand; (2) it constrains the development of sophisticated "lead users"[3] that could stimulate innovation; (3) it also limits the scope for technological spillovers;[4] and (4) the limited size of the national knowledge and capital base restricts the choice of industries in which such small nations might successfully specialize.

Taiwan's experience, however, tells a different story: SMEs have been the main carriers of its rapid development. Despite the dominance of SMEs, Taiwan today has the most broadly based computer industry in Asia outside of Japan. The country has diversified beyond core PC-related products into a variety of related high-growth market segments; it has improved its domestic production capabilities for a number of high value-added components; and it has been able to move beyond manufacturing into a range of higher end support services.

This chapter inquires into how this was possible. Its message can be summarized by paraphrasing John Stopford (1996), "innovations in strategy and organization can change the 'rules of competition' and overturn many scale advantages to permit David to grow in the shadow of Goliath." I argue that two factors have been critical for this outcome: active, yet selective and continuously adjusted industrial development policies; and a variety of networking linkages with large firms, both domestic and foreign. I show how government policies facilitated the initial market entry of SMEs and were adjusted over time to promote continual upgrading and adjustment. Industrial development policies on their own, however, are insufficient to explain Taiwan's success.

Taiwanese computer companies also benefited from the specific form of the production networks they created. These offer a variety of linkages that facilitate learning and capability formation. Such linkages include strong ties with large Taiwanese business groups, foreign sales and manufacturing affiliates and an early participation in international production networks (IPNs) established by foreign electronics companies. By and large, these features that sustain Taiwanese leadership in many segments of industrial electronics have been little altered by the Asia crisis. If anything, the crisis has reinforced Taiwanese advantage: benefiting from a domestic economy least affected by the region's economic problems, Taiwanese firms have invested aggressively to enhance their regional position and expand the scope and capability of their production networks.

## Taiwan's achievements: a broad range of capabilities

During the 1990s, Taiwan established itself as a world-class supply source for a variety of electronic hardware products. It is the world's largest supplier of computer monitors, motherboards, switching power supplies, mouse devices, keyboards, scanners, and a variety of add-on cards. In 1996, almost 60 percent of the world's desktop PCs were either made in Taiwan or contained a motherboard made by a Taiwanese company.[5] Since 1994, Taiwan also has become the world's largest manufacturer of notebook PCs. Most of these computers are sold to American and Japanese computer companies which re-sell them under their own logo, but 70 percent of the computers sold under such OEM arrangements have been designed by Taiwanese companies.[6] Taiwanese computer firms have clearly developed significant design capabilities.

Progress has been equally impressive in the field of electronic components. Taiwan today has hundreds of passive component makers that have established a strong position relative to leading Japanese and US competitors. Taiwanese firms have also improved their position in the capital-intensive mass production of precision components, such as large-scale cathode ray tubes (CRTs) for computer monitors and sophisticated display devices (like active-matrix TFT–LCDs) for laptop computers. The same is true for integrated circuits. Although Taiwan's semiconductor industry at present accounts for hardly more than 3 percent of the world market, some of its firms have developed a strong position for a number of higher value-added IC devices, like chip sets, static RAM memories, mask ROMs (read-only memories), and EPROMs (erasable programmable read-only memories). In addition, Taiwan today has one of the world's leading silicon foundry companies, the Taiwan Semiconductor Manufacturing Corporation (TSMC), which is able to produce leading-edge ICs on very short production cycles, both for major international semiconductor firms and for smaller design firms (Liu *et al.* 1995).

Two recent structural changes show how Taiwanese firms have upgraded their capabilities: a rapid diversification beyond hard core PC-related products, and a shift from stand-alone manufacturing services to integrated service packages that cover a wide range of value-chain activities, including higher value-added support services. Taiwanese computer companies now have established themselves as competitive suppliers in a variety of complementary, high-growth market segments, some of which display considerably higher profit margins. Such diversification is evident in three areas: the development of so-called PC network products,[7] especially modems and network interface cards; multimedia accessories, such as compact disk read-only memory (CDROM) drives and add-on cards, and a variety of information services industries, such as multimedia software, system integration, turnkey systems, and network services. Most of these information services owe their existence to the convergence of previously separated technologies used for computing, communicating, and digital consumer applications, and require the capacity to combine various strands of technology to generate new applications and markets.

Taiwanese firms have also developed a capacity to provide a package of services across a wide range of value-chain activities, sustaining their position as preferred OEM suppliers to the industry. With the exception of R&D and marketing, practically all other stages of the value-chain can now be performed by Taiwan's OEM contractors. Moreover, Taiwanese firms are beginning to shoulder essential coordination functions.

Three characteristic examples of these processes of diversification and the provision of integrated service capabilities are scanners, computer monitors, and turnkey production arrangements [Malaysian Industrial Classification (MIC) 1997a]. Scanner production demands optical, mechanical, and electronic technologies and capabilities. Taiwan has accumulated expertise in all three and has become the world's largest supplier of scanners. With a firm grip on all stages of the value-chain, from R&D and production to marketing and after-sales service, Taiwan is positioned to defend its leadership position as a "one-stop shopping center" for scanners.

Since 1993, Taiwan has been the world's largest producer of monitors. Monitor production is highly sensitive to scale economies. Not surprisingly, Taiwan is now faced with intense competition from Korean *chaebol*, which are clearly superior in terms of standard mass production. Some firms have tried to establish themselves as suppliers of higher end and environmentally friendly monitors, with limited success. Much more successful has been a second response: to move beyond manufacturing to the supply of integrated service packages. Taiwanese monitor producers are now able to provide their leading OEM customers with global manufacturing and sales support more rapidly than the slow-moving Korean *chaebol*. This shift to global support service packages has been driven by external developments, particularly IBM's

1996 decision to pull out of monitor production and to transfer large orders to two leading Taiwan-based monitor producers. In order to guarantee a smooth transition, IBM requested that product be delivered and service provided direct to local markets to meet time-to-market requirements. Taiwanese suppliers not only deliver a hardware product (a computer monitor) directly to a particular market, they also provide a complex package of local support services that cover manufacturing, sales, and distribution.

A third example is the spread of "turnkey production arrangements" in the PC industry. In a recent contract with Taiwan's Mitac International, Compaq has outsourced all stages of the value-chain except marketing.[8] Mitac is responsible for the design and development of new products, as well as for manufacturing, transport and after-sales services at its manufacturing facilities in Taiwan, China, Britain, Australia, and the United States; Mitac's greatest attraction for Compaq was the presence of plants and sales subsidiaries in most of the world's key computer markets.

Taiwan's achievements would be impressive for any country; they are even more impressive for a small island, about one-third the size of New York State. With a population of about twenty-one million people, roughly half the size of South Korea, Taiwan lacked a large and sophisticated domestic market, specialized capabilities and support industries, and the science and technology (S&T) infrastructure necessary for developing a broad set of electronics products. From the outset, Taiwan's PC industry depended heavily on international markets and access to foreign technology. Penetrating foreign markets and absorbing imported technology is not automatic, however; it requires conscious efforts to develop a variety of domestic resources and capabilities.[9] How do small enterprises develop such capabilities?

## The dominance of SMEs: a source of flexibility

SMEs have been the main carriers of Taiwan's rapid development and remain important today. In 1993, SMEs accounted for 96 percent of the total number of companies, 69 percent of total employment, and 55 percent of Taiwan's manufactured exports (Chen *et al.* 1995). Taiwan today is home to more than 4,000 electronics firms that produce a broad mix of PC-related products and electronic components. With a few exceptions, such as the Tatung group, almost all of these companies started out as small enterprises.

The role of SMEs as engines of growth and industrial transformation sets Taiwan apart from South Korea, where huge and highly diversified conglomerates (*chaebol*) have been the main carriers of the development of the electronics industry.[10] Almost without exception, the *chaebol* have targeted those segments of the electronics industry that require huge investment outlays and sophisticated mass production techniques for fairly homogeneous products such as microwave ovens (MWOs), TV sets, VCRs, computer monitors, picture tubes, and computer memory, especially dynamic random access memory (DRAM). The result has been a heavy focus on assembly-type mass production activities related to lower end consumer products and standard electronic components, and weakness in more design-intensive sectors of the computer industry.

Why have Taiwanese firms succeeded in the computer industry while their much larger and resource-rich Korean counterparts have largely failed? The answer lies in the fundamental characteristics of an industry in which high volatility and uncertainty put a premium on flexibility and the capacity to adjust to abrupt and frequently unexpected changes in demand and technology. Small firm size is even an advantage.[11] By combining incremental product innovation with incredibly fast speed-to-market, Taiwanese firms have been able to establish a strong international market position relatively early in the product cycle.

The primary source of this flexibility appears to be the specific organization of the domestic supply base in Taiwan, especially for parts and components. Two main features of this domestic supply base have contributed to the flexibility of Taiwanese producers, the first being an extreme form of specialization. By engaging in single tasks and by producing, purchasing, and selling in small lots, subcontractors avoid heavy fixed capital costs. This, in turn, makes it relatively easy to shift production at relatively short notice, and with a minimum of costs. The second feature is a certain network structure of multiple, volatile and short-term links that involve only limited financial and technology transfers. Spot-market transactions play an important role, but so do "temporary spider web" arrangements that are assembled for the duration of a particular job.[12]

The result of these characteristics is an extreme form of open and volatile production networks, arguably even more so than the highly flexible production networks that characterize California's Silicon Valley.[13] Firms maximize the number of jobs in order to compensate for the razor-thin profit margins; as a result, they avoid being locked into a particular production network. Domestic supplier networks thus have been highly flexible and capable of rapid change but are short-lived and foot-loose.

If flexibility constitutes one prerequisite for Taiwan's competitive success in computers, economies of scale and scope and speed-to-market have been of equal importance.[14] Entry barriers have increased for those stages of the value-chain that are of critical importance for competitive success, including particularly component manufacturing, where production-related scale economies remain important. But the epicenter of competition has shifted beyond manufacturing to R&D and other forms of intangible investment required to complement price competition with product differentiation and speed-to-market. Only those companies that are able to get the right product to the highest volume segment of the market at the right time can survive. Being late is a disaster, and often forces companies out of business.

In sum, what really matters for competitive success are substantial investments in the formation of a firm's technological and organizational capabilities. How were Taiwanese computer companies able to successfully compete in an industry where size-related advantages are of critical importance? And, more specifically, what kind of organizational innovations have enabled Taiwanese firms to overcome their size-related disadvantages?

In order to answer these questions, we need to examine issues of specialization and coordination. Andersen (1996) has recently provided an interesting theoretical explanation why excessive specialization may involve substantial trade-offs.[15] He shows that as an economy becomes more specialized it increases the pressure for standardization. This, in turn, may constrain innovation.[16] The solution to this dilemma is the establishment of tight linkages between firms along the supply chain that enhance the prospects for inter-firm learning, for instance between end product manufacturers and component suppliers.[17]

To understand how Taiwan avoided the dangers of excessive specialization and established tight inter-firm linkages, it is important to correct some popular misconceptions of the Taiwanese model. This is not an economy characterized by atomistic competition. SMEs do play an important role, yet they survive as a result of a combination of four forces: government policies that facilitated market entry and upgrading; strong linkages with large Taiwanese firms and business groups; the presence of foreign sales and manufacturing affiliates; and early participation in international production networks.

## The role of industrial development policies

Although Korea and Taiwan share many similarities, the two countries have chosen very different policy approaches. In the early 1960s, the Taiwanese government introduced aggressive programs to encourage investment by domestic as well as foreign companies.[18] In line with similar programs in Korea, these statutes provided generous tax incentives and laid down rules to facilitate the acquisition of land for industrial use by investors and access to utilities. Four features, however, distinguished Taiwan's approach.

First, no limits were set on the number of firms within each industry group, with the exception of a few mining and utility industries. Any domestic firm could invest and enjoy the same tax and other privileges if they complied with the regulations. This open policy gave rise to intense domestic competition and was conducive to a diversified industry structure.

Second, the government actively promoted the development and modernization of Taiwan's SME sector. The first of such policies "The Rule for Promotion of Small and Medium Enterprises" was promulgated in 1967 and was subsequently revised several times as Taiwan's SMEs grew. Government assistance to SMEs included market promotion, management rationalization, cooperation, and promoting strategic alliances, loans, and upgrading technology and labor training.[19] Third, there was no discrimination against smaller firms *within* the SME category. Any firm, irrespective of size, could participate and was treated equally. This neutral policy was an important foundation for the development of Taiwan's large pool of vibrant and entrepreneurial SMEs.

Finally, virtually equal treatment was granted to domestic and foreign investment, with the exception of some majority shareholding regulations applicable to foreign firms and strict foreign exchange control regulations governing domestic firms. This balanced policy attracted foreign investment without producing the "crowding-out" that occurred in Singapore, where domestic firms have played a minimal role in the manufacturing sector.[20]

In sum, Taiwan's development strategy generated forward and backward linkage effects while relying on "market-augmenting" policies that reduced risk and uncertainty rather than market-repressing policies that increased fragmentation and rent-seeking (Johnson 1987: 141). Taiwan's policy approach was not a static one, however; as the requirements of industrial upgrading changed over time, so did the nature of state intervention. This process of change has been well documented and need not be recounted here.[21]

## The role of inter-firm linkages

Although governmental policy emphasized small firms, these firms suffered a variety of size-related organizational weaknesses. However, these weaknesses could be offset provided that firms are part of a dense network centered around a core firm (Ernst and O'Connor 1989; Wong 1991; Ernst and O'Connor 1992; Ernst 1994a). Close interaction with the core firm can facilitate learning and capability formation. To the extent that the core firm takes charge of product and process innovation as well as marketing, the small firm does not have to mobilize the substantial financial and human resources required to overcome high entry barriers to these activities.

Contrary to conventional wisdom, large firms have played a central role in the coordination and development of the Taiwanese production system. After the Second World War, the Taiwanese government took over the Japanese enterprises that had been established during the fifty years of colonial rule (1895–1945). In contrast to Korea, the government did not privatize these firms; instead, they were run as public enterprises. By developing a strong public enterprise sector, Taiwan developed companies large enough to enter the highly capital-intensive production of basic materials, while at the same time avoiding the dominance of private conglomerates (Schive 1990; San and Kuo 1997;).

Linkages with large firms have played an important role in the development of Taiwan's SME sector. To start with, SMEs depend on the supply of basic materials provided by large public enterprises at low cost and high quality (Wade 1990). Large firms have also acted as an important intermediary source of capital for SMEs. Taiwan's banks direct most of their funds to large domestic public and private firms who then on-lend money for equipment and working capital to smaller customers, subcontractors and suppliers at higher rates through trade credit and loans on the informal curb market.[22]

In addition, many SMEs are for all practical purpose members of a particular business group (Liu *et al.* 1994). The spread of such business groups partly reflects the impact of government policies; starting in the late 1950s, the government shifted its emphasis away from public enterprises to the private sector, providing guidance and essential externalities. This has set the stage for the growth of private firms. The growing capital requirements and technological complexity that accompanied the rapid industrial transformation of the island produced new forms of business organization; as electronics took over from textiles as the leading industrial sector, it set in motion an erosion of Taiwan's traditional form of business organization: the loose networks of family-owned SMEs. On the one hand, family firms were desperate to retain profitability. They were forced to venture across product lines and to move from industries with declining margins, like textiles, to the much more profitable electronics sector. On the other hand, loose networks of family-owned SMEs proved unable to raise the capital required for increasing fixed investment and R&D: as late as 1992, only 20 percent of a sample of Taiwanese manufacturing firms were engaged in R&D.[23]

Attempts to cope with these two conflicting pressures produced a peculiar Taiwanese form of business organization: cross-sectoral business groups. These business groups are very different from the large, hierarchical conglomerates, the *chaebol*, that are typical of South Korea,[24] but they also differ from the *keiretsu* system that has dominated much of Japan's industry. In Taiwan, business groups typically consist of a loose network of mostly medium-sized companies that produce a variety of products for different markets, with one core company exercising financial control.

The Automata Design Inc. (ADI) business group provides a typical example.[25] Founded in 1979, the company is run by the Liao Jian-cheng family. From trading and construction it first moved into shoe manufacturing for international mass merchandisers. Around the mid-1980s, the family decided to move into electronics. The breakthrough came in 1993, thanks to big orders from Compaq. Despite success in computer monitors, the owners maintain their diversification strategy. ADI has continued to expand its position in shoe manufacturing while at the same time investing in a number of new small start-up companies in software, system design, and in a variety of unrelated commercial activities.

The shift to business groups has been most pronounced in the electronics industry. This is hardly surprising, given the critical importance in this industry of economies of scale and scope. But in Taiwan's case, there are two additional reasons why SMEs became integrated into larger business groups: linkages with foreign customers through international subcontracting and OEM arrangements; and linkages with international supply sources, especially for key components. As a result of these linkages, size became essential to secure economies of scale and scope and achieve sufficient bargaining clout with foreign customers and suppliers.

To fulfill an OEM contract, large Taiwanese companies like Tatung, First

International Computer (which is part of the Formosa Plastics group), Mitac, and Acer rely on hundreds of loosely affiliated domestic suppliers to which they can pass on an endless variety of low-margin yet quite demanding manufacturing and design tasks. The typical Taiwanese small computer company thus often gets involved with foreign firms only in an indirect way; large Taiwanese business groups increasingly dominate the direct interface with foreign customers. The same is true for the affiliates of foreign multinationals like Philips, Matsushita, DEC, and others that have substantial production platforms in Taiwan. A similar mechanism also works on the procurement side, especially for high-end key components like DRAMs, microprocessors, CRTs for computer monitors and liquid crystal displays (LCDs) for laptop computers. The insecurity of supply plays an important role in the formation of inter-corporate linkages. Roughly 85 percent of all semiconductors used in Taiwan are currently imported. Under "normal" circumstances, Taiwanese SMEs rely on the "spot market": they purchase these components from the branch offices or agents of foreign component vendors. But normal circumstances are rare in these component markets. When a serious component supply shortage occurs, Taiwanese SMEs will be the worst hit. Foreign vendors will either require sharp price mark-ups or refuse to deliver.

For SMEs, the only hope is to survive in the shadow of the large Taiwanese PC manufacturers. During a typical supply shortage, the large Taiwanese manufacturers will expand their procurement orders well beyond their real needs.[26] By buying large quantities of components before price wars actually materialize, firms seek to buffer their effects; one could call this the "component future trading" effect. Firms also seek to hedge against opportunism on the part of foreign suppliers. Major Taiwanese PC companies simply must keep large safety inventories of key components as a risk minimization strategy. Third, during shortages, foreign component suppliers normally only supply their strategic customers. For Taiwanese PC makers it is of critical importance to get on such "strategic customer" lists. The way to do this is to inflate their component orders above their real needs to convince foreign suppliers that the Taiwanese customers are big and important.

As a result of these purchasing strategies, Taiwanese PC makers regularly get bogged down with large inventories of key components. The product composition of these inventories keeps rapidly changing, with newer component generations vying for precious inventory space with older ones. Taiwanese PC makers are thus under strong pressure to resell parts of their component inventories to local SMEs. Most of these re-sales are components "one-generation-behind-the-leading-edge." Prices charged are higher than the prices paid by the large PC maker to the foreign supplier, but lower than those charged on the spot market.[27]

In sum, the only way for Taiwanese PC-related SMEs to survive periodic supply shortages for key components is to stay in the shadow of the large domestic PC makers and to accept the crumbs that the big guys are willing to share with them. The prices charged for these crumbs are substantial. Yet, what matters from the perspective of the SME is that they can get access to these vital components and that the prices they pay are lower than those they would pay in the spot market. This situation obviously puts a tremendous pressure on the existing Taiwanese SME population: the only SMEs that can survive are those that succeed in ruthlessly cutting costs and overheads while accepting the most exacting contract conditions in terms of delivery times. The result is a high turnover of the existing SME population: at any given point in time, a large number of firms go bankrupt, although an equally large number of firms emerge as new start-up companies.

During the late 1990s, the importance of big business groups has further increased, blurring the division between small and large firms. Taiwan's electronics industry has recently witnessed a rapid increase in concentration. In the PC industry, the top ten firms today control roughly 80 percent of total production, and some of the most powerful Taiwanese business groups (Formosa Plastics, HwaHsin, China Steel, YFY Paper) have now also entered the production of key components, like DRAMs, CRTs, and displays.[28] These changes raise a new challenge: what changes are necessary in Taiwan's industrial structure so that the scale advantages of large firms can be combined with the speed and flexibility of smaller firms?

## New forms of inter-firm linkage

We have seen that family-owned SMEs, based on informal social networks, have dominated the Taiwanese electronics industry. This system had considerable advantages, both in terms of cost and flexibility, as long as the goal was catching-up. Transaction costs were low, as family-run enterprises cooperated on the basis of informal social contacts. Outsourcing could be performed at much lower cost, risks could be substantially reduced, and information circulated much more quickly.

This type of arrangement is now coming under increasing pressure, and appears to be ill-equipped to deal with the new competitive requirements. Family bonds erode, especially when the firm has to move production overseas and loose networks between family-owned SMEs are unable to raise the capital required for increasing fixed investments and R&D outlays.

Taiwanese SMEs increasingly need to develop a variety of linkages with more powerful third parties, like Taiwanese business groups or foreign firms. In addition to project-specific alliances with larger firms, these linkages have taken five forms:[29] informal "peer group" networks; hierarchical center-satellite systems; business associations; industrial parks; and variations in the business group model, centered around a holding company. It is difficult to say which of these different linkage arrangements are most effective for coping with the dual challenge of upgrading and internationalization. We find that Taiwanese SMEs as well as the government have pursued a plurality of approaches in parallel, rather than concentrating exclusively on one particular linkage. In this section we focus on linkages with domestic firms, yet, as most of the domestic firms are part of much larger international production networks, we cannot avoid dealing now with some of these international linkages.

### Informal "peer group" networks

Taiwanese SMEs have always relied heavily on informal social networks for access to resources, capabilities, and knowledge that they are unable to mobilize on their own. Over time, the focus of these networks has shifted from labor, capital, and basic market information to technological knowledge and brand name recognition. Originally, these networks were restricted to family and kinship relations. They are now rapidly being substituted by professional "peer group" networks. This is especially true for the electronics industry, where resource and capability requirements are much more demanding than in traditional industries, and where participation in international knowledge networks is of the essence.

Informal peer group networks come in a variety of forms. Typically, classmates (especially in elite schools) and former colleagues (especially in foreign affiliates) form tight networks that can be instrumental in the creation of start-up companies. For example, Taiwanese SMEs rely heavily on informal information exchange with former classmates for the generation of tacit knowledge on specific engineering and marketing problems and when they need confidential information on potential partners or competitors. Interviews at Acer for instance showed that even today, when this company has long moved beyond its earlier SME status, senior managers still prefer to contact former teachers or classmates when they have to deal with a specific engineering, marketing, or management problem rather than a commercial consultancy firm or a technology research institute.

Acer actually has been a master in the formation of such informal networks; much of its success arguably is due to the scope and depth of its peer group linkages. Founded in 1976 as Multitech International Corp. with a registered capital of just $25,000 and eleven employees, the company's first activity was to run a training center for computer engineers. In the first three years, more than 3,000 engineers were trained who later were to occupy important positions in Taiwan's nascent computer industry. As a result, Acer was able to establish early on an extensive network of social contacts within Taiwan's computer community. These contacts have become an important asset. Since 1986, Acer Sertek Inc, the company's domestic sales, marketing, and service arm, has trained more than 170,000 Taiwanese students in computer use. Similar stories abound for foreign companies as well: RCA, the incubator of Taiwan's semiconductor industry, Philips, IBM Taiwan, AT&T Taiwan, Matsushita, Toshiba, Sanyo, and Fujitsu.

## *A hierarchical center-satellite system*

One attempt to overcome the disadvantages of small firm size has been the government's Center-Satellite (CS) Program, launched in 1984, in response to the private sector's unwillingness to vertically integrate production through either merger or inter-firm cooperation. The objective of this program has been to eliminate cut-throat competition and destructive price-cutting practices by encouraging closer, interdependent, and long-term ties between larger "center" firms (upstream suppliers, final assemblers, large trading companies) and their "satellites" (especially component suppliers).

The CS program is an attempt by the Taiwanese government to copy the Japanese *keiretsu* system. It is run by the semi-official Center-Satellite Development Industrial Coordination Center (San 1995). In each CS system, the central plants assume the responsibility to coordinate, monitor, and upgrade the operations of their satellite plants. In order to strengthen these links, the government provides a variety of financial, manpower training and technical engineering assistance to both the central plants and the satellites.

On paper, the CS system is attractive, as it addresses the needs of both large and smaller companies. For center companies, the expected benefits include a lower fixed investment burden due to outsourcing and the sharing of investment outlays; access to the specialized capabilities of satellites; cost reduction due to lower wages paid by satellites; economies of scale and scope, especially if satellites supply the needs of several central firms; and the use of satellites as a buffer against market fluctuations. For satellites, expected benefits include assured orders; access to materials and components; access to technology and improved learning possibilities; and access to markets.

Most assessments conclude that the CS program so far has been only partially successful.[30] Yet, these assessments need to be placed in a broader context. During the late 1990s, the CS program has generated an increasing variety of linkages between SMEs and large firms, linkages that frequently extend beyond national boundaries. Government policies to promote CS networks were particularly successful in accelerating the outward investment of SMEs to Southeast Asia and China. Once a foreign lead company of an OEM network had invested in these regions, it exerted a powerful pressure on Taiwanese satellites to follow suit and to move their production offshore. In many cases, this has had the unanticipated effect of "hollowing-out" the domestic supplier system.

In order to correct and avoid such negative impacts, both government policies and firm strategies are currently being adjusted. Government policies now pay more attention to assisting SMEs to upgrade their domestic activities. This applies especially to incentives for technology diffusion and product-related R&D: incentives for training, policies to improve infrastructure and access to telecommunications services, and policies to improve financial services. For their part, firms are striving to diversify and internationalize their ownership, and to reap broader benefits from international specialization and the building of proprietary assets.

### Business associations and industrial parks

Business associations traditionally have played a very important role as vehicles to expand and deepen Taiwan's domestic production networks in the computer industry. These arrangements are now rapidly being internationalized. The government is actively promoting the establishment of "Taiwanese Businessmen's Associations" in the main investment locations of Southeast Asia, i.e. Malaysia, the Philippines, Thailand, Indonesia, and Vietnam. These associations are supposed to perform a variety of functions that normally fall under the responsibility of home country governments. Their primary tasks are to facilitate the exchange of information and experiences, to conduct marketing studies of various Southeast Asian markets, to organize investment promotion seminars and establish Chinese-language schools for the children of Taiwanese expatriate managers.

Similarly, as has been widely argued, industrial parks and, later on, science parks have played a major role in the development of Taiwan's locational advantages. This organizational innovation is now being transferred abroad, especially to the southern coastal provinces of China and Southeast Asia. During the late 1990s, there has been a rapid proliferation of special business zones and industrial estates that are geared primarily to the needs of Taiwanese small and medium-sized computer companies.

### Business groups centered around a holding company

Many Taiwanese computer companies have experienced very rapid growth since the last industry shake-out in 1992; the challenge now is to develop an organization that enables them to combine the advantages of size with the flexibility and speed-to-market advantages of decentralization. For PC manufacturers, the main role model is the client-server model.[31] A rapidly growing company like Acer or Mitac spins business units into independent profit centers, creating a federation of loosely connected companies united by four factors: access to common core technologies; access to the holding company's financial resources; access to its knowledge base, market intelligence and technology scanning capabilities; and a common brand name. This type of organizational innovation makes it possible to keep high value-added operations and core capabilities in Taiwan while dispersing sales, marketing, procurement, product integration, and service operations around the world in close proximity to the main growth markets.

Each of the different members of a "client-server organization" is separated by product lines and by geographic region, and each operates independently from the other. This allows them to make decisions quickly in response to market changes and to define the market segments where they feel fit for leadership. At the same time, however, all of these businesses have ready access to the full range of products and support that the lead company provides.

One important element of this re-organization is a new approach to overseas PC assembly. Acer provides an example.[32] In order to reduce cost and increase speed-to-market for new products, Acer has established fifteen modular assembly sites around the world. Each of these assembly subsidiaries is located close to important markets and performs only very limited activities: it receives PC housings and floppy disk drives by sea, with motherboards flown in directly to ensure delivery of the newest technologies. Central processing units (CPUs), hard drives, and memory are sourced locally to fill individual user requirements, and the modular components are assembled quickly according to a standardized procedure. This strategy allows Acer to maintain control over product quality and keep inventory to a minimum while providing fast assembly of competitively priced PCs that always contain the latest microprocessor generation.

The Taiwanese "client-server" model comes strikingly close to the basic philosophy of many proponents of corporate re-engineering, especially the model that IBM's previous chairman John Akers had tried to implement for the ailing giant before he was ousted.[33] Yet, the basic motivation of firms like Acer has been fundamentally different from those of IBM; the goal is not to reduce the cost of excessive centralization, but to overcome some size-related barriers to upgrading and internationalization without repeating the mistakes of excessive integration characteristic of US, European, and Japanese firms.

## Participation in international production networks

Inward FDI played an important catalytic role during the critical early phase of the development of Taiwan's electronics industry. It exposed Taiwanese workers and managers to new organizational techniques, which, although not necessarily "best practice," contributed to gradual erosion of traditional, highly authoritarian and ultimately inefficient management practices. The need to comply with some minimum international quality standards gave rise to learning effects that spilled over to a wide spectrum of local enterprises as a result of the high turnover in Taiwan's skilled labor market. A questionnaire survey of 318 Taiwanese electronics firms found that 104 of these companies had high-level managers and engineers with work experience in foreign electronics firms (San 1990).

Of these, roughly 43 percent felt that their working experience with foreign firms was helpful for their management skills, 31 percent said that it was useful for product design and development, and almost 30 percent that it enhanced their capacity to generate market information.

Inward FDI also contributed to the development of local suppliers, at least for domestic market-oriented production. These FDI-related linkages first emerged in the early 1960s in consumer electronics, and a bit later in components, telecommunications, and computing. A combination of protection and local content requirements, directed especially at Japanese consumer electronics manufacturers, forced these companies to pull along their main Japanese component suppliers. Together, they systematically groomed local vendors and established a broad range of local supplier networks.

Although inward FDI played the important catalytic role, it was the rapid proliferation of international outsourcing arrangements that enabled extraordinary developmental leverage: these arrangements include subcontracting, consignment assembly and various forms of OEM contracts,[34] and are no longer confined to parts and components but involve high-value-added support services such as product customization, product design and production technology.

As Chapter 3 suggests, American computer companies like Apple, IBM, DEC, Compaq and HP have been pioneers in the subcontracting of component manufacturing, contract assembly, the spread of OEM, and more recently ODM arrangements that enable them to concentrate on what they do best. As we saw in Chapter 4, Japanese computer companies only followed suit during the early 1990s, once their tight grip over their domestic market was challenged by the aggressive price war strategies of American computer companies.[35]

Similarly, since the early 1990s, Taiwanese OEM suppliers have shifted a growing share of their production to low-cost production sites in Southeast Asia and China. Since 1992, Taiwan's PC industry has experienced an extremely rapid expansion of overseas production.[36] In value terms, the ratio of overseas production out of Taiwan's total PC production has increased from 10.4 percent in 1992, to 14.9 percent in 1993, 20.6 percent in 1994, and 27.2 percent in 1995.[37] For 1996, the OPR is estimated to have increased to almost 30 percent. Throughout this short period, annual growth in overseas production value was consistently over 70 percent, which implies that overseas production today plays a critical role for the success and failure of Taiwan's PC industry.

Most of the overseas production of Taiwanese computer companies is concentrated in neighboring regions in China (most of it in China's southern coastal provinces) and in Southeast Asia. For instance, out of the ninety-five overseas production sites of Taiwanese PC firms that have been registered by the Malaysian Industrial Classification (MIC), seventy-five production sites, i.e. almost 80 percent, have been located in East Asia (exclusive of Japan). China alone has attracted forty-one investments, i.e. 43 percent of the total.[38]

The logistic complexity of the new Taiwanese IPNs is not simply a result of their geographic spread; it is also a function of an increasingly complex division of labor.[39] Each IPN combines different, hierarchically structured and closely interacting subnetworks. For example, an American computer company such as IBM or Compaq is linked to first-tier contractors, for instance an American disk drive producer like Seagate with its IPN, or large Taiwanese OEM contractors like Acer. At the next level, we find medium-sized, specialized Taiwanese contractors like Delta Electronics, a major producer of switching power supplies that has production facilities in Thailand, China and Mexico. At the lowest levels, we find a myriad of subproduction networks each centered around a small Taiwanese subcontractor many of which have redeployed production to China or Southeast Asia.

The complexity of such arrangements becomes clear when we look at the major customers list of a firm like Delta Electronics.[40] This list reads like a *Who's Who?* of the computer industry and covers twenty-four leading computer companies from the United States, Japan, Europe, and Taiwan.[41]

In sum, Taiwanese firms in the electronics industry are deeply embedded in complex IPNs that involve transactions between a large number of different national production systems. The increasing complexity of IPNs, however, has also allowed small enterprises from a small nation to participate and upgrade their position over time.

### The evolution of Taiwanese production networks

Taiwan's involvement in the OEM business dates back the mid-1960s and IBM's decision to begin sourcing from Taiwanese suppliers. A long period of capability formation followed, which left Taiwanese firms in a strong position to build OEM relationships in the PC business as it evolved. In the early PC days, Taiwanese firms were involved only in very simple OEM arrangements. The focus was on low-end desktop PCs and labor-intensive peripherals, like computer mouse and keyboards. The OEM customer provided detailed technical "blueprints" and technical assistance to allow the Taiwanese contractor to produce according to specifications.

There is a broad consensus that Taiwanese firms were able to reap substantial benefits from this easy phase of OEM. For example, in a late 1980s survey of forty-three Taiwanese OEM suppliers (twenty-seven domestic and sixteen foreign invested), roughly 70 percent acknowledged that OEM contracts were useful in transferring production technologies and in acquiring product design capabilities (San Gee 1990: Table 4.1). Yet, these simple forms of OEM also had substantial drawbacks. Suppliers became "locked into" OEM relationships that hindered independent brand name recognition and marketing channels. Profit margins were thinner in OEM sales than own brand sales, which in turn makes it difficult for suppliers to muster the capital needed to invest in R&D required for the development of new products.

In response to these drawbacks, a number of Taiwanese computer companies tried to expand their share of original brand manufacturing (OBM) sales. In 1988, for example, the share of Taiwan brand-name to total PC sales stood at roughly 28 percent; by 1989 it had risen to 40 percent.[42] Yet, the transition to OBM turned out to be difficult, and only a handful of companies were able to succeed; most others failed and are now content to consolidate and upgrade their position as OEM suppliers. The story of this upgrading process can be seen through the lens of Taiwan's best-known computer company, Acer.

Acer's involvement in the PC cloning business dates back to 1983, when it was among the first Taiwanese companies to introduce an IBM XT/PC compatible. In the same year, Acer had organized Taiwan's first international distributors' meeting, attended by delegates from over twenty countries. Building strong links with foreign distributors and OEM customers subsequently became an important priority, complementing Acer's strong domestic roots.

The years following 1986 brought a number of early successes. MPUs (32 bit) were just beginning to appear on the market, and Acer was able to beat IBM in announcing a 32-bit PC based on Intel's 386 MPU. During the same year, Acer's subsidiary Continental Systems, Inc. (now Acer Peripherals) received two successive excellence rewards from Integrated Telecom Technology (ITT), acknowledging the high quality of its OEM products. After changing the company name to Acer in 1987,[43] the company got approval to list on the Taiwan stock exchange in 1988.

Acer's export success was wholly dependent on OEM sales, however. These early triumphs led Acer's management to believe it could reduce this dependence and jump to producing its own brands. In 1988, Acer hired a senior IBM executive to reorganize the company with the explicit goal of transforming it into a global competitor. Expectations were running high. IBM was still considered the industry's role model; by copying key features of IBM, Acer could speed up its leapfrogging effort. In particular, the idea was to increase the company's vertical integration and generate a critical mass of proprietary assets that would enable Acer to develop its own brand name image.

This effort failed miserably. The IBM manager assumed that change could be imposed from above by forcing consensus on the local management. Such an aggressive top-down approach ran into stubborn opposition by Acer's managers and engineers, who were used to a substantial amount of decision autonomy. More important, however, was the fact that Acer simply did not have the resources that are necessary to implement such a strategy.

The peak of leapfrogging euphoria came in 1989, when Acer shipped its one-millionth computer and was ranked for the first time by Datamation among the top 100 information technology (IT) companies in the world; Acer was chosen as one of the "corporate stars of the future" by the *Wall Street Journal*, and it was chosen by Texas Instruments (TI) as its joint venture partner for DRAM production in Taiwan. Insiders knew that TI's decision was based on the lavish financial package that Acer, in cooperation with the Taiwanese government, was able to offer.[44] For a broader public, however, the tie up with TI conferred tremendous prestige.[45]

The shift in strategy was supposed to occur quickly. Acer projected that the share of OEM sales would decline from 40 percent of total sales in 1988 to 25 percent in 1992. Not only did Acer intend to compete through its own brand, but it also wanted to broaden its product portfolio. This led to a rapid succession of acquisitions, which almost ended in disaster. In 1987, Acer acquired Counterpoint Computers with the intention of using it to build a strong position in minicomputers, but the follow-up costs of technology development and marketing were way above Acer's expectations. Counterpoint lost $15 million in 1989 alone, almost as much as the $17 million that Acer had paid for the firm, and the firm was closed down. Undeterred, Acer tried again the following year, by acquiring Altos, an American producer of UNIX-based multiuser systems. At the time, the expectation was that Altos' UNIX experience and distribution channels would help Acer to speed up its product diversification.[46] Bought for $94 million, the firm recorded a mere $125 million in sales in 1990, and was incurring heavy losses. Such losses continued for a few more years, but this time Acer also benefited. By acquiring Altos, the company was able to develop its computer networking capabilities and to enter the PC server market.[47]

The awakening came in 1991 when Acer posted a loss ($23 million) for the first time. Acer's overambitious diversification strategy came at the worst possible moment. The PC industry worldwide was swept by a crippling price war, as a result of which almost all companies faced a serious profit squeeze.

Taiwan's computer industry was particularly hard hit and went through a major shake-out. During the second half of 1991, fifty to sixty Taiwanese computer companies went out of business each month.[48] Most of these firms were small companies. One could argue that this was a healthy development, as it indicated a long overdue consolidation of this industry. Moreover, the disappearance of small firms from a sector under pressure seems to be a fairly normal occurrence in Taiwan; many of them reappear making something else or at a foreign location. Since 1991, however, a number of larger Taiwanese PC companies like Acer were in serious trouble too; some, such as Autocomputer, actually went out of business.

The spread of intense price wars constituted a major challenge for the Taiwanese computer industry, and readjustment came at a heavy cost. The big players pursued aggressive price-cutting strategies, with the result that cost reduction became the most critical issue in the computer industry. This posed a serious challenge for Taiwanese firms. In order to sustain their position as OEM suppliers, they had to implement drastic additional cost reductions at a time when Taiwan's traditional cost advantages were rapidly eroding. Fueled by the appreciation of the New Taiwanese dollar (NT), the cost of land and labor in Taiwan exploded in the early 1990s, with the result that Taiwan lost its comparative advantage as a low-cost production site. At the same time, Taiwan faced serious competitive threats both from below and from above. New low-cost competitors have entered the fray in Southeast Asia and China, and South Korea has strengthened its position as a supplier of scale-intensive components, like DRAMs, monitors, CRTs, and display devices. Furthermore, Japanese firms, which have lost market share at home and in export markets, have now begun to fight back and to develop much more aggressive global market penetration strategies.

As a result, Taiwan's OBM products came under fierce attack. The OBM share of Taiwan's PC exports fell from 30 percent in 1992 to 22 percent in 1993.[49] Taiwan's computer industry thus did not have much choice but to fall back on its strength as OEM suppliers; most firms made a conscious effort to consolidate their position in this field.[50]

Acer pursued a different approach. While it consolidated its position as an OEM supplier, it simultaneously continued to pursue an aggressive OBM strategy. Rather than trying to reduce its reliance on OEM contracts, the objective now is to quickly increase the OEM share to 50 percent. This part of the strategy has worked well. For desktop computers, Acer is one of the five Taiwan-based producers that have collectively come to dominate the OEM market: Tatung, Acer, DEC's Taiwan affiliate, FIC and AST's local affiliate. In addition to its strong position in desktop PCs, Acer has also become a major OEM supplier of notebook computers for Apple and Canon. The result has been that, in 1994, the OEM share of Acer's PC sales had risen again to 35 percent.

Acer's strategy is to leverage its OEM business to generate the necessary financial resources to pursue its OBM strategy and to further upgrade Acer's capabilities, especially in design and computer networking. The logical consequence is a focus on mass production rather than on niche markets. Acer's goal is to become one of the world's highest volume producers of peripheral equipment, key components, subassemblies, and design services, both for Acer's worldwide computer assembly plants and for leading international computer companies like Apple, Canon, and Fujitsu. Acer describes its own competitive strength as "...the ability to market affordably-priced products quickly due to innovative production and distribution strategies, a component supply approach, a flexible and independent organization and economies of scale in manufacturing."[51]

Meanwhile, Acer's OBM strategy tries to combine the following not always consistent goals: to establish a credible global brand image for a broad mix of "affordably-priced products"; to improve its ability to market such products quickly and to adapt them in response to changing market requirements; to penetrate secondary markets in Asia, Latin America, and elsewhere in order to gain economies of scale and to use these countries as a test-ground for refining its globalization strategy. In these markets, Acer aims to price its products 10–15 percent below Compaq's prices. Gradually, Acer would build its product and marketing capabilities in a few very limited "market niches." Acer's acquisition of some American computer companies, like Altos, was one element of this approach, but much more important is the shift to digital consumer electronics, and, possibly, Acer's pioneering role in the field of software design and distribution. These objectives serve the overriding concern of developing an independent global brand image.

Until 1995, there was good reason to believe that this dual strategy would work: between 1993 and 1995, Acer's share price has almost quintupled.[52] And in 1995, the group's consolidated sales revenues were $5.8 billion, up from $690 million in 1989. This quick and impressive turnaround owes a great deal to sheer luck, and to industry-specific factors that were beyond Acer's control. Probably of greatest importance has been the strong demand for DRAM chips, which has pushed up profit margins for this product. Without the windfall profits of TI–Acer's DRAM joint venture, Acer would probably still suffer from its overambitious diversification strategy. In 1993, 90 percent of Acer's net earnings were generated by TI–Acer, and its share in Acer's 1995 net earnings was still as high as 45 percent. This, however, has drastically changed since 1990. As a result of the free fall of DRAM prices, TI–Acer has ceased to act as a provider of cash for Acer's OBM strategy.

As for Acer's core PC business, profit margins have improved. The surprise success of Acer's multimedia home personal computer in 1994 helped to improve the company's position.[53] In 1995, Acer became one of the top ten PC suppliers to the US market: in the eighteen months that ended in June 1995, Acer more than doubled its market share of PCs sold in US stores to 7 percent. Since then, however, not much has moved. In 1995, the US market still accounted for roughly 26 percent of Acer's worldwide sales, and in 1996 Acer America went into the red again, losing $42.3 million during the first six months.[54] While Acer has retained its top position in a number of rapidly growing yet still quite secondary markets, such as Indonesia, Malaysia, Mexico and South Africa, the overall growth of sales revenues for computers has slowed down and Acer has still not succeeded in expanding its OBM market share in Japan and China. Margins in the computer business are also low – 4 percent – and as a result, Acer's 1996 net profits were substantially lower than Acer's own forecast. These results are simply too meager to support Acer's ambitious upgrading strategy.[55]

All of this does not imply that Acer's strategy has failed altogether. Rarely has a company grown so fast, and rarely has a small firm from a small nation been able to build up such a broad range of capabilities and to introduce far-reaching organizational innovations during a relatively short period of time. Yet, it also shows that there is no easy and quick shortcut to success and that leapfrogging is an illusory concept that should be discarded.[56] Developing a firm's capability base is a time-consuming and laborious process: at each stage of its growth, new barriers arise that require a period of consolidation. The more Acer progresses and grows, the more demanding will be the barriers with which it has to cope. This excludes a frontal attack on the market leaders. Attacking from the sidelines is the only realistic option. This is certainly true as long as Acer has not yet reached a size that qualifies it for Fortune 500 membership. The key to Acer's success is that it has pursued a gradual market penetration strategy: it avoids direct confrontation and pursues markets where the market leaders are not present.[57] Acer's OBM strategy thus remains primarily focused on non-OECD markets, and at the same time it continues to upgrade its capabilities as an OEM supplier.

This shows that Chandler is right in emphasizing the difficulties of overcoming the first mover advantages of large transnationals (Chandler 1990). Yet, Acer's story also shows that a small firm from a small nation can enter and grow in the rapidly moving computer industry, provided that it pursues a realistic market penetration strategy.

Developing a global brand image is costly and involves extreme risks. Acer's approach to "attack from the sidelines" and to focus its OBM strategy on non-OECD markets is one realistic response to this dilemma. As for market penetration in the United States, Japan, and Europe, Taiwanese computer firms will have to rely however for quite some time on OEM contracts. This is why upgrading Taiwan's OEM position is currently the appropriate strategic priority. Let us look at some examples.

During 1993, Taiwan became the main OEM supplier of PC-related products for leading American and European computer manufacturers and distributors.[58] Compaq for instance now sources its monitors from ADI, Philips Taiwan, and TECO; notebooks from Inventa, power supplies from Lite-on and Delta, and mouse devices from Logitech Taiwan and Primax.

Probably the most interesting arrangement is that with Inventa, a company that has earned a reputation for innovative notebook design and that has already supplied notebooks on an ODM basis to Dell and Zenith, now an affiliate of the French computer firm Bull. Inventa is part of the family-owned Inventec business group that is involved in a wide range of products and services, but is most well known for calculators and telephones. In 1994, the group's consolidated revenues were $450 million, with Inventa contributing more than one-third. Inventa has only a few hundred employees in Taiwan, with a large share of engineers.

As part of the Inventec group, however, Inventa has access to low-cost volume production facilities that the group has established in China and Southeast Asia, primarily Malaysia. A second attraction of such networks are the sophisticated quality control procedures characteristic of Inventec's manufacturing facilities. For the last fifteen years, Inventec has made TI's calculators and had to cope with TI's stringent quality requirements. But probably the most important reason for Compaq to link up with Inventa is the company's specialized design capabilities for notebook computers.[59] In 1994, Compaq was only fourth in the notebook market behind IBM, NEC, and Toshiba. By using Inventa's notebook design, Compaq expected to be able to leapfrog the market leaders, without being forced to commit its own limited engineering resources.

Logitech Taiwan provides another illustration of how complex IPNs have become in the computer industry,[60] but also the high volatility of the OEM business and the need to continuously upgrade product mix and capabilities. Founded in 1981 in Switzerland and incorporated a few months later in the United States, Logitech is the world's largest producer of computer tracking devices (mice and trackballs). In 1987, Logitech shifted production to Taiwan and established a large-volume production line in Hsinchu Science Park. Taiwan's main attraction was that it offered a well-developed supply base for parts, qualified people, and a rapidly expanding PC industry. In 1995, however, Logitech shifted all of its production from Taiwan to China. The result has been a drastic decline in Taiwan's share of the global mouse market from almost 75 percent in 1994 to 65 percent in 1996 (MIC/III 1997a: 30–1). At the same time, Logitech continues to use the same Taiwanese suppliers that have now set up shop close to Logitech's new location in China.

Over time, Compaq's OEM arrangements with Taiwanese firms have considerably increased in complexity. In a recent "turnkey production" contract with Mitac, Compaq has outsourced all stages of the value-chain for some of its desktop PCs, except marketing for which it retains sole responsibility. Other foreign computer companies have followed Compaq's example. For instance, IBM has recently signed a preliminary agreement with the Acer Group where Acer will use its international production network in developing countries to assemble lower end IBM desktop and laptop PCs and to distribute and service them. Such "turnkey production" arrangements constitute an important innovation, and show how rapidly OEM relationships have moved beyond production to encompass an increasing variety of high-end support services. The spread of such broad cross-value chain arrangements shows that leading foreign computer companies are confident that Taiwan's computer industry is now sufficiently well integrated to serve as a one-stop shopping center.[61]

As they begin to respond to the American IPNs, Japanese PC manufacturers have also increased their OEM contracts with Taiwanese firms for desktop PCs, motherboards, terminals and monitors, and a variety of other PC-related products. NEC for instance gets monitors and motherboards from Tatung and Elite; Fujitsu has relied primarily on OEM supplies from Acer, and Epson; Canon, Hitachi, Sharp, and Mitsubishi have all become major OEM customers. In 1994, this was followed by a massive increase of OEM contracts for notebook computers.

As a result of these developments, the share of OEM/ODM out of Taiwan's total desktop PC production has increased, in volume terms, from 37 percent in 1995 to 53 percent in 1996.[62] For notebook PCs, the share of OEM/ODM reached 82 percent in 1996.

For two reasons, these developments benefit rather than harm Taiwan's computer industry. First, Taiwan's OEM clients now include the top ten worldwide industry leaders, which are at the cutting-edge of product development. Close interaction with these industry leaders provides Taiwanese firms with a constant flow of precious feedback information on product design, new architectural standards, leading-edge production technology, and sophisticated quality control and logistics procedures. Close links with these industry leaders acts as a powerful vehicle for a further strengthening of the learning and innovation capabilities of Taiwanese computer firms.

At the same time, we have seen that OEM contracts have now become much more demanding: they require a broad range of sophisticated capabilities that cover most if not all stages of the value-chain. Taiwanese firms now need to provide more sophisticated services, including design and global supply chain management.[63] While in 1993, roughly half of all PCs supplied by Taiwanese OEM suppliers were based on Taiwanese designs, this share today has increased to more than 70 percent.[64]

Of even greater importance is a tendency to extend OEM contracts to include an integrated package of higher end support services, as illustrated in the "turnkey production" contracts of Compaq with Mitac, and of IBM with Acer. This implies that, with the exception of hardcore R&D and strategic marketing, Taiwan's OEM supplier community must be able to shoulder all steps in the production chain and the coordination functions necessary for global supply chain management.

Changing OEM relationships are producing a new division of labor between large Taiwanese computer majors and SMEs, patterns that have been reinforced by the Asia Crisis. Large firms appear to rely more on OEM contracts, whereas SMEs are much more active in ODM. For instance, OEM orders for desktop computers are all concentrated on a select group of large companies, i.e. Tatung, Acer, DEC Taiwan, FIC, and MITAC. The same is true for other scale-sensitive products such as monitors and modems. This sounds counterintuitive, but OEM contracts come in large orders; they typically generate razor-thin profit margins. Economies of scale and scope are of critical importance, and large firms are better placed to reap such economies. Time and again, we thus find that Chandler's insistence on the continuous importance of scale and scope economies makes perfect sense, even in a fast moving sector like the computer industry (Chandler 1990). Moreover, only a large firm can avoid becoming overly dependent on one particular customer. Smaller firms may find it too risky to depend on large OEM contracts, as each of these contracts normally surpasses their maximum production capacity. They prefer to shift to ODM contracts where they have greater chances to sustain a diversified customer base and charge higher prices. In other words, SMEs are under greater pressure relative to large Taiwanese firms to improve their design capabilities to become credible niche market players within the overall OEM market. Many of these SMEs will not succeed, but those that do have good chances to grow and to improve their competitive position.

## Conclusion

This study shows beyond doubt the benefits from participating in IPNs; however, those benefits do not come automatically. Reaping them requires far-reaching institutional and organizational innovations that enable small firms from a small nation to overcome their size-related disadvantages. Taiwan's industrial development policies have played an important role, as did close interaction with large domestic firms.

The great advantage of Taiwan's computer industry has been the incredible speed with which it has been able to respond to changes in markets and technology. Such quick response and flexibility now needs to be supplemented with industrial deepening – the development of a domestic supply base for key components and improved product differentiation capabilities.

Apart from strengthening their domestic R&D capabilities, Taiwanese firms also need to locate R&D laboratories as listening posts abroad in the relevant centers of excellence in the United States, Japan, and Europe. To do this requires a variety of joint ventures and strategic alliances with major international electronics firms. Simultaneously, a concerted effort is required to move beyond an exclusive focus on hardware production and to complement this with attempts to strengthen domestic capabilities in information services industries.

All of this will require time. What matters is that Taiwan has succeeded in developing a critical mass of capabilities that will help this small island economy to cope with future challenges. The Taiwanese model in the computer industry provides clear evidence that David can grow in the shadow of Goliath, and that small enterprises can succeed in global competition.

## Notes

1  Since Stephen Hymer's pioneering contribution in 1960 (Hymer 1976), theories of the firm implicitly assume that only large, diversified multinational enterprises can compete in industries that combine high capital intensity, high knowledge intensity, and a high degree of internationalization. For concise statements of this consensus position, see Caves (1982), Chandler (1990), and Dunning (1993).
2  Important contributions are Walsh (1987), Freeman and Lundvall (eds) (1988), and Maskell (1996a).
3  Von Hippel defines "lead users of a novel or enhanced product, process, or service" as those that "...face needs that will be general in the market place, but...(who) face them months or years before the bulk of that marketplace encounters them..." and who will "...benefit significantly by obtaining a solution to those needs" (Von Hippel 1988: 107).
4  Technological spillovers are assumed to be mainly domestically generated by innovation theorists (Lundvall 1992) as well as by "new growth" theorists (Grossman and Helpman 1991, 1993). If this is so, then large countries will benefit more from an investment in R&D than smaller countries, where some of the spillovers of R&D are likely to benefit its trading partners (Zander and Kogut 1995).
5  *AITR*, January 1997, p. 3.
6  Information provided by MIC/III.
7  "PC network products" are defined as "products that are used for LANs (local area networks), PSTN (public switched telephone network), ISDN (integrated services digital network), ASDL (asymmetric digital subscriber loop), and cable modems. Main products include "network interface cards, hubs, bridging switches, modems and routers." Definitions are taken from *Electronic Computer Glossary*. Add-on cards include sound, video and graphics cards. Of these, video cards display higher than average profit margins.
8  Information provided by MIC/III, October 27, 1995.
9  There is a rich body of research, based on the assumptions of evolutionary economics, that specifies what type of capabilities are required and how the development of such capabilities affects firm organization. (Important contributions include Penrose 1959; Nelson and Winter 1982; Dosi *et al.* 1988;

Lundvall 1988, 1992; Carlsson and Stankiewicz 1991; Teece *et al.* 1992; Foray and Lundvall 1996; Zander and Kogut 1995; Malerba and Orsenigo 1996.) For an application of this theoretical approach to research on developing countries, see Ernst *et al.* (1997a) and Ernst and Lundvall 1997). In this view, competition centers around a firm's ability to build capabilities quicker and at less cost than its competitors. This literature thus constitutes an important progress relative to traditional "industrial organization" debates: capability-based theories of the firm are much better qualified to explain the dynamics of competition than contractual theories of the firm, as put forward by Williamson, with their focus on static allocation efficiency. [Williamson (1975, 1985) and Milgrom and Roberts (1992) are the relevant sources on contractual firm theories. Much of the literature on firm capabilities, however, focuses on large multidivisional corporations and fails to discuss how small enterprises can develop such capabilities.

10   For a detailed analysis, see Ernst (1994c, 1998; Guerrieri *et al.* 2000).
11   For the underlying argument, see Acs and Audretsch (1992). For a critical assessment, see Harrison (1994).
12   For details, see Shieh (1990) and Lam and Lee (1992: 112). Individual firms often bid for contracts beyond their own capacities; once a supplier gets the contract, it calls on other firms, often competitors, to help fill the order.
13   For an analysis of Silicon Valley-type production networks, see Saxenian (1990).
14   Chandler (1990) remains the most authoritative source. Economies of scale and scope in the computer industry are analyzed in Flamm (1988, 1990), Ferguson (1990), Ernst and O'Connor (1992), and Ernst (1997a).
15   A related argument about the dark side of specialization can be found in Prahalad and Hamel (1990), who argue that excessive specialization, typical for the multidivisional form of firm organization, may undermine the firm's core competencies.
16   "While standardization appears to be a necessary consequence of the attempts of economic agents to exploit economies of scale and to avoid dealing with impossible amounts of information, this may also lead to difficulties for innovative activities." (Andersen 1996: 98).
17   The primary source for such "user-producer linkages" remains Lundvall (1988, 1992).
18   The Statute for Investment by Foreign Nationals was first promulgated in July 1954 to attract foreign companies. In November 1955, this was followed by the Statute for Investment by Overseas Chinese whose purpose was to tap into the experiences and capital of the Overseas Chinese communities in Hong Kong and Southeast Asia. Finally, the Statute for the Encouragement of Investment was enacted in September 1960 (San and Kuo 1997).
19   Ministry of Economic Affairs (MOEA) 991).
20   For an analysis of such crowding-out affects on potential domestic investment in Southeast Asia, see Lim and Peng E. F. (1991).
21   See, for example, San and Kuo (1997), G. San (1995), Kobayashi (1995), Meaney (1994). Kajiwara (1993). Liu (1993). Schive (1990, 1993). and Wong (1995).
22   Ministry of Economic Affairs (MOEA), 1991.
23   Questionnaire survey, conducted in July 1992, for the Ministry of Economic Affairs, covering a sample of 4,137 private manufacturing companies in Taiwan. See Liu *et al.* (1994: 51).
24   Note, however, that changes occur even in Korea. In response to the collapse of a major *chaebol* (the Hanbo group) and a looming banking crisis, all *chaebol* are now forced to reconsider basic features of their organization. Take for instance the Daewoo group: its officially declared debt in 1997 was more than three times its equity, and it had committed itself to more than 100 foreign investment

projects, worth at least $3 billion. The group's chairman, Kim Woo Choong, declared that Daewoo would evolve "in a cluster of independent firms, each led by professional managers." *The Economist*, 8 February 8 1997, p. 81. With the Asian financial crisis, the group collapsed.

25 Author's interviews, Taiwan, May and November 1995.

26 Author's interviews, Taiwan, May and November 1995.

27 A similar system apparently works for leading-edge components: while price levels, of course, are substantially higher than for the more vintage-type components, they still tend to be below price levels on the spot market.

28 Interviews at ERSO/ITRI, December 1994 and May 1995.

29 This classification is an attempt to develop further some ideas that have been introduced by a variety of Taiwanese authors. Important contributions include Lee (1995); Liu *et al.* (1994).

30 San (1995) and Wade (1990: 167).

31 The following is based on interviews with Acer, Mitac, and FIC between 1992 and 1995.

32 Similar approaches have been developed by other leading Taiwanese computer manufacturers like Mitac and FIC.

33 Acer hired an IBM executive to assist its reorganization in 1988, with little success; however, the crisis of 1991 spurred a new round of organizational innovation. *BW*, 27 November 1995, p. 73.

34 Definitions of what constitutes an OEM (original equipment manufacturing) contract keep changing. Probably the most widely accepted definition refers to arrangements between a brand name company (the customer) and the contractor (the supplier) where the customer provides detailed technical blueprints and most of the components to allow the contractor to produce according to specifications. Using this definition of OEM arrangements, we can then distinguish ODM (original design manufacturing) as arrangements where the contractor is responsible for design and most of the component procurement, with the brand name company retaining exclusive control over marketing.

35 Until the mid-1980s, Japanese computer firms were actually major OEM suppliers to American computer companies. We will see in a moment what factors have enabled Taiwanese firms to bypass Japanese companies as leading OEM suppliers.

36 The following figures are courtesy of MIC/III.

37 In 1995, keyboards had the highest overseas production ratio (OPR), with 86 percent of Taiwan's total production value being produced overseas. Other products with high OPRs are: power switching supply (77 percent), monitors (almost 50 percent), motherboards (37 percent), and mouse devices (24 percent). For 1966, the greatest increase in overseas production was expected for CDROMs and mouse devices.

38 Questionnaire survey by MIC/III, conducted in 1996.

39 The concept of an "international production network" is an attempt to capture the spread of broader and more systemic forms of international production that cut across different stages of the value chain and that may or may not involve equity ownership. Such networks constitute an important organizational innovation that enable multinational corporations to cope with the conflicting requirements of specialization and coordination. The concept allows us to analyze the globalization strategies of a particular firm with regard to the following four questions: (1) Where does a firm locate which stages of the value chain? (2) To what degree does a firm rely on outsourcing? What is the importance of inter-firm production networks relative to the firm's internal production network? (3) To what degree is the control over these transactions exercised in a centralized or in a decentralized manner? (4) How do these different elements of the IPN

hang together? For details, see Ernst (1992, 1994a,b; 1997a), Ernst and Guerrieri (1998), and Ernst and Ravenhill (1999).

40  Interview at Delta Electronics, 7 June, 1995.
41  Acer, Alcatel, AST, Apple, Canon, Compaq, DEC, Epson, Hewlett-Packard, Hitachi, IBM, Intel, Microtek, Matsushita, Mitsubishi, Motorola, National Cash Register (NCR), NEC, Philips, Rockwell, Synoptics, Tatung, Thomson, and Toshiba.
42  *Eurotrade*, Taipei, Vol. 2, January 1990, p. 32.
43  Acer is Latin for "sharp, acute, able and facile."
44  TI's strategy is to choose wafer fabrication locations where most of the investment costs are shouldered by local governments. See Ernst (1994a).
45  By 1989, Acer's consolidated sales revenues were less than $690 million and it had around 5,500 employees.
46  *BT* (Singapore), 11 February 1992.
47  A recent review of high-quality servers for small workgroups concludes that the Acer Altos 800/P is "a solid choice with somewhat weak software" that compares well with the products offered by such industry majors as Compaq, Hewlett-Packard, and DEC. "Centralized storage. Small workgroup servers – Hardware Review," *PCC*, vol. 8, no. 11 (November, 1995), p. 140.
48  *CENS*, 4 December 1991.
49  *AITR*, March 1994, p. 8.
50  See our discussion below.
51  *The Acer Group Profile* 1994, p. 4.
52  "Acer's Edge: PCs to Go," *Fortune*, 30 October, 1995.
53  Its US affiliate was among the first firms to anticipate the demand for home multimedia computers – high-end systems with CDROM drives that play compact disc-based software with sharp graphics and stereo sound. Much of this was good luck. Acer just happened to have the right product at the right time ready for the right market. Zielinger, M. "Ace in the Hole. Taiwan's Acer makes surprising comeback in America," *FEER*, 26 January 1995, p. 52.
54  Sales of its heavily promoted Aspire multimedia *FEER*, 6 February 1997, p. 60. The Aspire was launched, amidst great fanfare, in September 1995. It was praised for its innovative design which includes a monitor integrated with a stereo speaker system and microphone, and was meant to herald Acer's successful transformation into a global consumer electronics company. For a description of these aspirations, see cover story on Acer, *FEER*, 25 July 1996, pp. 74–80.
55  BZW Securities estimate, quoted in the *FT*, 10 February, 1997.
56  For an early critique, see Ernst and O'Connor (1989: Chapter II).
57  Kotler *et al.* (1985) remains the classic source.
58  The following information on OEM contracts is courtesy of MIC/III.
59  *WSJ*, 3 February 1995, p. B6.
60  The following is based on Jolly and Bechler (1992) and author's interviews.
61  For IBM, Acer's main attraction is its "global operations," its strong presence in developing countries, and its "ability to tailor its products to each market." IBM intends to buy in up to $2 billion worth of PCs over a period of three years. *WSJ*, 6 December 1996.
62  These and the following figures on OEM/ODM shares are from MIC/III, 1997c.
63  For the concept of "global supply chain management," see Lee and Billington (1995) and Levy (1995).
64  Design, in this context, includes the capacity to make quick changes in the configuration of motherboards in order to be able to integrate the latest microprocessor generation. Although this is a very demanding requirement, it is quite different from the capacity to define architectural standards and create new markets.

# References

Acs, Z. J. and Audretsch, D. B. (1992) *Innovation and Small Firms*, Cambridge, MA: The MIT Press.

Andersen, E. S. (1996) "The Evolution of Economic Complexity: A Division-of-Coordination-of Labor Approach," in E. Helmstaedter and M. Perlman (eds) *Behavioral Norms, Technological Progress, and Economic Dynamics. Studies in Schumpeterian Economics*, Ann Arbor: The University of Michigan Press.

Carlsson, B. and Stankiewicz, R. (1991) "On the Nature, Function and Composition of Technological Systems," *Journal of Evolutionary Economics*, 1(2): 93–118.

Caves, R. E. (1982) *Multinational Enterprise and Economic Analysis*, Cambridge: Cambridge University Press.

Chandler, A. (1990) *Scale and Scope: The Dynamics of Industrial Capitalism*, Cambridge, MA: Belknap Press.

Chen, T.-J. *et al.* (1995) *Taiwan's Small- and Medium-Sized Firms' Direct Investment in Southeast Asia*, Taipei: Chung-Hua Institution for Economic Research.

Dosi, G. Freeman, C. Nelson, R. Silverberg, G. and Soete, L. (eds) (1988) *Technical Change and Economic Theory*, London: Pinter.

Dunning, J. (1993) *Multinational Enterprises and the Global Economy*, Wokingham, UK; Reading MA: Addison-Wesley.

Ernst, D. (1983) *The Global Race in Microelectronics*, Frankfurt and New York: MIT, Campus Publishers.

—— (1992) *Networks, Market Structure and Technology Diffusion – A Conceptual Framework and Some Empirical Evidence*, report prepared for the OECD secretariat, Paris: OECD.

—— (1994a) "Network Transactions, Market Structure and Technology Diffusion – Implications for South-South Cooperation," in L. Mytelka (ed.) *South-South Cooperation in a Global Perspective*, Paris: OECD.

—— (1994b) "Carriers of Regionalization? The East Asian Production Networks of Japanese Electronics Firms," *BRIE Working Paper 73*, University of California at Berkeley: BRIE.

—— (1994c) *What are the Limits to the Korean Model? The Korean Electronics Industry Under Pressure*, Research Paper, University of California at Berkeley: BRIE.

—— (1997a) *Data Storage Industry Globalization Project Report 97-02*, San Diego: University of California Graduate School of International Relations and Pacific Studies.

—— (1997b) "Partners in the China Circle? The Asian Production Networks of Japanese Electronics Firms," in B. Naughton (ed.) *The China Circle*, Washington, DC: The Brookings Institution Press.

—— (1998a) "Catching-up, Crisis, and Industrial Upgrading. Evolutionary Aspects of Technological Learning in Korea's Electronics Industry," *Asia Pacific Journal of Management* 15(2).

—— (1998b) "High-Tech Competition Puzzles. How Globalization Affects Firm Behavior and Market Structure in the Electronics Industry," *Revue d'Economie Industrielle*.

Ernst, D. and Guerrieri, P. (1998) "International Production Networks and Changing Trade Patterns in East Asia. The Case of the Electronics Industry," *Oxford Development Studies*, 26(2).

Ernst, D. and Lundvall, B.-Å. (2000) "Information Technology in The Learning Economy – Challenges for Developing Countries," in E. Reinart (ed.) *Evolutionary Economics and Income Inequality*. London: Edward Elgar.

Ernst, D. and O'Connor, D. (1989) *Technology and Global Competition. The Challenge for Newly Industrialising Economies*, Paris: OECD.

—— (1992) *Competing in the Electronics Industry. The Experience of Newly Industrialising Economies*, Paris: OECD.

Ernst, D. and Ravenhill, J. (1999) "Globalization, Convergence, and the Transformation of International Production Networks in Electronics in East Asia," *Business and Politics*, 1(1).

Ernst, D., Mytelka, L. and Ganiatsos, T. (1998) "Export Performance and Technological Capabilities – A Conceptual Framework," in D. Ernst, T. Ganiatsos and L. Mytelka (eds) *Technological Capabilities and Export Success – Lessons from East Asia*, London: Routledge.

Ferguson, C. H. (1990) "Computers and the Coming of the US Keiretsu," *Harvard Business Review*, July–August: 55–70.

Flamm, K. (1988) *Creating the Computer. Government, Industry and High Technology*, Washington, DC: The Brookings Institution Press.

—— (1990) "Cooperation and Competition in the Global Computer Industry," paper prepared for the working group meeting on the "Globalization in the Computer Industry," Paris: OECD.

Foray, D. and Lundvall, B.-Å. (1996) "The Knowledge-based Economy: From the Economics of Knowledge to the Learning Economy" in *Employment and Growth in the Knowledge-based Economy*, Paris: OECD.

—— (1996) "Capabilities and the Theory of the Firm," *DRUID Working Paper 96–8*, Copenhagen Business School, Department of Industrial Economics and Strategy.

Freeman, C. and Lundvall, B.-Å. (eds) (1988) *Small Countries Facing the Technological Revolution*, London: Pinter Publishers.

Grossman, G. M. and Helpman, E. (1991) *Innovation and Growth in the Global Economy*, Cambridge, Mass.

—— (1993) "Endogenous Innovation in the Theory of Growth," Working Paper 4527, Cambridge, MA: National Bureau of Economic Research (NBER).

Guerrieri, P., Jammarino, S. and Pietrobelli, C. (2000) *SME Clusters in Globalized Industries. The Case of Italy and Taiwan*. University of Rome: La Sapienza.

Harrison, B. (1994) *Lean and Mean. The Changing Landscape of Corporate Power in the Age of Flexibility*, New York: Basic Books.

Hymer, S. H. (1976) *The International Operations of National Firms: A Study of Direct Investment*, Cambridge, MA: MIT Press.

Johnson, C. (1987) "Political Institutions and Economic Performance: The Government-Business relationship in Japan, South Korea and Taiwan," in F. Deyo (ed.) *The Political Economy of the New Asian Industrialism*, Ithaca, NY: Cornell University Press.

Jolly, V. K. and Bechler, K. A. (1992) "Logitech: The Mouse that Roared," *Planning Review*, 20(6).

Kajiwara, H. (1993) "Taiwan's Electronics Industry: From an Import Substitution and Export Oriented Industry to a Highly Advanced Industry," in R. Inoue, H. Kohama and S. Urata (eds) *Industrial Policy in East Asia*, Tokyo: JETRO.

Kobayashi, S. (1995) "Current Situation of Taiwan's Economy and Future Issues," *Rim: Pacific Business and Industries*, 29(3):45–49, Tokyo: Sakura Institute of Research.

Kotler, P., Fahey L. and Jatvsripitak, S. (1985) *The New Competition. Meeting the Marketing Challenge from the Far East*, Englewood Cliffs, NJ: Prentice Hall International.

Lam, D. K. K. and Lee, I. (1992) "Guerrilla Capitalism and the Limits of Static Theory: Comparing the Chinese NICs," in C. Clark. and S. Chan (eds) *The Evolving Pacific Basin in the Global Political Economy. Domestic and International Linkages*, Boulder & London: Lynne Rienner Publishers.

Lee, C. J. (1995) "The Industrial Networks of Taiwanese SMEs," Manuscript, Taipei, Taiwan: Chung-Hua Institution for Economic Research.

Lee, H. L. and Billington, C. (1995) "The Evolution of Supply – Chain Management Models and Practice at Hewlett-Packard," *Interface*, 25(5).

Levy, D. (1995) "International Sourcing and Supply Chain Stability," *Journal of International Business Studies*, 26(2): 343–360.

Lim, L. and Pang E. F. (1991) *Foreign Direct Investment and Industrialisation in Malaysia, Singapore, Taiwan and Thailand*, Paris: OECD.

Liu, C. Y. (1993) "Government's Role in Developing a High-Tech Industry: the Case of Taiwan's Semiconductor Industry," *Technovation*, 13(5).

Liu, P. C., Liu, Y. C. and Wu, H. L. (1994) "Emergence of New Business Organization and Management in Taiwan," *Industry of Free China*, 82(5): 33–62.

Liu, J. Luo, T. and Weng, A. (1995) *Semiconductor Industry Update*, Taipei, Taiwan: Corporate Banking Group.

Lundvall, B.-Å. (1988) "Innovation as an Interactive Process: From User–Producer Interaction to the National System of Innovation," in G. Dosi, C. Freeman, R. Nelson, G. Sivberg and L. Socte (eds) *Technical Change and Economic Theory*, London: Pinter Publishers.

—— (ed.) (1992) *National Systems of Innovation: Towards a Theory of Innovation and Interactive Learning*, London: Pinter Publishers.

Malerba, F. and Orsenigo, L. (1996) "The Dynamics and Evolution of Industries," *Industrial and Corporate Change*, 5, 1.

Maskell, P. (1996a) "Learning in the Village Economy of Denmark. The Role of Institutions and Policy in Sustaining Competitiveness," *DRUID Working Paper 96–6*, Copenhagen Business School, Department of Industrial Economics and Strategy.

—— (1996b) "The Process and Consequences of Ubiquification," paper prepared for the DRUID workshop, January 1997, Copenhagen Business School, Department of Industrial Economics and Strategy.

Meaney, C. S. (1994) "State Policy and the Development of Taiwan's Semiconductor Industry," in J. Auerbach, D. Dollar and K. L. Sokoloff (eds) *The Role of the State in Taiwan's Development*, Armonk, New York: M. E. Sharpe.

Milgrom, P. and Roberts, J. (1992) *Economics, Organization and Management*, Englewood Cliffs: Prentice-Hall International.

Ministry of Economic Affairs (MOEA) (1991) *Small and Medium Enterprises White Paper*, Taipei.

Nelson, R. and Winter, S. G. (1982) *An Evolutionary Theory of Economic Change*, Cambridge MA: Bellknap Press.

Penrose, E. T. (1959) *The Theory of the Growth of the Firm*, Oxford: Oxford University Press.

Prahalad, C. K. and Hamel, G. (1990) "The Core Competence of the Corporation," *Harvard Business Review*, May–June (3): 79–93.

San G. (1990) "The Status and an Evaluation of the Electronics Industry in Taiwan," *OECD Technical Papers*, 29, Paris: OECD.

—— (1995) *Technology Support Institutions and Policy Priorities for Industrial Development in Taiwan, R.O.C.*, report prepared for the Ministry of Economic Affairs, Taipei, Taiwan: Chung-Hua Institution for Economic Research.

San, G. and Kuo, W. (1997) "Export Success and Technological Capability: Textiles and Electronics in Taiwan," in D. Ernst, T. Ganitasos and L. Mytelka (eds) *Technological Capabilities and Export Success – Lessons from East Asia*, London: Routledge.

Saxenian, A. L. (1990) "Regional Networks and the Resurgence of Silicon Valley," *California Management Review*, 33: 89–112.

Schive, C. (1990) "The Next Stage of Industrialization in Taiwan and South Korea," in G. Gereffi and D. Wyman (eds) *Manufacturing Miracles: Paths to Industrialisation in East Asia and Latin America*, Princeton: Princeton University Press.

—— (1993) "Industrial Policies in a Maturing Taiwan Economy," Taipei: Council for Economic Planning and Development.

Shieh, G. S. (1990) *Manufacturing "Bosses": Subcontracting Networks under Dependent Capitalism in Taiwan*, Dissertation, University of California at Berkeley, Department of Sociology.

Stopford, J. (1996) "Implications for National Governments," in J. Dunning (ed.) *Globalization, Governments and Competition*, Oxford: Oxford University Press.

Teece, D., Pisano, G. and Shuen, A. (1992) "Dynamic Capabilities and Strategic Management," *WP 90–8*, Consortium on Competitiveness and Cooperation, Berkeley.

Von Hippel, E. (1988) *The Sources of Innovation*, New York and Oxford: Oxford University Press.

Wade, R. (1990) *Governing the Market: Economic Theory and the Role of Government in East Asian Industrialization*, Princeton: Princeton University Press.

Walsh, V. (1987) "Technology, Competitiveness and the Special Problems of Small Countries," *STI Review*, 2, Paris: OECD.

Williamson, O. E. (1975) *Markets and Hierarchies: Analysis and Antitrust Implications*, New York: The Free Press.

—— (1985) *The Economic Institutions of Capitalism*, New York: The Free Press.

Wong, P. K. (1991) *Technological Development through Subcontracting Linkages*, Tokyo: Asia Productivity Organization (APO).

—— (1995) "Competing in the Global Electronics Industry: A Comparative Analysis of the Strategy of Taiwan and Singapore," paper presented at the international conference on "The Experience of Industrial Development in Taiwan," Taiwan: National Central University.

Zander, U. and Kogut, B. (1995) "Knowledge and the Speed of the Transfer and Imitation of Organizational Capabilities: An Empirical Test," *Organizational Science*, 6(1).

# 6 Technological capabilities and the Samsung Electronics network[1]

*Youngsoo Kim*

Korean electronics firms have been aggressively involved in learning and knowledge accumulation since the 1980s. Their consumer products, including color television sets (CTVs), video cassette recorders (VCRs), and microwave ovens (MWOs), were able to remain competitive in the low-end segment of world markets until the late 1980s, generating the cash flow needed to support development of more advanced technologies. In recent years, however, Korean products are meeting increased competition, particularly from Japanese producers, who have recovered their competitiveness by investing in low-cost offshore production.

Increased overseas production has been a major component of Korea's strategic response. Korean production networks in Asia now extend beyond the ASEAN region to China and India. The ratio of overseas production to total production has increased sharply in recent years, from 19 to 27 percent for CTVs and from 16 to 17 percent for VCRs during the period 1992–4. However, those of their Japanese electronics counterparts increased even faster, from 67 percent to 86 percent for CTVs and from 36 to 71 percent for VCRs during the same period (see Table 6.1), keeping competition intense in the cost-driven struggle for low-end markets.

Perhaps a better comparison would be with another of Asia's newly industrialized countries. The internationalization of Korean electronics production also appears to have lagged behind that of Taiwan. Outward foreign direct investment (FDI) by Korean electronics firms lagged behind their Taiwanese rivals. The cumulative FDI by the former amounted to US$0.85 billion (Electronic Industry Association of Korea 1993), whereas for the latter it was US$1.05 billion.[2]

In 1993, the three major Korean producers, Samsung, Goldstar, and Daewoo, announced their intention to increase their overseas production ratio (OPR) from an average of 20 percent in 1993 to 60 percent by 2000 (*KED*, 21 July 1993). This chapter will focus on the experience of Samsung, which has the highest OPR of the three.[3]

The chapter is arranged chronologically, focusing both on the forces driving Samsung to develop offshore networks and on the struggle to adapt the nature of its networks to its capabilities. Particular attention will be placed on the networks connecting its offshore affiliates in East Asia.

*Table 6.1* Overseas production ratio of the Korean and Japanese electronics industries

|         | 1991 | 1992 | 1993 | 1994   | 1995 |
|---------|------|------|------|--------|------|
| *CTV*   |      |      |      |        |      |
| Korea   | NA   | 19%  | 20%  | 27%    | 28%  |
| Japan   | 63%  | 67%  | 72%  | (86%)* | NA   |
| *VCR*   |      |      |      |        |      |
| Korea   | NA   | 16%  | NA   | 17%    | 20%  |
| Japan   | 29%  | 36%  | 48%  | (71%)† | NA   |

Note
Overseas production ratio in the table is the ratio of the unit quantity produced overseas divided by the total unit quantity produced overseas and in the home country.
*Sharp's overseas production ratio.
†Sanyo's overseas production ratio.

Sources: Electronics Industry Association of Japan (EIAJ), Tsuda and Shinada (1995), *Junja Shinmun* (28 February 1994), Electronics Industry Association of Korea (23 February 1995), *Hankuk-ilbo* (10 April 1995), *Jungang-ilbo* (24 February 1995).

The firms involved are all part of the Samsung Group, a highly diversified conglomerate. The core electronics producer is Samsung Electronics Company (SEC), and its affiliated firms are Samsung Electron-Devices Company (SED), Samsung Electro-Mechanics Company (SEM), and Samsung Corning Company (SC). The sources for this study are primarily internal Samsung publications, including monthly bulletins relating to international production, technological development, and organizational processes, as well as interviews that were conducted at Samsung in Seoul during November 1994. The organization of Samsung's international production networks (IPNs) in ASEAN were also reviewed during July 1995.

The first section examines the 1970s, after Samsung's entry into the electronics sector. The focus was on the development of mass production capability, and international linkages were used to acquire product designs and marketing outlets, allowing Samsung to concentrate its resources on the development of mass production capability. The second section looks at Samsung in the 1980s. The majority of the group's resources were channeled into the highly demanding production of advanced semiconductors. Although the effort was eventually successful, it appears to have retarded the development of design and marketing capabilities for its mass-production goods, leaving the group dependent on foreign sources of product design and distribution. The decade also saw the company's initial foray into international production to cope with trade pressure in its major markets, and explores how the group's internal organization was poorly adapted to the needs of overseas operation and to the task of organizational learning. The third section considers Samsung in the 1990s. Samsung has been pursuing a variety of strategies, including internal organizational reform, rapid expansion of offshore production, and aggressive acquisition of technology.

Table 6.2 provides an overview of the profile of the group in each decade. The fourth section examines Samsung's Asian production networks in detail. Initial investments were for consumer goods for both export and local markets. The networks were promptly integrated backwards and linked to the networks of other producers in the region. The final section provides a brief summary of the findings about Samsung's production networks, along with an analysis of the directions the firm must go if it is to remain competitive in a rapidly changing environment.

## Samsung in the 1970s: from textiles to televisions

Samsung was first incorporated in 1938 by Lee Byung-Chull, and its main business line was trade. The trading function has continued to be important, first with imports and later with exports, starting in the mid-1970s. Samsung had become one of Korea's top ten firms by 1950.

In the mid-1950s Samsung entered two manufacturing sectors: sugar in 1953 and textiles in 1956 (SED 1990). Domestic demand was huge, and Samsung could start production using imported equipment from Japan and Germany. It was not until 1969 that the firm entered the electronics industry, with the incorporation of SEC.

*Table 6.2* Samsung's technological capabilities and features of international production

| 1970s | 1980s | 1990s |
|---|---|---|
| *Key activities* | | |
| Conglomerate diversification | Entry into DRAM market | Organizational reform, internationalization |
| *Main sources of capabilities* | | |
| J/V partners, original equipment manufacturer (OEM) buyers and overseas training | OEM buyers, foreign licensing, reverse engineering | Acquisitions, strategic alliances, in-house R&D |
| *Level of technological capabilities* | | |
| Capabilities in mass production (TVs) | Broader product range (VCR, MWO, DRAM, components), but very weak in ability to introduce a major change of product | Continued weakness in product development |
| *International production and scope of interaction* | | |
| | US and EC for low-end markets (limited success) | International production of low-end items in peripheral regions |
| | Centralized intra-firm interaction | Moving toward decentralized intra- and inter-firm interaction |

Samsung's entry into the electronics industry had four important features that continued to characterize Samsung's electronics activities into the 1980s: an emphasis on mass production, reliance on foreign technology, a follow-the-leader strategy, and government support. First, its electronics business was significantly influenced by the two manufacturing activities of textiles and sugar. Both industries required a large scale of operation, and Samsung developed know-how through learning-by-doing for more than a decade before it entered the electronics industry. Secondly, its business started with imported foreign technology, having a close relationship with Japanese electronics firms. Having been educated in Japan, Lee Byung-Chull was able to establish informal contacts. Originally Samsung had considered cooperation with American firms, but it finally chose Sanyo and NEC as joint venture partners because of the language difficulties inherent in learning about the American technology (SEC 1989). Thirdly, Samsung entered the Korean electronics industry as a market follower. Another Korean firm, Goldstar Electrical, had started assembling vacuum tube radios for a US firm in 1959 and had built up export capabilities for ten years before Samsung entered the industry. Finally, Samsung enjoyed government support for its expansion into electronics. In 1968, the Korean government introduced the Electronics Industry Promotion Law, marking the beginning of official support for the industry.[4]

Samsung's initial strategy was nothing more (or less) than the mimicking of its Japanese rivals. Its aim was to become a vertically integrated electronics firm, "...from materials to components to end-products, including consumer and industrial electronics" (SEC 1989).[5] However, entry barriers were so strong that the government set a condition for Samsung that all products should be exported (SEC 1989).

Given its lack of previous experience in electronics, Samsung had no choice but to be simultaneously involved in learning a number of different technologies. To accomplish this, it turned to foreign sources of technology in management, production, and marketing. It created several joint venture companies with foreign technology suppliers such as NEC, Sanyo, Corning Glass Works, and other companies. It also reached numerous agreements to assemble electronics products for foreign original equipment manufacturer (OEM) buyers, who provided it with design and engineering support as well as with an international market. Investment in design and international marketing remained limited while Samsung concentrated on improving its production capability through such measures as the training of technicians in Japan.

A series of joint ventures allowed Samsung to rapidly achieve its goal of becoming a vertically integrated producer of television sets.

In December 1969, the recently established SEC established one joint venture firm, Samsung-Sanyo, with Sanyo (40 percent) and Sumitomo Trading (10 percent) and in January 1970 established another joint venture company, Samsung-NEC, with NEC (40 percent) and Sumitomo Trading (10 percent).

According to the two joint venture agreements, Samsung alone had local market sales rights, and Sanyo and NEC had the export rights. However, it was not until the mid-1970s that Samsung was allowed to distribute its products within the domestic market and reap higher profits as a result of domestic market protection. Samsung thus had to rely on foreign linkages from the very beginning of its electronics endeavors.

In March 1973, Samsung-Sanyo Parts, from which SEM originated, was set up. Its shareholders were Samsung-Sanyo, SEC, and Sanyo. This company was to produce parts for televisions, including tuners, deflection yokes, transformers, and condensers. In December 1973, Samsung formed another 50:50 joint venture company with Corning Glass Works of the United States in order to produce glass bulbs for the production of cathode ray tubes (CRTs). Foreign linkages thus permitted Samsung to achieve a high level of vertical integration in the production of televisions in a remarkably short time. Furthermore, apart from the first three years of the venture with Corning, all ventures were under Samsung's management control (SC 1994).

Its joint venture partners provided significant training to Samsung's employees. An early example is NEC. The first intake of sixty-three Samsung-NEC employees was sent to NEC in Japan, from September 1969 to February 1970, in order to master the skills of assembling technologically simple products. In 1970, about twenty employees went to Japan for training with vacuum tubes and black and white CRTs, which Samsung-NEC was successfully assembling by the end of the year (SEC 1989). In accordance with a technical assistance agreement, NEC technical experts came to Korea annually to train eighty Samsung-NEC technicians (SED 1990). Starting in 1977 when NEC licensed Samsung-NEC to produce color picture tubes, several groups of Samsung-NEC technicians were once again sent to Japan for one to four months' training. Foreign training has remained a feature of Samsung's partnerships in a variety of electronics fields, including Sanyo (radios and television sets), ITT (telecommunication switches), and Honeywell (semiconductors).

Although Sanyo divested its shares with Samsung, NEC and Corning Glass Works are still shareholders in SED (a CRT producer) and SC respectively.

SEC expanded and improved its assembling capability, producing nearly ten million black and white TV sets by the end of the 1970s, by which time Samsung was exporting a considerable volume of television sets to the United States, its only significant overseas market. On the strength of its mass-production capability and the Korean government's support for exports, SEC was able to seize a fairly high share of the US market (although far less than its Japanese counterparts), particularly in low-end products. SEC's exports were significantly concentrated on the US market – USA (77 percent), Canada (7 percent), Europe (3 percent), South America (3 percent) and others (10 percent).[6] The products exported were black and white TV sets (43 percent), color TV sets (44 percent) and audio products (9.6 percent).

Most sales were through OEM channels. OEM buyers provided Samsung with product design, quality control, and engineering support, leaving Samsung to increase its manufacturing capability through the intensive training of employees, particularly shop-level technicians.

Apart from the NEC and Sanyo channels, Samsung tried to get access to other international distributors.[7] As growing connections with international direct marketing channels increased its bargaining power, Samsung was able to ease the restrictions initially imposed by its joint venture partners. When the agreement with Sanyo was renewed in 1972, the original export marketing restriction, which had been unfavorable to Samsung, was terminated.[8]

In addition to assembled products, Samsung also engaged in the direct sale of components to other firms. As SEC's quantity of production increased, its demand for core components produced by its affiliated part suppliers such as SED, SEM, and SC increased accordingly.[9] However, SEC was not able to purchase all the components produced by the affiliates, who were obliged to find non-Samsung customers in Korea or Japan.[10]

Samsung expanded its OEM channels and capabilities by adding two new products – VCRs and microwave ovens. Samsung tried to get access to technology for the two products in the mid-1970s, but gaining foreign licensing was more difficult than for television sets. Therefore, Samsung had no choice but to get it through "reverse engineering" (SEC 1989: 248–250). In 1976, SEC formed a product development team that began to dismantle a Panasonic microwave oven. The project was successfully completed in 1978. In 1979, Samsung succeeded in developing its own VCR through reverse engineering. According to Jun and Han (1994: 317) Samsung still showed no improvement in creative development unless a similar sample or manual was available as the basis.

Samsung further diversified its business line into the telecommunications sector through a 1977 joint venture with General Telephone and Electronics (GTE) of the United States.[11]

But even as its product engineering and assembly capabilities improved, the Samsung group's development of market knowledge was stymied by its internal organization, further stunting the creation of original product designs. Samsung Corporation, the group affiliate involved in general overseas trading, distributed the electronics products manufactured by SEC through international branch offices (Cho 1983). According to an interview, SEC's expansion into foreign marketing had been blocked by Samsung Corporation, whose priority was the increase of export performance in order to meet the export-led industrialization policy. It was not until 1978 that SEC was actively engaged in overseas marketing through its own sales affiliate established in the United States.

Yet, intra-firm interaction between the US-based sales affiliate and the Korea-based production site was not effective. The affiliate belonged to the department handling export marketing, not to the production department. Once again, SEC was not able to recombine knowledge of the US market with that accumulated in Korea. In short, there was no organizational support for links between production and international marketing.

One cause may be the profit-center system that was introduced in 1975 to stem the losses incurred for the first five years of operation (SEC 1989).[12] Each affiliate operated independently in its own interests, and the same was true for each business division. Autonomy was limited by the central control of the chairman's secretariat.

The profitcenter system led to at least two negative effects. First, the strategic direction of each affiliate put much more importance on the short-term than on the mid- and long-term.[13] The system was reinforced by an employee evaluation system that focused on short-term performance which remained in place up to the early 1990s (Samsung 1993). Second, the system generated unproductive competition rather than cooperation between affiliated organizations within the group, and between organizations within a firm.

Despite the organizational difficulties it experienced, Samsung made considerable progress during its first decade in the electronics business. But the next decade would see Samsung's electronics operation reach new levels of sophistication.

## Samsung in the 1980s: technological upgrading

The 1980s saw Samsung expanding and diversifying. Table 6.3 shows how the company's revenues were expanded first by the addition of microwave ovens, then VCRs, and later by successive generations of memory chips. We will begin the review of this critical period in the firm's history with integrated circuits (ICs), which have become its primary focus, before returning to the history of its product divisions which are, in fact, the source of Samsung's IPNs in Asia.

### Integrated circuits

Samsung's vertical integration strategy was extended quite early to embrace semiconductor technology, which was to be SEC's key focus in the 1980s. In 1974, Samsung acquired Korea Semiconductor Company (KSC), a joint venture between Korea Engineering & Manufacturing Co. and Integrated Circuit International, a US firm that manufactured simple ICs ("chips") for electronic watches. This time, Samsung acted well ahead of its rival Goldstar, which entered the market by acquiring Daehan Semiconductors in 1979.

The firm hoped that internalization of core components technology would reduce its heavy dependence on Japanese suppliers (SEC 1989). SEC suffered from the outside purchase of core components because its production quantity of CTVs and VCRs was limited by component availability. In the late 1970s, Kim Kwang-Ho [chief executive officer (CEO) of the electronics division], who had worked for the TV production department, was transferred to the semiconductor sector. It seems that his primary mission was to develop core ICs such as the "chroma IC" that were then imported from Japan. The mission

*Table 6.3* Samsung Electronics Corporation: major export products in the 1980s (US$ millions)

|  | 1982 | 1983 | 1984 | 1985 | 1986 | 1987 | 1988 |
|---|---|---|---|---|---|---|---|
| CTVs | 88.2 | 151.7 | 196.7 | 141.9 | 221.6 | 353.8 | 408.9 |
| VCRs | – | – | 2.6 | 134.5 | 297.4 | 401.7 | 581.7 |
| MWOs | 59.8 | 95.2 | 149.5 | 127.4 | 238.8 | 308.4 | 367.1 |
| REFs | 12.5 | 10.8 | 16.0 | 24.0 | 34.4 | 53.6 | 89.8 |
| W/Ms | 0.7 | 1.0 | 1.4 | 2.5 | 5.6 | 13.4 | 18.1 |
| A/Cs | 0.2 | 2.3 | 2.5 | 1.6 | 1.9 | 12.4 | 14.6 |
| EPBXs | – | – | – | – | 0.4 | 0.5 | 1.6 |
| Keyphones | – | 0.8 | 0.2 | 5.2 | 13.2 | 62.0 | 48.4 |
| Fax | – | – | – | – | – | – | 2.2 |
| Computers | – | – | 0.02 | 0.8 | 7.9 | 22.5 | 69.5 |
| Watch chips | 8.1 | 7.7 | 12.8 | 13.1 | 27.5 | 21.1 | 21.9 |
| Linear ICs | 4.6 | 5.9 | 10.9 | 15.8 | 22.0 | 37.3 | 45.6 |
| Transistors | 1.2 | 1.2 | 7.6 | 13.7 | 17.8 | 38.8 | 50.0 |
| 64 kb DRAM | – | – | 5.5 | 12.4 | 33.2 | 21.7 | 76.9 |
| 256 kb DRAMs | – | – | – | 27.0 | 50.3 | 134.2 | 253.4 |
| 1 Mb DRAMs | – | – | – | – | – | 6.0 | 221.3 |

Note

MWOs, microwave ovens; REFs, refrigerators; W/Ms, washing machines; A/Cs, air conditioners; EPBXs, electronics private branch exchanges; Fax, facsimile machines.

Source: SEC (1989: 1032, 1036, 1053, 1057, 1067).

was accomplished in November 1981, followed by another important development – the motor drive IC – in 1982.

To successfully achieve its objective, Samsung once again tried to learn foreign technology through a broad range of formal and informal contacts. The acquired technology was internalized through learning-by-doing, backed by a large pool of resources. The decade-long effort to develop semiconductor capabilities may well have limited learning and knowledge accumulation in other areas.

In 1983 Samsung expanded beyond production for its internal needs and entered the merchant market for DRAMs, which require the most advanced manufacturing technologies and huge capital outlays. As for its initial entry to electronics, government support was a factor, with a semiconductor promotion law enacted in 1983. To the extent that the company was known to be naturally very cautious on entering new business ventures (Jun and Han 1994), the entry decision would not have been made without nearly a decade of successful chip manufacturing experience.

Samsung was able to shorten its learning process by a variety of interactions with foreign technology sources.

In June 1983, Samsung licensed a DRAM design from Micron Technology, a medium-sized American producer.[14] Samsung claims that it was the only source of DRAM design after contact with various firms including Texas Instruments (TI), Advanced MOS, Motorola, NEC, Toshiba, etc. For the process development of 64 kb DRAM, Samsung was fortunate to get access to Sharp, which was the only source of process technology such as 16 kb SRAM and 256 kb ROM technology. In November 1983, a 64 kb DRAM chip was developed at Samsung, and in mid-1984 mass production started.

Samsung placed great importance on informal learning and training in addition to the purchase of foreign technology. This provided Samsung with an opportunity to overcome problems whenever critical situations occurred. For instance, when, out of "309 individual manufacturing process steps, it succeeded in managing all the steps except eight key process steps," it overcame the obstacle by adding "three experts who had participated in the project of 64 kb DRAM in the United States and been trained at Micron Technology" [Samsung Semiconductor and Telecommunications Company (SST) 1987: 203]. Japanese technology advisers who had maintained a relationship with the ex-chairman, Lee Byung Chull, consulted the firm about semiconductor technology and market trends. Similarly, the current chairman Lee Kun Hee's informal networks with technology sources were significantly beneficial during the development of the 4 Mb DRAM.

But inter-personal networks were insufficient to develop capabilities in a demanding field where Korea was so far from the center of activity, necessitating the globalization of Samsung's technology development.

Soon after its entry in the DRAM market, Samsung set up a research institute – Samsung Semiconductor Inc. (SSI) – in Silicon Valley. SSI's first objective was to develop 64 kb and 256 kb DRAMs. The office began producing silicon wafers in 1985 with 300 engineers and was expanded in 1987 to study IC applications in computers, office and telecommunications equipment. That same year, SEC opened its Tokyo Design Centre for ICs.

SSI became an important platform for collecting information about up-to-date technology and markets as well as a training post for Korean engineers. Samsung was also able to recruit several Korean DRAM experts educated in the United States who would play an important role in helping Samsung to develop and commercialize DRAMs.

The company adopted a dual strategy for development of the 256 kb DRAM generation after extensive "reverse engineering" of Micron's design (Ernst 1994a: 81). Two teams, one in Silicon Valley and the other in Korea, simultaneously started the same work. In October 1984, the Korea-based team developed a 256 kb DRAM sample. In early 1985, the Silicon Valley team developed one, and this was the sample adopted for mass production (Ernst 1994a).[15]

The DRAM case provides one of the most important examples of Samsung's practice of creating new capability by quickly combining new knowledge and information from foreign sources with its accumulated current skill base. As it developed subsequent generations – 1 Mb DRAM (July 1986), 4 Mb DRAM (February 1988), 16 Mb DRAM (September 1990) – Samsung mastered the necessary capabilities bringing it ever closer to the frontier of innovation. In the early 1990s it became the world's largest producer of DRAMs, and was one of the first companies to ship engineering samples of the 64 Mb generation in 1995.

Foreign linkages have continued to be important. Samsung's development of the 64 Mb and 256 Mb generations was undertaken in close cooperation with NEC.

Samsung's progress in internalizing DRAM know-how improved its ability to develop ICs for its consumer electronics, industrial, and tele-communications products. By the late 1980s, SST was able to produce sixty-one kinds of telecommunications ICs, for use in phone sets, computers, private automatic branch exchanges (PABXs), and facsimile machines. Similarly, SEC could produce a total of thirty-seven kinds of ICs for use in its VCRs (*SMM* January 1987). As a result, it was freed from dependency on Japanese suppliers for these core components.

The mastery of IC technology meant not only the internalization of supply but also the development of new capabilities to be deployed in new and existing products. In 1988 SEC developed the 2-micron bipolar process, which combined with other breakthroughs leading to its development of VCR motor control ICs, which improved the quality of the picture and sound of its VCRs (*SMM* March 1989). Samsung developed voice synthesis ICs in 1989 for use in robots, automobiles, microwave ovens, refrigerators, washing machines, and electronic toys.

However, the success in DRAM came at a price. The combination of long-term investment commitments and cyclical demand from downstream users meant that DRAM prices were unreliable. A sustained price drop in the mid-1980s led to huge losses, reducing the cash flow to other group affiliates.[16]

### The OEM trap

Because of the drain on resources inflicted by the IC operation during much of the 1980s, other divisions and affiliates had few strategic options except that of exploiting the company's previously developed strength in production. Except for a short-term investments generating immediate cash, other investments were strictly controlled by the chairman's secretariat. Relatively little effort was spent on product development or strategic marketing, and Samsung's emphasis remained on the mass production of relatively low-end products. Another important characteristic of the group's operation in the 1980s was the internal production of core components. SED became one of the world's largest producers of CRTs. The strategy was extended to newer products such as VCRs and microwave ovens, for which Samsung produced most of its own magnetrons.

The development of product design capabilities was undermined by the company's major commitment to ICs. Of course, SEC had a minor change capability that required an ability for doing "reverse engineering," but was very weak in major change capability.[17] As a result, it continued to use foreign sources of technology even for its main export products, which were seen mainly as a means of generating cash to support the IC project.[18]

Nevertheless, Samsung slowly built an institutional infrastructure to increase its internal technological capability. Three directions were pursued. First, it acknowledged that the objective was to set up an integrated R&D organization, and then the company expanded Korea-based R&D centers involved in the assimilation and adaptation of acquired foreign technology.

The Samsung Advanced Institute of Technology (SAIT) was created to interlink several affiliates, but, at least initially, it was unable to transcend the demand for projects which were commercially exploitable in the short-term (Koh 1992). Second, Samsung established foreign-based R&D centers that could provide it with new technologies, up-to-date information, and training for Korean R&D personnel. These were used mainly for ICs and, starting in the late 1980s, for computer-related technologies.[19] The third form of effort was continued collaboration between SEC and its affiliated components suppliers.

The ability to use R&D to build new capabilities was constrained by accounting perspectives. Research projects were held to extremely short-term objectives, preventing the development of know-how beyond what was needed for simple adaptation to mass production requirements.

Table 6.4 shows a typical example of how the company evaluated the impact of R&D on sales and profits, placing a strong emphasis on immediate sales growth.

Another victim of Samsung's concentration on ICs may have been its international marketing capabilities, which remained weak. Samsung started distribution of its own brand products making minor changes from models it had built from designs provided by Japanese customers, but success was limited. SEC gradually established a network of foreign sales affiliates. It would typically set up a foreign branch office, and then the office turned into a sales subsidiary when it had accumulated a certain degree of foreign market knowledge. However, the hierarchically integrated organization structure restricted the interaction of its own foreign sales channels with Korea-based production sites, limiting feedback from customers to factories. Accordingly, OEM channels remained dominant in the company's sales. (Table 6.5).

Samsung maintained close relationships with OEM buyers such as JC Penney, Sears Roebuck, GTE, Toshiba, IBM, Hewlett-Packard, RCA, and Crown Corporation. However, its clients were generally not providing Samsung with leading-edge product design, and Samsung did little to upgrade its internal capabilities in this area, confining itself to low-end market segments.

In the early 1980s, the US market was by far the most important for Samsung, but by the end of the decade it had greatly increased the geographic diversity of its distribution channels, particularly in Europe and Southeast Asia (see Table 6.6).

*Table 6.4* Samsung Electronics Corporation: measures of R&D expenditure and its effect (1980–83) (million won)

|  | 1980 | 1981 | 1982 | 1983 |
|---|---|---|---|---|
| R&D expenditure (A) | 768 | 1,323 | 2,092 | 2,417 |
| Attributed sales increase | 2,099 | 36,137 | 22,028 | 133,406 |
| Profit (B) | 277 | 691 | 2,116 | 28,976 |
| Net profit (A – B) | –491 | –632 | 24 | 26,559 |
| Net profit (accumulated) | –491 | –1,123 | 1,099 | 25,460 |

Source: SEC (1989: 284).

*Table 6.5* Samsung Electronics Corporation exports (US$ millions)

|  | 1984 | 1985 | 1986 | 1987 | 1988 |
|---|---|---|---|---|---|
| OEM export (A) | 443 | 483 | 813 | 1,130 | 1,205 |
| Total export (B) | 669 | 743 | 1,146 | 1,727 | 1,840 |
| OEM ratio (A/B) | 66.2% | 65% | 70.9% | 65.4% | 65.5% |

Source: SEC (1989: 1037).

*Table 6.6* Samsung Electronics Corporation exports by region (%)

|  | 1982 | 1984 | 1986 | 1988 |
|---|---|---|---|---|
| North America | 62.1 | 75.6 | 62.4 | 35.5 |
| Europe | 7.1 | 6.5 | 19.1 | 26.0 |
| South America | 9.3 | 6.0 | 7.3 | 8.0 |
| Southeast Asia | 8.2 | 6.9 | 6.2 | 20.0 |
| Oceania | 2.2 | 1.6 | 1.6 | 1.5 |
| Middle East/ Africa | 11.1 | 3.4 | 3.4 | 8.6 |

Source: SEC (1989: 1036).

In the early 1980s, CTVs imported from Japan, Korea, and Taiwan became a controversial trade issue in the United States and Europe (Bellance 1987), and Korean firms faced antidumping duties on their CTV exports.[20] SEC had no alternatives but to protect existing export markets mostly in the United States and the European Community (EC).

In order to protect its access to the US market (Jun 1987), SEC set up an affiliate producing CTVs in the United States in 1984 (two years after its domestic rival, Goldstar, had made a similar move), transferring production capability accumulated at home.[21]

The experience proved unsuccessful and the firm started to divest from the United States in 1989 and shift to Mexico as part of a low-cost strategy. There were two main reasons for the retreat: the US production organization failed both to develop high-end products for the American market and to link with local components suppliers, continuing to rely on components from its Korean factories.

In general, the US affiliate failed to upgrade overall capabilities in strategic marketing. There was no effective interaction between the marketing and production departments. This case is totally different from that of its Japanese rivals who had superior technological capabilities; they succeeded in providing high-end products and linked well with local component suppliers.[22] In short, SEC's failure was because SEC was forced by trade issues to set up an international production platform in the US without the prior accumulation of capabilities in product design and development.

## Samsung in the 1990s: challenge and response

The 1990s have presented Samsung with a number of challenges requiring adaptive strategies. The key strategic shift is from "quantitative" to "qualitative" growth. This has been manifested in a series of organizational reforms and in new approaches to technology management. Another major thrust of recent years has been an increasingly aggressive globalization of production.

### Declining competitive advantage leads to organizational restructuring

In recent years, Samsung has had to cope with a very changed environment from the world it faced twenty years earlier as it entered the electronics business. On the one hand, its investments in semiconductors paid off handsomely. But on the other hand, its traditional cash-generating product lines – in which it has considerable sunk investments – began to face serious challenges in both foreign and domestic markets. In 1993 Samsung Chairman Lee Kun-Hee described the electronics business as suffering from cancer.

One aspect of this decline is a series of changes that have occurred in the markets which Samsung serves. First, Samsung's major export markets for consumer electronics in the United States and Europe have become saturated. The reduced growth in demand has severely increased price competition, and has increased the importance of smaller markets with specialized demand – turning Samsung's marketing weakness into a major problem (Ernst and O'Connor 1992). Second, Korea's domestic electronics market, which had long been protected from foreign competition, has been liberalized as Korea prepares to join the ranks of industrialized nations, eroding an important source of profits.

Liberalization of imports by the Korean government has led global players to enter the Korean domestic market, which had long been protected from foreign electronics products. In 1989, import quotas on consumer electronics goods were removed. From July 1991, foreign retail distribution outlets were allowed to possess up to ten stores with less than 1,000 square feet in size (Jun 1992) – far bigger than the 100–130 square feet that local Korean outlets usually occupied (*SEMM* April 1991). By 1993 there was a plan to cut the average tariff rate to below 10 percent for all imported electronics goods (Bloom 1992).

Samsung conducted an internal analysis of Taiwan's market liberalization (*SEMM* April 1991). It found that Taiwanese producers lost huge market shares when faced with competition from Japanese brand products. The market share of Japanese goods between 1986 and 1990 rose from 18.5 percent to 77.5 percent for CTVs, from 43.3 percent to 86 percent for VCRs, from 35.5 percent to 62.2 percent for refrigerators, from 48.7 percent to 72.1 percent for washing machines, and from 21.6 percent to 40.7 percent for air-conditioners.

In 1991, imported electronics goods accounted for 5 percent of the Korean market, but that figure was expected to increase to 15 percent (*SEMM* April 1991). This was a threat to Korean electronics firms, considering that Samsung, Goldstar and Daewoo were fighting to increase their market share by 1 or 2 percent per year. During the early 1990s, virtually every major producer has developed and begun to implement plans for penetrating the Korean market.

Meanwhile, international economic forces had further eroded Samsung's competitiveness. Generalized system of preferences (GSPs) privileges were withdrawn from Korean electronics goods by the United States and the EC in 1988 (EIAK 1989: 255). At the same time, the won had appreciated about 20 percent against the dollar, making exports from Korea less attractive to their major markets.

Such demand-side developments are particularly troublesome to a firm like Samsung, which followed a "market-pull" approach rather than the "technology-push" strategy of product innovators like Japan's Sony (Yu 1989). Samsung's low-end products were increasingly squeezed out of the market by more sophisticated goods that were nonetheless price competitive. Furthermore, the speed of technological obsolescence has accelerated, with shorter product cycles making it more difficult for a mass production-oriented firm like SEC to amortize its production set-ups.

A shift of resources from OEM to own-brand production made matters worse because, unbacked by adequate product development capabilities, it was doomed to failure. In the 1990s, the share of Samsung's sales attributable to own-brand merchandise has actually risen to about 60 percent, but this is due in large part to an absolute decrease in OEM business.

Samsung's leadership responded with two sets of initiatives. One change is increased internationalization, which will be considered in a separate section. The other initiatives involved organizational reform designed to overcome the lack of coordination and cooperation between different organizations within and across group member firms (Samsung 1993; Jun and Han 1994). Particular attention has been paid to the essential realm of technology management.

Starting in the early 1990s, SEC undertook a gradual organizational integration to increase coordination between production, marketing, and research both within and across product lines. In 1991, Samsung set up a strategic management section in SEC, which was in charge of planning, internationalization and strategic technology management (*SEMM*, August 1991). In December 1992, SEC's multiple product sectors were fully integrated under a single CEO, Kim Kwang Ho, previously head of semiconductor operations (*SMM* December 1992).[23] In January 1993, SEC restructured further by merging the audio and video business divisions (*SEMM* January 1993). In mid-1993 Samsung started to initiate more radical reform than it had done before.[24] In October 1994, Kim Kwang Ho was appointed as head of all electronics affiliates, including SEC, SED, SEM, and SC.

One of the key reasons for this consolidation was to improve the dissemination of knowledge throughout the group. An integrated technology management division was established in 1993 (*SEMM* January 1993).

During the 1990s, internal improvement in DRAM technology has generated technological spillover effects, so a number of core components were being developed and produced because of the advanced production capability.[25] Samsung says that the semiconductor sector created technological synergy for use among all of its related businesses. For instance, the development of DRAM process technology caused the level of Samsung's overall precision process technology to improve significantly (SST 1987).

Yet, until the early 1990s, SEC had done little to upgrade its capabilities in product design and development. This lapse became particularly dangerous as competition increased in its non-component product markets. Furthermore, product design capability was an important complement to the internationalization of production; as low value-added goods were increasingly produced offshore, new and better products were needed to avoid the hollowing out of production in Korea.

As competitive conditions changed in the electronics market, foreign licensing of important technologies and designs became more difficult. Samsung, flush from the achievement of profitability in its semiconductor business, began to acquire new capabilities through the outright acquisition of, or direct investment in, foreign firms.[26]

Table 6.7 shows that the acquisitions and strategic investments dating from the time when Samsung's boldest organizational reforms were being implemented covered a broad range of technology such as telecommunications, computers and semiconductors.

In addition to improving its competitiveness in consumer electronics, the investments reported in Table 6.7 make clear Samsung's desire to diversify further into the information technology sector. Samsung reports that in 1994 the structure of its sales was consumer electronics (38 percent), semiconductors (40 percent), and information systems (22 percent) (SEC 1995b). However, the share of information systems would be more or less 15 percent if a large proportion of components such as CRTs and computer

Table 6.7 Samsung Electronics Corporation: 2 years of investments (April 1993 to February 1995)

| Name of firm | Date | Scope and content |
|---|---|---|
| Array Microsystems (US) | April 1993 | SEC acquired 20% of Array and established cooperative arrangement in digital process chip technology used in multimedia products. |
| Harris Microwave Semiconductor (US) | May 1993 | HMS specializes in gallium arsenide chips and is one of the world's leading makers of optical semiconductors |
| LUX (Japan) | May 1994 | Acquisition (51%) of Japanese hi-fi audio maker:<br>LUX: development and sales<br>SEC: manufacturing and sales |
| Control Automation Inc. (US) | June 1994 | Acquisition (51%) of the CAD/CAM software technology company |
| ENTEL (Chile) | September 1994 | Investment (15.1%) in the largest operator of telecommunications systems |
| Integrated Telecom Technology (US) | December 1994 | Acquisition (100%) of ITT that specialized in ATM technology |
| Integral Peripherals (US) | January 1995 | Investment (4%) in shares of US-based firm specializing in HDD technology; joint development of HDD products |
| AST Research (US) | February 1995 | Investment (40.25%) in shares of US-based computer company; broad range of commercial relationships including supply and pricing of critical components, joint product development, cross-OEM arrangements and cross-licensing of patent |

Source: SEC 1995b.

monitors were excluded from it. Samsung's computer business had experienced only low growth despite a series of investments and alliances struck in the 1980s with leading US firms such as Hewlett-Packard, Micro-Five Corp. IBM, and Control Data. SEC's system design capability has lagged behind that of its Taiwanese rivals, and SEC's OEM ratio for computer products was much higher than that of Taiwanese firms.[27] Its position in computer systems outside of Korea was particularly weak.

The recent major investment in AST Research provides Samsung an alternative means of overcoming its internal weakness in the computer business.[28] The agreement enables Samsung to share the AST brand name and to sell memory chips to AST. SEC is actually not entitled to be directly engaged in AST's management for the first four years of acquisition (*Junja Shinmun* 9 March 1995).

However, Samsung's acquisition of foreign firms (except perhaps LUX and Control Automation Inc.) was not aimed at ameliorating Samsung's internal weakness in product design and development, but at acquiring frontier technologies seen as essential to the production of next generation products.

### Internationalization of production

Although Samsung's organizational strategy for the 1990s revolves around consolidation, the strategy for its physical production facilities involves increasing movement offshore (Samsung 1993: 145).

Samsung's earliest overseas production efforts were a Portuguese joint venture operation started in 1982, a US subsidiary established in 1984, and a subsidiary set up in Mexico in 1988. They had competencies in the production of CTV sets and many core components. By the end of 1988 it also had twelve sales subsidiaries outside Korea.

After unsatisfactory results with US production, Samsung focused more intensely on establishing low-cost manufacturing plants in Mexico, peripheral Europe, and Southeast Asia. Several factors stimulated this move. We have already discussed above the various factors eroding Samsung's competitiveness, including market saturation, loss of preferential tariff status, and appreciation of the won. But an important motivation may have come from the strategies of its rivals.

Moves by Japanese and other Korean electronics firms seem to have induced Samsung to adopt a "follow-the-leader" strategy.[29] In the mid-1980s, Japanese companies such as Matsushita, Toshiba, Sony, and Sanyo started to move into Southeast Asia to establish production subsidiaries. For instance, Matsushita's foreign investment projects in Southeast Asia and China numbered five in 1987, four in 1988, three in 1990, four in 1991, three in 1992, and eight in 1993 (Itoh and Shibata 1994).

The consumer electronics goods produced by Japanese overseas affiliates started to penetrate into the low-end global market where Korean firms had predominated (although not under their own names) until the late 1980s. Here was a strong challenge for Samsung. The Japanese brand products made in the ASEAN region were cheaper than the products made in Korea. In the case of microwave ovens, the cost of the Sanyo product, manufactured in Southeast Asia for the OEM market, was 13 percent cheaper than that made in Korea.

The same is true for the components. Matsushita started to produce CRTs and tuners in Southeast Asia, and expanded into China (*Nihon Keizai Shimbun* 21 April 1992). Sony built a color CRT plant in Singapore (*Nihon Keizai Shimbun* 27 November 1989). Toshiba, Matsushita, and Hitachi also established CRT production in the United States. Similarly, Asahi Glass and Nippon Electric Glass (NEG) set up overseas operations.

Strategies based on international production were also adopted by Samsung's Korean rivals. In 1988, Goldstar signed a contract with the Chinese government to acquire 165,000 square meters of land in the Zhuhai Economic Zone for the construction of a manufacturing plant to produce CTV sets and audio equipment to be sold on the Chinese market (*NNB* 20 May 1988). Around the same time, Goldstar moved into Thailand with Samsung right behind.

Finally, it should not be overlooked that Samsung's recent thrust into offshore production was enabled by its successful accumulation of technological capabilities which could now be transferred. Nearly all of Samsung's foreign affiliates are engaged in the production of standardized products, utilizing mass production capability transferred from Korea. It has been able to build on its initial forays into foreign production. Recently SEC transferred Park Byung Moon, who had been a head of an Indonesian affiliate for a couple of years, to India, where it is setting up a new CTV plant.

Samsung's highly centralized structure has limited the transfer of technological capabilities to overseas affiliates, even as they face new competitive requirements. Samsung's affiliates have been forced to interact with a growing variety of economic actors, including those within the group. Hence, each organization in the network requires greater autonomy to avoid bureaucratic paralysis in the network as a whole. In early 1995, shortly after a wave of administrative consolidation had swept over its Korea-based operations, Samsung extended the concept to its offshore production networks by designating five regional headquarters around the world.[30] Of the five, two were in Asia. Their locations – Singapore and Beijing – reflected the relative separateness of the two offshore production networks that had been created by Samsung in the region.

In particular, SEC's in-house R&D operations have continued to be highly centralized. The hierarchical integration has failed to provide researchers and engineers with satisfactory R&D circumstances. According to company surveys (reported in Koh 1992: 36), Samsung engineers complained most about an unsatisfactory R&D working environment (54 percent), being overloaded with projects (30 percent), insufficient time for the feasibility study of future projects (27 percent), and being overwhelmed with documentation and paperwork requirements (26 percent).

Many of the organizational problems that hindered the development of effective product innovation in the past continue to plague SEC. Koh (1992: 36–7) reported that production departments are seldom involved in the early stages of new projects, that projects were chosen by the corporation on the basis of their expected short-term impact on individual strategic business units, that projects reflecting a longer term outlook were likely to be suppressed by marketers or by the strategic business units themselves, and that communication was poor among marketing and engineering departments and the company's R&D center.

Perhaps to decentralize some of its innovatory activities away from this inauspicious environment, SEC went overseas, establishing foreign design centers in order to upgrade its product development capability. The centers have been established in each of Samsung's main market regions to help develop products better suited to local needs, following a pattern already well-established by its Japanese rivals.[31]

The first such center was established in the consumer electronics bastion of Osaka in 1991 with five employees for audio and video products. The following year, a center was set up in Frankfurt, Germany, for the development of products to be distributed in Europe. In 1994 SEC set up Samsung Design America in the United States for consumer electronic products for the US market in cooperation with a local design corporation, IDEO (US). In early 1995, SEC established a product planning post in Southeast Asia for the development of regionally marketable product models. Its activity has currently been limited to collection of market information with only three Korean personnel.

Table 6.8 shows evidence suggesting that Samsung's regional focus began to pay off rapidly in its European market.

SEC's market development activities were confined to the United States and Europe. It is not surprising that recognition of the Samsung brand name in Asia is relatively weak.

*Table 6.8* Local market share of Samsung brand products

| Product | Country | 1991–2 (%) | 1993 (%) |
|---|---|---|---|
| Microwave ovens | Spain | 4.5 | 11.1 |
| Microwave ovens | Netherlands | 16.0 | 24.2 |
| Facsimile machines | UK | 15.0 | 21.0 |
| VCRs | Spain | 10.7 | 16.6 |
| Cordless phones | Sweden | 20.0 | 23.0 |

Source: The author's interviews with SEC in Korea during November 1994.

## Samsung's production networks in Asia

### Overview

Asia has been an important destination for Samsung's direct investment for a number of reasons. In addition to the company's interest in recovering cost competitiveness by utilizing the low-cost resources available in Southeast Asia, it was also pursuing some of the major customers for its components as well as some of the world's most dynamic markets.

Table 6.9 shows how Samsung's network in Asia spread rapidly since 1989, when it opened a TV assembly plant in Thailand for low-end products. Samsung's production in Asia ranges from end-products to components, and has spread from ASEAN to China, Vietnam, and India. Currently, the regional network has two central nodes located in Singapore and Beijing.

A Singapore based purchasing office was established in 1991 to speed up the internationalization of production, in part by being a supplier of low-cost parts for Korea-based production sites. Ironically, the purchasing office has directly bought components from Korea-based components suppliers because it is cheaper than going through SEC headquarters in Korea. The office has grown dramatically since its creation and was eventually able to satisfy Singapore's requirements for the preferential tax treatment granted to regional headquarters.

The vertically integrated operations in China were set up more quickly than those in Southeast Asia, possibly reflecting the firm's increased confidence in overseas production. Since 1994, Samsung has announced the creation of other integrated production complexes in its strategic markets.[32]

To date, interaction between Samsung's two Asian subnetworks has been mostly limited to CRTs sent from Malaysia to a China CTV affiliate and Chinese-made VCR components sent to a Thai affiliate. This is because the two subnetworks were originally designed to serve two largely separate Asian markets. The key intermediary is the Singapore-based purchasing office, which purchases and distributes a huge amount of components among the Samsung affiliates and those of their Japanese counterparts in the regions.[33] However, the most important intra-firm transactions are still highly centralized, occurring between the affiliates and the Korea-based product division, or between the affiliates and the Korea-based global marketing division (in charge of export arrangements).

The separateness of the two subnetworks may prove a competitive disadvantage. Japanese producers in the region usually divide their product mix geographically according to the subsidiary's technological capability, facilitating the achievement of scale economies. By comparison, Samsung's production networks in Asia are still at a primitive stage, incorporating certain redundancies.

The weakness of Samsung's performance in the consumer goods sector meant that it found itself with excess capacity in its overseas plants. In practice, this has meant that the offshore plants are underutilized – in spite

Table 6.9 Evolution of Samsung's international production networks in Asia

| | 1989 | 1990 | 1991 | 1992 | 1993 | 1994 | 1995 |
|---|---|---|---|---|---|---|---|
| Thailand | CTV | | | | VCR tuner<br>FBT<br>DY (SEM) | | W/M<br>sales |
| Indonesia | | REF | VCR, Audio | | | | CTV, sales |
| Malaysia | | | MWO<br>CRT (SED) | | CRT glass (SC) | | Monitors |
| Singapore | | | IPO | | | | RHQ |
| China | | | | Audio products<br>Audio<br>components<br>Keyboards (SEM)<br>VCR transformers<br>(SC) | VCR<br>VCR<br>components | Tuners<br>VCR heads,<br>motors (SEM) | CTV |
| Vietnam | | | | | | | CTV |
| India | | | | | | | CTV |

Note
REF, refrigerator; W/M, washing machine; FBT, flyback transformer; DY, deflection yoke; CRT, cathode ray tube; CPT, color picture tube; MWO, microwave oven; IPO, international procurement office; RHQ, regional headquarters. All affiliates established by SEC except as indicated.

Source: The author's interview and Samsung internal publications (various years).

of their vocation to improve cost-competitiveness – because Samsung's employee evaluation system is oriented to performance at the plant level, making employees resistant to transferring production overseas when no activity would fill the void at the Korean plant.

This has been much less of a concern in the case of plants producing components, which have been able to sell the majority of their output to other firms operating in the region, particularly Japanese affiliates. Samsung's Asian networks have thus been able to build on the company's past history of OEM relationships with Japanese companies. For example, two component-producing subsidiaries – SEM-Thailand and SED-Malaysia – supply more than 80 percent of their output to Japanese companies.

In fact, Samsung's Asian television production network has been deeply enmeshed virtually from its inception with those established earlier by Japanese firms. For example, not only does the CRT producer SED-Malaysia sell the bulk of its output to nearby Japanese affiliates of Sanyo, Matsushita, Sharp, and Funai, it also sources about a third of its total components from mostly Japanese suppliers such as NEG and Asahi.[34] Clearly, the establishment of offshore production has led to complex interdependence between Samsung and its Japanese competitors.

It was the presence of its Japanese customers that permitted Samsung to reduce the risk inherent in starting capital-intensive production overseas. For example, having already become a successful supplier of CRTs to Japanese CTV producers, SED could be reasonably certain that its Malaysian affiliate could meet demanding Japanese quality assurance requirements (*SEM* 1990: 238). SED-Malaysia fills a specific role in the regional division of labor of Japanese firms; by providing 14-inch CRTs, it permits the component subsidiaries of Japanese producers to specialize in larger, more higher value-added picture tubes.

Samsung's production presence in Asia is increasingly connected to marketing objectives. To that end, the firm has established ties with mainland and overseas Chinese partners, typically as a prerequisite for market entry, in addition to establishing its own distribution channels. Its local joint ventures are thus the mirror of those it established in Korea in the 1970s with Japanese partners, trading production know-how for market access – only now the know-how is Samsung's.

In at least one case, an affiliate established for the local market (in Indonesia) was forced by poor performance to shift to exports. But more generally sales were able to shift from export to local markets.

So far these locally oriented operations have achieved local and even regional linkage between production and marketing activities, but design and product development activities still belong to organizations in Korea: "…we continue to move Korea-based manufacturing sites overseas. Instead, leave the concept of design, development, research institutes at home" (Samsung 1993: 145). But this has left a void in affiliates for which the local market is important. For instance, the Indonesian affiliate distributing CTVs to the local market is searching for locally marketable products that differ from the products designed in Korea for global markets.

In early 1995 SEC formed a new product planning post at its Singapore-based regional headquarters. The team was to concentrate on supporting product design and development activities targeted to the Asian regional market. Yet, there is no sign that this team has actively interacted with the group affiliates (or with non-affiliated organizations). Yet SEC is under pressure to carry out product design closer to individual markets as Japanese and European rivals have increasingly done, frequently co-locating product design with offshore production. Recently, a new executive officer who had worked for the department in charge of product development has been assigned to the Indonesian refrigerator affiliate, signaling a possible decentralization of product development within the region.

The component producing affiliates are also experiencing product design difficulties. They currently lack the capability to implement minor changes requested by non-affiliated customers in the region and are forced to forward all requests back to Korea. Samsung is thus unable to compete effectively with numerous other rivals that have already decentralized such capabilities. Thus one of Samsung's continuing challenges is to make the leap from mass to flexible production.

But even as they try to exploit local markets, Samsung's Asian affiliates are part of a global production network, supplying a considerable number of components to Samsung affiliates in Europe and America. Examples include SEM-Thailand which has supplied parts to SEC in Europe, Brazil, and Korea; SED has exported 14-inch CRTs to Mexico; SEC-Indonesia has assembled PCBs for a Portugal based VCR plant; and SED-Malaysia has been supplying electron-guns for CRTs to SED-Germany and SED-Mexico.

Much as its Japanese partners did in the 1970s, Samsung has trained the employees in its Asian affiliates, often by sending them to Korea, or by sending Korean trainers to the affiliate. The Korea-based plants play a central role in Samsung's regional technology network. This differs from the practice of Samsung's Japanese rivals in the region, whose training sites are increasingly offshore.

In 1990 forty technicians from the recently established refrigerator plant in Indonesia were sent to a Korean factory for three months. One-third of the workers at Samsung's mivrowave oven plant in Malaysia were also trained in Korea, and Korean technical instructors also trained local workers (*SEMM* January 1993). A major glass bulb factory in Malaysia sent local technicians to Korea for training both before and after operations started (SC 1994: 315). The heads of production lines at a components plant in Thailand received more than three months' training in Korea, and fifteen Korean technical instructors were dispatched to train local employees (*SMM* September 1989).

Little is known about the level of local linkages of Samsung's affiliates. One Indonesian affiliate reported local content ratios of 15 percent for audio components and only 5 percent for VCRs in 1992, its first year of production. At the Thailand CTV affiliate, the initial level of local content was about 10 percent. Within several years, the ratio of components sourced from local and nearby regional suppliers had risen above 50 percent. It was also reported that three Korean components suppliers moved to Malaysia to supply Samsung's microwave oven plant, showing that local content does not necessarily mean linkages to locally owned firms. The Malaysian CRT plant is also anticipating the arrival of Korean suppliers. Dongguan Samsung Electro-Mechanics, a producer of audio components and computer keyboards in China, procures 80 percent of its materials from Korea versus 19 percent in China.

### Southeast Asia

Samsung's operations in Southeast Asia started out somewhat tentatively, primarily focusing on assembling final goods for exports. As the company developed its capabilities to set up offshore production, it added output in core components requiring a larger initial commitment of resources. The experience of its network creation in Southeast Asia undoubtedly simplified the subsequent creation of other intra-group networks in China and in Europe.

Thailand was the starting point for Samsung's entry into Southeast Asia. In 1987 SEC set up a branch office in Bangkok. In 1988 it established a joint venture company – Thai Samsung Electronics (TSE) – with Saha Pathana Interholding, one of the three biggest business groups in Thailand (*SMM* March 1989). SEC had a 51 percent share, and Saha Pathana 49 percent. SEC provided the management, technology, machinery, and brand name, whereas Saha Pathana provided the land and local manpower, as well as knowledge of the local market. TSE started producing CTVs in 1989, with production rising steadily 500,000 per year in 1994 (*SEMM*, June 1994). VCRs were added in 1993, and washing machines two years later. TSE intended to distribute half of its output to the local market, and the rest to the United States and the EC through SEC's marketing channels (SEC 1989: 626). The goal of 50 percent local sales had not quite been achieved by 1994, but the level has gradually increased.

Soon after setting up production in Thailand, Samsung established a 50:50 joint venture in Indonesia for refrigerator production with Maspion, a local distributor of consumer electronics products. Once again Samsung provided equipment, know-how, and a brand name, and Maspion provided a plant, labor, and land (*SMM* March 1989). Originally the project was designed with the expectation that local market would absorb much of the output. Despite a capacity of 60,000 units per year, production reached only 11,000 units in the first year, 1990, and 20,000 in 1991. In 1992, the affiliate, Samsung Maspion Indonesia, changed its strategy and targeted regional and global markets, supported by its own overseas sales network. This strategy was successful and the affiliate has made a profit since July 1992.

In 1991, the pace of investment picked up. A second affiliate in Indonesia was established to produce VCRs and CD players for export.[35] Samsung controls 80 percent of PT Samsung Metrodata Electronics. The minority partner is Metrodata Indonesia, which had previously been the sole distributor of Samsung products such as monitors and office equipment. Production started in August 1992. The audio output was exported mostly to Europe and elsewhere in Asia. Video products were exported worldwide, but in Europe a previously established VCR affiliate in Spain foreclosed much of that market. Most of the production was sold under the Samsung brand name, but it also undertook OEM sales with GE, Akai, and other companies. In early 1995 the affiliate started to manufacture CTVs for the local market.

1991 was also the year that Samsung began production in Malaysia. One investment was an export-oriented plant producing microwave ovens, Samsung Electronics Malaysia, a wholly owned subsidiary. All its products are exported to the United States, Australia, and Europe through Samsung's international marketing subsidiaries. Very recently, the affiliate was busy preparing to produce microwave ovens to be sold on the local market.

Also established in Malaysia Samsung Electron Devices (Malaysia), its first backward integration in the region, and its first offshore production of CRTs anywhere in the world. By 1989, SED was exporting more than 60 percent of its CRT production, mostly to Japan, Southeast Asia, Hong Kong and China (SED 1990: 490). SED Malaysia, a wholly owned subsidiary was set up with an annual capacity of 1.7 million units, which has since been doubled, along with increases in the plant's automation level. Given the strong level of demand in the region, it is not surprising that the operation achieved profitability after only six months of operation. Less than 20 percent of its output went to Samsung's Thai television affiliate, with the rest being sold to nearby affiliates of Sanyo, Funai, PTI, Thomson, and other companies.[36] By this time, clearly, Samsung had mastered the organizational skills needed to move production offshore.

This success undoubtedly helped Samsung decide to undertake a second round of backward integration in the region (SC 1994: 565). In 1992, Samsung received approval from its US partner Corning Glass Works to establish a glass bulb plant in Malaysia near the CRT affiliate. Once again, this was Samsung's first offshore production for this product. Initially, it had sought to reduce the risk by setting up a joint venture with Asahi Glass, a major Japanese producer. But when Asahi decided not to go ahead with the project, SC proceeded on its own, investing $25 million (SC 1994). Starting in 1993, Samsung Corning (Malaysia) assembled panels and funnels imported from SC-Korea, with an annual capacity of 2.5 million units. SC-Malaysia has diversified its product lines from 14-inch glass bulbs to 20 and 21-inch glass bulbs. It also plans to increase its vertical integration by building a glass fusion plant (SC 1994: 316). SC-Malaysia is also expected to produce bulbs for plants established by the other major Korean CRT producers, Orion and Goldstar, in Indonesia, China, and Vietnam (SC 1994: 561).[37] SC-Malaysia planned to expand its production capacity to 3.6 million units by 1995, investing an additional US$200 million (*SEMM* August 1992).

Another component operation was started in 1993, this one in Thailand. SEM-Thailand, a wholly owned subsidiary of SEM was actually announced in late 1990, but did not begin operations until 1993 because it had to be sure of market demand (Jun and Kang 1994). It produces a variety of components, such as deflection yokes and flyback transformers for CTVs, and oil condensors for microwave ovens, plus other parts for audio-visual equipment (*SMM* September 1989). Its production capacity in 1993 was 1.4 million tuners, 2.4 million deflection yokes and 3.9 million flyback transformers (EIAK 1993). Only about 10 percent of its output went to Samsung's local CTV affiliate, with the rest being distributed to unaffiliated companies in the region, particularly Japanese manufacturers such as NEC, Toshiba, and Sharp, along with small supplies to Samsung's Malaysia-based microwave oven plant and its Indonesian affiliate, Samsung Metrodata.

Table 6.10 summarizes Samsung's investments in Southeast Asia.

## China

Samsung's network in China is actually divided into two relatively separate pieces, one of which is located at Tianjin, and the other in Guangdong Province. A new electronics complex has recently been announced for the Singapore-sponsored Suzhou Township, located about halfway between Samsung's southern and northern China plants.

In the early 1990s, Samsung selected Tianjin, which is close to Korea, as a strategic FDI location. SEC rapidly set up integrated operations to build first VCRs then CTVs. Samsung Aerospace Industries joined in this location to produce cameras for the local Chinese market.

Tianjin Samsung Electronics (TSEC) was SEC's fourth offshore VCR plant,

*Table 6.10* Samsung's affiliates in Southeast Asia by country

| Country | Affiliate name | Products (establishment date) |
| --- | --- | --- |
| Thailand | Thai Samsung Electronics | CTVs, VCRs and washing machines (1988) |
| | SEM-Thailand | CTV and VCR components (1990) |
| Indonesia | Samsung Maspion Indonesia | Refrigerators (1989) |
| | Samsung Metrodata Electronics | VCRs and audio products (1991) |
| Malaysia | Samsung Electron Devices (Malaysia) | CRTs (1991) |
| | Samsung Electronics Malaysia | Microwave ovens (1991) |
| | Samsung Corning (Malaysia) | CRT glass bulbs (1992) |

and its second in Asia. It was established in early 1993 as a 50:50 joint venture with a state-run electronics firm. A total of US$64 million was invested in the vertically integrated project, which produces VCRs, VCR decks, and VCR drums. In 1995 it produced 400,000 VCR sets. Half of its products are being sold locally, and the remainder are going to Australia and the former Soviet Union.

Just prior to the VCR affiliate, Samsung Corning set up a plant to produce rotary transformers for VCRs, a product it had made in Korea since the late 1980s (SC 1994). In late 1992, after the approval of Samsung-Corning's US partner, SC-Tianjin started to produce rotary transformers with a capacity of 800,000 units, which was rapidly expanded in the following months. From 1993, it added more sophisticated products such as four-channel rotary transformers, in addition to the two channel type (SC 1994). SC-Tianjin planned to expand to a capacity of 5 million units per year by 1995 (SC 1994: 561).

In December 1993, SEM established Tianjin Samsung Electro-Mechanics, an 80:20 joint venture with one of the state-run electronics corporations, to manufacture a variety of components that could be used in the VCRs produced nearby and in the CTVs that were soon to be produced. The total investment required was US$60 million. Production started in May 1994 with the following capacities: 3.6 million TV and VCR tuners; 2.4 million VCR heads; 3.6 million precision motors; 600,000 computer spindle motors (*SEM* January 1994). This is of course much more than can be absorbed by Samsung's local affiliates.

In 1994, SEC formed Tianjin Tongguang Samsung Electronics, a 50:50 joint venture with the same partner as the VCR plant, to produce color TV sets. SEC invested US$30 million for a production capacity of 1 million sets. It is the largest of Samsung's overseas CTV plants, and recent annual output was 800,000 units, absorbing about one-third the tuner capacity of the nearby components plant.

Samsung Aerospace Industries appears to have made an unrelated opportunistic investment by setting up a 50:50 joint venture to produce cameras with a large local camera manufacturer, Tianjin Camera. The total investment was a relatively small US$10 million. The target markets are China, Hong Kong, Thailand, and Singapore. Its future expansion will be mostly dependent on the marketing efforts of the Chinese partner.

In southern China, Samsung established a smaller network for audio products. First came components, with Dongguan Samsung Electro-Mechanics, a wholly owned subsidiary in Guangdong Province. It was technically the first offshore plant of Samsung's SEM branch, having been established in mid-1990, at the same time as several other Korean companies invested there, but production did not begin until 1992. An expansion in 1994 raised production capacity: from 400,000 audio decks to 800,000; from 1.8 million audio speakers to 4 million; and from 100,000 computer keyboards to 300,000. Most of the output is shipped to Southeast Asia, China, America, and Korea (EIAK 1993).

Starting in late 1992, SEM's Dongguan affiliate began supplying audio components to Huizhou Samsung Electronics, another Guangdong affiliate. SEC owns 90 percent of the shares in this company, and its Chinese and Hong Kong partners hold 5 percent each. In November 1992, Huizhou SEC started production of audio products. Its capacity in 1994 was 540,000 units, and 15 percent of its production is sold on the local market.

Samsung is also involved in the Chinese telecommunications market. Samsung Sandong Telecommunications was set up in 1994 to assemble time division exchange (TDX) central office switches for local use, which had been developed by Samsung in cooperation with the Korean government. The joint venture with two local partners, one of which is a state-run tele-communications corporation in Sandong, represents an investment of US$20 million. It is currently producing 370,000 TDX switches.

In 1994, Samsung announced a $100 million dollar investment plan for Suzhou Township. The initial plants would be devoted to household appliances and the assembly of transistors and linear ICs for use in consumer electronics. SEM said that it would manufacture oil condensers and air-conditioning motors there as well.

Table 6.11 summarizes Samsung's investments in China.

## Summary and conclusion

This case study of Samsung reveals a dynamic interaction between firm capabilities and IPNs. In the early stage, when Samsung was building capabilities, foreign linkages were needed for technology and marketing. As

*Table 6.11* Samsung's affiliates in China by region

| Region | Affiliate name | Products (establishment date) |
| --- | --- | --- |
| Tianjin | Samsung Corning Tianjin | Rotary transformers (1992) |
| | Tianjin Samsung Electronics | VCRs, VCR decks and VCR drums (1993) |
| | Tianjin Samsung Electro-Mechanics | VCR drum motors, tuners (1993) |
| | Samsung Aerospace Industries | Cameras (1994) |
| | Tianjin Tongguang Samsung Electronics | CTVs (1995) |
| Guangdong | Dongguan Samsung Electro-Mechanics | Speakers, keyboards, etc. (1990) |
| | Huizhou Samsung Electronics | Audio products (1992) |
| Suzhou | Suzhou Samsung Electronics | Refrigerators, microwave ovens, washing machines and air-conditioners (1994) |

the group's capabilities grew, it ventured into international production. However, its capabilities in mass production were inadequate for ensuring the success of its initial efforts to bypass trade barriers in its major markets by building offshore production bases there. It was only following a reorientation of its international production to low-cost operation in peripheral areas that it was able to correctly match its current capabilities with its network structure. Meanwhile, it has reoriented the nature of its non-production linkages with foreign firms to help foster the development of the design and marketing capabilities it has lacked in the past, frequently through acquisition.

Internally, the Samsung Group's electronics activities have suffered from an almost complete de-linkage between production (in Asia), marketing (in the United States and in the EC), and design and development (in Korea) since the 1970s. This chapter tends to confirm the argument by Kogut and Zander (1993: 635) that the key to successful international production is "...to recombine the knowledge acquired at home with the gradual accumulation of learning in the foreign market." Thus Samsung's affiliates in Southeast Asia were gradually able to increase the percentage of output sold in the local market, relying at first mostly on exports. Yet the continued centralization of product development has slowed the learning process in offshore affiliates.

Given the weakness of product development in the Korean electronics sector, it is possible that centralization is necessary during the period in which major innovation capabilities are acquired. But we have already seen that this leaves offshore production centers vulnerable as they try to penetrate local markets in competition with rivals who use minor change capability to tailor products for local customers.

The different technology management pattern established by Samsung's Japanese rivals seems to be relevant. The major Japanese consumer electronics firms have decentralized minor product change capabilities at many of their production affiliates in Southeast Asia, increasing the flexibility of their production networks and freeing up engineering resources in Japan for more valuable work.

Samsung's IPNs are also different from those of Taiwanese firms. While Samsung tends to focus on economies of scale, largely in consumer electronics products manufactured in a vertically integrated system, Taiwanese firms focus on economies of networking in the region that permit a large degree of flexibility for adapting to the rapidly changing information technology market. Thus, we can note in passing that this research supports the idea that IPNs have developed in divergent, rather than convergent ways.[38]

Korean industrial policies have been important for facilitating, and even inciting, the firms' international competitiveness by requiring foreign firms to transfer technology in exchange for market access, supporting exports, protecting the home market, and supporting research. However, policy errors have also occurred. The first was nearsightedness in creating a top-heavy industrial structure mimicking that of Japan but without that economy's underlying dynamic of continuous upgrading of product design. The second involved the creation of a Korean innovation system with a relative weakness in basic research, which may prove a major problem as Korea nears the technology frontier and can no longer license or buy all it needs from more advanced countries.[39]

FDI has helped Korean firms maintain their competitiveness in low-end goods, but they have not completely succeeded the transition in to higher value production at home that is required after a massive relocation of productive resources. They have partly responded by finding new, more complex products to mass-produce, such as advanced flat-panel displays. But this merely postpones the transition to market-driven product development that will be necessary for continued competitiveness.

The recommendations of Ernst (1994a) that the Korean government should shift from "export-led market expansion" to "FDI-led market expansion," and national innovation policies from "sectoral targeting" to "diffusion oriented policies" appear sound. At the same time, the government must fundamentally change its traditional education system, which is extremely uniform and no longer relevant under the new competitive requirements in order to build up the creative capability of human resources as suggested by Kim (1991).

The challenge for Samsung (and for other Korean electronics firms) in the context of its IPN is to successfully develop and transfer adaptive product design know-how to its offshore affiliates. Improvement in the competitive advantage of overseas affiliates is directly dependent on how quickly a firm can create and diffuse required capabilities that properly adapt to changing conditions. Deeper linkages within Samsung's organizational network both in Asia and around the world will be needed to face the next round of competition in the electronics sector.

## Notes

1 The author would like to thank D. Ernst (University of California, Berkeley), Sung-Tack, Park (Korea Institute for Industrial Economics & Trade), M. Hobday and K. Pavitt (University of Sussex), S. J. Nicholas (University of Melbourne), K. Iijima and D. Tachiki (Sakura Institute of Research), I. Vertinsky (University of British Columbia), C. A. Bartlett and D. J. Collis (Harvard Business School), J. Cantwell (University of Reading), and T. Abo (University of Tokyo) for their helpful assistance and comments. Special thanks go to P. Drysdale, H. Hill, and M. Dodgson (The Australian National University) for their special guidance and kind support. I am also grateful to T. M. Kim and C. S. Yoon for their assistance. The author is indebted to Samsung Economic Research Institute and Samsung managers with whom I conducted interviews in China, Korea, and Southeast Asia. The views expressed, and any remaining errors, are solely the responsibility of the author.
2 This is based on the figures published by the Investment Mission, Ministry of Economic Affairs, Republic of China in 1992. It is generally believed that the real figures are far bigger than the ones published because of unreported flows to mainland China.

3 The value of its offshore production in 1994 was US$1,050 million, compared with US$550 million for Goldstar, and US$50 million for Daewoo (*KED*, 29 August 1994).

4 It is also not surprising that Samsung entered the international DRAM market in 1983, the year when the government again promoted the semiconductors promotion policy.

5 Samsung (SEC 1989) claims that to achieve this, it needed a large industrial complex in which to build several plants. It therefore bought a single block of land of about 1.5 million square meters, which was larger than Sanyo's electronics complex in Japan in the late 1960s.

6 Owing to this unbalanced distribution in the market, in 1984, SEC was forced to establish its CTV production plant in the United States, although its capability was not mature enough to operate it. Four years later, it disinvested from the United States, whose market is the most important for electronics products.

7 SEC's first subsidiary, Tokyo Samsung Engineering Co. got access for SEC to Mitsubishi in 1971 and SEC obtained an order for 5,000 black and white TV sets for the US market under the brand name of "Uncle Sam." In 1973, SEC exported black and white TV sets to MGA of the United States and electronic calculators not only to Casio but also to Hermek in Europe and Hatzlack in the United States. In 1974, SEC contracted with Beltrans, European buyer, to export radios (SEC 1989: 171). In 1975, SEC's compact stereos were exported to AGS of Canada as were radios to Zenith on an OEM basis. The first export of CTVs was in April 1976 to Panama. In 1978 SEC established sales channels with Zenith of the United States and exported amplifiers on an OEM basis (SEC 1989).

8 The termination of the original contract must have been one of the main reasons that Sanyo divested from the joint venture and withdrew its share from Samsung. This is in contrast to the relationship with NEC, which still held about 10 percent of its share in SED, and Corning Glass Works that holds a considerable proportion of shares in SC.

9 The localization ratio of components for black and white TV sets increased from 60 percent to 90 percent (SEC 1989: 177). In July 1978 the linear IC was developed (SST 1987: 177). In September 1978 the IC package assembly became available, because lead frames for the IC were produced. The initial semiconductor operation supplied only a small proportion of Samsung's internal demand, so a large quantity of ICs were still imported for several years (SST 1987: 179).

10 These early sales linkages enabled Samsung's foreign affiliates to interact with Japanese organizations in Southeast Asia from the start of overseas production in the early 1990s.

11 SEC had a 51 percent share and GTE had a 49 percent share of the company. Samsung-GTE produced and marketed electronic private automatic branch exchanges (EPABXs), which had been developed by the Korea Institute of Science and Technology (KIST). Furthermore, Samsung decided to acquire the Korea Telecommunications Company (KTC), a state-run telecommunications corporation established in 1977 to produce electronic switching exchanges (ESS) for the local Korean market in collaboration with BTM of Belgium, a subsidiary of ITT (SST 1987).

12 These were turbulent years. SEC had five different CEOs between 1969 and 1975 (SEC 1989).

13 See Yu (1989) and Koh (1992), who have identified Samsung's short-term strategic view.

14 There were two strategic reasons for Micron Technology: it desperately needed cash, and intended to established a low-cost second-source, enabling Micron to keep its own investment at a minimum. (Ernst 1994a: 79).

15 Samsung had considerable trouble in producing the 256 K chip. It was not until

April 1986 through trial and error that it managed to start mass production.

16  In October 1984 the 64 K DRAM was exported to the United States and Europe. Samsung, however, seriously suffered from the huge loss because its price fell drastically from 3 US$ in 1984 to 20 cents in 1985. This continued until the end of the 1980s. Many Samsung affiliates suffered a tight cash flow because millions of dollars of group money was poured into its semiconductor business (Business Korea, March 1992: 66).

17  See Bloom (1992), Ernst (1994b) and Hobday (1995) for details of the Korean electronics weakness on design and product development,

18  Examples are hi-fi VCRs over three years (1987), for which Toshiba sent SEC technical advisers (SEC 1989); two of the licensing agreements with Sanyo were for microwave oven technology, over five years (December 1984), for which Sanyo sent technical experts to train SEC's employees (SEC 1989); In May 1985, SEC made a five-year licensing agreement with Matsushita for magnetron production technology, for which Matsushita dispatched technical experts to SEC and SEC sent its technical personnel to Matsushita-Japan for training (SEC 1989: 371); in August 1983 Sony licensed Samsung to produce VHS VCRs over five years.

19  In 1988 SEC acquired the Micro Five Corporation of the United States to complement technological capability in the computer sector and set up Samsung Software America (SSA) in Boston. The objective was to acquire advanced software technologies but also to establish a US marketing base for computer exports. In October 1989 SEC established Samsung Information Systems America Inc. (SISA) in San Jose, California, to support export activities and gather further technology for information and telecommunications products (Koh 1992).

20  The dumping rate was preliminarily charged on three leading electronics firms: 3.87 percent (Goldstar), 3.05 percent (Samsung) and 1.77 percent (Daewoo). Their export growth in three consecutive years from 1983 to 1985 remained without significant change.

21  In 1982 Samsung had implemented a pilot project in Portugal, where it established its first overseas production joint venture in cooperation with Portuguese and British partners, in order to gain international production experience (SEC 1989).

22  See Kinugasa (1982) for the case of the Matsushita's international production strategy in the United States.

23  The head of the consumer electronics sector was transferred to SEM, and the head of the telecommunications sector was transferred to the Samsung Advanced Institute of Technology.

24  The reform was initiated by Lee Kun Hee, who was called the Samsung group's chief visionary officer, and by Kim Kwang Ho, who set the strategic goals. (*Business Times*, 19 February 1994). The three main strategic goals were quality-first management, globalization, and multifaceted integration.

25  Ernst and O'Connor (1992) state that DRAMs are the best technology driver among alternative IC types. For other spillover examples, see SST (1987).

26  Samsung continued to engage in strategic alliances, particularly in the IC field, where it could now exchange its advanced production capabilities for complementary technology.

27  In 1989, SEC's OEM ratio of computer products was as high as 80 percent, whereas in 1992, 50 percent of SEC's total revenues generated by computers and monitors came from OEM deals, with firms like IBM, Hewlett-Parkard and Packard Bell. Taiwanese PC producers' OEM ratio between 1987 and 1991 varied between 41 percent and 47 percent (Ernst 1994a: 69–70).

28  However, the deal was only achieved because AST was in dire financial straits,

leaving some doubt about the quality of the assets Samsung obtained for its $300 million.

29  The concept is developed in Knickerbocker (1973). For FDI of Korean electronics firms, see Jun and Simon (1992).

30  America regional headquarters (HQ), consisting of five sales affiliates, two production affiliates and four branch offices; Europe regional HQ, with eight regional sales affiliates, five production affiliates and five branch offices; China regional HQ, which has two sales affiliates, four production affiliates and four branch offices; Southeast Asia regional HQ, with two sales affiliates, four production affiliates and eight branch offices; and Japan regional HQ, consisting of one sales affiliate and one branch office (SEC 1995b).

31  See Baba and Hatashima (1995) for the recent trend of product development activities by Japanese electronics firms in East Asia.

32  Two examples in Mexico and the UK are (1) Tijuana integrated electronics complex is building factories in a land area of 600,000 square meters. This complex was scheduled to be completed in 1996. It will contain a number of production subsidiaries belonging to SEC, SEM, SED, SC, and Samsung Aerospace; (2) Wynyard industrial complex in the UK, where Samsung plans to invest US$720 million, is building factories. The complex will cover an area of 750,000 square meters. It plans to start producing microwave ovens, personal computers, monitors, fax machines, color CRTs, wireless phones, and DRAMs (*SMM* November 1994).

33  The purchasing office has been extended to form a link not only between two subnetworks and the Korea-based non-affiliated component suppliers, but also between the Korea-based production sites and a number of non-affiliated economic actors in the region.

34  Source: the author's interviews with Samsung Asian affiliates during July 1995. These relationships suggest that the "opening" of Japanese production networks in Asia since the early 1990s is due at least partly to the emergence of Korean component suppliers in Southeast Asia rather than to the use of locally-based suppliers. For a discussion about Japanese electronics firms' IPNs in Asia, see Ernst (1994b).

35  Samsung had previously opened offshore VCR factories in the UK (1987) and Spain (1989).

36  This is based on the interview undertaken in July 1995 and see also Jun and Kang (1994).

37  In January 1993 Orion Hanel Picture Tube Co. Ltd was incorporated in Vietnam with a production capacity of 1 million color picture tubes and 600,000 units of black and white CRTs. Production was scheduled to begin in December 1995. Goldstar plans to set up a color CRT plant in China (EIAK 1994). Orion and Goldstar are also planning to build CRT plants in Indonesia.

38  For similar conclusions, see Stopford (1995) and Ernst (1995).

39  Several authors have identified a number of basic sectoral weaknesses of the national innovation and educational system in Korea (Kim and Chung 1991; Kim and Kim 1991; Kim 1991; Bloom 1992; Ernst and O'Connor 1992; Ernst 1994b). In particular, Kim (1991) argues that "one of the major mistakes made by the Korean government in developing a national system of innovation has been its under-investment in higher educational institutions...making all universities primarily undergraduate teaching-oriented rather than research-oriented...As a result, Korea has failed to develop a stock of highly trained scientists and engineers who will be necessary in the 1990s in order for Korea to sustain its international competitiveness."

# References

Baba, Y. and Hatashima, H. (1995) "Capability Transfer of Japanese Electronics Firms to the Pacific Rim Nations: Towards Open global Manufacturing?," in E. M. Doherty (ed.) *Japanese Investment in Asia: International Production Strategies in a Rapidly Changing World.* San Francisco, California: The Asia Foundation.

Bellance, R. (1987) *International Industry and Business: Structural Change, Industrial Policy and Industrial Strategies*, London: Allen & Unwin.

Bloom, M. (1992) *Technological Changes in the Korean Electronics Industry*, Paris: OECD.

Cho, D. S. (1983) *Hankuk-eui Jonghap-Muyeok Sang-sa (Korean General Trading Companies)*, Seoul.

Electronic Industry Association of Korea (EIAK) (1989) *Junja Kong-up Samsip-nyun-sa* (The 30 Year History of Electronic Industry), Seoul.

—— (1993) *Junja Sanup haewoi-tuja-upche directory* (Directory of Foreign Investors of Electronics Industry), December, Seoul.

—— (1994) *CPT Sanup Dong-hyang* (The Current Trend of CPT Industry), Seoul.

Ernst, D. (1994a) *What are the Limits to the Korean Model? The Korean Electronics Industry Under Pressure,* University of California at Berkeley: BRIE.

—— (1994b) "Carriers of Regionalisation: the East Asian Production Networks of Japanese Electronics Firms," *Working Paper 73*, University of California at Berkeley: BRIE.

—— (1995) "Mobilizing the Region's Capabilities? The East Asian Production Networks of Japanese Electronics Firms," in E. M. Doherty (ed.) *Japanese Investment in Asia: International Production Strategies in a Rapidly Changing World.* San Francisco, California: The Asia Foundation and BRIE.

Ernst, D. and O'Connor, D. (1992) *Competing in the Electronics Industry. The Experience of Newly Industrialising Economies*, Paris: OECD.

Hobday, M. (1995) "East Asian Latecomer Firms: Learning the Technology of Electronics" *World Development,* 23(7): 1171–1193.

Itoh, M. and Shibata, J. (1994) "A study of the operations of Japanese firms in Asia: the electrical machinery industry," a conference paper presented at the Twenty-First Pacific Trade and Development (PAFTAD 21) in Hong Kong.

Jun, Y. (1987) "The reverse direct investment: the case of Korean consumer electronics Industry," *International Economic Journal,* 1(3): 91–104.

—— (1992) "Strategic Responses of Korean Firms to Globalisation and Regionalism Forces: the Case of the Korean Electronics Industry, Global Business Seminar," paper prepared for the conference "The Impact of Globalisation and Regionalisation on Corporate Strategy and Structure Among Pacific Rim Firms," August 3–7, 1992, Sapporo, Japan.

Jun, Y. and Han, J. (1994) *Cho-u-ryang Ki-up-euro Ka-nun-kil* (A Way toward a Best Firm: The Growth and Change of Samsung), Seoul.

Jun, Y. and Kang, S. (1994) *Samsung-junja Bumun-eui Kuk-jae Network Jun-ryak: Dongnam-a Saeng-san Network Sare* (International Networking Strategy of Samsung Electronics: A Case of Production Networking in Southeast Asia), Seoul: Chung Ang University.

Jun, Y. and Simon, D. (1992) "The pattern of Korea's foreign direct investment: implications for the internationalisation of China's economy," in Ross Garnaut and Liu Guoguang (eds), *Economic Reform and Internationalisation: China and the Pacific Region,* Australian National University and Allen & Unwin.

Kim, I. and Chung, S. (1991) "R&D Cooperation Between Large Manufacturing Companies and Suppliers," Science and Technology Policy Institute, Korean Advanced Institute of Science and Technology (KAIST) mimeograph 1991.

Kim, I. and Kim, C. (1991) "Comparison of Korean to Western R&D: Project Selection Factors for New Product Development," Science and Technology Policy Institute, Korean Advanced Institute of Science and Technology (KAIST) mimeograph, Taejon.

Kim, L. (1991) "National System of Industrial Innovation: Dynamics of Capability Building in Korea," Working Paper 91–1, Seoul: Business Management Research Centre, College of Business Administration, Korea University.

Kinugasa, Y. (1982) "Japanese firms' foreign direct investment in the US: the case of Matsushita and others," in A. Okochi and T. Inoue (eds) *Overseas Business Activities*, Tokyo: University of Tokyo Press.

Knickerbocker, F. T. (1973) *Oligopolistic Reaction and Multinational Enterprise*, Boston: Harvard University Press.

Koh, D. J. (1992) "Beyond Technological Dependency, Toward an Agile Giant: The Strategic Concerns of Korea's Samsung Electronics Co. for the 1990s," MSc thesis unpublished, Science Policy Research Unit, University of Sussex.

Kogut, B. and Zander, U. (1993) "Knowledge of the Firm and the Evolutionary Theory of the Multinational Corporation," *Journal of International Business Studies*, 24(4): 625–646.

Samsung (1993) *Samsung Sin-kyung-yeong: Na-bu-teo Byun-haiya-handa* (The New Management of Samsung: get myself changed), Seoul: Samsung group.

Samsung Electronics Co. Ltd (1989) *Samsung Junja 20-nyun-sa* (The 20 Year History of Samsung Electronics), Seoul.

—— (1995a) *Guide to Out Bound Presentation Kit*, Global Operations Division.

—— (1995b) Samsung Electronics in Brief.

*Samsung Jun-ki Sa-bo*: Samsung Electro-Mechanics' Monthly Magazine (*SEMM*) (1994) January–December.

*Samsung Jun-ja Sa-bo*: Samsung Electronics' Monthly Magazine(*SEMM*) (January 1990 to December 1994).

Samsung Electron-Devices Co. Ltd (1990) *Samsung Jun-kwan 20-nyun-sa* (The 20 Year History of Samsung Electron-Devices), Seoul.

Samsung Corning (SC) Co. Ltd (1994) *Samsung Corning 20-nyun-sa* (The 20 Year History of Samsung Corning), Seoul.

*Samsung Sa-bo:* Samsung Monthly Magazine (*SMM*) (January 1980 to December 1994).

Samsung Semiconductor and Telecommunications Co. Ltd (1987) *Samsung Ban-do-he-tong-sin Sip-nouns* (The 10 Year History of Samsung Semiconductors), Seoul.

Stopford, J. M. (1995) "Competing Globally for Resources," *Transnational Corporations*, 4(2) (August): 34–57.

Yu, S. (1989) "Korean Electronics Enterprises: Growth and Strategies," in D. Kim and L. Kim (eds) *Management Beyond Industrialisation: Readings in Korean Business*, Seoul: Korea University Press.

# 7 Riding the waves

## Technological change, competing US–Japan production networks, and the growth of Singapore's electronics industry

*Poh-Kam Wong*

## Introduction

As described elsewhere in this book, several East Asian countries outside Japan have emerged as major production platforms for the global electronics industry since the 1970s. Driven by global competition, firms from advanced countries in general and US and Japanese firms in particular have increasingly extended their supplier bases and production networks to the various countries in East Asia. In 1993, the four Asian NIEs, ASEAN, and China together already accounted for 13 percent of global electronics production, or about 40 percent of Japanese output (Elsevier 1996). With nearly all these countries achieving double-digit growth over the last three years and Japanese production stagnating, the share of non-Japan East Asian output in global production has increased substantially since then. Along with rapid expansion in output, there has also been a significant transformation in the nature of activities being carried in these countries.

This chapter focuses on one aspect of this changing structure of Asian production networks for the global electronics industry – the emergence and growth of Singapore as a major hub in South East Asia. By examining the dynamics of growth of Singapore's electronics industry over the last three decades, this chapter seeks to provide new insights into the shifting patterns of competitive interactions between US and Japanese production networks. In particular, we argue that the rise of Singapore is largely due to its ability to leverage the competing but overlapping production networks of major US and Japanese electronics firms. It is this ability to "ride the waves" of technological and organizational changes emanating from the United States and Japan that enabled Singapore to differentiate itself from other competing locations in East Asia – the North Asian NIEs of Korea, Taiwan and Hong Kong as well as the Southeast Asian "tigers" of Malaysia and Thailand.

This chapter is organized as follows. The first section profiles the historical growth of Singapore's electronics industry, highlighting a number of salient features that distinguish it from other competing locations in East Asia. The second section analyzes in more details the competing yet overlapping contributions of major US and Japanese firms to the development of Singapore's electronics industry, and the salient differences in organizational characteristics and strategic orientations between US and Japanese operations in Singapore. The third section examines the recent emergence of indigenous electronics firms in Singapore and their changing roles in the US–Japan competitive nexus. Finally, the fourth section examines the contributing role of the state in promoting Singapore as a regional hub for electronics, and provides some concluding observations concerning future directions of US–Japan competition in electronics, and their implications for Singapore in particular and Asian production networks in general.

## The rapid growth of the electronics industry in Singapore

Since the late 1960s, when electronics firms from the United States and Japan first began to redistribute production to Asia, Singapore has been a major node in the production networks of the global electronics industry. Despite the continuous spreading of the US and Japanese production networks to other countries in East Asia in general and Southeast Asia in particular, Singapore has continued to maintain an eminent, though changing, position in Asia. Indeed, successive waves of investments by multinational corporations (MNCs) from the United States, Japan, and Europe have intensified Singapore's integration into the global production networks of these firms (Economic Committee 1986; Borrus 1993; Lee 1993; Angel 1994).

The remarkable pace of growth of Singapore's electronics industry can be seen from the summary statistics in Table 7.1. Between 1960 and 1996, electronics manufacturing output grew at over 25 percent per year in current prices, or over 20 percent in real terms. The aggregate electronics industry output reached S\$63 billion in 1996, constituting over 52 percent of the total manufacturing output in Singapore, making it by far the largest industrial sector in Singapore today.

Along with quantitative growth, Singapore's electronics industry has also undergone tremendous qualitative transformation. Between 1970 and 1995, the industry has moved from simple technology, labor-intensive operations to highly automated, skill-intensive operations, as reflected by an average increase in labor productivity (as measured by value-added per worker in constant price) of over 5 percent per year during the 25-year interval. Reflecting the significant rise in capital and technology intensities over the years, fixed asset per worker also increased dramatically (see Wong *et al.* 1997 for details).

The qualitative transformation of the electronics industry can also be seen in the shifting sectoral composition of the industry over the years (see Tables 7.2 and 7.3). Although consumer electronics and basic electronics component assembly and testing activities dominated in the earlier years, the growth of the industry over the last decade has been fueled mainly by the manufacturing of computer-related products (PCs, hard disk drives, printers, CDROMs), and more advanced electronics component-manufacturing operations (semiconductor wafer fabrication, disk media, advanced circuit board assembly, and precision electro-optical components).

*Table 7.1* Performance of Singapore's electronics industry, 1960–95

(a) Aggregate growth in electronics industry, 1960–95 (in nominal prices)

| Year | Output | Value add | Employment | Share of total manufacturing (%) | | |
|------|--------|-----------|------------|--------|-----------|------------|
| | | | | Output | Value add | Employment |
| 1960 | 17.1 | 7.9 | 1252 | 3.7 | 5.5 | 4.6 |
| 1970 | 283 | 127.4 | 13586 | 7.3 | 11.7 | 11.3 |
| 1980 | 5344 | 1668.9 | 71727 | 16.9 | 19.6 | 25.1 |
| 1990 | 27878.1 | 7716.6 | 122797 | 39.1 | 35.7 | 34.9 |
| 1995 | 57872.75 | 11987.9 | 126891 | 51.1 | 44.6 | 34.3 |

(b) Average growth comparison per year (%) – electronics industry versus total manufacturing

| Year | Electronics industry | | | Total manufacturing | | |
|------|--------|-----------|------------|--------|-----------|------------|
| | Output | Value add | Employment | Output | Value add | Employment |
| 1960–70 | 32.4 | 32.1 | 26.9 | 23.6 | 22.6 | 16.0 |
| 1970–80 | 34.2 | 29.3 | 18.1 | 23.3 | 22.8 | 9.0 |
| 1980–90 | 18.0 | 16.5 | 5.5 | 8.5 | 9.8 | 2.1 |
| 1990–95 | 15.7 | 9.2 | 0.7 | 9.7 | 4.5 | 1.0 |
| 1960–95 | 26.1 | 23.3 | 14.1 | 17.0 | 16.2 | 7.7 |

Source: EDB, Report on the Census for Industrial Production, 1960–95.

*Table 7.2* Sectoral composition of Singapore's electronics industry, 1970–95 (%)

| Subsectors | 1970 | 1975 | 1980 | 1990 | 1995 |
|------------|------|------|------|------|------|
| Consumer electronics | 100 | 30.6 | 38.8 | 17.7 | 7.8 |
| Electronics components | 0 | 69.4 | 54.4 | 35.2 | 27.6 |
| Computers and peripherals | 0 | 0 | 5.4 | 42.3 | 47.0 |
| Telecom and others | 0 | 0 | 1.2 | 4.8 | 17.6 |
| Total | 100 | 100 | 100 | 100 | 100 |

Source: Calculated from EDB, Report on Census of Industrial Production, 1970–95.

Not only is the electronics industry of critical importance to the entire Singapore economy, it has also become an indispensable hub for the industry within the Southeast Asian region, which itself has been rapidly expanding over the last two decades. The share of Southeast Asia in total East Asian electronics has risen from less than 5 percent in the 1970s to over 15 percent in the 1990s (Scott 1987; Elsevier, various years). Within Southeast Asia itself, Singapore emerged as the single most important location of electronics production, accounting for over half of the region's output in the mid-1980s. Despite escalating costs and increasing spread of electronics production to

*Table 7.3* Detailed sectoral structure of Singapore's electronics industry, 1996

| Subsectors | Output (S$ billions) | % |
|---|---|---|
| Data storage | 18.31 | 29.0 |
| Computer | 12.61 | 20.0 |
| Printers and other office equipment | 5.36 | 8.5 |
| Consumer electronics | 4.97 | 7.9 |
| Communications | 2.94 | 4.7 |
| Semiconductor | 12.08 | 19.1 |
| Passive components, PCBs and display devices | 3.39 | 5.4 |
| Contract manufacturing and others | 3.46 | 5.5 |
| Total | 63.16 | 100 |

Source: EDB, Press Release in conjunction with EDB Annual Briefing on the Electronics Industry on 20 January 1997.

lower cost locations in the region throughout the second half of the 1980s and the first half of the 1990s, Singapore has nonetheless maintained its status as the largest center for electronics production, with about 43 percent of the Southeast Asian region's total electronics output in 1995. Moreover, Singapore's share was significantly higher for those electronics subsectors that were more technology or capital intensive (e.g. over 60 percent in computer and office automation equipment).

The continuing importance of Singapore as a production platform for electronics is in strong contrast to Hong Kong, another city-state in East Asia. Historically, Hong Kong started from a more favorable position in the early 1970s, with a significantly larger electronics production base than Singapore. Through the years, however, Hong Kong steadily declined as an electronics production center relative to Singapore: the ratio of electronics output of Hong Kong to Singapore's changed from more than 1.00 throughout the 1970s and early 1980s to 0.84 in 1985 and 0.61 in 1990. By 1995, Hong Kong's electronics output was only 25 percent of that of Singapore's (Elsevier 1996). The ratio was much worse for the more technology-intensive sectors of semiconductors, computers, and peripherals.

Singapore's electronics industry development also stands in strong contrast to Korea and Taiwan, where electronics manufacturing has also grown rapidly (Wong 1995a). Whereas electronics growth in Korea and Taiwan has been achieved primarily through indigenous firms, Singapore's electronics industry has, until recently, been largely driven by MNCs (Table 7.4). Despite the lack of a domestic market, and having a less sophisticated prior indigenous industrial base and a less well-developed technical manpower base compared with Taiwan and Korea, Singapore nonetheless managed to catch up quickly to become a highly competitive location for technologically advanced electronics manufacturing in East Asia. The next section analyzes in more details the different roles and contributions of Japanese and US electronics MNCs.

*Table 7.4* Indicators of foreign MNCs' dominance in Singapore's electronics industry

(a) Foreign share of equity investment in Singapore's electronics industry, 1980–93

| Year | Electronics industry (%) | Total manufacturing (%) |
| --- | --- | --- |
| 1980 | 91.0 | 67.1 |
| 1987 | 96.7 | 70.8 |
| 1990 | 93.5 | 69.4 |
| 1994 | 84.8 | 62.6 |

Source: 1980 estimated from Economic Development Board (EDB) cumulated investment data; 1987–94 Department of Statistics (1996).

(b) Ownership structure of electronics firms, 1993

| Ownership structure | Number of firms | % |
| --- | --- | --- |
| 100% local | 50 | 18.9 |
| > 50% local | 62 | 23.5 |
| 50:50 joint venture | 4 | 1.5 |
| > 50% foreign | 16 | 6.1 |
| 100% foreign | 132 | 50 |
| Total | 264 | 100 |

Source: Report on the Census of Industrial Production 1993 (unpublished).

## Competing and overlapping production networks of US and Japanese electronics firms

### Brief overview of the historical trends in US and Japanese electronics manufacturing investment in Singapore

The bulk of foreign investment in electronics manufacturing in Singapore had come from the United States and Japan throughout the industry's growth. Although the first major foreign electronics assembly operation in Singapore – a TV assembly plant – was established by a European firm, Philips, before 1965, the real growth of the industry in Singapore started in 1967 when Texas Instruments (TI) set up its first offshore semiconductor assembly plant in Singapore. Within a few years, TI was joined by several major US and European semiconductor assembly firms, including National Semiconductor (1969), Harris Semiconductor (1969), SGS-Thomson (1969), and Siemens (1970). These were quickly followed by a wave of new investment in consumer electronics, electrical appliances, and office equipment manufacturing by MNCs such as Black & Decker (1970), HP (1970), and Smith Corona (1972) from the United States and Sanyo (1972), Matsushita Refrigeration Industries (1972), Asahi Electronics (1972), Murata (1972), Hitachi (1973), Aiwa (1974), and Toshiba (1974) from Japan (Ernst 1994).

It is interesting to note that major investments in semiconductor assembly activities by the Japanese majors did not begin until the second half of 1970s and the early 1980s, lagging behind the US pioneers by more than five years. NEC Semiconductors started operation in Singapore in 1976, Matsushita Denshi in 1978, and Fujitsu Microelectronics not until 1986. However, even though the early US semiconductor pioneers did expand their production activities significantly in the decade that followed, it was Japanese consumer electronics and electronic components/devices companies that dominated new electronics manufacturing investment throughout the second half of the 1970s and the first half of the 1980s. For example, the Matsushita group added four new plants (manufacturing audio electronics, transformers and power supplies, micromotors and precision engineering components/automation equipment) during 1977–8, in addition to the previously mentioned refrigerator compressors and IC assembly plants (the latter also established in 1978). Hitachi established TV tubes and electronic component plants in 1978 and 1979, and JVC and Kenwood started in 1978 and 1979 respectively. The few notable major new investments by US electronic firms during this period were all in electronic components [Delco Electronics (1978) and Molex (1977)] or communications and computer peripherals [Motorola (1983) and Seagate (1982)].

After the spurt of Japanese consumer electronics and components growth began to subside towards the mid-1980s, a new wave of growth of electronics investment began to take shape from around 1986 onwards, this time driven by the rapid growth in computer-related products and largely dominated by US firms. First and foremost, Singapore emerged as the major hub for magnetic HDD assembly over the period of 1985–90, with major new investments by practically all the major US non-captive HDD producers (Seagate, Conner, Western Digital, Maxtor, Micropolis) (Wong 1997). A second cluster evolved around PC assembly, led initially by Apple Computer and later by Compaq and HP. A third cluster evolved around printers led by HP. Following in the footsteps of these major US investments, a number of Japanese companies also began to invest in computer and related peripherals manufacturing in Singapore from the mid-1990s. For example, Epson began to manufacture terminal printers in late 1993 and more recently inkjet printers; Matsushita started manufacturing fax machines using thermal, inkjet, and laser printing technologies, and MKE, Hoya, and Mitsubishi Chemicals established manufacturing operations in data storage products [HDD assembly, disk media, and compact disk readable (CD-R) media respectively].

Each of these clusters, in turn, contributed to the rapid growth of a wide range of electronics supporting industries, particularly PCBs and their assembly (PCBA), precision metal and plastic components, surface treatment and key module subassembly. Although some of these electronics supporting firms initially started as suppliers to the Japanese consumer electronics firms, their major growth impetus came mainly with the new wave of computer-related products; I will return to this issue in more detail below.

Although much of this precision engineering and other electronics supporting industry growth took the form of indigenous enterprises, it has also attracted some new investments by Japanese firms manufacturing key components and US firms specializing in contract manufacturing. In particular, Japanese investment in electronics supporting industries in Singapore expanded rapidly in the second half of 1980s, partly driven by the yen appreciation and partly by the need to serve the rapidly growing Japanese consumer electronics assembly operations in Malaysia and Thailand. This involves both backward integration by large Japanese electronics firms as well as new investments by small and medium-sized Japanese suppliers. For example, Sony Precision Engineering Centre (SPEC) was set up in Singapore in 1987 to manufacture a full range of key components and modules, including optical pick-up devices, lenses, and components for CD and CDROM, magnetic heads, drums and precision parts for VCRs, and electronic guns for color TV sets. Examples of Japanese electronics supporting SMEs that came during this period include Kohoku Electronics and Tokyo Pidgeon Manufacturing. In contrast, electronics supporting firms that came during this period were fewer and primarily in contract manufacturing [e.g. Adaptec and SCI in PCBA using surface-mount technology (SMT)].

Even as the US-led computer industry growth was sustaining its healthy growth in Singapore throughout the 1990s, another new wave of electronics investment began to take shape from around the middle of the 1990s – that of semiconductor wafer fabrication. In this latest wave, it is interesting to note that MNCs from the United States, Japan, and Europe as well as indigenous Singapore firms are all playing significant roles. In contrast to the earlier investments, the Singapore government has played a much more active role in the growth of the wafer fabrication industry by being a significant co-investor in several of the new projects (see more details below).

While highlighting these successive waves of investments into new and typically technologically more intensive product clusters, it must also be noted that most existing US and Japanese firms had, within the same product mandates, also been upgrading their manufacturing operations and process technologies to produce increasingly higher end products or more recent generation of products. For example, Hitachi Electronic Devices Singapore (HEDS) had moved from assembling smaller sized TVs in the late 1970s to being Hitachi's largest and most advanced overseas plant assembling large screen TVs and high-end computer monitors. Seagate had shifted from labor-intensive E-block subassembly and PCBA to the final assembly of entire HDDs, and from low-end drives to the most advanced drives produced by the company. TI quickly advanced from assembling and testing of simple bipolar devices to more complex metal oxide semiconductor (MOS) logic devices and MOS memory devices in the 1970s, went into 64 kb DRAM production in the early 1980s, and progressed rapidly to 16 Mb DRAM in the early 1990s; it also diversified into flash memory EPROMs in the 1990s.

Overall, we can thus observe that major US and Japanese electronics firms have used Singapore extensively for their offshore manufacturing operations. However, three differences between US and Japanese firms can be discerned. First, the sectoral pattern of concentration of US firms appears to vary quite significantly when compared with Japanese firms, in accordance with the relative strengths of the respective countries in the global markets. The United States dominates in computer-related industries, Japan dominates in consumer electronics and key modules/devices, and the two countries have more or less equal representation in semiconductors.

Second, with the exception of consumer electronics, where Japanese dominance has been overwhelming, Japanese firms appear to have lagged behind US firms in coming to Singapore for each of the major new waves of new industrial cluster development identified above (semiconductor assembly and test, data storage, computer assembly, printers).

Third, the orientation of the Japanese manufacturing operations appear to be somewhat different from their American counterparts. Although reliable statistics are not available for the period before 1980, export data for the year 1981 and 1991–4 show clearly that US electronics firms export a much larger proportion of their output (98 percent in 1981, 90 percent over 1991–4) than Japanese firms (72 percent in 1981, about 65 percent over 1991–4) (see Table 7.5). Moreover, whereas US electronics firms exported a significant proportion of their output back to their home market (87 percent in 1981, about 60 percent over 1991–4), Japanese firms exported less than 10 percent of their output back to Japan. It is also interesting to note that Japanese firms in Singapore exported proportionately more to the neighboring ASEAN than US firms. The overall pattern of export destination suggests that US electronics firms in Singapore were primarily producing for the global market, whereas a significant proportion of Japanese firms' output (38–45 percent over 1991–4) were regionally oriented, i.e. consumed in Singapore or within the ASEAN region. Although a detailed breakdown by product categories is not available, it is quite certain that the bulk of this regional consumption is not final consumption, but intermediate parts and components flows, either intra-firm or inter-firm.

In addition to, and related to, these three differences, Japanese and US electronics firms in Singapore also differ significantly in terms of their pattern of input sourcing, diversification into non-manufacturing activities, and technology interactions with the host economy. These are discussed in greater detail below.

### Local and regional sourcing pattern of US and Japanese firms

A key aspect of IPNs is the extent to which the network of supply of components and parts along the production value chain are localized. Are there inherent advantages in locating the supply base in close geographic proximity to the usage point, or do economies of scale favor concentration of the supply base at one or a few locations globally, even if these are quite distant from the usage points? Obviously, the economies of local content sourcing vary significantly with the type of electronics products (e.g. assembling and testing of semiconductors is likely to have much lower local content economies than PC assembly) and the nature of the intermediate inputs concerned (e.g. direct parts versus tool- and die-making services). It may also vary over time as technological complexity increases or as the competitive context changes. For example, as a component becomes increasingly complex and expensive (e.g. disk media) and assembly yield becomes an important differentiating factor, there may be a need to have close geographic proximity with the manufacturers (HDD assembler) to improve responsiveness and to fix yield problems. The converse may also be possible: as a component technology becomes mature and standardized, the need for close proximity between the supply base and the usage point may decrease.

The definition of "local" sourcing is also problematic for a small city-state like Singapore. Being in such close geographic proximity to peninsular Malaysia (Johor lies across a causeway, and Penang and Kuala Lumpur are within one and a half hours flight time), there may be little difference to manufacturing operations if a component is manufactured in Singapore or in Malaysia. For more mature products, the sourcing network could be extended even further, for example to Thailand and Indonesia, and for truly standardized items, geography may not matter at all. Consequently, the "local" supply base for electronics manufacturing firms in Singapore should more properly be interpreted as encompassing regional networks that span all of Southeast Asia.

Last, but not least, the "locality" of a supply network must conceptually be distinguished from its indigeneity. "Local" suppliers can in principle be either indigenous firms or foreign-owned firms. This point is particularly important in distinguishing Singapore from Taiwan. As Ernst points out in Chapter 5, American firms in Taiwan have benefited substantially from their cultivation of an indigenous Taiwanese supply base that has become increasingly sophisticated over time. In Singapore, however, the "local" supply base encompasses not only Singaporean firms, but a dense network of Japanese and American component and subassembly operations.

Comprehensive industry-wide census data on sourcing origins of electronics firms in Singapore are unfortunately not available. However, using import statistics of electronics goods (SITC 75–77) as a proxy measure of cross-border intra-industry linkages (in view of the relatively small domestic end-user market of Singapore), it is interesting to note that Singapore's import of electronics products from ASEAN as a share of total imports has increased substantially from 14.2 percent in 1980 to 25.8 percent in 1990 and 33.3 percent in 1996. In addition, several existing empirical studies (see, for example, Wong 1991; 1992) suggest that MNC electronics production in Singapore has substantial stimulation effects on the development of a wide range of local electronics supporting industries: precision plastic parts, metal stamping, mould making and die casting, precision machined metal parts and components, electroplating and finishing, tools, jigs and fixtures, lead frames, PCBs and their assembly, and industrial automation equipment. The aggregate output of these supporting industries amounted to S$5 billions in Singapore in 1995, close to 10 percent of the output of the electronics industry itself (Wong *et al.* 1997).

Comprehensive statistics on the sourcing pattern of electronics firms by nationality of ownership are not available. However, the few empirical studies of the procurement practices of Japanese electronics firms in general and in Singapore in particular suggest that Japanese firms tend to be much more likely to source from Japanese suppliers than firms of other nationalities (see, for example, Yamashita 1991; Kobayashi 1992; Takayasu and Ishizaki 1995; Ernst 1997a,b; Itagaki 1997). Interviews by the author with the senior managers of more than a dozen indigenous supplier firms to the electronics industry in Singapore further confirmed this. Indeed, many Japanese suppliers to the Japanese electronics majors have replicated their supplier–buyer relationships in Japan by investing in Singapore to serve their buyers' manufacturing plants in Singapore or in the ASEAN region. Moreover, some of the larger Japanese electronics majors have vertically integrated backwards by establishing their own component production facilities in Singapore. This higher intra-Japanese sourcing propensity is also reflected in Table 7.5, which shows a significantly higher share of electronics output from Japanese firms in Singapore going to other firms in Singapore and other ASEAN countries (36 percent and 9 percent, respectively, in 1994 vs. 10 percent and 2 percent for US firms).

In contrast, the same interviews with managers of local electronics supporting industries suggest that US firms exhibited a higher propensity to engage in external sourcing, including a higher degree of willingness to try out local indigenous suppliers of various precision engineering parts and contract manufacturing services. In more recent years, this local sourcing has extended to automation services, logistics and warehousing services, and even design services. For example, Apple computer had substantially outsourced PCBA and final assembly activities to indigenous contract manufacturing firms such as Venture and Richgold, and both HP and Compaq had engaged services of indigenous logistics firms, such as YCH, to do final configuration/packaging/outbound logistics (HP) or inbound logistics and knock-down kit assembly (Compaq). Conner (now part of Seagate) worked extensively with local baseplate supplier MMI to develop extrusion techniques for making HDD baseplates, and now is the now largest buyer of these baseplates.

Many of the local supporting industry firms interviewed reported greater difficulty qualifying to supply Japanese firms than their US counterparts. However, a number of firms that have succeeded in supplying to Japanese majors indicated that Japanese firms tend to emphasize long-term supplier relationships more than US firms do. These firms also indicated that they

*Table 7.5* Geographic destination of electronics export from Singapore, 1980 and 1990–4

| | Sales (M$) | % Singapore | % USA | % EU | % Japan | % ASEAN | % E. Asian | % Other Asian | % Other | Total export(%) |
|---|---|---|---|---|---|---|---|---|---|---|
| *European MNCs* | | | | | | | | | | |
| 1981 | 1,041,869 | 8.69 | 5.39 | 52.59 | 0.27 | 18.35 | 0.00 | 0.00 | 14.79 | 91.31 |
| 1991 | 3,434,615 | 12.51 | 13.12 | 56.35 | 4.11 | 4.37 | 6.12 | 0.00 | 5.95 | 87.49 |
| 1992 | 3,637,434 | 13.64 | 13.21 | 48.62 | 2.25 | 4.32 | 6.22 | 0.09 | 11.66 | 86.36 |
| 1993 | 4,010,074 | 13.58 | 8.38 | 46.23 | 2.25 | 11.06 | 7.26 | 0.00 | 11.23 | 86.42 |
| 1994 | 4,180,886 | 19.78 | 13.80 | 41.88 | 2.89 | 9.31 | 7.30 | 0.08 | 4.97 | 80.22 |
| *Japanese MNCs* | | | | | | | | | | |
| 1981 | 1,625,720 | 27.87 | 24.09 | 21.5 | 8.37 | 4.62 | 0.72 | 0 | 12.84 | 72.13 |
| 1991 | 7,242,573 | 31.64 | 16.54 | 15.18 | 12.65 | 6.84 | 6.43 | 0 | 10.73 | 68.36 |
| 1992 | 7,000,268 | 34.68 | 16.26 | 11.1 | 11.23 | 7.84 | 7.38 | 0 | 11.43 | 65.32 |
| 1993 | 7,616,831 | 33.99 | 17.56 | 7.13 | 10.89 | 12.61 | 6.07 | 0 | 11.75 | 66.01 |
| 1994 | 9,919,251 | 36.4 | 19.72 | 10.88 | 10.69 | 9.1 | 5.79 | 0 | 7.38 | 63.6 |
| *US MNCs* | | | | | | | | | | |
| 1981 | 2,789,605 | 1.76 | 87.24 | 7.37 | 0.79 | 0.49 | 0 | 0 | 2.36 | 98.24 |
| 1991 | 16,056,822 | 9.02 | 61.05 | 13.37 | 2.09 | 4.64 | 5.46 | 0 | 4.28 | 90.98 |
| 1992 | 18,901,068 | 9.65 | 54.75 | 19.33 | 2.89 | 3.7 | 6.05 | 0 | 3.61 | 90.35 |
| 1993 | 24,198,497 | 7.89 | 57.2 | 16.4 | 4.51 | 2.58 | 9.86 | 0 | 1.57 | 92.11 |
| 1994 | 29,807,735 | 10.04 | 60.54 | 14.93 | 5.49 | 2.25 | 5.76 | 0.18 | 0.81 | 89.96 |

Source: Unpublished data from EDB's Census of Industrial Production as presented in Davis (forthcoming).

have invested substantially in relationship-specific assets that are co-specialized with their Japanese buyers, including recruiting senior managers who have worked in Japanese firms and who speak Japanese fluently, adopting total quality management (TQM) methods familiar to Japanese firms, and maintaining frequent interactions at the managerial level.

### Extensions beyond manufacturing – trends towards an integrated regional hub role

Besides continuous advancement in the technological sophistication of electronics manufacturing operations in Singapore by successive waves of new MNC investments as well as upgrading of existing plants, major US and Japanese electronics firms have also deepened their operations in Singapore into a wide range of non-manufacturing activities over the years. Here again, despite some similarities in overall diversification trends between Japanese and US firms, closer examination reveals significant differences in corporate strategies.

Diversification and growth of electronics MNCs into non-manufacturing activities in Singapore can involve one or more of the following five additional regional hub functions: regional marketing and sales; regional technical support and training; regional procurement; regional logistics and distribution; and product or process R&D. Although there is no necessary linear progression in these functions, they do represent a common sequence or route undertaken by many of the MNC electronic majors. Regional marketing and sales typically represents the earliest form of expansion into non-manufacturing activities undertaken by many MNCs as far back as the 1970s. Regional technical support and training and procurement followed in many cases in the 1980s, and regional logistics and distribution functions have become more prominent since the late 1980s. Good examples of the former include Motorola University corporate office for South East Asia (training), HP Regional Response Centre (technical support), and IBM (international procurement), and representative examples of the latter include Sony Logistics and Asia Matsushita Logistics from Japan and Apple and Compaq from the United States (regional logistics hub). Product and/or process R&D represent a more recent phenomenon, and has only begun to be undertaken in significant numbers since the early 1990s. Between 1993 and 1995, R&D expenditure by electronics MNCs in Singapore rose from S$248 million to S$352 million or 19 percent per year [calculated from National Science & Technology Board (NSTB) various years].

In addition to this functional diversification, some of the MNCs have chosen to establish regional headquarters (RHQ) or operational headquarters (OHQ) in Singapore to manage their regional operations. The geographic reach of these OHQs can range from Southeast Asia to include Northeast Asia (Japan excluded), South Asia and Australia–New Zealand. These regional OHQs typically also serve to integrate one or more of the non-manufacturing operations of the company in Singapore. A good example is the Matsushita group, which established its OHQ in Singapore (Asia Matsushita Electric Singapore or AMS) in 1989 to coordinate its Southeast Asian manufacturing operations and to integrate regional sales and logistics distribution. Other representative examples of MNCs with RHQ in Singapore include Motorola (1994) and HP (1995), Hitachi (1990), and Sony Display Devices (1996). An indication of the extent of regional headquartering by MNCs in Singapore is that more than 100 companies have been awarded OHQ or business headquarters (BHQ) tax incentives by the government since the introduction of the schemes in 1986 and 1994. Electronics MNCs probably accounted for at least half of these.

Last, but not least, an as yet small but growing number of MNC operations in Singapore have also achieved world product charter (WPC) status, taking over the full management responsibility of particular product lines from product planning, commercialization launch to distribution and sales worldwide. For example, HP Singapore currently holds three WPCs: one for hand-held personal computing devices (including calculators and palm-tops), one for portable inkjet printers, and one for wide-format printers. Other companies that have been granted world product mandates include Motorola (for Asian language pagers), Thomson Consumer Electronics (for TVs of given format), and Philips (for given audio products). It is notable, however, that there is as yet no Japanese operation in Singapore that has achieved WPC status.

Overall, although both US and Japanese electronics firms have broadened their operational activities in Singapore beyond manufacturing alone, the pattern of diversification into non-manufacturing activities has been somewhat different. Japanese firms appear to make greater use of Singapore as a regional marketing, sales, technical support and regional coordinating center than US firms do, but, by and large, major decisions remain dependent on corporate headquarters in Japan. In contrast, US firms appear to have gone further in giving autonomous decision-making power to their regional operations in Singapore, particularly in the setting up of lead manufacturing plant and regional/world product charter in Singapore. US firms also appear to have been more aggressive in extending into R&D activities and devolving manufacturing process technology development responsibilities to Singapore in general.

The contrast in management control is reflected in the extent of indigenization of top management in the US versus Japanese subsidiary operations in Singapore. To date, there is not a single Japanese electronics manufacturing plant in Singapore where the topmost manager is not Japanese [although a number of Japanese regional sales offices in Singapore (e.g. NEC) do have Singaporean managing directors]. In contrast, many US electronics firms in Singapore have promoted indigenous Singaporeans to the most senior management post in their Singapore manufacturing operation (e.g. HP, Motorola, Apple Computer, Compaq, and IBM Data Storage). Indeed, some

US electronics MNCs have deployed their Singaporean managers to head up new manufacturing operations in the region (e.g. Motorola and Conner assigned Singaporean managers to start up their new factories in China).

### Technology linkage with host economy

Another key difference observed between US and Japanese electronics firms is the pattern of technology flows between the corporate headquarters and the local subsidiaries on the one hand, and the technology flows between these local subsidiaries and other firms and institutions in the host economies on the other. As reported in Wong (1996; 1998), a recent survey covering nineteen US and thirteen Japanese electronics-related manufacturing subsidiaries in Singapore found that the US firms exhibited significantly higher technological innovation intensities than their Japanese counterparts, as measured by indicators such as R&D spending as a percentage of total sales, the proportion of employees with university degrees in S&T, and the relative ranking of new product development versus improving existing products.

Although both US and Japanese attached similar degree of importance to technology transfer from their parent headquarters as a source of technology, US firms generally assigned markedly higher importance to several other channels of technology acquisition than Japanese firms: joint R&D with local public research institutes and universities; joint R&D with other companies; joint ventures with other firms; acquisition of other companies owning the relevant technologies; incorporating the technologies of suppliers; learning from the technical specifications and feedback from buyers; and recruiting experienced scientists and engineers (Wong 1998). Overall, US electronics firms exhibited a much higher extent of technological collaboration and interactions with other firms and R&D institutions in Singapore than their Japanese counterparts did.

By and large, the above findings are consistent with widespread industry informant perception that Japanese subsidiaries in East Asia tend to depend primarily on technology transfer from their parent headquarters. Although Japanese subsidiary firms do emphasize technological learning by the local workforce, this is geared primarily towards absorbing, adapting, and improving the process technologies transferred from Japan, rather than seeking out alternative sources of technologies from within the host country or elsewhere (Itagaki 1997). The manufacturing plants of Japanese subsidiaries in Singapore typically upgrade to making more advanced products by adopting the entire product line process technology already perfected in Japan. In contrast, many US firms have their lead manufacturing plants in Singapore, with prime process engineering responsibility to develop the process lines to make the products assigned from parent headquarter. Indeed, some of the US companies no longer have volume manufacturing capacities in the United States and rely on the Singaporean lead manufacturing plants for critical production ramp-up (see, for example, Wong 1997). Some of these Singaporean plants of US firms also play the role of "engineering transfer station;" they provide the process engineering capabilities to establish volume production of new products, but once these production processes are stabilized, they are then transferred to other less advanced locations.

The difference between US and Japanese firms in terms of technological impact on the host economy is thus somewhat subtle. Because Japanese firms tend to be global leaders in manufacturing process technologies, their subsidiary plants in East Asia primarily get their manufacturing process technologies transferred from Japan, and hence exhibit a high degree of dependency on Japanese headquarters. In contrast, US firms tend to focus on product technology development, and increasingly rely on their overseas manufacturing subsidiaries to develop (or co-develop) the manufacturing process technologies, or to outsource substantial part of their manufacturing activities to specialized contract manufacturers. This translates into less direct process technology transfer from the parent headquarters, but more innovation efforts at the subsidiary plant and increased interactions with local firms and R&D institutions. This mandate to seek more technological inputs from the host economy itself may have the indirect effect of stimulating development of local technological capabilities.

### Competitive performance of US versus Japanese electronics firms

As argued by Michael Borrus in Chapter 3, the different production network strategies of US and Japanese electronics firms in East Asia are likely to have had a causal impact on their global competitive performance. Although it is not possible to make causal inferences about competitive performance at the global level from financial performance at the level of subsidiary operations in Singapore, it is interesting to note that US electronics firms appear to have reported higher profitability performance than Japanese firms, at least in the most recent years for which data are available. As can be seen from Table 7.6, of the seventeen large US and forty-four large Japanese electronics manufacturing firms in Singapore for which data are available, the US firms registered significantly higher return on sales (ROS) and return on assets (ROAs) performance than Japanese firms did over the three-year period from 1992/3 to 1994/5. Although it is possible that part of this difference may be due to differences in transfer pricing and other international accounting practices of US and Japanese firms, the data are at least not inconsistent with the argument of Borrus at the global level.

## The emergence of indigenous electronics firms

As mentioned in the first section, the role of indigenous firms in Singapore's electronics industry had been negligible until the 1980s. Unlike Taiwan and Hong Kong, Singapore lacked an initial injection of experienced

*Table 7.6* Profitability of major electronics-related MNCs in Singapore, 1992/3–1994/5

| Nationality | 1992/3 | | 1993/4 | | 1994/5 | |
|---|---|---|---|---|---|---|
| | Return on sales | Return on assets | Return on sales | Return on assets | Return on sales | Return on assets |
| US | 7.5 | 13.6 | 9.4 | 16.4 | 9.8 | 15.8 |
| Japan | 1.7 | 4.0 | 2.0 | 4.6 | 2.3 | 5.9 |
| Europe | 1.3 | 3.0 | 3.3 | 8.0 | 3.9 | 8.7 |

Note: Data pertain only to companies that are known to be involved in electronics manufacturing and exclude companies classified by the publisher as electronics but which only undertake sales and marketing or which are holding companies/headquarter operations where revenues pertain to sales in the region.

Source: Estimated by author from Datapool, *Singapore Industrial Companies 1000*, 1994 and 1996 editions.

manufacturing entrepreneurs from mainland China during the early years of political independence. Neither did Singapore send large numbers of students to the United States for training in electronics technology as did Taiwan, Hong Kong, and South Korea. The influx of foreign manufacturing investments did provide training and exposure to a large number of Singaporean engineers and technicians, but much of this was in manufacturing process technology, not in product technology know-how, which, by and large, still resided in the corporate headquarters in the United States, Japan, and Europe. It is thus not surprising that the transfer of technological know-how through these manufacturing investments translated first into the development of indigenous firms in the electronics contract manufacturing (i.e. "OEM" subcontracting) and supporting industries, rather than in "original design manufacturing" (ODM) or "original brand manufacturing" (OBM).

In spite of this, there has been a rapid growth of indigenous electronics firms since the late 1980s. There are now about thirty indigenous electronics-related firms in Singapore with annual sales of over S$100 million, of which about ten are in the S$500 million league (Wong *et al.* 1997). Although still significantly smaller than what has emerged in Taiwan and Korea, this indigenous sector is playing an increasingly significant role in the production networks of Southeast Asia and beyond.

We can discern three distinct groups among these indigenous firms. The first, and by far the largest, consists of firms that are primarily contract manufacturers or precision engineering firms providing parts, components, automation equipment, and process engineering services to the electronics industry. Practically all of them first emerged as local suppliers to electronics MNCs operating in Singapore, and later succeeded in upgrading their technological capability in response to their customers' increasingly sophisticated demands. Since the late 1980s, many have also been able to internationalize their operations by moving to lower cost overseas locations such as Malaysia, Indonesia, and China. These overseas operations typically supply not only their original MNC customers in Singapore, but also increasingly MNC manufacturing plants that are rapidly expanding into these sites as well.

In so doing, these firms were able to leverage two advantages over indigenous firms in these less advanced host economies. First, they had a first mover advantage of learning economies, having developed more advanced manufacturing process capabilities through their relationships with the most advanced MNC manufacturing plants in the region. Second, having established long-term supplier–buyer relationships with their customers in Singapore, they were often able to replicate those relationships when their customers shifted their lower end manufacturing activities out of Singapore. The most successful examples of companies in this group are Venture Manufacturing and Flextronics (in PCBA), Amtek Engineering (in metal stamping), and MMI (HDD baseplate machining). Indeed, a company like MMI has completely hollowed out its manufacturing operations to Malaysia, with its Singapore headquarter undertaking only product development and process engineering activities.

The second group consists of indigenous companies that have achieved some degree of success in OBM. In contrast to the first group of companies, which developed their competitive advantages in manufacturing process technology and operational capability, firms belonging to this second group were able to develop their own product technology and commercialization/ marketing capability, rather than as component suppliers or contract manufacturers. The most successful among this group of companies is Creative Technology, the global market and technological leader in PC audio-cards. Although Creative Technology had pursued an OBM strategy from the start, a more typical route is for successful contract manufacturers to forward integrate into own product innovation; Goldtron [global system mobile communication (GSM) phones] and Flextech (semiconductor packaging) provide interesting examples of this strategy.

Whereas the first two groups comprise indigenous private enterprises, the third group consists of state-owned enterprises that have been explicitly directed to enter targeted electronics sectors perceived as strategic to Singapore, including defense-related sectors where government control is considered critical, or capital intensive sectors like semiconductor wafer fabrication where the entry barriers are high and MNCs on their own might not be willing to invest in Singapore. The strategic intent to develop indigenous technological capabilities in sectors seen as critical to future national competitiveness may also have been an important motivation of the government. The Singapore Technologies (ST) Group represents the most prominent and biggest of such state enterprises targeted at a range of high-tech industries including aerospace, electronics systems integration, computer software, and semiconductors.

It is under the direction of the government that three major indigenous semiconductor wafer fabrication firms have been established in Singapore in the 1990s. The first, Chartered Semiconductor Manufacturing, was set up as a state-owned enterprise to compete in the "third-party" ASIC wafer-foundry market. The second, Tech-Semiconductor, started as a joint venture of the Economic Development Board (EDB) with TI, Canon, and Hewlett-Packard in the DRAM market. The third, Tri-Tech, was established to compete in the IC design market. The formation of Tech-Semi is significant in that it represented a new attempt by the government to attract high-tech investment by MNCs through the offering of tax incentives and equity capital to share the risk with foreign investors. Two more recent cases of this approach are the joint investment in a new S\$1.33 billion DRAM wafer-fabrication plant by the EDB, Hitachi, and Nippon Steel, and another joint venture involving EDB, Chartered Semiconductor Manufacturing, and HP to enter into ASICs wafer fabrication.

The pervasive presence of MNC electronics firms in Singapore may have had the effect of stunting the growth of indigenous enterprises in the early years, by bidding away non-tradeable resources such as industrial land and human resources (Lee and Low 1990). However, there is now substantial evidence that the close proximity of a large number of "world-class" MNCs has helped stimulate the growth of a whole host of local electronics supporting industries (Wong 1992; 1994; 1995b). An increasing number of these firms are seeking to develop their own product technology capability (Wong 1998). Moreover, green-field high-tech start-ups driven by similar forces of techno-entrepreneurship, as are observed in Taiwan, are also beginning to occur in Singapore, albeit on a smaller scale. Both groups are leveraging on the strong and competitive local supply base in Singapore, as well as increasing incentives and assistance from the government in the forms of R&D grants, technology transfer from public research institutes/universities, and other high-tech infrastructural supports such as science park facilities and incubator schemes (NSTB 1996).

## Conclusion: how small economies can successfully ride the global technological waves

Our analysis of the growth of Singapore's electronics industry illustrates the need to understand the development of an Asian production network as the result of a complex interaction at three level of changes: (1) macro-level changes in technology and market demand; (2) micro-level changes in the form of strategic and organizational responses of individual firms; and (3) "meso-level" changes in the form of home and host government policies. Although technological change and shifting competition between leading firms from different national home bases represent the underlying sources of "carrier waves," the specific manner by which these waves ripple across East Asia is influenced strongly by competition between host governments in attracting FDI and inducing technology transfer/development of host technological capabilities.

Although Singapore's initial ability to attract MNC investment to locate their production in Singapore in the 1960s could be attributed partly to fortuitous timing and the lack of serious competition due to the generally inward-looking industrial policies prevalent among developing countries at the time, her ability to consistently attract these new investments to Singapore throughout the 1970s, 1980s, and 1990s has also depended crucially on the role of the state in making Singapore a viable location for electronics manufacturing and related activities. This is particularly true given continuously rising costs, labor shortages, and increasing competition from other countries in Southeast Asia and elsewhere for similar investments.

Much has been written on the role of government policies and institutions in enabling Singapore to ride the successive waves of new MNC investments and upgrading into ever higher value-added manufacturing activities involving more advanced technologies (see, for example, Natarajan and Tan 1992; Low *et al.* 1993; Soon and Tan 1993; Schein 1996; Goh 1996; EDB 1997) and need not be repeated here. What is interesting to note in the context of this chapter is that, despite the significant differences in the internationalization strategies of Japanese and US electronics firms, Singapore has been able to become an important regional node for the two somewhat distinctive production networks that have been spurned by US and Japanese firms. Indeed, the development of Japanese and US production networks has been complementary in sustaining the continuous growth of Singapore's electronics industry in general and in fostering the growth of a highly competitive and flexible and diverse total business infrastructure for the electronics industry: a wide range of world-class electronics supporting industries; a highly efficient and flexible regional logistics, procurement, transport and communications infrastructure; a well-developed financial and administrative infrastructure; and a large pool of highly skilled, experienced professionals to service the entire business value chains of product development, process engineering, manufacturing, marketing, distribution, and technical services. It is perhaps this diverse source of agglomeration economies that may help sustain Singapore's overall competitiveness in the future, rather than any single factor.

At the same time, the competing yet overlapping interactions of US and Japanese production networks in Singapore also illustrate the existence of mutual complementarities between the two: despite their greater use of non-Japanese local suppliers, many US electronics manufacturing operations in Singapore continue to source from Japanese suppliers located in Singapore, either directly (for various key components and devices) or indirectly (many of their non-Japanese suppliers in Singapore still depend on Japanese precision engineering equipment).

Finally, the extensive co-location of US and Japanese production systems in Singapore is bound to invite comparative benchmarking of their management approaches and manufacturing strategies. This comparative benchmarking, coupled with the growing importance of the indigenous Singaporean cluster and the consequent inevitable increase in strategic alliances that will be developed between this cluster and the foreign MNCs, is likely to contribute towards convergence of management practices and strategies between the Japanese and US firms. Already, Japanese firms in Singapore have been found to be more "westernized" than their counterparts in Thailand and Malaysia (Itagaki 1997), whereas US firms in Singapore had extensively adopted JIT, TQM, and other Japanese manufacturing practices.

As highlighted in Chapters 5 and 6, Taiwan and Korea have both emerged as new autonomous sources of technological innovations that are beginning to rival US and Japanese electronics firms in selected sectors. Our analysis in this chapter has shown that an indigenous innovative electronics sector is beginning to emerge in Singapore as well. As the weight of the lead user market of US–Japan is increasingly being balanced by the growing market of non-Japan East Asia, and as the advanced East Asian NIEs increasingly invest in R&D and product innovation, future competition between Japan and the United States will increasingly take the form of stronger alliances between the US and Japanese firms with firms from the advanced East Asian NIEs.

## References

Angel, D. (1994) "Tiger Bonds? Customer-Supplier Linkages in Semiconductor," *Regional Studies*, 28(2): 187–200.

Borrus, M. (1993) "The Regional Architecture of Global Electronics: Trajectories, Linkages and Access to Technology," in P. Gourevitch and P. Guerrieri (eds) *New Challenges to International Cooperation: Adjustment of Firms, Policies, and Organizations to Global Competition*, San Diego: University of California at San Diego.

Department of Statistics, Singapore. *Yearbook of Statistics*, various years.

Economic Committee (1986) *The Singapore Economy: New Directions*, Singapore: Ministry of Trade and Industry.

*EDB Yearbook* (various years) Singapore: Economic Development Board.

*Electronics Industry in Singapore* (1996) Singapore: Economic Development Board.

Ernst, D. (1994) "Mobilizing the Region's Capabilities? The East Asian Production Networks of Japanese Electronics Firms," in E. M. Doherty (ed.) *Japanese Investment in Asia: International Production Strategies in a Rapidly Changing World*, San Francisco: The Asia Foundation, 29–56.

—— (1997a) "Patterns for the China Circle? The Asian Production Networks of Japanese Electronics Firms," in B. Naughton (ed.) *The China Circle*, Washington DC: Brookings Institution.

—— (1997b) "From Partial to Systemic Globalization: International Production Networks in the Electronics Industry," BRIE Working Paper 98.

Goh, K. S. (1996) "The Technology Ladder in Development: The Singapore Case," *Asia Pacific Economic Literature*, 10(1): 1–12.

Itagaki, H. (ed.) (1997) *The Japanese Production System: Hybrid Factories in Asia*, London: Macmillan.

Kobayashi, H. (1992) *Tōnan Ajia no Nikkei Kigyo* (Japanese Affiliated Companies in South East Asian Countries), Tokyo: Nihon Hyoronsha.

Lee, T. Y. and Low, L. (1990) *Local Entrepreneurship in Singapore: Private and State*, Singapore: Time Academy Press.

Lee, T. Y. (1993) *Overseas Investment: Experience of Singapore Manufacturing Companies*, Singapore: McGraw-Hill.

Low, L. Toh, M. H. Soon, T. W. Tan, K. Y. and Hughes, H. (1993) *Challenge and Response: Thirty Years of the Economic Development Board*, Singapore: Times Academic Press.

Ministry of Trade and Industry, Singapore (various years) *Economic Survey of Singapore*, Singapore: National Printers.

Natarajan, S. and Tan, J. M. (1992) *The Impacts of MNC Investments in Malaysia, Singapore and Thailand*, Singapore: ISEAS.

National Science & Technology Board, Singapore (1996) *National Science and Technology Plan: Towards 2000 and Beyond*. Singapore: NSTB.

National Science & Technology Board, Singapore (various years) *National Survey of R&D*, Singapore: NSTB.

*Report on the Census for Industrial Production*, various years, Singapore: Economic Development Board.

Schein, E. (1996) *Strategic Pragmatism: The Culture of the Economic Development Board of Singapore*. Cambridge, MA: MIT Press.

Scott, A. (1987) "The Semiconductor Industry in Southeast Asia: Organization, Location and the International Division of Labor," *Regional Studies*, 21(2): 49–68.

*Singapore Investment News* (various issues) Singapore: Economic Development Board.

Soon, T. W. and Tan, C. S. (1993) *Singapore: Public Policy and Economic Development*, Washington DC: World Bank.

Takayasu, K. and Ishizaki, Y. (1995) "The Changing International Division of Labor of Japanese Electronics Industry in Asia and its Impact on the Japanese Economy," *RIM-Pacific Business and Industries*, 1, 27: 2–27.

*The Straits Times*, Weekly Edition, various dates.

UNCTAD (1997) *World Investment Report 1997: Transnational Corporations, Market Structure and Competition Policy*, New York, United Nations.

Wong, P. K. (1991) *Technological Development Through Subcontracting Linkages*, Tokyo: Asian Productivity Organization.

—— (1992) "Technological Development Through Subcontracting Linkages: Evidence from Singapore," *Scandinavian International Business Review*, 1(3): 28–40.

—— (1994) "Singapore's Technology Strategy," in D. F. Simon (ed.) *The Emerging Technological Trajectory of the Pacific Rim*, New York: M. E. Sharpe.

—— (1995a) "Competing in the Global Electronics Industry: A Comparative Study of the Innovation Networks of Singapore and Taiwan," *Journal of Industry Studies*, 2(2): 35–61.

—— (1995b) "Technology Transfer and Development Inducement by Foreign MNCs: The Experience of Singapore," in K. Y. Jeong and M. H. Kwack (eds) *Industrial Strategy for Global Competitiveness of Korean Industries*, Seoul: Korea Economic Research Institute: 130–159.

—— (1996) "From NIE to Developed Economy: Singapore's Industrial Policy to the Year 2000," *Journal of Asian Business*, 12(3): 65–85.

—— (1997) "Creation of a Regional Hub for Flexible Production: The Case of Hard Disk Drive Industry in Singapore," *Industry and Innovation*, 4(2).

—— (1998) "Technology Acquisition Pattern of High-Tech Firms in Singapore," Singapore: NUS-CMT Working Paper.

Wong, P. K. Phang, S. Y. *et al.* (1997) *Development of Internationally Competitive Indigenous Manufacturing Firms in Singapore*, Tokyo: Foundation for Advanced Studies of International Development.

Yamashita, S. (ed.) (1991) *Transfer of Japanese Technology and Management to the ASEAN Countries*, Tokyo: University of Tokyo Press.

*Yearbook of World Electronics Data* (various years), Amsterdam: Elsevier.

# 8 Japan and the United States in the Malaysian electronics sector

*Greg Linden*

Malaysia provides a rich entry point for examining the differences between American and Japanese production networks in the electronics sector. In 1990, Malaysia's export-oriented electrical/electronics sector accounted for over 25 percent of the country's manufacturing output and 30 percent of manufacturing employment (Rasiah 1995: Table 5.3). Furthermore, the sector is dominated by foreign capital; in 1990 the foreign share of fixed assets in electrical/electronics was 89 percent (ibid.: Table 5.2).

Building on its initial attractiveness as a source of low cost land and labor, an economy once dominated by tin mines and rubber plantations has come to occupy an intermediate role in the regional division of labor, somewhere in the technological gap between Indonesia and Taiwan. Malaysian factories supply a range of components to other network nodes in the region and assemble a variety of final goods for shipment to destinations across the globe. Industrial policies introduced over the last decade have helped induce affiliates to upgrade their activities by assembling more valuable and complex products and by adding ancillary activities. Malaysian managers and engineers are increasingly called upon to help launch factories in other developing countries. Local suppliers have emerged in support industries, such as the injection molding of plastic parts, and also as subcontractors for assembly.

We will compare US and Japanese affiliates across five categories of behavior: linkages to the local economy, development of local human resources, introduction of higher value-added activities such as product design, capital deepening, and management autonomy. We must be careful not to ascribe all differences to the nationality factor alone. The present study permits us to hold constant certain key explanatory factors for affiliate behavior, namely the host country's policies and resources. As we proceed, we will try to account for other significant factors that might lead to observed national differences.[1]

It should not be surprising that some differences between American and Japanese affiliates cannot be explained apart from their differing ownership. The organizational differences of the parent firms are so great that it would be hard to imagine that this would not affect the operation of overseas plants. For example, Japanese electronics firms have much more rigid personnel practices, are more vertically integrated, and have tighter linkages with home country suppliers than US firms do. On this basis, we would expect Japanese offshore affiliates to favor Japan-based suppliers and to have limited management autonomy relative to the corresponding behaviors in US-owned affiliates. In Malaysia, these expectations are more or less fulfilled.

We begin by reviewing the policies governing foreign direct investment (FDI) in Malaysia and the history of FDI in the Malaysian electronics sector. The main body of the paper reviews evidence on affiliate behaviors in Malaysia drawn from the BRIE FDI database, company interviews, and other primary and secondary sources.[2] The final section summarizes the findings and concludes.

## Foreign investment: policy and response

Malaysia opened itself to foreign investment soon after gaining independence from Britain in 1957. Under an import substitution policy, tariffs were raised and tax benefits granted to selected industries. Because of the limited domestic market and requirements for taking on local partners, the response of foreign investors was disappointing.

With the Investment Incentives Act of 1968 and the Free Trade Zones Act of 1971, Malaysia adopted a formula that had been used elsewhere in the region: to make itself an attractive platform for export-oriented investment through exemptions from various taxes and duties. Electronics was made a "pioneer industry" in 1971. Exporting manufacturers were offered up to ten years of tax exemption, freedom from joint venture requirements, subsidized industrial estates, free trade zones (FTZs), investment guarantees, and unhindered profit repatriation. FTZ firms were also kept union-free for many years (Rasiah 1993: 130).[3]

In 1981, government leadership was taken over by the current Prime Minister Mahathir Mohamad. He installed a Japan-style technocracy, emphasizing the development of heavy industry as part of a "Look East" policy aimed at assimilating the lessons of Japan and Korea (Lim and Fong 1991: 22). In the mid-1980s, a downturn in world prices for the country's commodity exports, coinciding with a drop in foreign and domestic investment, seriously undermined the new policy. The government responded by easing the restrictions and strengthening the incentives for both foreign and domestic investors. Japanese electronics firms were at the forefront of the subsequent wave of FDI.

After approximately ten years of expansion by the Malaysian electronics sector, the Asian financial crisis has posed a new challenge to the country's policy-makers. The trading value of the Malaysian Ringgit (RM) was caught in the wake of Thailand's July 1997 decision to stop defending its currency. From the level of roughly RM 2.5 to the dollar, which had held since 1992, the currency's value slid steadily to as low as RM 4.7 to the dollar in early 1998.

Malaysia's leadership responded in September 1998 with the unorthodox imposition of capital controls and a fixed exchange rate of RM 3.8 to the dollar. Whereas the capital controls affected the country's access to loans and portfolio investment, the impact on direct investment in manufacturing was less noticeable. The drop in FDI may also have stemmed in part from the general decrease in regional demand and the weakened circumstances of many of the region's potential investors. Data from the Malaysian Industrial Development Authority (MIDA), the lead agency for attracting foreign investment, show that applications (as opposed to approvals) for manufacturing investments by foreign companies fell only about 12 percent between 1997 and 1998 and continued to arrive steadily in 1999 (*BT*, 3 February 1999).

Investors in the export-intensive electronics sector have generally been supportive of the country's capital controls, which do not pose any barrier to the processing of export earnings through foreign currency accounts. In fact, as other regional currencies begin to recover, the fixed Ringgit appears increasingly competitive. The head of Sony Malaysia has said that the controls "should be maintained" (*The Star*, 11 May 1999).

Figure 8.1 shows the levels of investment approvals for new plants and expansions in the electrical/electronics sector from 1987 through 1998. Although a gradual upward trend can be discerned for the period as a whole, the regional crisis that began in 1997 appears to have significantly depressed investment activity. The downturn appears to be more severe than, but not different in kind from, earlier cycles, and it does not seem destined to have any lasting impact on the organizational behaviors of concern in this study.

Table 8.1 shows the nationality of foreign paid-in equity in 1986 and 1996 as reported by MIDA. Even before the yen appreciation of the mid-1980s,

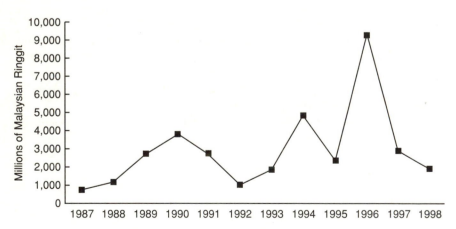

*Figure 8.1* Approved foreign investments in the Malaysian electrical/electronics sector. Source: MIDA.

*Table 8.1* Top four investors by nationality in Malaysia's electrical/electronics sector

| Percent of total paid-up capital | | Percent of fixed assets (book value) |
| --- | --- | --- |
| *1986* | *1996* | *1996* |
| Japan (28%) | Japan (52%) | Japan (39%) |
| Singapore (21%) | Taiwan (15%) | United States (23%) |
| Hong Kong (7%) | Singapore (13%) | Singapore (14%) |
| United States (7%) | United States (9%) | Taiwan (9%) |

Source: MIDA.

Japanese firms were the top investors, which indicates that "vintage effects" (the influence of the relative age of affiliates) may be relatively unimportant in the Malaysian case; Japanese companies were generally slower than US companies to invest overseas, but electronics firms were among the earliest investors and Southeast Asia one of their earliest destinations. By December 1996, the Japanese share of sectoral paid-up capital had risen to 52 percent, while the US share remained below 10 percent.

The data on paid-up capital overstate the difference between US and Japanese investments in the sector. In terms of fixed assets (at book value) at 31 December 1996, the Japanese share was 39 percent versus 23 percent for US-owned affiliates.

Table 8.1 also shows the importance of some of East Asia's newly industrialized economies (NIEs). Like Japan, the "tigers" faced appreciating currencies, rising wages at home, plus loss of trading benefits under the generalized system of preferences (GSPs) starting in 1988. The biggest jump in the FDI share was by Taiwanese investors. Neighboring Singapore has also been an important source of FDI for Malaysia.

Malaysia's electronics FDI falls into several overlapping phases distinguished by product category. The first phase was integrated circuit (IC) assembly, dominated by American firms. A second wave beginning in the late 1980s was mainly consumer electronics and related components. A third phase, much smaller than its predecessors, is currently taking place for computing hardware.

The first wave of export-oriented investments in Malaysia was for the assembly of ICs, a product that still dominates the country's electronics exports. Just as Malaysia's northern state of Penang was developing its first free trade zone (FTZ), semiconductor firms were extending the globalization of their labor-intensive assembly operations.

US chip firms had established numerous assembly plants elsewhere in East Asia during the 1960s. But it was only in the next decade, after a 1971 official promotional mission to California's Silicon Valley, that investors turned to Malaysia. Over the next three years, Malaysian IC assembly operations were initiated in Penang's new FTZ by the US firms National Semiconductor,

Intel, Advanced Micro Devices, and Texas Instruments (TI) and Japan's Hitachi.[4] Other plants were established in and around Malaysia's capital, Kuala Lumpur, by Motorola, Harris, RCA, Toshiba, and NEC. Each of these companies employs over 1,000 workers – and some have grown to employ several thousands.

In the early 1980s, 85 percent of the output of the Malaysian electronics sector consisted of components – primarily ICs (O'Connor 1993: 212). This concentration exposed the economy to the cyclicality of the semiconductor industry, including a severe downturn in the mid-1980s. Policies to attract investment in other electronics sectors helped to reduce the weight of semiconductors to about 40 percent by 1995 (*The Star*, 18 June 1996). Yet despite the government's desire to rely less on ICs, it has permitted several additional producers to start assembly, such as Italy's SGS in 1986, Integrated Device Technology in 1987, Japan's Fujitsu in 1988, Taiwan's Advanced Semiconductor Engineering in 1991, and Korea's Samsung in 1994. Malaysia ranks consistently in the world's top five exporters of ICs, and ICs remain Malaysia's most important electronics export.

In 1986, the Promotion of Investments Act took a more targeted approach that relied on bureaucratic decisions about the value of particular products for the country's economic development. This policy change coincided with profound changes in Japan: an appreciating currency, rising domestic wages, and serious competition from producers in Korea and Taiwan. These circumstances created a surge of FDI from Japan in search of lower cost production sites for lower technology product segments, which Malaysia was well placed to receive.

Consumer products are actually the oldest sector for foreign investment in the Malaysian electronics industry. In the mid-1960s, Matsushita and Sanyo invested in joint ventures producing electrical appliances and televisions for the domestic market in response to the import-substitution incentives.[5]

After the policy switch to export promotion, among the first firms to invest were producers of car radios, such as Germany's Robert Bosch and Japan's Clarion. However, investments in consumer products were infrequent during the 1970s and early 1980s. Then from 1986 to 1989, Sanyo, Matsushita, Sony, NEC, Hitachi, Mitsubishi Electric, and Sharp established new operations for the manufacture of TVs, VCRs, and microwave ovens for export. Europe's Grundig also arrived in 1988, joining Thomson and Philips, which had invested earlier. The 1990s saw the arrival of Samsung (microwave ovens) and Daewoo (washing machines) from Korea.[6]

Malaysia has become one of the world's biggest exporters of home-use air-conditioners. Color television exports have grown quite rapidly since the late 1980s and, along with radios, are among Malaysia's top five electronics exports. However, this success has raised resistance to Malaysian exports. The EU has placed anti-dumping tariffs on microwave ovens and color TVs from Malaysia and elsewhere in East Asia (*BT*, 23 January 1996).

Trade pressure arises from Malaysia's role at the heart of the region's "triangular trade,"[7] in which Japanese components are assembled into final goods in East Asian affiliates for shipment directly to markets in North America and Europe. Another factor besides rising trade barriers is disrupting this pattern, namely that more of the goods produced by offshore affiliates in East Asia are sold within the region, which has grown in importance as an end market. In particular, as the quality of goods produced offshore has grown, Japanese firms are importing a small but growing portion of the output back to Japan. For example, in 1990, Matsushita's television affiliate in Malaysia began shipping to Japan 100,000 sets of a small size that it had ceased producing there, rising to 300,000 in 1991 – about a quarter of the affiliate's total production. These "reverse imports," as they are often called, are designed in part to ease the trade imbalance between Japan and Malaysia.

After 1985, for the same reasons as consumer electronics, non-IC component investments also greatly increased. Malaysia is, for example, among the top exporters of discrete semiconductors, such as diodes and transistors. Early component investments came primarily from Japanese firms, such as Koa Denko (resistors – 1973), Matsushita (TV parts – 1973), and Mitsumi (transformers – 1973).

Table 8.2 gives an indication of the variety of component investments that followed the currency realignments of the mid-1980s.

Some of the output, such as cathode ray tubes (CRTs, the principal component in TV sets), is used locally. For ten Japanese component firms who supplied this information to the Electronics Industries Association of

*Table 8.2* Recent FDI in non-semiconductor components

| Item | Representative manufacturers |
| --- | --- |
| Micro-motors | Mabuchi (1989), Mitsumi (1987), Matsushita (1990), Sankyo Seiki (1990) |
| Small liquid crystal displays | Vikay (Singapore, 1986), Casio (1991), Seiko Epson (1991), Varitronix (Hong Kong, 1991) |
| Air conditioner compressors | Matsushita (1987), Hitachi (1989) |
| Cathode ray tubes for color TV sets and computer monitors | Matsushita (1990), Chung Hwa Picture Tube (Taiwan, 1990), Samsung (Korea–1991) |
| Miscellaneous electronic components | Matsushita (1988), TDK (1989), Thomson (France, 1989), First Resistor and Condensor (Taiwan – 1990) |
| Printed circuit board assembly | Wearnes Technology (1989), Venture Manufacturing (1990), Richgold (1992) – all from Singapore |

Note
All firms Japanese except as indicated.

Japan, the share of components produced in Malaysia that are sold there stayed the same or rose between 1990 and 1993, suggesting that inter-multinational company (MNC) linkages are deepening. Still, much of the output from these plants is exported for assembly elsewhere, keeping Malaysia tangled in the web of IPNs that criss-cross the region.

The most recent influx of investment has been from producers of computers and peripherals, but Malaysia's record of attracting such investments is mixed. In HDDs, for example, major producers had already settled on Singapore as the key manufacturing base in the early 1980s, leaving Malaysia with a relatively small share. Leading producers of personal computers such as Apple and Compaq had also settled in Singapore by the time Malaysia renewed its export promotion policies in 1986. Furthermore, Japanese producers were slower than the Americans to move production of computing hardware offshore; now that they are doing so, Thailand and the Philippines are among the chief destinations.

Nevertheless, Malaysia has experienced a number of important investments in the sector. Computer keyboards are being made by Fujitsu (1988) and Taiwan's Acer (1990) and Silitek (1991). Floppy disk drives are being manufactured by Alps (1989), Mitsumi (1989), Sony (1990), and TEAC (1990). In 1994, Sony and TEAC added CDROM drives to their Malaysian output. Taiwan's Acer (1990) and Lite-On (1991) produce computer monitors, as does Korea's Samsung (1995). Matsushita, Hitachi, and NEC began production of monitors at existing TV plants in 1994. Several MNC affiliates also produce fax machines (Brother, 1989; Canon, 1989; and Toshiba, 1990).

Although Singapore is the world capital of HDDs, Malaysia has not been completely shut out. Its biggest success has been in the core components for HDD – heads and disks. Leading US producers Conner, Seagate, and Applied Magnetics opened head plants in Penang in the late 1980s. Market leader Komag started a disk plant in 1993. Construction on another disk plant was commenced by Fuji Electric in 1997. Disk substrates are being made by Kobe Precision (1992), with 1996 investments by Sumikei and Akashic Kubota (the latter of which was sold to Stormedia of the United States in 1997). HDDs have been assembled in Penang by Conner Peripherals (later acquired by Seagate) since 1991. Hewlett-Packard, Western Digital, and Digital Equipment all started HDD production in 1994, although the Digital Equipment plant was closed, and the Hewlett-Packard operation was discontinued in 1996.[8]

## MNC affiliate behavior in Malaysia

In this section, we will review the available data on affiliate behaviors on five dimensions: linkages to local firms, human resources development, higher value-added activities, capital deepening, and management autonomy. Each subsection will provide background on relevant Malaysian policies, after which the available evidence will be used to provide a preliminary evaluation of the hypothesis of national differences between investors.

### Linkages

Linkages to local firms are one of the most important characteristics of foreign manufacturing affiliates for the host economy. Backward linkages involve ties to suppliers of inputs and services. Forward linkages include distribution and marketing. MNC activity also involves purchases from service sectors such as power, telecommunications, construction, and transportation, but manufacturing linkages are typically viewed as the main conduit for potential technology transfer.

Stories abound of local suppliers growing through relationships with both Japanese and US-based MNCs. The typical firm starts out with a link to one major customer, often one for whom the local entrepreneur has worked in the past (Rasiah 1995: 168). It is not unusual for a small firm to remain in the orbit of a single customer indefinitely, but if a local firm is well run, it will expand its customer base. The best firms also diversify their products and develop export markets.

The initial wave of investments in the electronics sector occurred in semiconductor assembly, which offered relatively little scope for backward linkages because it uses a small number of highly specialized inputs. It was not until the 1980s that the automation of IC assembly and, more importantly, the wave of investments in consumer goods beginning after 1985 opened new opportunities for local vendors of precision-engineering services, plastic and metal parts, circuit boards, and packaging – sectors where the capital expenses are modest enough to permit small-scale firms to enter.

Local sources of inputs were also increasingly favored by MNCs to reduce cost as appreciating currencies made Japanese- or Taiwanese-manufactured components relatively more expensive, and to raise efficiency by permitting implementation of "just-in-time" supply lines and rapid correction of design changes or quality problems. However, if Malaysian firms were not ready to provide components of the necessary quality, MNCs often found it easiest to bring in suppliers from offshore.

Official Malaysian policy has done little until quite recently to support local firms as suppliers to MNCs. Quite the contrary, the protection designed to help state-supported plants in upstream heavy industry (e.g. steel, petrochemicals, and paper) raised input costs for all firms outside the FTZ (Jomo and Edwards 1993: 29). The development of local suppliers was further hindered by onerous regulations governing commerce between the FTZs and the rest of the country (Rasiah 1995: 80). Not surprisingly, FTZ firms frequently chose to rely on imported components, which were available free of duties and regulatory hassle. Ethnic tensions probably also discouraged the development of domestic firms, as Chinese capital – which has been important in manufacturing elsewhere in the region – was funneled into the commodity sector, real estate development, or offshore investments.[9]

During the 1970s, Malaysian policy paid little attention to local content in the electronics industry, much less to linkages with local firms. Policies to encourage foreign firms to increase backward linkages were sometimes announced but were unsupported by actual measures and were further undermined by the recession of the mid-1980s (Rasiah 1995: 81). Measures taken to support small local firms have been criticized for being poorly publicized, mired in bureaucracy, and lacking in transparency. As a result, smaller Malaysian firms still frequently lack access to credit, technology, training, and marketing assistance (Jomo 1993: 5). In addition to this, small firms must compete for skilled labor in the same tight market as the high-paying MNC affiliates.

It was not until recently that meaningful policies were really put in place to support local vendors and stimulate ties to MNCs.[10] For example, in 1993, the government made "linkage development" a criterion for qualifying for tax incentives in the electronics sector (*BT*, 11 August 1993).

The most important initiative is the vendor development program (VDP), which teams MNCs with local suppliers with the goal of speeding up the natural development of the suppliers. The VDP was instituted in 1988 for the automotive sector and extended to the electronics sector in 1992. The program was revised in 1993 to include financial institutions as partners to help the vendors expand and update their facilities to meet MNC requirements. A government agency is responsible for coordinating an agreement in which the MNC assures a market for the vendor and the partner bank provides a loan based on the market assurance.[11] The MNC typically also helps the vendors upgrade technologies and provides training in process and quality control.

Sapura, a Malaysian telecom firm, and Japan's Sharp were the original "anchor companies" in the electronics VDP (*BT*, 11 August 1993). By 1994, thirty-seven of forty-three firms with a VDP were in the electronics sector.[12] One participant is Sony Electronics Malaysia, an audio equipment affiliate started in 1987, which established a VDP in 1993 in cooperation with a local bank (*PDN*, April–June 1994). Fifteen SMEs participate, supplying mostly plastic parts (*NST*, 22 March 1996). Packaging and metal stamping vendors are also supported.

As of December 1994, nineteen of fifty-nine vendors in the VDP (which also covers the automotive and wood-based sectors) did injection molding of plastic components, eight did circuit board assembly, seven did metal stamping or fabrication; the remainder were in non-electrical sectors.

It has been suggested that Japanese firms would develop fewer linkages to the local economy because of their tight business group relations with other Japan-based firms. Although this may be difficult to assess quantitatively, the evidence suggests that Japanese firms have made much more use of Japan-affiliated suppliers than American firms have made of

US-affiliated ones. Furthermore, local suppliers to American firms seem to be involved in more technologically sophisticated processes, with more significant technology transfer from the MNC affiliate.

First we will look at evidence on Japanese linkages to the Malaysian economy.

Rasiah (1995: 110) reports that Japanese firms in the electrical/electronics sector were particularly likely to relocate their Japanese suppliers to Malaysia to raise local content rather than cultivating local suppliers. For example, Sony's Malaysian plants source about 50 percent of their inputs locally, but only 20 percent of that is from Malaysian companies (*NST*, 22 March 1996). Furthermore, Guyton (1996) surveyed forty Japanese firms producing consumer electronics and related components in Malaysia and found that they were much more likely to provide technical assistance to Japan-based suppliers than to locally owned firms.

Matsushita Electric Industrial (MEI) – Japan's largest producer of mass-market electronic and electrical goods – provides a good case study of the linkage building process for consumer products. Matsushita's Malaysian air-conditioning group – with its roots in a 1972 affiliate producing for the Malaysian market – employs over 5,000 and produces about one-quarter of the group's worldwide output of this product (*BT*, 15 September 1994). In pursuit of cost efficiencies, Matsushita has aimed at a high level of local content, either by producing components in-house, coaxing its Japanese suppliers to move with it, or transferring technology to local firms. The core components – motors and compressors – are now made in-house, along with critical molds and dies, leaving lower valued inputs to outside suppliers. The Japan-affiliated firms that supply Matsushita in Malaysia make products such as insulation and copper tubes.

Local firms have been supported by technology transfers from some of MEI's Japanese suppliers, and Matsushita has provided "guidance in areas such as quality control techniques, cost saving know-how and methods for mold and die maintenance" (ibid.). But the results with local firms have reportedly been less than satisfactory, with quality below that of Japan-affiliated suppliers.

In 1991, MEI's Malaysian air-conditioning affiliates had ninety-five main suppliers (fifty-three locally owned, twenty-five Japanese affiliates, thirteen Malaysian–Japanese joint ventures and four European or American firms) from which it purchased $150 million in components (ibid.). Local suppliers are more numerous than the others, but generally engaged in lower technology activities. Nevertheless, the support that Matsushita has provided its local suppliers is unquestionably very valuable.

Many other examples of Japanese support for local suppliers can be found. A local metal stamping firm, Atlan Industries, was started in 1977 as a one-man operation for supplying metal components to the then recently established audio equipment joint venture of Japan's Sharp (*PDN*, April–June 1994). Atlan expanded and later diversified vertically into tool and die making. It has also added many other (mostly Japanese) customers, including Sony, NEC, Toshiba, Casio, and Matsushita. It exports both within the region and to the United States. Its most important relationship is now with Sony, which helped an Atlan subsidiary adopt automated transfer press technology from other Japanese firms, then invited it to set up in Indonesia as a supplier to Sony's new plant there.

Japanese firms have also been important clients for board assemblers. PCBs lie at the heart of all consumer electronics and information equipment, from radios to computers. Firms that master board assembly are potentially able to expand into additional manufacturing services such as full assembly of the final product. However, small firms face increasing challenges as they strive to reduce dependence on one or two initial clients. MNCs typically commit to less than one year of future orders, adding considerable risk to supplier investment plans. Early customers will usually offer some guidance in quality control, but higher level technology transfer through product design may be minimal. Direct financial assistance is rarer still, although local suppliers have benefited from loans through the Japanese Overseas Development Assistance program.[13]

The plastic parts industry has especially flourished with the wave of Japanese consumer electronics investment, and many local firms have benefited. Luster Industries, for example, produces plastic parts for audio equipment. Luster was started in 1986 with 120 workers, and its workforce has grown to 1,650 (*The Star*, 9 January 1996). Some of its output is exported to France and Japan as well as within Southeast Asia. It also set up a joint venture in Indonesia with Singaporean and local partners to supply a Japanese calculator manufacturer.

However, the plastic parts industry also provides an example of how the transplanted Japanese suppliers can make it difficult for Malaysian firms to develop a client base. By 1995 there were some 300 locally and foreign-owned firms in Malaysia capable of making plastic parts (Salleh 1995). As of December 1996, 42 percent of the paid-up capital in Malaysia's "plastic products" sector (which includes more than just electronics suppliers) was foreign, of which about 40 percent was Japanese. The second biggest nationality was Singaporean (25 percent), with the US share at about 1 percent.

One of the earliest Japan-based suppliers, Kohno Plastics, was brought in by Matsushita in 1980 (*BT*, 4 July 1988). By 1988, there were only five firms in Malaysia molding plastic, and Matsushita felt compelled to develop in-house capacity for its air-conditioner affiliate (ibid.). By mid-1989, four more Japanese firms had come to Malaysia to supply Japanese assemblers (*BT*, 10 January 1989), and new ones continued to arrive thereafter, such as Nifco (1991), Nippo (1993), and Dai-Ichi Kaken Kogyo (1994). These small and medium-sized Japanese suppliers are moving offshore to survive as their customers increasingly expand outside Japan.

Turning to the American side, the evidence suggests that US-based firms are likely to transfer more advanced technologies to their local suppliers. For example, Motorola, one of the largest American firms in Malaysia, has supported the development of firms supplying sophisticated components to its radio frequency (RF) products affiliate. One example is QDOS Microcircuits, which began supplying advanced "flex circuits" to Motorola and now also supplies the product to Siemens and Hewlett-Packard in Penang and to ten MNCs outside Malaysia (*The Star*, 1 April 1996). Another such firm is Bakti Comintel. Under a government program, Motorola transferred surface mount technology for PCBs to Bakti in 1993. The firm now supplies products directly to eleven Motorola sites worldwide, and has also branched into final assembly of cordless and office phones, with other customers such as Sony (*The Star*, 10 July 1996).

In the key state of Penang, the IC sector – which is dominated by American firms – gave rise to an important group of machinery suppliers. The story is the epitome of the positive spillover from FDI through linkages. As automation increased among IC assemblers beginning in 1979, so did the need for machinery parts. The frequent re-tooling that occurred as a result of changes in technology, plus the weight of the machines involved, made transport time and cost a major deterrent to using offshore suppliers (Rasiah 1995: 146). Furthermore, the large fixed investment required, such as the need for computer-numeric controlled machine tools, was so large relative to each MNC's internal needs that it was more cost-effective to outsource production than to use internal machine shops (ibid.). This provided an opening for local suppliers.

The Penang machine firms went from "backyard workshops" (Rasiah 1995: 184) to become preferred suppliers in a high-technology industry. By 1987, the Penang machinery cluster was supplying about 20 percent of the molds and dies used by the electronics sector (Rasiah 1993: 140). Services offered include mold making (for plastic IC packages), precision turning of machine parts, stamping, die making (for lead frames), and cutting.

By 1985, there were twenty-two locally owned metal engineering firms supporting the Penang electronics sector, along with seven "plastic engineering" and six packaging firms (Rasiah 1989: 71). The total complex employed over 2,400 workers, compared with a total Penang electronics workforce of about 26,000 (ibid.: 68). The complexity of machines supplied also grew, from stamping and other basic equipment in the 1970s to high precision machine tools and factory automation equipment later on (Rasiah 1995: 167).

A frequently cited success story is that of Eng Technology, which was established as a family business in 1974, making jigs and machined parts as part of machinery maintenance for the IC assembly firms. After a few years, it was able to invest in precision equipment and was able to upgrade through working with the engineering staff of its clients as well as through "self-development" (Teh 1989). The company further diversified into automation machinery and metal stamping. As its reputation spread through the production networks of its clients, it was able to begin exporting in 1984 and now exports more than half its output (ibid.). Diversification has continued, and Eng has become an important supplier of precision parts to the disk drive industry. Although Eng is exceptional, it is far from unique. Other firms, such as Loh Kim Teow and Wong Engineering, have followed similar trajectories.

But we must be careful about concluding from the machinery example that American firms are more likely to support local suppliers. Rasiah also reports that at least three IC firms in his sample had "tried unsuccessfully to attract foreign machinery firms to relocate in Malaysia" (Rasiah 1995: 222), suggesting that the linkages arose out of this foreign supplier unwillingness rather than from any US preference for developing local capabilities.

And even though US firms may not bring US suppliers with them, they may bring firms from elsewhere in the region. For example, a small American consumer electronics producer, Avnet, faced the same shortage of available plastic molders as the Japanese when it came to Malaysia in 1988.[14] It utilized the available local suppliers, but also induced a Singapore firm to set up a Malaysian affiliate (*BT*, 4 May 1988).

The semiconductor firms have also supported a second set of local suppliers – local subcontractors for chip assembly. The first, Carsem, was founded in 1984 with an equity investment from a national investment fund. In 1991, two other major firms were established – Unisem and Globetronics, the latter having been started by an ex-Intel employee. The three companies collectively employ several thousand workers.

In summary, the evidence is hardly clear, but Japanese firms seem to rely more heavily on relocated suppliers from their home country, supporting the general belief about the effect of Japanese business ties.

Another "national" difference is in the type of industry supported. Whereas the Japanese firms, active in consumer electronics, focus on metal-stamping, plastic injection and board assembly, American firms are more likely to develop suppliers in precision machinery and advanced components. However, much of this difference is inherent in the type of product made by the affiliates – consumer products by the Japanese and ICs by the Americans.

### Human resource development

The "human resource development" dimension considers training of production and technical workers. Training imparts skills that, at least to some extent, will be transferable to other firms. At least as important is the potential for employees who have acquired skills in a multinational affiliate to work at or even to start a local firm. Rasiah documents that over 10 percent of the employees of ten local machinery firms had prior work experience in the eight semiconductor firms in the same study (Rasiah 1995: 183), and that the owners of seven out of nine local machinery suppliers had prior work experience at one of the MNCs among their customers (ibid.: 168).

In 1988, the government introduced double deduction for training expenses, plus a special annual allowance for dedicated training facilities. In 1992, the Human Resources Development Fund (HRDF) was created. Firms with over fifty employees are required to contribute 1 percent of wages to the fund, and they can receive grants or loans from it for approved training programs. The government seeded the fund with US$ 18.8 million (*SCMP*, Supplement, 28 August 1993).

In 1989, the state government of Penang, which has been the pacesetter in terms of providing policy support to the electronics industry, created the Penang Skills Development Center (PSDC). The PSDC, created in response to a growing shortage of skilled workers, is a public–private partnership that upgrades the skill level of production workers and technicians in both foreign- and locally owned firms. The innovation has been slow to diffuse to other states, even those with electronics production.

In 1995, the government added new incentives for technical and vocational training institutes, which now qualify for an investment tax allowance of 100 percent for a period of ten years (*BT*, 15 March 1995). Firms responded to the incentive. National Semiconductor, for example, opened a "learning center" at its Penang plant with an auditorium, five training rooms, a video-conferencing room, a computer laboratory, a technical laboratory, and a library (*The Star*, 20 November 1995).

Meaningful quantitative comparisons are hard to make because, whereas American firms in Malaysia have undertaken a number of high profile training initiatives, Japanese firms are known for superior on-the-job training of production workers. Whereas American training is typically based on knowledge codified in manuals, Japanese training relies more on personal contact (Guyton 1996: 185).

Motorola's RF products affiliate is one of the most publicized trainers in the Malaysian electronics industry, and is frequently held up as a good example. In 1989, it announced that it would build a training center in Malaysia that would bring lectures from its Chicago Training Institute via satellite (*BT*, 29 August 1989). Motorola's Malaysian affiliates set aside between 4 and 5 percent of the payroll for training programs, well over the corporate-wide goal of 2 percent (*BT*, 30 August 1994).

In the American-dominated IC sector, increased automation has led to increased skills for production workers, who are now trained in statistical process control and other features of total quality management (Rasiah 1995: 151). Training frequently involves a trip to the MNC's home country (or regional headquarters) for several weeks. The sixteen firms in the Malaysian–American Electronics Industry (MAEI), with over 45,000 employees, reported sending over 500 employees for overseas training in 1992 (MAEI 1994).

The MAEI firms report that they were already spending about 3 percent of combined wages and benefits for training between 1991 and 1993 (MAEI 1995) – well above the 1 percent targeted by the government's HRDF – but that this fell off sharply in 1994 to 1.5 percent and was expected to stay lower, with the explanation that "concentrating more on internal training...[lowered] the costs...of training greatly" (MAEI 1996).

Technical training is particularly important for the development of local capabilities. Here, too, American firms have publicized their efforts. Advanced Micro Devices (AMD), for example, has trained hundreds of managerial and technical staff over the twenty-five years of its operation (Rasiah 1995: 153). In 1991, Motorola's RF products affiliate launched a project, unique within the company's global network, to train production workers through a combination of classroom and on-the-job training to become electro-mechanical technicians because of the increasingly short supply of skilled labor (*BT*, 2 July 1991).

The share of "technical and supervisory" employees in total employment is relatively high at US-owned firms. The share at AMD doubled from 8 percent in the 1970s to over 16 percent by 1990 (Rasiah 1995: 152). At Intel, the share of engineers in total staff has risen from under 3 percent in 1980 to more than 16 percent by 1994 (*WSJ*, 30 September 1994). In the MAEI, of which these companies are members, 15 percent of employees were classified as "technical and supervisory" in 1994, up from 12 percent in 1990 (MAEI 1996).

Within many IC firms, considerable expertise has been developed, to the point that Malaysian engineers are sent overseas to start new plants at sister affiliates and have also been sent to the United States to help transfer production know-how developed in Malaysia (Salih and Young 1989: 61). Harris, for example, sent five Malaysians to help start a new plant in China, including one who will become plant manager (*BT*, 12 June 1995). Motorola has sent 27 Malaysians overseas, including general managers in the Philippines and Mexico (*BT*, 12 December 1994).

Comparable evidence is unavailable for Japanese firms. Technical training is clearly important. Guyton (1996) reports that both large Japanese electronics firms and their smaller Japan-based suppliers in Malaysia send technicians and engineers on regular training visits to headquarters – up to seven people per year for up to six months each (Guyton 1996: 177).

However, Malaysian managers in Japanese affiliates who had previous experience in American or European firms were likely to complain of the slow pace of technology transfer (ibid.: 185). And in an unpublished survey with which the author was associated, three Japanese consumer electronics firms reported ratios of technical and supervisory workers of only 6, 8, and 9 percent. This evidence collectively suggests that Japanese firms in Malaysia are generally operating at a lower level of technology than their American counterparts, hence providing less valuable training.

In summary, the evidence suggests that training of line workers is probably roughly comparable between American and Japanese firms given their very different styles. At the technical level, however, training may be somewhat more important among American firms. This could be attributable to the lower level of technology of the products produced by many Japanese affiliates. Nationality, *per se*, cannot be said to be determinant.

## Higher value-added activities

The "higher value-added activities" dimension considers whether affiliates are engaging in development, design, procurement, distribution, and marketing services in the host country, with the ultimate goal being that the Malaysian operation becomes an "integrated manufacturing center" encompassing the full range of activities from design to marketing. The implication is not that every worker in these non-manufacturing departments is a highly paid professional, but rather that these corporate functions typically involve at least some workers with specialized skills that are as integral to economic growth as manufacturing capabilities.

Malaysia has faced a particular challenge in this realm because of its proximity to Singapore. The nearby city-state was chosen early by most MNCs for many ancillary activities because of its well-developed infrastructure and its history as a trans-shipment point (see Chapter 7 by Wong). Many Malaysian policies have been based on similar initiatives adopted earlier in Singapore.

Sales-related activities are rare in Malaysian manufacturing affiliates and are not encouraged by any targeted policies. In the 1970s, when the industry was dominated by IC assembly, for which the primary markets were outside the Asia–Pacific region, there was probably little scope for locally based marketing.

As East Asia itself becomes a major market for ICs and other electronics products, local affiliates are more likely to assume post-manufacturing functions. Rasiah (1995: 137), for example, mentions the 1990 establishment of a marketing department at an IC assembly and test affiliate. Several years later, TI opened a sales and marketing office in Penang, separate from its plant in another state (*The Star*, 8 February 1996).

As the IC sector added final testing to its assembly operations, more sophisticated distribution operations were put in place because chips were shipped directly to customers rather than to an intervening testing site. By the mid-1980s, all seventeen semiconductor producers operating in Malaysia conducted testing operations (UNCTC 1987), creating a greater need for sophisticated distribution operations, although the option was in some cases foreclosed by the existence of a Singapore distribution center.

Another type of support activity that can be added to manufacturing is procurement. Matsushita's TV plant in Malaysia added a procurement office in 1990, which sources components from 120 companies in Malaysia and Singapore and provides them to twenty-one of the group's affiliates all over the world. Furthermore, good relations with the government helped Matsushita avoid taxes on this parts-trading business (*NW*, 20 June 1994).

In October 1996, Malaysia introduced a formal program to promote the creation of "international procurement centers" (IPCs). Incentives included special allowances for expatriate employees, foreign currency accounts, and local equity partnering requirements. Within two years, sixteen IPCs, of which fourteen were Japanese, had been created (*Bernama* 27 August 1998).[15]

The impact of Singapore on Malaysia's prospects for the upgrading of its multinational affiliates can be seen clearly in the example of regional headquarters. Malaysia's OHQ incentive aims to attract offices supplying services to at least three offshore affiliates outside Malaysia. The services must include financial management, R&D, and training along with three of the following: general administration, business planning, procurement, technical support, marketing control, or information management. The incentives include a preferential tax rate of 10 percent for five years (with a possible five-year extension) on fees paid by the affiliates to the OHQ, plus reduced oversight on currency transactions and the use of expatriates.

The Malaysian policy was put into place in 1989. It is very similar to a Singapore policy introduced in 1986 (Perry 1992). The two policies differ in degree, with Singapore being more generous in areas such as length of benefits and use of expatriates (*NST*, 24 October 1995).

Singapore had approved thirty-three OHQs by 1991 (Perry 1992: 291). It currently has regional headquarters for many electronics firms with affiliates in Malaysia, including Sony, Hitachi, NEC, Toshiba, Motorola, Hewlett-Packard, and Samsung. By contrast, Malaysia had approved only seven OHQ by 1993, when Singapore's total had risen to forty (*BT*, 8 November 1993). The first electronics OHQ in Malaysia was Avnet, a small American firm, which reported that its main objective was to be able to bring in skilled foreign workers for its manufacturing operations (*BT*, 23 May 1991). Japan's Sharp received OHQ status in 1995 and will undertake R&D, procurement, and distribution of parts for service (*The Star*, 22 December 1995). Neither Avnet nor Sharp has manufacturing operations in Singapore, which suggests that a simple regional production network is the prerequisite for a firm to choose Malaysia for a regional headquarters.

One particularly well-publicized higher value-added activity is R&D. Research incentives that have been introduced by the government since 1988 include double deduction for expenses, 50 percent tax allowance and import duty exemption for capital equipment, and expanded use of expatriates. In practice, however, many important types of R&D are not covered by these incentives, including most work performed in-house, such as product development.[16] The MAEI firms report an aggregate ratio of R&D to value-added greater than 0.7 percent from 1989 until 1994 (MAEI 1995, 1996), but only about half the members conduct research locally.[17] Comparable data are not available from Japanese electronics firms.

Although there is no obvious reason for nationality to matter in determining the amount of research undertaken at the plant level, the evidence in Malaysia suggests that American firms undertake more process engineering and the Japanese more product design. The difference can probably be attributed to their concentration in different product areas.

Process engineering is the most common type of research activity undertaken by American firms, followed by improving reliability (MAEI 1996). All fifteen IC firms (mostly US-based) interviewed by Rasiah (1995) reported "substantial process research facilities in Malaysia" and "substantial contributions towards improving the process technology utilized in their other subsidiaries and parent plants" (Rasiah 1995: 18).

Hewlett-Packard, which has been manufacturing optoelectronic and communication components in Penang since 1972, began a process engineering program in 1991. The Penang center – currently employing about twenty engineers – is linked to similar centers in the United States, Japan, and Europe (*ET*, 17 February 1994). Its first task was to develop automation prototypes (MAEI 1994). Product development is scheduled to be introduced in the future. Since 1991, Intel's Penang operation has had corporate responsibility for all new IC package and process development (MAEI 1994), and another semiconductor firm, Harris, set up a research center in 1994 for the development of processes, equipment, and IC packages (*BT*, 12 June 1995).

Japanese IC firms have generally not publicized this type of activity in their Malaysian affiliates. In consumer electronics, Sharp's audio equipment affiliate reports having designed its process equipment locally, but this is the only case we have discovered. Part of the problem may be production network density – both Sony and Matsushita, for example, manufacture factory automation equipment in Singapore.

The picture for product design is reversed – Japanese firms appear to be more active than the Americans. Most design work in Malaysia involves the adaptation to local conditions of basic designs previously generated by the parent corporation. Although adaptive design is an important task, and one which had been previously performed at the parent firm, it is much less sophisticated and critical to the firm than new product development, which still typically takes place in the home country.

The placement of product design in Malaysia makes use of the relatively low-cost local engineering talent. For final assembly firms, it also permits easier "design-in" of cheaper components made nearby, replacing more expensive imports from Japan or the NIEs. Furthermore, it is a reflection of the growing importance of the regional market.

One notable American design operation is at Motorola, which transferred technology for research in RF products to its Penang affiliate in 1976. The center now employs over 100 engineers. Initial work involved only minor changes in existing designs, but in 1983, local engineers completed the full design of a pager (*PDN*, January–March 1994). The affiliate's biggest success was a walkie-talkie developed in 1988 for use in industrial applications such as for security guards; Penang set the specifications for the US, European, and Japanese markets. In 1994, the Penang lab was named Motorola's "Asia Design Center" with responsibility for mechanical, electrical, software and design engineering of radio-based communications products for the regional market (*ET*, 17 February 1994).

Other American design programs are located in the IC and components sector. In 1992, Intel announced that it would open a design center for microcontrollers (*ST*, 13 November 1992).[18] The center, opened in 1994, employs about 100 engineers. It is Penang's first IC design operation, and is also responsible for planning, manufacturing, marketing, and customer service (*ET*, 7 October 1993). Other IC design operations have been established by Harris and Altera.[19]

Among Japanese component firms, Hitachi has added IC design for regional customers at an affiliate established in 1972 (*NW*, 11 April 1992), and TDK designs coils and other electronics components to customer specifications with assistance from its Japanese headquarters in an affiliate established in 1989 (*BT*, 9 May 1994). But most product design in Japanese firms is in the consumer electronics sector.[20]

Sharp has been designing TVs for the regional market in Malaysia since 1989 and has announced that an affiliate for consumer audio products will begin taking over more basic design projects from its Japanese headquarters. Matsushita and Sony have also started Malaysian centers designing televisions for the regional market. In 1992, Matsushita established the Air Conditioning Research & Development Center, where it will gradually increase the center's share of worldwide design responsibilities. In 1994, Hitachi announced that it was "localizing" its VCR division in Malaysia, also implying more advanced product development capabilities. All told, these operations employ about two hundred Malaysian engineers in product design activities.

To summarize, the existing data suggest that American firms undertake more process engineering in their Malaysian affiliates, while Japanese firms conduct more product design. This is due in part to their respective product emphases (components versus consumer goods). Motorola's RF products plant is the exception that proves the rule since it is one of the few US firms producing final goods with an important regional market, and it is also one of the few American firms engaged in product design. Singapore may also be an important factor in that Japanese firms with regional bases on the island tend to locate their regional process engineering there. "Vintage effects" stemming from the average age differences of US and Japanese affiliates do not seem to be important since the ancillary activities discussed above have been introduced in manufacturing affiliates as quickly as four years after their date of establishment.

## Capital deepening

Although one of the primary goals of the export-oriented policies introduced in 1968 was increased employment, capital investment also received favorable treatment. For example, after the expiration of a firm's "pioneer" tax-free status, all fixed assets could "be depreciated as if they were new" over five years (Spinanger 1986: 152).[21]

In 1986, the government created the Investment Tax Allowance, which grants allowances up to 100 percent of capital expenditure on approved projects. Accelerated depreciation was still permitted for other "qualifying" capital expenditures (Rasiah 1995: 101). These allowances were alternatives to pioneer status, and did not distinguish between simple expansion and labor-saving investment.

A push toward greater automation came with the 1996 budget, which doubled the fee imposed on firms for the use of foreign workers, from RM 600 to RM 1,200 per year in the case of semi-skilled employees (*NST*, 28 October 1995). Given that the 1994 average annual wages in the consumer electronics sector were RM 10,260 (*BT*, 2 May 1995) this tax was non-trivial.

American IC firms are generally considered to be the most highly automated in the electronics sector. The percentage of production machinery that was automated at AMD rose from nil in 1978 to over 80 percent by 1990 (Rasiah 1995: Table 6.6). Intel assembles three times as many chips as it did ten years ago with the same number of workers (*WSJ*, 30 September 1994).

By contrast, the consumer electronics sector is less automated. Rasiah reports that worker–machine ratios in European consumer electronics firms in Penang are typically still 1:1 versus from 1:4 to 1:12 in the semiconductor plants (Rasiah 1995: 126).[22] Guyton (1996) reports that Japanese electronics firms in Malaysia are considerably less automated than their counterparts in Japan, frequently employing labor-intensive conveyor-belt assembly techniques (Guyton 1996: 178).

A look at recent data confirms this view only partially. Table 8.3 shows historical cost data on fixed assets per employee for the two primary Malaysian Industrial Classification (MIC) codes in the Electrical/electronics sector. At risk of oversimplification, we can use this "noisy" data as shorthand for characterizing an American-dominated IC sector and a Japanese-dominated consumer electronics sector.[23]

The capital–labor ratio of "ICs and other components" is higher than that for consumer electronics, as expected. The continued growth of the capital–labor ratio for components accords well with firm-level evidence that shows

*Table 8.3* Fixed assets (at book value) per employee in the electronics sector (Ringgit per employee; annual growth rate)

|  | *1988* | *1989* | *1990* | *1991* | *1992* | *1993* | *1994* |
|---|---|---|---|---|---|---|---|
| MIC 38321: Radio, TV, and sound equipment | 11,449 | 16,980 48% | 24,464 44% | 28,356 16% | 29,277 3% | 32,441 11% | 33,819 4% |
| MIC 38329: ICs and other components | 20,303 | 22,705 12% | 27,205 20% | 31,663 16% | 34,838 10% | 37,230 7% | 41,473 11% |

Source: Department of Statistics, various years.

that automation has not yet been fully implemented by semiconductor firms. Hitachi Semiconductor began introducing computer-integrated manufacturing in 1992 (*BT*, 3 July 1992). National Semiconductor places its Penang operation "in the 60 to 70 percent bracket among MNCs in the region" in terms of automation (*The Star*, 20 November 1995). Motorola's Seremban plant, which makes discrete semiconductors and conducts simple wafer fabrication, has also reported that automation levels still have room to increase (*The Star*, 1 April 1996).

Whereas the growth rate of capital intensity in the components sector has been relatively steady, the capital–labor ratio of consumer electronics has not. The flood of new Japanese investments that reached its peak in 1989 appears to have greatly increased the capital intensity in the consumer sector, but the subsequent decline in annual growth rates suggests that this was a one-time effect and that capital deepening may be slower in the consumer than in the semiconductor sector. More detailed study would be needed to determine whether this is attributable to technological features of the products involved or to nationality-based differences in production methods.

### Management autonomy

To what extent are local personnel promoted to management positions and given autonomous decision-making authority? This question is important because policy-makers may have more opportunity to influence decisions that are made by locals, including the timing of lay-offs or the decision to replace imported inputs by developing a local supplier. Anuwar and Wong (1993) found that managers in local affiliates could play "a major initiating and lobbying role" in investment decisions, by leveraging their combined knowledge of local conditions and of internal corporate decision-making apparatus. Decisions about technology and equipment sourcing are usually made at the corporate headquarters level, but sourcing of inputs is more likely to be localized and subject to influence by the identity of the local manager (ibid.: 113).

We first consider management autonomy, which appears to be more limited in Japanese than in American firms. Anuwar and Wong (1993) surveyed twenty-six MNCs operating in Malaysia, including ten from the electronics sector. In discussing management, they report that in at least two companies, Malaysian managers "complained that the Japanese practiced exclusive management control, where local Malaysian managers are not adequately consulted" (ibid.: 109). Another study found that "In Japanese, Taiwanese, and Hong Kong firms – mainly involved in the textile and apparel industries – foreign personnel even made important decisions on day-to-day operations," whereas "day-to-day operations in American firms are under control of local management." Although "strategic decision making is still done abroad...local management has an important role in decisions about capacity, targets, and the inputs to be used" (Rasiah 1993: 130).

The oldest electronics affiliates in Malaysia are Japanese, dating back to the import substitution period of the 1960s and producing mature products for the domestic market. Because of their local focus and their age, we might expect these firms to have a great deal of decision-making autonomy. The evidence suggests, however, that the Japanese parent retains tight control despite the participation of local capital. For example, Matsushita Electric Co. (Malaysia), established in 1965, produces a broad range of household appliances and is only 43 percent owned by the Japanese parent, MEI. But since 1988, it has been progressively drawn back into MEI's expanding regional production network, and MEI announced that in response to tariff reductions in Malaysia, it will concentrate on a much narrower range of products, spinning off the others to affiliates in the region which have competitive scale (*Nihon Keizai Online*, 12 July 1996).

Guyton (1996) reports that sixteen of seventeen Japanese consumer electronics firms interviewed were bound to the parent company by formal technology transfer agreements, including technical assistance agreements, patent licensing, and turnkey contracts (Guyton 1996: 175). Most of these agreements included restrictions on where raw materials and capital equipment could be sourced (ibid.: 184). Guyton also reports that Malaysian subsidiaries of Japanese electronics firms generally have a shorter training–promotion cycle for local managers than that used at the headquarters – three to five years versus twelve years (ibid.: 176). This may bias Japanese superiors against granting much authority to the relatively inexperienced local managers.

Although American firms are generally considered to be more autonomous, it is probably a question of a "longer leash." For example, American disk drive firms Seagate and Conner (later acquired by Seagate) were hit with claims by the US Internal Revenue Service for $120 million in back taxes because their East Asian subsidiaries – including those in Malaysia – were headless extensions of the parents rather than the "arm's-length" subsidiaries suggested by the income accounting used on the companies' US tax returns (*CRN*, 28 August 1995).[24]

Two American IC firms interviewed by the author in 1995 about the hypothetical choice of a local subcontractor by a Malaysian affiliate both said that the decision would need to be approved at a higher level. For one firm, this was a regional headquarters. For the other firm, lacking such an office, the decision needed to be approved in California. This difference suggests that MNCs with denser offshore networks are more likely to locate decision-making closer to the affected location.

One study notes the presence of a vintage effect for autonomy. Sim (1977) reports an early in-depth study of matched firms from seven sectors, including electrical and electronics. The firms were matched for many characteristics including age, products, technology level, and market focus. Authority within Japanese firms was found to be the least dispersed both to the affiliate from the parent and within the affiliate itself. However, Sim also notes that "age was the most significant factor," so that older affiliates had greater autonomy. It seems reasonable to expect that differences in autonomy will diminish, if not vanish, over time.

We next turn to the promotion of local personnel to management positions, where a somewhat stronger distinction between Japanese and US firms appears. Anuwar and Wong (1993: 109) report that Malaysian affiliates are still typically run by expatriates. However, American and European firms are generally promoting Malaysians to "next-in-line senior positions," whereas Japanese companies tend to retain "a higher proportion of expatriates at the senior level." Sim's (1977) matched pairs study also found a greater use of expatriate managers in Japanese than in US-owned affiliates.

The issue acquired prominence in 1994 as the criticism of Japanese promotion practices appeared in the media. At a press conference, a spokesman for the Japan–Malaysia Economic Association stated that locals were not promoted because they have yet to acquire the management skills to be in senior-level management (*BT*, 28 July 1994). The following month, a spokesman for the Japanese Chamber of Trade and Industry in Malaysia (JACTIM) was more diplomatic, saying that a barrier to putting Malaysians in charge is that few speak enough Japanese to communicate with home offices in Japan (*RAPBR*, 11 August 1994). Furthermore, JACTIM reported that in 144 Japanese-invested manufacturing firms in Malaysia, 39 percent of general managers, 73 percent of managers, and 99.4 percent of supervisors were Malaysians (*BT*, 12 August 1994). These figures confirm that the barriers to local managers in Japanese firms are situated mainly at the highest levels. As of 1992, no Japanese firm in Malaysia had a Malaysian managing director (*NW*, 5 September 1992).

In the 1995 *Directory of Overseas Corporations* published by the Electronics Industry Association of Japan (EIAJ 1995), 100 out of 141 Malaysian electronics affiliates of Japanese companies report the number of Japanese managers at their plants. The overall average is five Japanese managers per 1,000 employees, and they make up roughly half of the total managers. Within the forty-one largest affiliates employing from 700 to 4,000 workers, however, the average number of Japanese managers to employees is a much lower 1.5. An ordinary least-squares regression on this high-employment group finds no evidence of a "vintage effect" for the employment of Japanese managers.[25]

Systematic data for American firms were unavailable, but anecdotal evidence abounds. A 1980 survey of six US-owned electronics plants in Malaysia noted only thirteen non-Malaysians for 19,000 employees, a ratio of less than one per 1,000 (Lester 1982).[26] AMD had only one American on the staff during most of the 1980s – the managing director (Rasiah 1995: 223). At Intel (2,000 employees), all managers – including the managing director – have been Malaysian natives "for many years" (Anuwar and Wong 1993: 109), and Malaysian managing directors were also in place at three other US semiconductor firms (Rasiah 1993). In 1992, TI had three expatriates for 2,800 employees (*BA*, September 28 1992).

In summary, nationality appears to influence the management practices of Malaysian affiliates, with Japanese firms keeping expatriates in the top positions and granting less decision autonomy to local managers. Research in a non-English-speaking country would be needed to determine the extent to which remaining differences are language-based rather than the result of cultural differences.

## Summary and conclusion

This chapter used evidence from a Malaysian case study to explore the extent to which nationality might determine affiliate behavior. Table 8.4 summarizes the findings and lists the probable causes of observed national differences. It shows that nationality mattered for linkages with local suppliers, for management practices, and, possibly, for capital deepening. In each case, the Japanese practice may be less conducive to Malaysian growth than if a more American-style practice were substituted.

The implication for Malaysian policy-makers is not, of course, that one nationality of investor should be favored over another. Rather, the findings should be used to direct efforts where they will do the most good. It may be hard to convince a Japanese subsidiary to install a local employee as managing

*Table 8.4* Summary of findings

| Behavior | Observation | Probable cause |
|---|---|---|
| Linkages | Japanese firms use more re-located home country suppliers | Nationality |
| | Japanese firms support more plastic and metal parts firms, Americans support more machinery firms | Product characteristics (consumer electronics versus ICs) |
| Human resources development | Technical training may be less widespread in Japanese firms | Product characteristics (mature technology) |
| Higher value-added activities | American firms do more process engineering | Network simplicity (fewer Singapore affiliates) |
| | Japanese firms do more product design | Mature products and regional market focus |
| Capital deepening | American firms are more highly automated | Nationality or industry characteristics |
| Management practices | Japanese subsidiaries have less autonomy | Nationality magnified by a vintage effect |
| | Japanese firms don't promote locals to top positions | Nationality |

director, but Japanese firms are likely to respond well to exhortations to work with skilled local suppliers or incentives to increase local engineering of minor product changes.

Nationality-based differences can be expected to persist for the foreseeable future, but the increasing cross-border networking of firms in the electronics industry appears to be blurring the distinctions. As an example, consider Komag, the world's leading merchant supplier of the disks in HDDs. California-based Komag has been an exemplary investor since its arrival in Penang in 1992. It supports local firms, brought a companion investment from Kobe Steel (one of its key suppliers), and has been an important "anchor" investor in the new industrial park in the Malaysian state of Sarawak on the island of Borneo.

But is Komag an American company? Two Japanese firms – Asahi and Kobe Steel – each own more than 10 percent of the company and each has a seat on its board of directors. And these links were forged under the guidance of the company's native-Taiwanese chairman (*IB*, March 1992). Is this a dynamic American technology company? A Japanese *keiretsu* affiliate? An overseas Chinese business? Such cases are rare now, but the globalization of industry guarantees that business cultures will become more widely diffused, reducing – but probably never eliminating – identifiable nationality-based differences.

## Notes

1  Unfortunately, some causal factors cannot be separated from nationality in the present study. In particular, the closeness of Malaysia to Japan compared with its distance from the United States makes proximity effects impossible to distinguish from those of nationality (i.e. corporate culture). To isolate the effects of distance, we would need to look at affiliates in a region more nearly equidistant from Japan and the United States, such as Europe. Similarly, some differences may be due to language barriers in Malaysia, where English is as common as Japanese is rare. We cannot isolate language effects in a Malaysian case study. The present study therefore uses "nationality" as shorthand for "corporate culture, language, or proximity." Chapters Four (Ernst) and Nine (Ernst and Ravenhill) in this book include regional-level discussion of the factors influencing affiliate behavior.

2  The sample includes the largest multinational producers of consumer electronics, electronic components, computers and peripherals, telecommunications equipment, and household appliances – over thirty firms from Japan, the United States, and Europe. In addition to extensive data gathering by BRIE from numerous publicly available sources, representatives of many of these firms were interviewed in Japan and California. Knowledge of their Malaysian operations has been augmented by confidential interviews undertaken in Malaysia in preparation for the government's Second Industrial Master Plan. The author was one of the interviewers employed by DRI-McGraw Hill, international consultant to the project.

3  Although FTZ workers eventually did earn the right to unionize, electronics firms were the last to do so. In-house unions were finally allowed in 1988 as a

compromise in response to the pressure of American unions calling for the United States to withdraw trade preferences from Malaysia (Rasiah 1995: 130).

4 Japanese controls on outward FDI were lifted in 1972.

5 Both companies still exist and are listed on the Kuala Lumpur Stock Exchange. Although they were typical for the time they were established, they are now unusual for Malaysia's electronics sector. Local capital was involved because of a requirement under Malaysia's import substitution policy; most other investments by major foreign electronics firms in Malaysia are wholly foreign-owned.

6 See Chapter 6 by Kim for a description of Samsung's production network in Southeast Asia.

7 Although this expression is in current usage, it is a misnomer. The triangular trade of the eighteenth century was a closed loop (sugar for rum for slaves for sugar), unlike the friction-generating unbalanced trade of current debates.

8 The Digital Equipment plant (along with all of Digital's hard drive business) was purchased by Quantum, a US drive producer, before it was closed. The facility was quickly acquired by another storage products firm, Iomega (*BT*, 29 July 1996).

9 Lim and Fong (1991: Chapter 4) provide an exhaustive list of possible reasons for the underdeveloped indigenous supply base in the electronics sector.

10 A critical exception to the rule is the Chinese-dominated state of Penang, which is the key site for Malaysia's electronics industry. Faced with a resource-poor state and high unemployment, the Penang Development Corporation (PDC – the lead agency for state level industrial policy) established Malaysia's first Free Trade Zone in 1972 and has continued to act several years ahead of the central government in pursuing industrial policy. The PDC was the leader, for example, in taking steps to match local suppliers with potential MNC customers. The Penang government has been very active in support of its local firms (predominantly ethnic-Chinese-owned) at least in part to offset the discrimination of central government policy (Rasiah 1995: 185).

11 The VDP was later upgraded under the name "Industrial Linkage Program" (*The Star*, 19 June 1996) and placed under a newly created cross-ministerial agency, the Small and Medium Industries Development Corporation.

12 The VDP data were provided at a government Web site in June 1996 but have since been removed. As of 1994, the most recent date for which data were available, twenty-five out of forty-three VDP firms were Japanese, but a breakdown by sector was not provided.

13 One example is Eastrade, a Malaysian company that supplies radios to Sony and other Japanese firms for sale under the Japanese brand names. Eastrade was able to upgrade its board assembly technology with the help of a Japanese loan.

14 Avnet is primarily a components distributor but also engages in limited manufacturing activities.

15 As early as 1988, Singapore had forty-four international procurement offices, primarily in the electronics industry. The number had grown to ninety-six by 1992, well before Malaysia launched its program (Linden 1994).

16 Product development is covered by the R&D incentives only if a separate subsidiary is established for the purpose, which Japanese firms are increasingly doing.

17 As much as 20 percent of MAEI member research was conducted outside Malaysia but financed by the affiliate.

18 Microcontrollers are "embedded" chips that give processing functionality to non-computer products, such as cars; it is typically a method for a company such as Intel to derive continued income from its older microprocessor designs.

19 Altera does not have a production affiliate in Malaysia – its manufacturing is

subcontracted to firms in other countries.

20  Except where indicated, sources for the information in the following paragraphs are various issues of *BT* and the Malaysian government's Web site (which has since been changed).

21  Tax relief is currently extended to only 70 percent of a pioneer firm's income, but at the same time the default corporate tax rate has been lowered from 40 to 30 percent.

22  The low man–machine ratio for semiconductor assembly does not apply to certain low volume processes that are still performed manually.

23  The caveats required in analyzing this data on assets per employee include the use of book rather than replacement value for the assets and the growing presence of Japanese and other firms in the components sector over the period.

24  The companies eventually settled for about a fifth of the claimed amount (*WSJI*, 15 May 1996; *DJNS*, 11 June 1996).

25  Within the fifty-nine affiliates employing between thirty and 700 workers, a statistically significant "vintage effect" appears. The coefficient suggests that these smaller affiliates employ one less Japanese manager per 1000 workers for every three years of age. This difference from the larger affiliates might reflect a "scale economy" in the use of Japanese managers, since the average number of managers in each "large" affiliate (1.9) is not much greater than in the smaller ones (1.5). This agrees with an earlier study's finding that Japan-centered control of the affiliate "is maintained through the use of Japanese personnel in top management or technical positions" (Sim 1977: 49).

26  In 1994, the forty-one larger affiliates from the EIAJ directory reported a total of 443 Japanese personnel (of which seventy-seven were managers) for 66,681 employees, a ratio of 6.6 per 1,000. The six firms with the lowest ratio from this group employed twenty-four Japanese for 11,746 employees, an expatriate ratio of two per 1,000 – more than double that reported for US affiliates in 1980. These six firms had an average age of eight years. A regression coefficient on affiliate age for the group of forty-one was barely significant (p = 5.6%) and suggests that an affiliate employs one less expatriate per 1,000 workers with every five years of age.

# References

Anuwar, A. and Wong, P. K. (1993) "Direct Foreign Investment in the Malaysian Industrial Sector," in K. S. Jomo (ed.) *Industrializing Malaysia*, New York: Routledge: 77–117.

Department of Statistics, Malaysia (various years) *Annual Survey of Manufacturing Industries*, Kuala Lumpur: Department of Statistics.

EIAJ (1995) "Directory of Overseas Corporations" [*Kaigai Hojin Risuto*], Tokyo: Nihon Denshi Kikai Kogyokai.

Guyton, L. (1996) "Japanese Investments and Technology Transfer to Malaysia," in J. Borrego *et al.* (eds) *Capital, the State, and Late Industrialization*, Boulder, CO: Westview Press, 171–202.

Jomo, K. S. (ed.) (1993) *Industrializing Malaysia: Policy, Performance, Prospects*, New York: Routledge.

Jomo, K. S. and Edwards, C. (1993) "Malaysian Industrialization in Historical Perspective," in K. S. Jomo (ed.) *Industrializing Malaysia,* New York: Routledge, 14–39.

Lester, M. (1982) "The Transfer of Managerial and Technological Skills by Electronic-Assembly Companies in Export-Processing Zones in Malaysia," in D. Sahal (ed.) *The Transfer and Utilization of Technical Knowledge*, Lexington, MA: Lexington Books, 209–24.

Lim, L. and Fong, P. E. (1991) *Foreign Direct investment and Industrialization in Malaysia, Singapore, Taiwan and Thailand*, Paris: OECD.

Linden, G. (1994) "Differences in US and Japanese Electronics FDI in East Asia: Evidence from the BRIE Database," BRIE Research Note #RN 3, Berkeley, CA: BRIE.

Malaysian-American Electronics Industry (various years) *Annual Survey*, Kuala Lumpur: MAEI.

Malaysian Industrial Development Authority (various years) *Annual Report*, Kuala Lumpur: MIDA.

O'Connor, D. (1993) "Electronics and Industrialization," in K. S. Jomo (ed.) *Industrializing Malaysia*, New York: Routledge, 210–246.

Perry, M. (1992) "Promoting Corporate Control in Singapore," *Regional Studies*, 26(3): 289–94.

Rasiah, R. (1989) "Technological Change and the Electronics Industry: The Impact on Penang in the 1980s," in S. Narayanan, R. Rasiah, M. L. Young, and Y. Beng Jong (eds) *Changing Dimensions of the Electronics Industry in Malaysia*, Kuala Lumpur: Malaysian Economics Association.

—— (1993) "Free Trade Zones and Industrial Development in Malaysia," in K. S. Jomo (ed.) *Industrializing Malaysia*, New York: Routledge, 118–46.

—— (1995) *Foreign Capital and Industrialization in Malaysia*, Ipswich, UK: St Martin's Press.

Salih, K. and Young, M. L.(1989) "Changing Conditions of Labor in the Semiconductor Industry in Malaysia," *Labor and Society*, 14: 59–79.

Salleh, I. M. (1995) "Foreign Direct Investment and Technology Transfer in the Malaysian Electronics Industry," in Nomura Research Institute and Institute of Southeast Asian Studies, *The New Wave of Foreign Direct Investment in Asia*, Singapore: ISAS: 133–59.

Sim, A. B. (1977) "Decentralized Management of Subsidiaries and their Performance: A Comparative Study of American, British and Japanese Subsidiaries in Malaysia," *Management International Review*, 2: 45–51.

Spinanger, D. (1986) *Industrialization Policies and Regional Economic Development in Malaysia*, Oxford: Oxford University Press.

Teh, A. E. L. (1989) "Ancillary Firms Serving the Electronics Industry: The Case of Penang," in S. Narayanan, R. Rasiah, M. L. Young, and Y. Beng Jong (eds) *Changing Dimensions of the Electronics Industry in Malaysia*, Kuala Lumpur: Malaysian Economics Association.

UN Center on Transnational Corporations (UNCTC) (1987) *Transnational Corporations and the Electronics Industries of ASEAN Economies*, New York: United Nations.

# 9 Convergence and diversity

## How globalization reshapes Asian production networks

*Dieter Ernst and John Ravenhill*

## Introduction: does globalization lead to increasing convergence?

Commentators writing from a variety of theoretical perspectives expect globalization to act as a powerful equalizer, both among nations and among firms.[1] Among nations, globalization imposes new constraints on the policy-making of national governments, constraints that force a convergence towards economic liberalization, balanced budgets, and lower expenditures on welfare (Schwartz 1994; Cerny 1995). Convergence is also expected among firms. Faced with similar constraints, firms will converge in their organization and strategies, irrespective of their national origin (Vernon 1971, 1977; Graham and Krugman 1989). Boyer (1996: 47) has succinctly summarized the underlying logic, "...everywhere firms facing the same optimizing problems find the same solution in terms of technology, markets and products, for there is one best way of organizing production – a single optimum among a possible multiplicity of local optima."[2]

It is the impact of globalization on firm strategies that we examine in this chapter. A significant literature has recently emerged in response to some of the overgeneralizations put forward by some enthusiast proponents of globalization. We believe, however, that several key weaknesses are apparent in how this literature discusses the impact of globalization on American and Japanese corporations.

Rarely does the literature look at how specific elements of the globalization process exert an impact on corporate structures and activities. Globalization is often left undefined; the linkages between its various elements and aspects of corporate behavior and governance remain unspecified. Moreover, the literature gives insufficient attention to the timing and dynamics of the globalization process. The globalization of the Japanese economy took off in earnest only in the mid-1980s, after the Plaza Agreement of the Group of Seven industrialized economies. In the late 1980s, the overseas subsidiaries of Japanese companies were newcomers to export-oriented production.[3] A static snapshot of the differences between American and Japanese corporations as reflected in data from the early 1990s therefore may capture variation that arises in a large part from the relative newness of the overseas operations of Japanese corporations. Finally, because the literature is preoccupied with differences between firms by nationality, it often overlooks other sources of variation in the behavior of firms.

We address these weaknesses in the existing literature. We look at how specific aspects of the globalization process have affected the operations of US and Japanese corporations. In particular, we are interested in the temporal dimension – how the behavior of firms has changed as, over time, their value chain has become more integrated across national boundaries. Our primary goal in this chapter is to examine the extent to which convergence has occurred in the 1990s between the organization of the Asian international production networks of Japanese and American firms in the electronics industry.

We focus on the electronics industry for several reasons. It is by far the most important single sector for both Japanese and US investments in East Asia. In the early 1990s, electronics accounted for about 45 percent of total US investment in manufacturing in the region, and about 25 percent of that of Japan. Moreover, it is an industrial sector where the subsidiaries established by Japanese and US investment are engaged in similar activities, that is in manufacturing primarily for export to third-country markets. By limiting our analysis to this one sector, we are able to compare like with like.[4] One problem with studies that use pooled aggregate data on foreign direct investment (FDI) is that this procedure groups subsidiaries established for diverse purposes, for instance wholesaling as opposed to manufacturing, as well as subsidiaries established at various points in time. Differences generated by nationality of ownership may be difficult to distinguish from those produced by sector of operation, the principal activities of the subsidiary, or the "vintage effect" (the length of time that a subsidiary has been established).

We first review the concept of the international production network (IPN) and discuss how IPNs interact with processes of globalization. We then document the differences, by nationality, between these networks at the beginning of the 1990s. In the third section, we seek to explain the sources of these differences. In the fourth section, we examine the forces that have induced changes in production strategies, primarily of Japanese firms. We show that an opening of Japanese production networks has occurred, and that this opening has produced a convergence on some variables towards their American counterparts. We give brief consideration to how the financial crises of 1997–8 may affect the evolution of production networks. In the concluding section, we argue that partial convergence coexists with persistent diversity relative to the behavior of US firms. Although nationality continues to matter, other factors affecting firm behavior have to be incorporated into the analysis to explain this outcome.

## International production networks and globalization: a conceptual framework

A rich body of literature shows that the behavior and organization of a firm are shaped by a highly complex combination of factors. These include geographic scope (dispersion); product range and diversity (including the number and extent of brands); market segmentation (commodities versus differentiated products) and pricing; size; degree of integration versus outsourcing; types of distribution channels; etc.[5] For each of these different factors, nationality acts as a constraining factor, in terms of the options available, but only within certain limitations. These limitations become clear only once the analysis moves from comparative statics to the dynamics of change.[6]

In examining the dynamics of firm strategies in East Asia, our focus is on IPNs. The concept of an IPN is an attempt to capture the spread of broader and more systemic forms of international production that cover all stages of the value chain; these may or may not involve equity ownership.[7] Firms break down the value chain into a variety of discrete functions and locate them wherever they can be carried out most effectively, where they improve the firm's access to resources and capabilities, and where they are needed to facilitate the penetration of important growth markets. By decomposing the value chain across national boundaries, firms attempt to combine scale economies with the flexibility of decentralization. The firm's overriding concern is to generate, across national borders, faster and more cost-effective interactions between different stages of the value chain. Since the 1960s, foreign electronics firms have rapidly expanded their production in East Asia.[8] The focus of network building shifted twice. In the second half of the 1980s, it moved from Northeast Asia (Korea, Taiwan, and Hong Kong) to the ASEAN region (primarily Singapore, Malaysia, and Thailand); and, since about 1992, from the ASEAN region increasingly to coastal China. The geographic coverage of linkages in Asian electronics production thus has substantially expanded. At the same time, firms have integrated their erstwhile stand-alone operations in individual host countries into increasingly complex IPNs.

In our analysis, globalization is a shorthand expression for the rapid increase in transnational flows of trade and factors of production that has led to a growing inter-penetration of national economies. Competitive forces have driven the process of globalization: more than in any other industry, competition in the electronics industry cuts across national and sectoral boundaries.[9] To compete in this industry, a firm must be present simultaneously in all major growth markets; dominance in a domestic market – even one as large as the United States – is no longer sufficient. Firms require the capacity to internalize on a global scale specialized assets and capabilities, such as technological knowledge, organizational competence, finance, production experience, supplier and customer networks, and market intelligence, that can lead to the timely development and to the effective commercialization of a wide variety of electronics goods and services. Of critical importance is whether the firm can build these capabilities quicker and at lower cost than its competitors.

Competition has led to a rapid geographic dispersion of the value chain, culminating in the spread of international production networks; today, the electronics industry arguably is among the most globalized of all industries. Take the example of the computer sector. It is normal for the supply chain of a computer company to span different time zones and continents. For instance, final assembly most likely is dispersed to major growth markets in the United States, Europe, and Asia: microprocessors are sourced from the United States; memory devices from Japan and Korea; motherboards from Taiwan; HDDs from Singapore; monitors from Korea, Taiwan, and Japan; keyboards and power switch supplies from Taiwan, etc. The electronics industry thus constitutes an excellent test case for research that inquires how globalization affects the transformation of IPNs.

IPNs are simultaneously the subject and object of the forces of globalization. The spread of these networks in East Asia during the 1990s has dramatically transformed not just patterns of trade[10] but also the production possibilities of economies in the region. IPNs accelerated the process of technology transfer, domestic firms enjoyed new possibilities for linkages to global markets, new regional centers of technological expertise emerged, and governments came under increasing pressure to provide the necessary domestic conditions perceived as essential to attract foreign firms. At the same time, IPNs have been a dependent variable in the process of globalization. Technological change, especially the shift to computer-based information networks, has acted as a powerful enabling force that has made globalization possible. Dramatic reductions in the costs of communication and of transportation facilitated the growth of an increasingly complex international division of labor. We discuss later in this paper how recent technological changes, e.g. the substitution of plastic for metal components in many areas of electronics, have further affected the distribution of activities within IPNs.

## Nationality and production networks

The debate about whether there are differences between Japanese and US FDI has a long if not altogether distinguished history. Many of the arguments made by early commentators, such as Kojima's (1978, 1986) distinction between the trade-enhancing nature of Japanese FDI and the trade-undermining characteristic of US FDI, and Ozawa's (1979) emphasis on the importance of relative factor endowments in driving Japanese FDI, have not withstood the test of time and empirical examination (for criticisms see Hill 1988, 1990; Ramstetter 1987).

The question posed by Mason and Encarnation (1994) "Does Ownership Matter?" continues to be a popular question in examining foreign investment and production networks. By the mid-1990s, a large literature pointed to significant differences in the way in which Japanese and American firms had organized their production networks in East Asia in the previous decade (Ernst 1994a; 1997a,b; Ravenhill 1998). For convenience, we group these differences under four headings: the localization of management; sourcing of components and capital goods; replication of production networks; and distribution of R&D activities.

### Management localization and autonomy

In the early 1990s, Japanese subsidiaries in other parts of Asia were far less likely than their US counterparts to employ local managers, to employ local personnel in senior technical roles, or to have nationals of the host country on their boards. Even where firms employed local managers, they were often "shadowed" by Japanese personnel and relegated primarily to the performance of public relations roles for the company. In their study of Japanese subsidiaries in Australia, Nicholas *et al.* (1995: 22–3) concluded that Japanese nationals dominated the upper echelons of management, and that "there was a systematic bias in favor of Japanese managers holding key management positions, especially those involving the implementation of the technology or human capital critical to the competitive advantage of the firm."

In part, the low levels of representation of local staff in management positions may stem from the replication of the lifetime employment system in overseas affiliates. This has two effects. First, if expatriates initially staff the subsidiary, any replication of the seniority system inevitably delays the transition to locally recruited managers – unless the senior staff are relocated elsewhere within the corporation. Even if such opportunities for transferring senior staff arise, however, many Japanese subsidiaries expect local recruits to complete a lengthy training and socialization period before they receive promotion. These company expectations generate the second effect: frustration on the part of locally recruited managers with their promotion prospects, which often leads to their seeking employment elsewhere. Several surveys of local managers in Trans-National Corporation (TNC) subsidiaries in Asia report that Japanese employers were viewed far less favorably than their American or European counterparts (Ernst 1994a: 16–17). Interestingly, in their Asian affiliates, Japanese firms seldom practiced the job rotation and quality-control circles for which they have won much admiration. Instead, a crude "Fordism" often prevailed.

The replication of the seniority system in Asian subsidiaries constitutes a structural explanation for the low levels of localization of management in Japanese companies. In addition, the lack of familiarity of most locals with the Japanese language, with corporate culture and with the networks within which the company operates are barriers to localization. Undoubtedly, however, corporate preferences were also a powerful factor acting against localization. Companies see the employment of Japanese managers as facilitating central control over essential operations. They also fear that localization of management will increase the risks of leakage of commercial secrets to the local economy.

Not only was the management in Japanese subsidiaries generally less localized than that of other TNC subsidiaries, but the management enjoyed far less autonomy in key areas of decision-making. Several studies have found that decision-making within Japanese TNCs tended to be hierarchical and centralized in the hands of headquarters. Managers of subsidiaries enjoyed little freedom of action on issues such as the sourcing of capital goods and components (Guyton 1996; Kreinin 1988). In Guyton's (1996) survey of Japanese affiliates in Malaysia, a majority of the Japanese companies reported that their parent companies dictated where machinery should be acquired (see also Sedgwick forthcoming). The lack of autonomy for local management leads to a second significant difference between Japanese and US subsidiaries:

### *Local sourcing*

The extent to which subsidiaries source locally is an important indicator of their integration into the host economy. Although no data are available that would enable systematic comparisons which control for date of establishment, industrial sector, etc., various studies have suggested that the subsidiaries of Japanese corporations, whether operating in industrialized or less developed countries, tended in the late 1980s and early 1990s to depend more heavily on imported capital goods and components from their home country than did subsidiaries of other TNCs.[11]

In some instances, local content in the production of Japanese subsidiaries in East Asia *declined* as companies moved from exclusive production for the local market to production for export markets. In 1992, over 60 percent of the components used by Japanese affiliates in the electronics sector in ASEAN countries and the NICs were imported, two-thirds of which were sourced from Japan (MITI data cited by Urata 1995: Table 7). The data on intra-firm transactions reflect the general preference for purchasing within the corporate network. These accounted for more than half of the purchases by Japanese affiliates in Asia in 1992; for the NICs, the figure was 60 percent (Urata 1995: Table 8). In contrast, arm's-length transactions accounted for well over 80 percent of all US exports to Asia (Encarnation forthcoming).

The ongoing reliance of Japanese subsidiaries on capital goods and components sourced from their parent companies was at the heart of the increasing trade imbalances in electronics products between Japan and other Asian economies in the first half of the 1990s. These trade imbalances were compounded by barriers facing independent companies attempting to export to the Japanese market, and by the fact that Japanese production networks in East Asia in the early 1990s produced primarily for local and third-country markets rather than engaging in reverse exports to Japan. In contrast, all major producing countries in East Asia enjoyed a substantial surplus in their electronics trade with the United States.

### Replication of production networks

Japanese companies had a greater propensity than their American counterparts to internalize their ownership-specific advantages through the replication of their domestic production networks when investing overseas. Although the sourcing by Japanese affiliates from local economies increased over time, this did not necessarily primarily benefit domestically owned firms but rather other Japanese subsidiaries. These companies often re-located to the region on the encouragement of other members of their *keiretsu* groupings. A study by JETRO in 1994 found, for instance, that nearly a quarter of the sixty-two Japanese affiliates in Malaysia interviewed had invested locally in response to a request of a Japanese assembler (JETRO 1995a). A survey by Manifold (quoted in Johnstone and Yamakoshi 1997: 6) found that 60 percent of Japanese subsidiaries in Indonesia, and close to 50 percent of those in Malaysia and Thailand, had ties to one or more *keiretsu* networks. The vintage effect here may cause a greater divergence rather than a convergence in the behaviors of Japanese and US subsidiaries as, over time, Japanese companies build a more complete local replication of their domestic supply networks.[12]

A rare survey that compared sourcing from locally *owned* with sourcing from locally *based* companies was conducted in Malaysia in 1987–9. It reported that even though there was an increase in the number of locally owned firms that supplied Japanese affiliates, the share in local procurement (itself less than a third of the value of total purchases) from locally *owned* companies remained constant at around 45 percent in these years. Meanwhile, the share sourced from locally based Japanese affiliates rose from 18.7 to 23.8 percent (Aoki 1992: 82, Table 5).

In turn, the replication of supply networks produced another inter-country difference in FDI: small and medium-sized enterprises (SMEs) had a greater share in Japanese FDI than in that of US companies. In general, the foreign investments by these smaller companies are less likely to be driven by the desire to exploit such ownership-specific advantages as proprietary technology than by the advantages that they enjoy by virtue of the nationality of their management and their established trading links with the large assembly companies. And their investment is more likely to be driven by location-specific advantages such as low labor costs. By 1993, Asia accounted for more than 90 percent of the worldwide investments by Japanese SMEs. This concentration has been attributed by JETRO (1995b: 20) to their search for inexpensive labor. SMEs are more likely than their larger counterparts to maintain management and key technical positions in the hands of home country nationals.[13]

### Centralization of R&D

Over the years, research has demonstrated that locally owned firms (or more accurately, companies that have their home base in a particular territory – see Porter 1990: 19) are more likely to carry out a greater range of activities, especially high value-added activities, in the national territory than are subsidiaries of TNCs. In Porter's (1990) words, "The home base will be the location of many of the most productive jobs, the core technologies, and the most advanced skills." The concentration of higher value-added activities in the home base results not only from the historical development of the company's activities and the local linkages built up over the years, but also, amongst other factors, from the availability of skilled personnel, from pressures from home country governments, shareholders, and workers, from the capacity for realizing lower transaction costs, and from concerns over the protection of proprietary knowledge. In particular, R&D activities tend to be concentrated in home countries. Dunning (1993: 303) reports that only nine percent of all R&D activities undertaken in 1989 by US TNCs was conducted by their foreign subsidiaries (only a modest increase over the 1966 share of 6 percent). Japanese companies were even less likely to give their overseas subsidiaries responsibility for R&D – only 5 percent of such expenditure was undertaken abroad (Dunning 1993: 303, citing an unpublished paper by L. S. Peters; Pauly and Reich 1997).

This general reluctance of Japanese companies to transfer R&D activities to overseas subsidiaries was reflected in their operations in East Asia. Various surveys have shown that Japanese firms seldom gave their Asian subsidiaries responsibility for more than incremental process improvements: product R&D was rare. Itoh and Shibata (1995: 196) reported that there were only two R&D facilities established by Japanese firms in Asia, both of which were in Malaysia: a joint venture between Sanyo, Mazda, and Ford for car stereo equipment (a venture that subsequently was reported to have foundered) and Matsushita's R&D facility for air-conditioning equipment.[14] The general conclusion that before the mid-1990s Japanese corporations undertook little R&D in their Asian subsidiaries stands. This contrasts with US subsidiaries whose parent companies increasingly delegated responsibility to them for product design and development, in some instances not just for local but global markets (Ernst 1997a).

Japanese and US subsidiaries in East Asia have differed significantly in their technology transfer to host economies and especially in their linkages with locally owned companies. This conclusion follows from several of the points made above: the dominance of Japanese nationals in key management and technical positions, the lack of autonomy the affiliates enjoy in sourcing, and the development of supplier networks involving local investment by Japanese SMEs. A rare attempt to examine issues of technology transfer in more detail is provided by Guyton (1996) in her survey of Japanese affiliates in Malaysia in the early 1990s. She found that Japanese companies were more likely to work closely with locally based Japanese suppliers on product specification and design than they were with locally owned companies. Moreover, less transfer of technology occurred from parent company to local subsidiary in Japanese firms than in their US counterparts. Malaysian employees of Japanese subsidiaries whom she interviewed who had previously worked for US or European subsidiaries reported that the parent companies had transferred more technology more quickly to local subsidiaries than was true of their current Japanese employers.

## Explaining national differences in production networks

Why did such significant differences exist between Japanese and US production networks in the first half of the 1990s? Social scientists naturally assume that organizations, including firms, adopt policies that enable them to pursue their goals in an efficient manner. A large literature, however, warns us against such assumptions (for example, Arthur 1989; March and Olsen 1989). Historical accidents and path dependency are pervasive. Such factors certainly played a role in the differences that we have observed between the production networks. But rational choices also explain the relatively closed nature of Japanese networks. We suggest five principal reasons for the differences in approach: the perceived advantages of the *keiretsu* networks of Japanese companies; the relatively late start of Japanese companies in export-oriented manufacture in electronics in Asian subsidiaries; corporate governance issues especially financial control; differences in the product mix; and the geographical proximity of Japan to Southeast Asia and China.

### *Perceived advantages of Japanese corporate networks*

A large literature exists on the potential efficiencies that come from Japan's corporate networks (Aoki 1988; Dore 1986; Gerlach 1992). In a period when companies faced new challenges in establishing export-oriented subsidiaries in other parts of Asia, it was natural that they should rely on familiar methods and linkages. Intra-firm trade enables corporations to exercise tight control over their subsidiaries, supply sources, and markets. By encouraging their traditional *keiretsu* suppliers to re-locate close to the new plants, the assemblers maintained linkages of proven worth. They also avoided the potential domestic embarrassment that may have arisen had they been perceived to be abandoning their long-standing commercial allies.

### *Japanese networks as latecomers*

The importance of existing network ties was magnified by the urgency with which Japanese companies had to re-orient their production in the mid-1980s faced, as they were, by rapidly escalating costs and by an increase in non-tariff barriers in the United States and Western Europe. Although Japanese electronics companies began overseas production in East Asia much earlier than their US counterparts, domestic market-oriented, rent-seeking production rather than export platform production remained the dominant focus until the mid-1980s. A quick response on a massive scale then became necessary to meet the challenge not only of the rapidly appreciating yen, but also of new competitors from Korea and Taiwan. We know from innovation theory that firms need time to develop their capabilities.[15] Time is of even greater importance for developing a firm's capacity to manage international production, hence the importance of the "vintage factor." Stopford (1995: 2), for instance, argues that firms progress over time from the simplest to more complex forms of international production networks as they learn how to manage them. Such learning also takes place in the foreign affiliates: as skills and resources accumulate within the various foreign units, new options and more complex projects can be undertaken without relying heavily on the parent organization for help and guidance (Stopford 1995: 16).[16] Developing local capabilities and linkages through "trial-and-error" is a time-consuming process. Latecomers to international production are likely to differ in their organizational approaches from firms that have had a much longer learning experience.

As latecomers to international production for export, Japanese firms minimized risks by centralizing management control in the parent company, and by relying heavily on the parent and other long-standing partners for the supply of capital goods and components. They did not have the luxury of engaging in the time-consuming process of developing local capabilities and linkages through "trial and error" procedures. The then relatively low levels of technological and productive capabilities of most Southeast Asian economies magnified the risks of doing so. As production was to be for the global market, quality-control considerations were paramount. With the switch to export-oriented production in the late 1980s, Japanese networks became more closed than previously. As noted, the share of components sourced from Japan increased. On one dimension, however, the move to export-oriented production brought Japanese networks closer to their US counterparts: Japanese companies increasingly insisted on majority control of their ventures. Previously, pioneering Japanese investors in the region, such as Matsushita, had been willing to enter minority joint ventures.

### Corporate governance

Until the "bursting of the bubble economy" in 1991, one of the key features of corporate governance in Japan was a lack of tight financial control (Dobson 1995; Stopford 1995; Kester 1996 ). This forced Japanese firms to establish other mechanisms for managing the activities of subsidiaries. Kester (1996: 118) distinguishes two types of corporate governance: those associated with the separation of ownership and control (the control of "agency costs"), and those associated with the establishment and maintenance of contractual exchange among separate enterprises. Kester (1996) suggests that:

> the chief shortcoming of Japanese governance is its low ability to control
> …agency costs….In modern Japanese business history, controlling agency
> costs has been of second-order importance….So long as attractive real

growth opportunities were abundant and product and factor market rivalry was fierce, corporate managers were likely to deploy resources in a highly disciplined way. High rates of real growth, moreover, can do much to attenuate disputes among corporate stakeholders by relieving pressures to compare one group's gains to those of another from a zero-sum perspective. So long as growth could be sustained, virtually all stakeholders benefited and conflict among them could be held to a minimum.

(Kester 1996: 126–7)

Japanese corporate governance thus differed fundamentally from the American approach, where elaborate capital-budgeting and financial-planning systems since the Second World War had become a key feature (Baldwin and Clark 1994). It is this fundamental difference in corporate governance rather than differences in the relative cost of capital (alleged or real) that explains why Japanese firms had better access than their US rivals to "patient" capital. This freedom from intense daily scrutiny by shareholders gave rise to high rates of capital investment and encouraged firms to develop overextended product portfolios. Firms experienced little pressure to control the use of capital: financial control mechanisms remained loose and embryonic compared to the sophisticated US techniques of global cash flow management.

The absence of tight financial control had important consequences for the organization of Japanese IPNs. Japanese firms were reluctant to let locals participate in decision-making, and relied heavily on expatriates to establish indirect centralized control. Consequently, most decisions taken at the level of the affiliate required continuous interaction with the management of the parent company. Centralized control over decision-making substituted for less direct financial direction.

## *Geographical proximity*

Japan's geographical proximity (and especially its location in roughly the same time zone) to other East Asian economies facilitated direct control by corporate headquarters over the new production networks – a luxury not enjoyed by their American counterparts. The scope for centralized control diminishes with increasing distance. Once a firm extends its value chain across national boundaries, it faces complex coordination problems and the risk of abrupt disruptions. Four sources of disruption can be discerned:

1    those caused by suppliers, either through late delivery or through the delivery of defective materials;
2    unforeseen fluctuations in demand and abrupt changes in demand patterns;
3    a variety of production problems that result from the transfer of immature products and production processes; and

4   abrupt changes in management decisions, for instance, last-minute corrections of product launch dates and performance features.

Firms have tried to reduce the likelihood of such disruptions – yet so far with only limited success.

In Asia, Japanese firms are in a much better position to manage these risks than American and European firms. Japanese firms were able to control their East Asian affiliates from Tokyo because the region is part of the same time zone. As a rule of thumb, a Japanese parent company historically has been willing to loosen and decentralize control only if the affiliate is more than six hours flying time away from Tokyo. Both in Asia and in Europe, American firms never had this option. Probably the distance factor is a principal reason why, early in their investments, companies such as Intel and Motorola were willing to grant a certain degree of decision-making autonomy to their Asian affiliates.[17]

### *Product mix*

Some of the observed differences in organization of production networks are explained by the very different product mix that Japanese and American electronics firms shifted to Asia. From the late 1960s, American firms in Asia concentrated on ICs (especially microprocessors and logic devices) and PC-related products, whereas Japanese firms, almost without exception, focused on lower end consumer electronics and related components. Microprocessors and PC-related products are highly differentiated products that require close and fast interaction with sophisticated customers. TV sets and household appliances, on the other hand, are homogeneous products.

Specific features of consumer electronics are important for the organization of Japanese production networks. Lower end consumer devices have a variety of characteristics that are conducive for the establishment of global export platform mega-plants. Their homogeneous character permits the realization of large economies of scale in which close interaction with customers is not required. They are characterized by a high divisibility. Different stages in the value chain can be easily separated, and fundamental changes in design methodology has facilitated offshore production, even for relatively complex components such as drums, video heads, and small motors. With but few exceptions (such as picture tubes), most components and subassemblies are also characterized by low transportation costs, and can be easily moved between different locations.

## Forces of change: the opening up of Japanese production networks

By the end of 1992, many of the major Japanese companies showed signs of reconsidering their approach to the management of their Asian production networks. In particular, they displayed a new willingness to give more autonomy to local managers, to delegate to subsidiaries greater responsibility for higher end, more knowledge-intensive support services, such as product and process customization and software engineering, and to increase their sourcing from local suppliers. By the mid-1990s, some Japanese networks had become substantially more embedded in the local economies. To what extent do the forces of globalization explain these changes in the management of Japanese networks?

A combination of factors exerted pressure on Japanese corporations to change the governance of their production networks. Some of these relate directly to the increasing internationalization of the Japanese economy. The Japanese government's loss of control over the exchange rate, symbolized by the dramatic appreciation of the yen after the Plaza Accord in 1985, not only launched the new wave of IPNs but continued to shape them profoundly. By the early 1990s, the cost of imported components from Japan was undermining the international competitiveness of the newly established subsidiaries in Southeast Asia. Such competitiveness was already under threat by the rapid advance of electronics producers in Korea and Taiwan, itself a reflection of the increasing globalization of production capabilities.

To increase local linkages necessitated granting greater autonomy to local managers. Before some firms changed their policies, Japanese procurement decisions were made by individual product divisions and profit centers in the parent through procurement offices that had strong ties with domestic suppliers. Procurement engineers were trained to handle the multilayered networks of Japanese suppliers, but had neither the incentive nor the expertise to search for, certify, and upgrade foreign suppliers. Under this system, it was difficult for managers of affiliates to override decisions made by the procurement offices in Japan. The system inevitably produced delays that were unacceptable in an era of shorter product life cycles. For example, once an affiliate located and certified a local supplier, it could take up to nine months for the parent company to approve the component.

In response to the need both to locate alternative sources of supply and to make more rapid decisions on procurement, Japanese companies began to establish regional procurement offices. One example is Hitachi, which in August 1993 established in Singapore a Center for the Promotion of Procurement in Asia. Other companies soon followed as Hong Kong and Singapore competed to establish themselves as the principal locus for regional headquarters of Japanese networks.

Data on the procurement activities of Japanese subsidiaries in ASEAN reflect the pressures for the opening up of production networks. These changed markedly between 1990 and 1995. Whereas, in 1990, Japanese subsidiaries in ASEAN engaged in manufacturing sourced 38 percent of their components from the local market and 44 percent from Japan, by 1994–5 the proportions had been almost exactly reversed (the figures were 45 percent and 37 percent respectively).[18]

Companies have also introduced new financial control systems. With greater scrutiny of finances from the center, corporations have been prepared to grant greater autonomy to subsidiaries. Moreover, the decreasing dependence of subsidiaries on the center for finance increased the scope for management autonomy. Until the early 1990s, most of the funds required for the expansion of Japanese regional production activities in East Asia came from remittances from the parent company in Japan. Reinvestments by overseas affiliates and equity links with local investors played a very minor role. This pattern is now beginning to change, especially in ASEAN countries. Most of these investments are now locally funded and do not involve a transfer of capital from Japan. Between 1989 and 1992, the ratio of reinvestments of Japanese affiliates to Japan's total FDI increased from 35 to 60 percent for ASEAN affiliates, and from 54 to 80 percent for newly industrialized economy (NIE) affiliates.[19] These figures are substantially above the ratios reported for affiliates in the United States and Europe (these increased from 15 to 24 percent, and from 10 to 17 percent respectively) (MITI, *Overseas Investment Statistics Overview*, Tokyo 1994). The high profitability of Japanese affiliates in Asia made the increasing reliance on local sources of capital possible: in fiscal year (FY) 1992, the ratio of "ordinary profit to sales" of Japanese overseas manufacturing affiliates was 5.1 percent in ASEAN, and 5.6 percent in Asian NICs. This was in sharp contrast to the situation in the United States and Europe where these ratios were minus 0.2 percent and minus 2.5 percent respectively. High profit margins coupled with perceived opportunities for further investment led to ASEAN having the largest share of any region in the profits re-invested worldwide by Japanese subsidiaries. In 1992, subsidiaries located in ASEAN accounted for 31 percent of all reinvested profits by Japanese firms (JETRO 1995).

Japanese companies also began to re-think the strategy of relying overwhelmingly on intra-firm trade for sourcing components. Although intra-firm trade generally reduces transaction costs, it also has disadvantages. In particular, it lacks the flexibility of arrangements with subcontractors that can permit swift responses to changes in technology or demand. Moreover, it denies firms the capacity to search for the lowest cost source of a product, and to pass on a share of the risk-taking to suppliers. Two developments facilitated the search for alternative suppliers. The first was the rapid growth in local capabilities in other parts of the region – in Korea, for instance, in computer memories and monitors, and in Taiwan in motherboards, monitors and a great variety of other PC-related products. Subsidiaries of Korean and Taiwanese firms followed Japanese networks into Southeast Asia and China. The second was the increased willingness of Japanese component suppliers, which had relocated to Southeast Asia or China, to sell beyond their traditional *keiretsu* partners. Squeezed by the assemblers' demands for reduced margins, and faced with an urgent need to recoup the costs of significant investments, component suppliers placed commercial considerations before long-standing loyalties.

Another aspect of the internationalization of the Japanese economy also prompted changes to procurement patterns: the liberalization of the domestic computer market. Before 1992 the Japanese market was an almost exclusive preserve for a handful of Japan's giant, diversified electronics makers, each of which had their own operating system and attendant software libraries. NEC controlled by far the largest fiefdom, with a seemingly impregnable 80 percent market share. Foreign companies, even the most powerful ones, nibbled in frustration at tiny pockets of demand for non-Japanese-language operating system machines – mainly among affiliates of foreign multinationals and banks that required foreign-language computers. This situation changed drastically when PCs (using Intel's 386 and 486 CPUs) became sufficiently powerful to handle Japanese language operating systems based on MS-DOS version five.

In addition, fundamental changes in the Japanese market helped to reduce the traditionally high entry barriers. Japanese companies, including the large corporations, have been under intense pressure to restructure in the 1990s recession; one consequence has been a shift to lower cost PC-based networking solutions, to the detriment of mainframe and microcomputer purchases. Gone are the days when Japanese corporate customers could indulge in brand loyalty to high-priced Japanese computer systems. In the current recession, brand snobbery had to give way to an increasingly price-conscious buying behavior and a taste for bargain shopping. Japan's shift to the open architecture DOS/V operating system, combined with the rapid price erosion for these machines, also has added a variety of new customers: Japanese SMEs can now afford to buy PC-based systems. Japan is also now experiencing for the first time the development of a large home PC market, mainly for multimedia-related desktops. These developments caused a rapid erosion of the market share of Japanese firms, especially for the home PC market, which, in 1994, grew by an estimated 35 percent. Domestically produced PCs accounted for only 9 percent of this growth, and the balance was either PC clones from Taiwan or brand name imports from the United States, Taiwan and Europe (Ernst 1997b).

Again, such liberalization may be seen as a result of globalization pressures – in particular, the move in international trade negotiations, encouraged by GATT's (General Agreement on Tariffs and Trade) success in lowering tariff barriers, to a focus on structural impediments to trade (Kahler 1996). It became clear that attempts to return to the status quo ex ante would no longer work. NEC and other Japanese computer manufacturers thus decided that attack was their only viable defense. In response to the successful penetration of the market by Compaq and other American PC manufacturers, Japanese companies have all significantly increased their purchasing of PCs, motherboards, terminals, monitors, and a variety of other PC-related products from Taiwanese computer companies. NEC, for instance, sources monitors and motherboards from Tatung and Elite. Fujitsu, Epson, Canon, Hitachi, Sharp, and Mitsubishi are all major original equipment manufacture (OEM) customers. Fujitsu's experience demonstrates the rapidity with which sourcing patterns changed. In 1994, Fujitsu sourced almost all of its PC-related components within Japan; in the first quarter of the following year, it imported 95 percent of the parts.[20] Ironically, the import incentives the Japanese government established (in response to protests from its trading partners at continuing trade imbalances) appear to have had their greatest impact on assisting the new regional procurement strategies of Japanese corporations rather than helping foreign corporations to penetrate the Japanese market.

The improved competence of Korean and Taiwanese firms in particular has affected Japanese networks in another way. Relatively low-cost overseas production no longer ensures the continuing competitiveness of Japanese companies in the face of new entrants into the industry. An example is Aiwa, which now produces close to 90 percent of its output offshore. The company failed, however, to complement overseas production with product upgrading and differentiation, and fell victim to increased competition from low-cost competitors (*FT,* 15 May 1996). The necessity of maintaining a technological edge has encouraged companies to take advantage of local centers of expertise and the growing supply of relatively low-cost engineers in the region. Increasingly, they are conducting higher end, knowledge-intensive support services, including engineering and product design, in the region. A greater reliance on outsourced components has reinforced this trend: "adaptive engineering" is required to incorporate these components into final products.

Finally, the growth in incomes in East Asian countries, itself again in part a product of globalization of production, has led to a significant increase in the size of local markets for electronics products. Asia is increasingly characterized by heterogeneous demand patterns and highly segmented product markets. Japanese firms have had to adapt their Asian production networks to the idiosyncrasies of each of these markets.

In summary, within a short period various mutually reinforcing changes have occurred to the environment in which Japanese production networks operate. To a significant extent, these changes have been driven by globalization. This includes the internationalization and liberalization of the Japanese economy itself. But it also includes developments to which the production networks themselves, as agents of globalization, have made significant contributions. Among the most important of these is the diffusion of technology and engineering skills.

We noted earlier how technological change has provided the enabling environment within which globalization occurs. Technological change has also had an impact on the operations of production networks. In particular, product life cycles (PLCs) in electronics have shortened. As conceptualized in the PLC theory, international production traditionally moved overseas only once a product had reached a certain degree of maturity; newer, leading-edge products normally remained confined to domestic production.[21] This is no longer the case today, as we can see from the computer industry. Firms have cut product cycles ruthlessly; time-to-market has become the single most important determinant of competitive success. An incremental and sequential process has been accelerated by product cycles as short as nine months. It simply does not make sense for PC vendors to transfer production to East Asia one year after the launch of a new product. To amortize such investment, computer firms must now shift the production of new products to Asia at the beginning of the product cycle.

Technological change has acted as another crucial enabling factor for an early transfer of the production of sophisticated products. Since the mid-1980s, fundamental changes in design methodology and the shift from metallic to plastic parts have facilitated the transfer of production of complex products to overseas locations. This finding runs counter to much of the established wisdom, which argues that the spread of microelectronics and new materials will make it more difficult to transfer industrial production to developing countries (Ernst 1997a). Technological trends thus have encouraged the transfer overseas of an increasing number of stages in the value chain. The more sophisticated operations Japanese subsidiaries now conduct reinforce the need for greater managerial autonomy and for greater integration into local economies. In other words, these trends are taking some Japanese networks down the path their American counterparts have pursued for a much longer period.

### Imitation and convergence

A final reason for the gradual opening-up of Japanese production networks is that some Japanese firms have consciously set out to imitate what they perceive to be successful strategies by their American counterparts. This desire for emulation not only characterizes the large, diversified business groups like Matsushita, Hitachi, Toshiba, NEC and Fujitsu but also medium-sized companies that have become global competitors like Kyocera, Canon, and Sharp, and many others whose names are less familiar to Western observers. As American computer and semiconductor firms have been able to consolidate their competitive position during the early 1990s, learning from the American experience has become a top priority for their Japanese counterparts. This is hardly surprising, in that US subsidiaries in Southeast Asia and the NICs have been even more profitable than their Japanese counterparts (as reported in MITI's 1996 Trade White Paper quoted in Johnstone and Yamakoshi 1997: 11). Japanese managers frequently mentioned Hewlett-Packard (HP), which conducts much of its R&D for its printers in Singapore, as a model they would like to emulate.[22] Other American role models frequently mentioned are GE, Compaq, and the successfully restructured IBM.

Imitation generates a complex process of hybridization where partial convergence coexists with persistent diversity. The fact that NEC has learned from Compaq's new strategy to combine price leadership with differentiation through a systematic rationalization of its IPNs, does not imply that NEC will develop in an *identical* manner. Although it has absorbed some elements of Compaq's approach, NEC has preserved some of its idiosyncratic features. For instance, Compaq has moved to an extreme form of outsourcing: in a contract with Taiwan's Mitac International, Compaq outsourced all stages of the value chain except marketing for which it retains sole responsibility.[23] NEC, however, prefers a much more gradual approach that enables it to balance some dispersion of value-chain stages with what it perceives to be necessary to maintain corporate coherence. To achieve this balance, at home NEC maintains an integrated set of high value-added manufacturing and knowledge-intensive support services that it considers necessary to exercise systemic control. At the same time, NEC supports a substantial two-way flow of personnel between its three major product units in Japan (i.e. telecommunications, computers, and components) and its overseas affiliates. Such systematic rotation is regarded as essential to establish a two-way learning process: (1) a transfer of NEC routines from Japan to overseas affiliates and suppliers, and (2) a continuous flow of feedback information on the functioning of these different nodes of its IPNs, including information on new trends in local capabilities and market requirements. In short, NEC remains distinctively different from Compaq with its focus on the generation and group-wide distribution of tacit knowledge.[24]

We could cite many other examples to support the argument that learning from the American experience is consistent with persistent diversity. Practically all the leading Japanese electronics firms over the last few years have attempted to learn from the American experience. The following example of Yokogawa Electronic shows that this is also true for second-tier, medium-sized companies (Ernst 1998c).[25] Yogokawa has long-standing links with two American companies, each of which in its own field is widely regarded as a pacesetter for organizational innovations. Since 1963, Yogokawa has had a joint venture with HP, originally for measurement equipment and control devices, and now for PCs and workstations. Since 1982, it has also had a joint venture with General Electric (GE), which has become a worldwide market leader for small-scale computed tomography equipment. Yogokawa's management has stressed the crucial importance of learning from US management practices.[26]

How did this emulation develop in practice? Does this desire to learn from American partners imply that Yogokawa is simply transforming itself into a clone of HP or GE? And, furthermore, has such learning been a one-sided affair where Yogokawa adopts features of its American partners, while the American partners remain unchanged? Clearly, not so. Yogokawa continues to differ from American firms in essential features of its organization. For instance, one important objective of the company's "global corporate management" doctrine is to balance increasing empowerment at every node of its IPN with corporate coherence. This brings us back to our earlier example of NEC: the key mechanism for providing such coherence is an elaborate scheme of information-sharing through constant rotation of human resources.

The focus is on the exchange of tacit knowledge embodied in skilled operators, technicians, engineers, and managers. This peculiar approach to human resource management continues to distinguish Japanese firms from most of their American competitors.

In Yogokawa's joint venture with HP, it is clear that learning has been a two-way process. Through this joint venture, HP not only was able to gain an early foothold in the Japanese market, on which it could later build when it began to penetrate Japan's computer market, but also was able to learn about some unique features of Japanese management. For instance, it was through this link with Yogokawa that HP became acutely aware – much earlier than many of its competitors – of organizational innovations in quality control in Japanese companies. This knowledge was one of the reasons why HP, in the early 1980s, was able, with full confidence, to criticize the decline in quality levels in the US semiconductor industry. HP was also able to reap similar learning effects in other areas in which Japanese firms have a proven record of strength, such as inventory management, human resource development and the acceleration of the design cycle for new products.[27]

These joint venture experiences indicate that the links which Japanese corporations have established with US companies certainly cannot be reduced to a one-way convergence to the US model. Instead, a case of mutual convergence or hybridization is evident, with both parties able to learn from one another, and to adapt elements of their partner's organization into their own organizational structures.[28]

### The impact of the Asian financial crises

How have the financial crises that beset East Asia in 1997–8 affected the evolution of IPNs in electronics? It is too soon to discern the longer term effects that the crises may have on the evolution of local industries. Some immediate effects that may have an impact over the medium term are, however, apparent.

Most worrisome is a significant erosion of the region's small and medium-sized suppliers (Ernst 1998a,b). Global OEM customers such as Compaq (for PC-related parts and subassemblies) and Seagate (for HDD-related supplies) have been quick to respond to the devaluation of local currencies and have requested substantial price reductions from their Asian suppliers. OEM suppliers do not have much choice but to comply. For the stronger ones this may be feasible, yet there is an important risk involved: once devaluation is reversed, Asian OEM suppliers will find themselves being caught in a high-cost production structure, but they will then be unable to back away from the price reductions that they have granted in response to the currency depreciation. There is a real danger that current price reductions may force many of these suppliers out of the market.

At the same time, however, Asian suppliers are under tremendous pressure to recapitalize in order to maintain their links with global OEM customers:

survival requires that these suppliers upgrade their product mix and their efficiency; they also need to proceed with a regionalization of their production base. This dual pressure has resulted in severe cash-flow problems, especially for smaller local suppliers.

The crisis also has very negative implications for the region's innovation systems. It has led to a substantial cutting back in the R&D efforts of some local firms, especially those in Korea. R&D expenditures fell in 1998 by 12.3 percent overall from the previous year. In some sectors, the fall was much more precipitous: in automobiles, chemicals, and medical research it was estimated to be closer to 50 percent. In semiconductors, Korea's largest single export earner, R&D fell by 20 percent. The Korea Industrial Technology Association suggests that 5,000 of a total of 75,000 jobs in R&D were lost in 1998. The number of patent applications in 1998 fell by close to 20 percent. Investment in plant also declined because of the economic crisis.

Although R&D expenditures were expected to rebound somewhat in 1999, the economic crisis may have a longer lasting impact on research capabilities. Several thousand researchers were reported to have been lured abroad in 1998 by more attractive employment opportunities. The Korean press noted with particular alarm that a number of chip designers had been recruited by Taiwanese companies that were competing with Korean firms. The loss of the tacit technology embodied in skilled personnel may be far more difficult to replace than an aging plant. One effect of the crisis might therefore be to redistribute capabilities away from the most severely affected economies to those that escaped relatively unscathed.

The financial crisis also had a profound effect on the capacity of Korean companies to invest abroad. According to UNCTAD data, foreign investment by Korean corporations had already declined in 1997 by nearly 10 percent compared with the previous year. In the first nine months of 1998, the foreign investments of Korean companies declined by a further 8 percent compared with the equivalent period in the previous year. Moreover, new investments of US$ 1.4 billion were partly offset by foreign divestments of US$ 900 millions.

These divestments, forced by capital shortages, are of particular importance in the development of technological capabilities. In the first half of the 1990s, Korean companies used foreign investment as an instrument to attempt to gain access to technology. Korean companies purchased chip manufacturers in the United States, and they purchased automobile design companies in the UK and Germany. How successful in the long term such investments would have been had yet to be demonstrated by the time of the crisis. Technology is in many instances "tacit," residing in the personnel employed by the companies. Whether skilled personnel would have remained with the companies under Korean ownership is uncertain.

With the onset of the financial crisis, however, Korean companies were forced to liquidate some of these investments. Most notable is Hyundai's sale of Symbios Logic in the United States for US$775 millions. Symbios, which Hyundai had acquired in 1995 from ATT, had been profitable throughout the period of Korean ownership, returning a net profit of US$69 millions in 1997. The longer term significance of the Symbios divestment lies in its role in Hyundai's efforts to move beyond DRAM production to non-memory chips, which generally enjoy higher profit margins.

Other divestments or postponement of investment plans by leading *chaebol* threaten their efforts at internationalization and at constructing their own marketing networks. In response to the economic difficulties brought on by the crisis, Samsung closed its European, US, and Southeast Asian regional headquarters and abandoned plans for sales of digital mobile phone equipment to Brazil because the project would have necessitated additional foreign borrowing. Hyundai postponed investment in a semiconductor plant in Scotland because it was unable to raise the required capital. Daewoo postponed investment in France in a plant to make glass for TV tubes and delayed its attempts to sell cars in the US market. In short, the financial crisis may have long-term effects on the efforts of domestic companies in the region to gain access to high technology, to diversify their markets, and to upgrade their production.

The crisis and the subsequent imperative for companies to reduce their debt ratios have also opened the way for increased foreign ownership of domestic electronics companies. Domestic companies have been forced to search for foreign partners with the capacity to provide injections of capital and technology. A prime example is the purchase by Royal Philips Electronics NV of 50% of Luck Goldstar's active matrix liquid crystal display business for approximately US$1.6 billion – a record foreign investment in Korea. It may be the case that European and US companies are better placed than their Japanese counterparts for such acquisitions given the current financial difficulties of some Japanese firms and the historical animosity towards them in some parts of the region.

Finally, changes in exchange rates arising from the crisis have made sourcing of components from some countries in the region even more attractive for Japanese and US networks alike. Facing increased cost pressures as PC prices continue to plummet, assemblers are likely to respond to the realignment of exchange rates brought about the crisis by seeking to increase the share of components sourced from Korea and Thailand in particular.

As argued in the Chapter 1, this obviously creates new opportunities for the spread of IPNs. However, the negative impact of the crisis on the region's knowledge base and industrial upgrading capacity may well act as an important constraint (Ernst 1999a).

## Partial convergence and persistent diversity: does nationality continue to matter?

Our study of the evolution of Japanese and US production networks in the electronics industry in East Asia in the 1990s has enabled us to identify how various forces that we associate with globalization – technological change, technology transfer, the shortening of product life cycles, trade liberalization, and the development of local centers of expertise – have shaped corporate decision-making. By focusing on change in one sector over a period of time, we were able to illustrate the dynamic process by which corporations of all nationalities have adapted to competitive forces.[29]

Pressures arising from the forces of globalization produced convergence in some firm strategies. Corporations not only learned from their own experiences but also from those of their competitors. In some instances, they attempted to emulate what they perceived as being industry best practice. The areas in which convergence occurred include the mix of products that are now produced in Asia and the increasing variety of value-chain activities that both American and Japanese firms have relocated to the region. Whereas in the past Japanese production in other parts of the region consisted overwhelmingly of consumer electronics, by the mid-1990s Japanese firms had joined their US counterparts in moving a substantial portion of PC production to the region. Japanese firms have also jumped onto the bandwagon of OEM contracts. During the early 1980s, when the US dollar appreciated rapidly, cash-strapped American firms were the first to experiment with new forms of international production that did not necessarily involve equity control. These provided substantial competitive advantages to American computer companies. Similarly, American firms were the first to take advantage of the growing concentrations of expertise in various areas of electronics production in East Asia by transferring increasing responsibility for R&D to subsidiaries. Again, this has proved to be a cost-effective strategy that some Japanese firms are beginning to emulate. The new responsibilities devolved to Japanese subsidiaries have inevitably required changes in management practices that have brought them closer to their American counterparts.

Japanese electronics networks have become more open – increasingly outsourcing components – and less centralized in their R&D and management practices. The vintage effect (the number of years a subsidiary has been established) appears to have been important in the opening up of networks – but so, in addition, have some of the forces of globalization. It is important to emphasize that the effects observed have been in plants that have been predominantly export-oriented. In other countries, where Japanese subsidiaries have produced primarily for the local market, aided by various tariff and non-tariff barriers, the vintage effect and an opening up of networks is far less evident (Kreinin 1988).[30]

Nationality of ownership continues to determine strategies in some areas. One example is in personnel management. Because of an unwillingness to promote local managers to top positions and because of the operation of a seniority system that inhibits rapid promotion, Japanese companies have found it difficult to recruit and retain quality managers and engineers in their Asian subsidiaries. Surveys have shown that most managers consider working conditions and promotion opportunities in US subsidiaries to be far more favorable, placing Japanese subsidiaries at a competitive disadvantage. The rapid expansion of the electronics industry in Southeast Asian has offered high-caliber personnel the opportunity for movement among employers. Extensive "job-hopping" is the name of the game, a phenomenon that Japanese corporations have found alien. The strategy for the training of engineers that many Japanese firms have adopted addresses this problem. Most of these engineers are hired internally. Based on a careful selection process, each affiliate develops a pool of highly motivated "technicians," which they then train over a period of five to seven years to become (sometimes unlicensed) engineers. In this manner, engineering skills are made firm-specific, reducing the likelihood of job-hopping behavior.[31]

In other areas, nationality may be far less important than other factors in causing firm convergence and divergence. For instance, the importance of proprietary technology may play an important role in decisions about the extent to which companies outsource component manufacturing. Firms that produce high-end products in which proprietary technology provides the essence of their competitive advantage are likely to be far less willing to outsource than are firms using standardized technologies. Seagate, the principal US producer of high-end HDDs, manufactures most of its components in-house. Other disk drive manufacturers (also located in Malaysia) in the high volume, low end of the market outsource many of their components. Similar differences are observable among Japanese companies. Sony, for example, has been particularly successful in establishing brand name recognition for its products in the markets of industrialized countries. Sony was under much less pressure to internationalize production than were its rivals, who lacked similar image recognition, and who concentrated on Asian markets. Sony has been reluctant to shift to export platform production in East Asia, instead investing heavily in the automation of its European and North American plants, including those in Mexico. Today Sony's Asian production networks are still relatively underdeveloped.

Our findings thus are that partial convergence coexists with persistent diversity; nationality of ownership is just one among various factors that determine corporate behavior and organization. These findings are in line with current debates on the theory of the firm and on international business strategy. Competitive requirements in an era of globalization have not only become more complex. They have also become universal in that they apply with equal force to American firms as well as to firms from Europe, Japan, South Korea, and Taiwan. This convergence in the basic parameters of competition, however, does not automatically translate into a convergence of business strategies and structure, a point that a growing literature in the field of business management emphasizes.[32]

In short, although globalization tends to increase convergence in some areas of international organization, persistent diversity is also apparent.[33] Organizations do not start with a clean slate. Path dependence constrains the strategies that firms can feasibly pursue. Our conclusion then is a tentative one – appropriately given the rapidity of change in the electronics industry in East Asia. Sound economic reasons as well as path dependency explain the differences in the IPNs of Japanese and US companies in East Asia in the late 1980s and early 1990s. The forces of globalization, including the activities of the production networks themselves, led to convergence between the networks on some essential dimensions in the mid-1990s. Yet, although in some areas we find important similarities, firms continue to diverge in their approaches to the organization of international production. Nationality continues to matter, an argument that implies that an economic analysis that excludes history and the development of institutions is ill equipped to address the question of globalization. But nationality is just one determining factor among others, and its relative importance is likely to decline over time as firms develop their capacity to manage their IPNs.

## Notes

1 For a typical example of a neo-liberal approach to globalization, see Ohmae (1991). For a critical review see Hu (1992).

2 These are not Boyer's own views. He argues that "This syllogism that equates globalization with convergence is logically flawed, and its premise may not correspond to the current state of the world economy." (Boyer 1996: 50), a conclusion with which we agree.

3 Much of the early Japanese FDI in manufacturing was directed towards import substitution behind protective tariffs.

4 A note of caution is appropriate here. As we discuss later, even within the electronics sector, US and Japanese subsidiaries in East Asia historically have had different specializations. One source of recent convergence is that Japanese corporations increasingly have moved into the same field, personal computing equipment, that US firms have traditionally occupied.

5 For a good overview, see John (1997).

6 Our focus on the dynamics of change is in line with the evolutionary, resource-based theory of the firm, based on Penrose (1959); Nelson and Winter (1982); Kogut and Zander (1993); Langlois and Robertson (1995); and Andersen (1996). For a recent overview, see Langlois and Foss (1997).

7 This concept allows us to analyze the globalization strategies of a particular firm by posing four questions: (1) Where does a firm locate which stages of the value chain? (2) To what degree does a firm rely on outsourcing and what is the importance of inter-firm production networks relative to the firm's internal production network? (3) To what degree is the control over these transactions exercised in a centralized or in a decentralized manner? (4) how do the different elements of these networks hang together? For details, see Ernst (1994b; 1997b; 1999b).

8 We define East Asia as including the economies of both Northeast and Southeast Asia.

9 In a recent survey, Vonortas and Safioleas (1997: 659) found that transnational strategic alliances occurred far more frequently in the computer sector than in any other industry sector.

10 Ernst and Guerrieri (1998) analyze how the spread of different IPNs in East Asia has affected the trade links of the region with the United States and Japan. This study documents that a far greater diversity of product groups is involved in Japanese in contrast to US trade links with East Asia. Of equal importance is

a second finding: the trade balances of the two countries with the region are radically different. A consistently high and growing trade deficit characterizes US trade links with East Asia in the electronic industry. This is true even for computers and components, the two sectors where the United States has re-established itself during the late 1990s as an uncontested leader. This is in stark contrast to East Asia's trade with Japan, where the latter enjoys large and rapidly growing surpluses. These differences can only be partially attributed to traditional macroeconomic factors that are the focus of standard trade theory. They can be better explained by some peculiar features of the international production networks that American and Japanese firms have established in East Asia. The chain of causation appears to work both ways. Changes in the organization of international production have led to changes in the composition of bilateral trade flows. Such changes in international trade patterns, in turn, lead to further changes in the organization of international production.

11 For the United States see Graham and Krugman (1989) and Congress of the United States (1994); for Australia see Kreinin (1988); on Malaysia see Guyton (1996); for Singapore see the study by Poh Kam Wong cited by Dobson (1993: 52–3) and Dobson's (1993) own survey of four TNC subsidiaries.

12 A trend also observed in Europe. See Mason and Encarnation (1994).

13 This argument applies *a fortiori* to Taiwanese investments – see Chi Schive (1990), Chen *et al.* (1995), and Ernst (1997b).

14 This estimate may be a modest understatement of the number of Japanese subsidiaries in the region in the first half of the 1990s that were undertaking some R&D activities. Ernst (1994a: 21) reports eleven instances of subsidiaries engaged in product development but cautions that it was unclear whether such development at the time amounted to anything more than simple product adaptation for the local market.

15 For a good overview, see Langlois and Foss (1997).

16 For a case study of such learning in the IPN of Samsung Electronics, see Chapter 6.

17 For a study of Intel's affiliate in Penang, see Ernst (1997a: Chapter IV).

18 The data have to be interpreted with some caution as they may also reflect increased sourcing from Japanese component suppliers that relocated to Southeast Asia in this period. The data, kindly supplied by Shujiro Urata, are taken from Ministry of International Trade and Industry, Wagakuni Kigyo no Kaigai Jigyo Katsudo (Survey of the Overseas Activities of Japanese Companies) # 21 (1992) and #25 (1996). Japanese automobile "transplants" in the US evince a similar pattern of expanded local sourcing over time – again with a substantial share coming from locally based subsidiaries of Japanese component manufacturers (Congress of the United States 1994: 21).

19 During the peak of the recession, when most Japanese electronics firms faced a serious profit squeeze, Japanese parent companies actually used sophisticated transfer-pricing techniques to transfer back home any profits made in Asia. Interview with Japanese venture capital firm, November 1993.

20 Japanese PC vendors undoubtedly perceive this new reliance on OEM purchases as an intermediate solution. It enables them to discontinue lower value-added production activities at home; their objective, however, is to set up their own supply base for some of these products in China and Southeast Asia. The rapid growth of OEM contracts, therefore, may well not last for long (although again contending forces may be at work, e.g. the extent to which components become "commodified"). For the time being, however, Japan's PC-related imports from East Asia continue to grow rapidly, and they are sourced from a variety of different international production networks.

21 For critical assessments of the product cycle model, see Bernard and Ravenhill (1995) and Cantwell (1995).

22  Author's interviews in the Japanese electronics industry, November 1995

23  Mitac in turn is responsible for the design and development of new products, as well as for manufacturing, transport, and after-sales services at its manufacturing facilities in Taiwan, China, Britain, Australia, and the United States, Compaq expects to save up to 15 percent in overall life cycle costs. Mitac's greatest attraction for Compaq is its plants and sales subsidiaries that are located in most of the world's key computer markets. Information provided by MIC/III, 27 October 1995.

24  For a theoretical foundation of the critical importance of tacit knowledge for Japanese management approaches, see Nonaka and Takeuchi (1995).

25  Established in 1915, Yokogawa Electronic has a strong position in measurement equipment and control devices, and has also successfully diversified into PCs, medical systems, software, engineering, and information services. Its consolidated group sales in 1996 were yen 280 billion with 29,000 employees – which places it squarely in the important group of medium-sized Japanese corporations that are often overlooked by foreign observers.

26  "[W]e are...able to learn...[from HP] many things like business strategy, American rationality and management style.... It is very valuable and profitable that we can learn business philosophy and management methodology from international top ranking companies. For example, our top management can meet and talk with Jack Welch, CEO of GE. Such an opportunity is very important and useful for considering our business strategy and management." Toshihiko Akaishizawa, director for strategic planning, Yogokawa Electronic, quoted in Teramoto *et al.* (1997).

27  See, for instance, the discussion in Ernst (1997a) of HP's innovative approach to global chain management, which, arguably, draws some of its inspirations from Japanese management approaches.

28  We need to emphasize, however, an important lacuna in existing research: to date little evidence is available about American subsidiaries in Asia mimicking the practices of Japanese companies. Our discussion of the case of Yogokawa Electronics has provided clear evidence of one instance of mutual convergence. To what degree American electronics firms have learned from some of the innovative Japanese human resource management practices, such as on-the-job training (OJT), quality control circles and information-sharing through frequent job rotation, has yet to be investigated. The same is true for other strengths of the Japanese management approach, such as inventory management and aggressive market penetration strategies in Asia's growth markets for electronics. American electronics firms, such as Motorola, Compaq, and Apple, have taken a keen interest in Japanese market penetration strategies in Asia (information provided by Dennis Tachiki, senior researcher at the Sakura Research Institute, Tokyo). It would also be of great interest to study whether SMEs in the American electronics industry have tried to learn from the internationalization strategies of Japanese SMEs.

29  We make no claims about how representative the East Asian production networks of Japanese and US electronics firms are of the behavior of US and Japanese companies' foreign investments more generally. As noted above, the proximity of other East Asian countries to Japanese headquarters facilitates certain patterns of interaction between parent and subsidiary that are more difficult for US companies operating in the region, and which would be more difficult for Japanese companies in other parts of the world. We also note that certain characteristics of consumer electronics production enables the construction of networks of geographically dispersed plants that would not necessarily be cost-effective in other industrial sectors. The study of a single sector over time, however, has the advantage of controlling for some of the variables that may

produce spurious correlations in aggregate analyses. One cost of our approach, however, is that some of the evidence, derived from case studies, that we offer is at best illustrative.

30  The same is true for American firms when their primary focus is on domestic markets. For some evidence, see Encarnation (forthcoming).

31  Information provided by Dennis Tachiki.

32  While noting that globalization has "…already led to converging transitions, and pointed to prospective organizational trends" Humes (1993: 24) acknowledges that this process still leaves sufficient latitude for organizational diversity. Ghoshal, whose well-known text with Bartlett (Bartlett and Ghoshal 1989) is often seen as providing strong evidence for increasing convergence amongst firm strategies, similarly argues in a co-authored paper with Nohria (Ghoshal and Nohria 1993) that matching organizational structure to environment and strategy does not preclude different approaches by individual companies. This message is captured in their article's title: "Horses for Courses: Organizational Forms for Multinational Corporations."

33  Recent research by Christensen and Drejer (1997) shows that this is true even for the financial sector, arguably the most globalized of industries, where the once clear-cut distinction between Anglo-Saxon and continental European/Japanese governance approaches has lost much of its earlier vigor. Globalization has placed different systems of corporate governance and of regulations in open competition with one another. Undoubtedly, strong convergence trends are evident. Yet significant differences continue to exist. In some areas it is possible to detect increasing diversity, due to a continuous hybridization of existing national institutional trajectories.

# References

Andersen, E. (1996) "The Evolution of Economic Complexity: A Division-of-Coordination-of Labor Approach," in E. Helmstaedter and M. Perlman (eds) *Behavioral Norms, Technological Progress, and Economic Dynamics. Studies in Schumpeterian Economics*, Ann Arbor: University of Michigan Press.

Aoki, M. (1988) *Information, Incentives and Bargaining in the Japanese Economy*, Cambridge: Cambridge University Press.

Aoki, T. (1992) "Japanese FDI and the Forming of Networks in the Asia–Pacific Region: Experience in Malaysia and Its Implications," in S. Tokunaga (ed.) *Japan's Foreign Investment and Asian Economic Interdependence: Production, Trade and Financial Systems*, Tokyo: University of Tokyo Press, 73–109.

Arthur, W. B. (1989) "Competing Technologies, Increasing Returns and Lock-In by Historical Events," *Economic Journal* 99: 116–31.

Baldwin, C. Y. and Clark, K. B. (1994) "Capital-budgeting Systems and Capabilities Investments in US Companies after the Second World War," *Business History Review* 1 (Spring).

Bartlett, C. A. and Ghoshal, S. (1989) *Managing Across Borders: The Transnational Solution*, Boston, MA: Harvard Business School Press.

Bernard, M. and Ravenhill, J. (1995) "Beyond Product Cycles and Flying Geese: Regionalization, Hierarchy, and the Industrialization of East Asia," *World Politics* 45, 2: 179–210.

Boyer, R. (1996) "The Convergence Hypothesis Revisited: Globalization but Still the Century of Nations?" in S. Berger and R. Dore (eds) *National Diversity and Global Capitalism*, Ithaca, NY: Cornell University Press, 29–59.

Cantwell, J. (1995) "The Globalisation of Technology: What Remains of the Product Life Cycle?" *Cambridge Journal of Economics* 19: 155–174.

Cerny, P. G. (1995) "Globalization and the Changing Logic of Collective Action," *International Organization* 49(4): 595–625.

Chen, T.-J., Ku, Y.-H., Liu, D. N., Chen, H. M., Liu, M. C., Riedet, J., Aguno, T. G., Raiff, M., Pussanussri, B. and Pangest, M. (1995) *Taiwan's Small- and Medium-Sized Firms' Direct Investment in Southeast Asia*, Taipei: Chung-Hua Institution for Economic Research.

Chi Schive (1990) *The Foreign Factor: The Multinational Corporation's Contribution to the Economic Modernization of the Republic of China*, Stanford, CA: Hoover Institution Press.

Christensen, J. L. and Drejer, I. (1997) *Finance and Innovation. System of Chaos?* DRUID Working Paper, University of Aalborg, Denmark.

Congress of the United States, Office of Technology Assessment (1994) "Multinationals and the US Technology Base," Washington, DC: US Government Printing Office, OTA–ITE–612, September.

Dobson, W. (1993) *Japan in East Asia: Trading and Investment Strategies*. Singapore: Institute for Southeast Asian Studies.

—— (1995) "East Asian Integration: Synergies between Firm Strategies and Government Policy," Toronto: Centre for International Studies, University of Toronto.

Dore, R. (1986) *Flexible Rigidities: Industrial Policy and Structural Adjustment in the Japanese Economy 1970–80*. Stanford, CA: Stanford University Press.

Dunning, J. (1993) *Multinational Enterprises and the Global Economy*, Wokingham: Addison-Wesley.

Encarnation, D. (forthcoming) "Asia and the Global Operations of Multinational Corporations," in D. Encarnation (ed.) *Investing in Asia: The Regional Operations of Japanese Multinationals*, Oxford: Oxford University Press.

Ernst, D. (1994a) "Carriers of Regionalization: The East Asian Production Networks of Japanese Electronics Firms," University of California, Berkeley, BRIE Working Paper 73, November.

—— (1994b) "Network Transactions, Market Structure and Technological Diffusion – Implications for South–South Cooperation," in L. Mytelka (ed.) *South–South Cooperation in a Global Perspective*, Paris: OECD Development Centre Documents.

—— (1997a) "From Partial to Systemic Globalization: International Production Networks in the Electronics Industry," San Diego: Graduate School of International Relations and Pacific Studies, University of California, Report Prepared for the Sloan Foundation project on "Globalization in the Data Storage Industry," jointly published as *The Data Storage Industry Globalization Project Report 97–02*, Graduate School of International Relations and Pacific Studies, University of California at San Diego.

—— (1997b) "Partners in the China Circle? The Asian Production Networks of Japanese Electronics Firms," in B. Naughton (ed.) *The China Circle*, Washington, DC: The Brookings Institution Press.

—— (1998a), "Catching-Up, Crisis and Industrial Upgrading: Evolutionary Aspects of Technology Management in Korea's Electronics Industry," *Asia–Pacific Journal of Management* 15(2).

—— (1998b), *Destroying or upgrading the engine of growth? The reshaping of the electronics industry in East Asia after the crisis*, background study prepared for the World Bank report *East Asia – The Road to Recovery*, The World Bank, Washington, DC, September.

—— (1998c), "Externalization and inter-organizational networks. How globalization transforms the Japanese model," in Daniel Dirks (ed.) *Japanese Management in the Low Growth Era. Between External Shocks and Internal Evolution*, Springer Verlag, Berlin and New York.

—— (1999a), *Moving beyond the Commodity Price Trap. How the Crisis Reshapes Upgrading Options for East Asia's Electronics Industry*, background study prepared for the World Bank report East Asia: Out of the Crisis, Into the New Millennium, The World Bank, Washington, DC.

—— (1999b) "Globalization and the Changing Geography of Innovation Systems. A Policy Perspective on Global Production Networks," *Journal of the Economics of Innovation and New Technologies*, special issue on "Integrating Policy Perspectives in Research on Technology and Economic Growth," edited by Anthony Bartzokas and Morris Teubal.

Ernst, D. and Guerrieri, P. (1998) "International Production Networks and Changing Trade Patterns in East Asia. The Case of the Electronics Industry," *Oxford Development Studies*, 26(2): 191–212.

Gerlach, M. (1992) "Twilight of the *Keiretsu*? A Critical Assessment," *Journal of Japanese Studies* 18(1): 79–118.

Ghoshal, S. and Nohria, N. (1993) "Horses for Courses: Organizational Forms for Multinational Corporations," *Sloan Management Review* 34(2): 23–36.

Graham, E. and Krugman, P. (1989) *Foreign Direct Investment in the United States*, Washington, DC: Institute for International Economics.

Guyton, L. (1996) "Japanese Investments and Technology Transfer to Malaysia," in J. Borrego, A. Alvarez and K. S. Jomo (eds) *Capital, the State and Late Industrialization: Comparative Perspectives on the Pacific Rim*, Boulder, CO: Westview Press.

Hill, H. (1988) *Foreign Investment and Industrialization in Indonesia*, Singapore: Oxford University Press.

—— (1990) "Foreign Investment and East Asian Economic Development," *Asian–Pacific Economic Literature*, 4(2): 21–58.

Hu, Yao-Su (1992) "Global or Stateless Corporations are National Firms with International Operations," *California Management Review* 34(2): 107–26.

Humes, S. (1993) *Managing the Multinational: Confronting the Global–Local Dilemma*, London: Prentice Hall.

Itoh, M. and Shibata, J. (1995) "A Study of the Operations of Japanese Firms in Asia: The Electrical Machinery Industry," in E. K. Y. Chen and P. Drysdale (eds) *Corporate Links and Foreign Direct Investment in Asia and the Pacific*, Pymble, NSW: Harper Educational, 187–202.

Japan External Trade Organization (1995a) "The Current State of Japanese Affiliated Manufactures in ASEAN," Tokyo: JETRO, Overseas Research Department 704–1312, June.

—— (1995b) "JETRO White Paper on Foreign Direct Investment 1995," Tokyo: JETRO, March.

John, R. (ed.) (1997) *Global Business Strategy*, London: International Thomson Business Press.

Johnstone, C. and Yamakoshi, A. (1997) "Strength without Dominance: Japanese Investment in Southeast Asia," *JEI Report* 19A (16 May): 1–12.

Kahler, M. (1996) "Trade and Domestic Differences," in S. Berger and R. Dore (eds) *National Diversity and Global Capitalism*, Ithaca, NY: Cornell University Press, 298–332.

Kester, W. (1996) "American and Japanese Corporate Governance: Convergence to Best Practice?" in S. Berger and R. Dore (eds) *National Diversity and Global Capitalism*, Ithaca, NY: Cornell University Press, 107–37.

Kogut, B. and Zander, E. (1993) "Knowledge of the Firm and the Evolutionary Theory of the Multinational Corporation," *Journal of International Business Studies* 34, 4.

Kojima, K. (1978) *Direct Foreign Investment: A Japanese Model of Multinational Business Operations*, London: Croom Helm.

—— (1986) "Japanese-Style Direct Foreign Investment," *Japanese Economic Studies* 14(3): 52–82.

Kreinin, M. (1988) "How Closed is Japan's Market? Additional Evidence," *The World Economy* 11(4): 529–42.

Langlois, R. and Foss, N. (1997) "Capabilities and Governance: the Rebirth of Production in the Theory of Economic Organization," Copenhagen: Copenhagen Business School, DRUID Working Paper 97–2, January.

Langlois, R. and Robertson, P. (1995) *Firms, Markets and Economic Change: A Dynamic Theory of Business Institutions*, London: Routledge.

March, J. and Olsen, J. (1989) *Rediscovering Institutions: The Organizational Basis of Politics*, New York: Free Press.

Mason, M. and Encarnation, D. (eds) (1994) *Does Ownership Matter? Japanese Multinationals in Europe*, Oxford: Clarendon Press.

Nelson, R. and Winter, S. (1982) *An Evolutionary Theory of Economic Change*, Cambridge, MA: Belknap Press.

Nicholas, S. *et al.* (1995) *"Japanese Investment in Australia: The Investment Decision and Control Structures in Manufacturing, Tourism and Financial Services,"* Canberra: Australia–Japan Research Centre, Australian National University, 17 July.

Nonaka, I. and Takeuchi, H. (1995) *The Knowledge Creating Company*, Oxford: Oxford University Press.

Ohmae, K. (1991) *The Borderless World: Power and Strategy in the Interlinked Economy*, New York: Harper and Row.

Ozawa, T. (1979) *Multinationalism: Japanese Style*, Princeton, NJ: Princeton University Press.

Pauly, L. and Reich, S. (1997) "National Structures and Multinational Corporate Behavior: Enduring Differences in the Age of Globalization," *International Organization* 51(1): 1–30.

Penrose, E. (1959) *The Theory of the Growth of the Firm*, Oxford: Oxford University Press.

Porter, M. (1990) *The Competitive Advantage of Nations*, New York: Free Press.

Ramstetter, E. (1987) "The Impact of Direct Foreign Investment on Host Country Trade and Output: A Study of Japanese and US Direct Foreign Investment in Korea, Taiwan and Thailand," in S. Naya, V. Vichit-Vadakon, and U. Kerdpibule (eds) *Direct Foreign Investment and Export Promotion: Policies and Experience in Asia*, Honolulu: East–West Resource Systems Institute, 223–57.

Ravenhill, J. (1998) "Japanese and US Subsidiaries in Asia: Host Country Effects," in D. Encarnation (ed.) *Investing in Asia: The Regional Operations of Japanese Multinationals*, Oxford: Oxford University Press.

Schwartz, H. (1994) "Small States in Big Trouble: State Reorganization in Australia, Denmark, New Zealand, and Sweden in the 1980s," *World Politics* 46(4): 527–55.

Sedgwick, M. (forthcoming) "Does Japanese Management Travel in Asia? Managerial Technology Transfer and Japanese Multinationals," in D. Encarnation (ed.) *Investing in Asia: The Regional Operations of Japanese Multinationals*, Oxford: Oxford University Press.

Stopford, J. (1995) "Regional Networks and Domestic Transformation: A New Challenge for Japanese Firms," Seoul: Institute of East and West Studies, Yonsei University, Third Conference on Economic Cooperation in Asia–Pacific Community, November.

Teramoto, Y. Iwasaki, N. and Takai, T. (1997) *Role of Inter-Organizational Networks: The Case of Japanese Corporate Groups,* Tokyo: Maison Franco–Japonaise and Deutsches Institut für Japanstudien.

Urata, S. (1995) "Emerging Patterns of Production and Foreign Trade in Electronics Products in East Asia: An Examination of a Role Played by Foreign Direct Investment," San Francisco: Asia Foundation, Conference on Competing Production Networks in Asia, April 27–8.

Vernon, R. (1971) *Sovereignty at Bay: The Multinational Spread of US Enterprises*, New York: Basic Books.

—— (1977) *Storm over the Multinationals: The Real Issues*, Cambridge, MA: Harvard University Press.

Vonortas, N. and Safioleas, S. (1997) "Strategic Alliances in Information Technology and Developing Country Firms: Recent Evidence," *World Development* 25(5): 657–80.

# Index

strategic response to competitive
pressures 141; technological
capabilities of Samsung network
141–70
Korea Semiconductor Company (KSC)
147
Korean Electronic Industry Association
141, 154, 166, 167
Korean Industrial Technology
Association 245
Kreinin, M. 231
Krugman, P. 226
Kuo, W. 116
Kyocera Wireless Corporation 242

LAM Research 6
Lasserre, P. 82, 90
Lee Byung-Chull 143, 144, 149
Lee Kun Hee (Samsung) 149, 153
Lee, T.Y. 177, 193
Lester, M. 220
Levy, D. 90
liberalization: computer market in
Japan 240; globalization and 240–1;
of trade 22–3
Lim, L. 199
Linden, Greg 22
Lite-on Corporation 130, 204
Liu, J. 112
Liu, P.C. 117
local content economies 184
locational patterns, Japanese networks
81
Logitech 130, 131
Loh Kim Teow 210
Low, L. 193
Luster Industries 208
LUX 156, 157

Mabuchi 203
Malaysia: affiliate behavior and
probable cause 221–2; capital
deepening 216–18; composition of
electronics trade 53; CPNs in 12, 14;
currency depreciation in 199–200;
fixed assets per employee 217;
foreign investment in 199–204; Free
Trade Zones Act 199; HDD
component manufacture in 204;
higher value-added activities 213–
16; human resource development
210–13; Human Resource
Development Fund (HRDF) 211;
indigenous management promotion

220; Investment Incentives Act 199;
Japanese affiliates in 219; Japanese
CPNs in 198–222; Japanese support
for local suppliers 207–8; local
linkages by foreign manufacturing
affiliates 205–10; local sourcing in
232; management autonomy 218–21;
MNC affiliates in 204–21;
nationality of investors 201;
operational headquarters in 214;
Penang IC assemblers 209; Penang
Skills Development Center 211;
Samsung in 165, 166; US affiliates in
219; US CPNs in 198–222; US
support for local suppliers 210;
vendor development program in 206
Malaysian Industrial Classification
(MIC) 112, 124, 217
Malaysian Industrial Development
Authority (MIDA) 200
Malaysian-American Electronics
Industry 211–12, 214, 215
March, J. 234
market organization 4–6
market share, local, of Samsung brands
159
Mason, M. 83, 229
Matsushita: aggressive strategies of 94;
Air Conditioning R&D Center 216;
China presence 98; compared with
Sanyo 91–2; CPN density 215;
desultory experience with MCA 9–
10; emulating IBM 59; foreign
investment projects in Southeast
Asia 157–8; imitation, convergence
and 242; interaction with US CPNs
89; large-scale producer 60; linkage
building, case study of 207; in
Malaysian electronic sector 202–4;
Malaysian governmental
cooperation 101; and "mini-Matsus"
99; representative of Japanese
approach 82; Singapore
developments 181; Singapore
research center 102; social contacts
in Taiwan 120; support for local
Malaysian suppliers 207–8, 213;
Taiwan production platform 118;
vertically integrated assembler 57
Matsushita, Konosuke 91
Maxtor Corporation 72, 181
MCA 10
Metrodata Indonesia 165
MicroFive Corporation 157